Sadat and Begin

Westview Replica Editions

The concept of Westview Replica Editions is a response to the continuing crisis in academic and informational publishing. Library budgets for books have been severely curtailed. Ever larger portions of general library budgets are being diverted from the purchase of books and used for data banks, computers, micromedia, and other methods of information retrieval. Interlibrary loan structures further reduce the edition sizes required to satisfy the needs of the scholarly community. Economic pressures on the university presses and the few private scholarly publishing companies have severely limited the capacity of the industry to properly serve the academic and research communities. As a result, many manuscripts dealing with important subjects, often representing the highest level of scholarship, are no longer economically viable publishing projects—or, if accepted for publication, are typically subject to lead times ranging from one to three years.

Westview Replica Editions are our practical solution to the problem. We accept a manuscript in camera-ready form, typed according to our specifications, and move it immediately into the production process. As always, the selection criteria include the importance of the subject, the work's contribution to scholarship, and its insight, originality of thought, and excellence of exposition. The responsibility for editing and proofreading lies with the author or sponsoring institution. We prepare chapter headings and display pages, file for copyright, and obtain Library of Congress Cataloging in Publication Data. A detailed manual contains simple instructions for preparing the final typescript, and our editorial staff is always available to answer questions.

The end result is a book printed on acid-free paper and bound in sturdy library-quality soft covers. We manufacture these books ourselves using equipment that does not require a lengthy make-ready process and that allows us to publish first editions of 300 to 600 copies and to reprint even smaller quantities as needed. Thus, we can produce Replica Editions as long as there is a demand for them.

About the Book and Author

Sadat and Begin:
The Domestic Politics of Peacemaking
Melvin A. Friedlander

The architects of the Camp David process expected their efforts to become a broad and inclusive framework for peace in the Middle East. Dr. Friedlander's book demonstrates how domestic factors affecting policy decisions made in both Cairo and Jerusalem prevented Sadat and Begin from embracing a structure that would yield a more comprehensive arrangement. Sadat, for example, confronted an anti-peace movement in Egypt, strengthened by then–Vice President Mubarak's ties to the military-security establishment and his alliance with members of the Arab nation's diplomatic corps. Begin was opposed by Israeli conservatives who saw the Camp David formulas as leading to a peace that would jeopardize Israel's security. Both leaders, Dr. Friedlander concludes, were able ultimately to guide their nations toward approval of the peace initiative primarily because of their mastery of techniques of domestic intra-elite bargaining.

Melvin A. Friedlander is a research associate at the Center for Conflict Resolution, George Mason University, and also serves as an adjunct professor at Georgetown University.

Sadat and Begin
the domestic politics
of peacemaking

Melvin A. Friedlander

Westview Press / Boulder, Colorado

A Westview Replica Edition

Published in 1983 in the United States of America by
Westview Press, Inc.
5500 Central Avenue
Boulder, Colorado 80301
Frederick A. Praeger, President and Publisher

Library of Congress Cataloging in Publication Data
Friedlander, Melvin A.
   Sadat and Begin: the domestic politics of peacemaking.
   (A Westview Replica Edition)
   Bibliography: p.
   1. Egypt—Foreign relations—Israel. 2. Israel—foreign relations—Egypt.
3. Egypt—Politics and government—1970-   . 4. Israel—Politics and govern-
ment. 5. Sadat, Anwar, 1918-   . 6. Begin, Menachem, 1913-   . I. Title.
DT82.5.I7F74   1983   327.6205694   82-21826
ISBN 0-86531-949-9

Printed and bound in the United States of America

10   9   8   7   6   5   4   3

To Mom, Dad, Sandy and the
children with love
and affection

"And if they incline to peace, incline thou also to it, and trust in Allah. Lo! He is the Hearer, the Knower."

Koran (Surah 8:61)

"How beautiful upon the mountains are the feet of him that bringeth good tidings, that publisheth peace..."

Isaiah 52:7

"Blessed are the peacemakers: for they shall be called the children of God."

Matthew 5:9

Contents

Acknowledgments

The largest part of this book was written during the winter of 1981 and spring of 1982. The study was submitted as a doctoral dissertation to the American University in the summer of 1982. Professors Alan Taylor, Amos Perlmuter and Aaron Miller were generous of their time and helpful with wise counsel during final stages of the preparation of the dissertation.

Field research in Egypt and Israel was conducted during visits to the Middle East in the summers of 1977 and 1981. The travel occurred just prior to the beginning and ending of active peace negotiations between the parties. The author found very different landscapes and attitudes existing in Egypt and Israel when he returned to the area after the four-year hiatus. These changing perceptions informed many of the judgments presented in the book. Yet a certain degree of optimism for the future is inherent in the evolution and continuation of relations between Cairo and Jerusalem portrayed in this book. Anwar Sadat is dead but his legacy remains. Menachem Begin is an embattled and controversial figure. But his commitment to an enduring peace with Israel's neighbors consistent with security for Jerusalem is undiminished. The author has great respect and admiration for both men, despite many differences with their policies and procedures. It is to their political mastery of events that this book is devoted.

Dan Patir, Yehiel Kadishai in Israel, Ali Dessouki in Egypt, former Secretary of State Cyrus Vance, Ambassadors Alfred Atherton, Samuel Lewis as well as Harold Saunders and Bill Quandt from the United States were liberal with their comments and suggestions. Leigh Bruce, formerly Associate Editor of Foreign Policy was a patient and skilled editor. Cherie Smith was a cheerful and excellent typist. The Defense Intelligence School with its superb faculty and staff was most supportive. And the many students of the educational institutions that I have been affiliated with provided needed inspiration to carry the project to its conclusion. Naturally all errors and acts of omission and commission are the author's responsibility.

Finally, this book is dedicated to Mom and Dad without whom the opportunity to begin the study could not have occurred and to my wife Sandy and our children, who saw the project to its completion during a most difficult period.

Melvin A. Friedlander
Potomac, Maryland
March, 1983

Introduction

The late Egyptian President Anwar Sadat's dramatic visit to Jerusalem and the ensuing Egyptian–Israeli peace treaty, signed on March 26, 1979, changed Middle East politics in ways that remain key to events in the area today. Nevertheless, the treaty has not produced a settlement in the West Bank and Gaza Strip and has failed to encourage other Arab States to join the peace process. Thus many in Arab, Third World, and European capitals perceive it as a seriously flawed document.

Yet no plan or set of recommendations has replaced the treaty. And despite the change in Cairo's leadership and domestic pressure in Egypt to move away from the relationship with Jerusalem, Israel returned the final portion of the Sinai to Egyptian control on time, fulfilling its treaty obligation.

Egyptian President Hosni Mubarak has tried to restore his country's standing in the Arab world and intensified the rhetorical battle with Israel. But thus far he too has observed the terms of the treaty. During last year's bloody conflict in Lebanon, Cairo did nothing to help Arabs materially against Israel.

But the fall of the shah of Iran, the Soviet invasion of Afghanistan, the war between Iraq and Iran, the assassination of Sadat, and the recent war in Lebanon provide ample and persuasive evidence that peace and stability in the Middle East remain little more than a distant prospect. At this writing the attempt to negotiate the withdrawal of all foreign forces from Lebanon and conclude a peace treaty between Beirut and Jerusalem seems stalemated. Palestinian and Israeli rejectionism have left American President Ronald Reagan's peace plan floundering, and internal Israeli politics threaten to paralyze Jerusalem's ability to move toward a broader peace. Under the circumstances, it would appear appropriate to reconsider the Egyptian–Israeli peace treaty, which only four years ago seemed to offer so much hope.

Anwar Sadat and Menachem Begin succeeded in guiding their nations toward approval of a peace treaty in large measure because each possessed an extraordinary capacity to manipulate and dominate his respective political establishment. Both Cairo and Jerusalem faced significant domestic turmoil in the first half of 1977. This turmoil made it necessary for Sadat and Begin to depart from established ideologies and policies. They thus raised the level of domestic conflict in order to gain lasting political benefits for their countries. But in order to win their gamble each ultimately had to control, rather than be controlled by his own country's domestic politics. This domestic imperative had a profound effect on the eventual shape of the treaty.

The Sadat Regime

Few analysts have identified internal Egyptian politics as a catalyst for seeking peace with Israel. Yet after the January 1977 food riots in Cairo divisions in Egypt widened and the domestic debate became increasingly bitter. The turmoil even threatened Sadat's presidency. The Egyptian leader's successful peace initiative -- abhorrent to many Arab leaders -- stilled domestic opposition for a time.

When Gamal Abdel Nasser died in September 1970, Sadat assumed the leadership of an 18-year old political system that was unraveling. Sadat was well aware of the defects in Nasser's method of rule; the former vice president was after all a key participant in the patron-client relationships that dominated all decision making. The new president moved swiftly in the first six years of his rule to eliminate his rivals and then to establish an elite loyal to him.[1]

Sadat, who consolidated his power base at the expense of Nasser sycophants, sought to build a regime with liberal tendencies.[2] His "State of Institutions" served his objective of destroying his enemies.[3] But it also suited his desire to revitalize Egyptian government, encourage a clash of competing interests, and search for new and more reliable talent to administer his programs.[4] Sadat's new system soon absorbed the technocratic and managerial elite, badly treated during much of Nasser's tenure.[5] They provided the expertise needed to design new policies and thus assure Sadat's rule.[6] Sadat owed his elevation to the presidency to the Egyptian constitution, according to which the vice president succeeds the president in case of death or other unexpected departure.[7] Through shrewd manipulation of personalities and institutions, he established his dominance of Egypt.[8]

Whereas Nasser relied exclusively on a small coterie of military officers to manage the country and his programs, Sadat chose to operate through large organizations -- party, parliament, press -- some new and some old. Sadat acted as umpire. His decisions were swift and usually final. He did not hesitate to abolish or restructure organizations if they became too powerful or unresponsive.[9]

An old boy network -- Duffa -- assured rapid promotion under each leader.[10] Intermarriage or a system of patron-client relationships -- Shillal -- and family ties also played a large role in political life under both Nasser and Sadat.[11] Nepotism and cronyism increased under Sadat,[12] but so did the dynamism of Egypt's political system.[13] The loosening of politics was not without its costs for Sadat. Public criticism -- confined under Nasser to veiled references or to the radicalized elements in the society, such as the left -- became more open.[14] Press censorship was lifted, and editorial criticism burgeoned.[15] The eminence grise of the Nasser era, Mohammed Heikal, was removed from the editorship of Al Ahram -- Egypt's most influential newspaper -- but remained a vocal critic of the Sadat regime from outside the country.[16] Sadat finally established a set of rules for the nation's editorialists. He threatened to silence any writer who violated the guidelines.[17] Nevertheless, dissent continued through more subtle channels. The Parliament, which had been accorded increased investigatory powers, became the instrument for official criticism of government policy. Dissident views were also circulated through Shillal, thus insulating the disobedient official from retaliation.[18]

The move to strengthen and multiply institutions reduced the power base of individuals and permitted Sadat time to devote his energies to governing. The organizations themselves, however, became more powerful and more able to alter or eliminate altogether irksome policies.[19] The military and security apparatus, for example, remained the most powerful institution in Egypt. As such, it represented the largest impediment and the greatest strength of the Sadat regime.[20] Sadat always took care to prevent any one officer from acquiring an independent power base and sought to reduce its direct influence on society.[21] Material incentives such as increased pay, promotion, and modernization of arms gave Sadat

the necessary leverage to manipulate the military.[22] Nevertheless, the vice presidency and interior ministry posts
remained in the hands of the military-security establishment.[23]

Sadat also sought to dominate the country's single party,
the Arab Socialist Union (ASU). Its leader under Nasser, Ali
Sabry, was in prison for attempting to oust Sadat in 1971.[24]
The president's brother-in-law, Mahmud Abu Wafia, took over as
secretary general of the party until February 1977.[25] But the
ASU apparatus was rooted in the Nasser style of politics.
Sadat simply ignored the party during his first years in
power.[26]

In the fall of 1976, however, he created a new party
system. Three parties -- of the left, center, and right --
were allowed to operate.[27] The change achieved several reforms
simultaneously. It splintered the party as a viable alternative power base. It eliminated the Duffa under Sabry. By
creating three mini-parties -- Minabar -- with diverse
ideological leanings, it encouraged Shillal to form on the
basis of principle and policy rather than expedience. It
allowed Sadat to break with the past and provide the West --
from which he sought aid and investment -- with evidence of
liberalization. It also weakened party control of the
parliament -- membership in the ASU had previously been
mandatory for all those seeking public office.[28]

Sadat's policies in the political arena were paralleled in
the economic sphere. Government control under Nasser had
failed to produce the economic independence for Egypt that its
supporters had forecast. As a result, Nasser had already begun
to move toward a mixed economy in the last years of his rule.[29]
When Sadat took power the economic system was nearly bankrupt.
Industrial expansion and agricultural production were in
decline. The nation was importing significant amounts of
capital equipment and food grains. Large-scale barter arrangements with the East remained the only short-term solution to
financing the country's huge purchases. The national debt had
climbed well above a third of gross national product.[30]

The material costs of war had contributed enormously to
Egypt's economic mess. Nasser sent a 60,000-man military to
Yemen in 1962 to fight alongside the Republicans against the
Royalists. The costs of maintaining this force during six
years of fighting more than a thousand miles away were
enormous. The 1967 Six Day War against Israel cost not only
men and materiel but also billions of dollars in lost revenue
from the closure of the Suez Canal. And Israeli occupation of

the Sinai deprived Egypt of earnings from oil production and increased its dependence on outside sources. Subsidies from Arab nations did not come near to covering these costs nor those incurred during the arms buildup before the 1973 conflict with Israel.[31]

Most important, Egypt received no Western high-technology assistance when Sadat took power. Egyptian military and trade deals with the Soviet Union and Eastern Europe discouraged Western governments from pushing potential private investors to do business with Egypt. Moreover, the climate for investment was particularly poor prior to 1973, as the so-called "War of Attrition" along the Canal provided little promise that stability would soon return to the area.[32]

Sadat moved quickly after the October 1973 War to secure large-scale Western investment but with less success than anticipated. The Sinai disengagement agreement negotiated by U.S. Secretary of State Henry Kissinger did not lead to Israeli return of the entire captured territories. Thus, renewed warfare seemed likely at some future date, and the environment for Western investors remained unfavorable. The Egyptian government nevertheless prepared legislation that eased earlier restrictions on foreign investment and private capitalization. The policy encouraged joint ventures between foreign firms and Egyptian state enterprises and established free trade zones to boost exports. Efforts to encourage foreign banking in local currencies almost foundered because of a requirement that Egyptians own a majority of the assets of any enterprise. Nevertheless, nearly two dozen banking groups applied for permission to open local branches, and another half dozen sought joint ventures with Egyptian government authorities.[33]

Despite the early promise of a large and varied flow of foreign investment, bilateral credits and loans formed the bulk of capital entering Egypt. Nearly two-thirds of all foreign investment went into tourism, mainly hotel and apartment construction. Most Western private investors preferred to provide management expertise to ventures financed entirely with Arab money.[34]

Consumer demand grew in the aftermath of the October 1973 War, but imports of basic commodities did not follow suit. Wheat, flour, sugar, and oil remained in extremely short supply. Luxury goods, however, became available in urban areas, where large numbers of foreign and Arab businessmen led a comfortable existence. The already burgeoning black market flourished,

flourished, adding to inflationary pressures. The rise of commodity prices worldwide worsened Egypt's economic plight.[35]

Egypt's resistance to International Monetary Fund (IMF) currency reforms and other stabilization measures ended in the wake of continuing economic reverses during 1976. The year had witnessed sustained foreign exchange shortages, imbalances in foreign trade, larger external debt servicing, low agricultural production, rapid population growth, and rising expenditures for the maintenance of a standing army numbering nearly a half-million men.[36]

The Sadat regime therefore endorsed the IMF proposals for restructuring the Egyptian economy, including a measure to reduce government subsidy payments. The program, which absorbed nearly one-sixth of national income, held down the prices of basic goods. Food subsidies accounted for two-thirds of the total amount. An emergency IMF loan of $130 million depended on adoption of the reform measure.[37] Dr. Abd-al-Moneium al Qaissuni, newly designated minister of finance and economy and former chairman of the Arab International Bank, announced on January 18, 1977 that the government would end or substantially cut subsidy payments for products such as sugar, flour, rice, oil, bottled gas, cigarettes, and beer.[38]

Riots broke out in major Egyptian cities the next day, January 19, resulting in 77 killed and more than 500 injured.[39] The army was forced to fire on its own countrymen, and a curfew was imposed. The regime quickly rescinded reductions in food subsidies but refused to eliminate wage increases for public sector employees.[40] The government bitterly attacked the left for allegedly inciting the masses. Sadat's public approval rating sank to its lowest point for imposing the IMF measures.[41]

The effects of the cuts in food subsidies occurred immediately in urban areas. But the nature of urban politics in Egypt ensured that corrective measures would also take effect rapidly in the cities. Government decisions took far longer to filter down to rural areas, however, as did measures to rectify or reverse a damaging policy. In great part this fact stemmed from the relative lack of effective rural representation in parliament, in Shillal, and in other centers of power.[42]

Nevertheless, the rural middle class emerged by the end of 1976 as an important constituency. Sadat had widened the technocratic-managerial elite early in his presidency. Many of the new members came from the middle class rural notability.

The ruling elite in the Nasser period were also drawn from this significant group. Ownership of small land holdings, usually 10 to 50 acres, qualified a person as a member of the rural notability. These notables dominated village affairs and could afford to send their sons to urban areas for their education. Most critical, these men retained important links to their family members who remained in the cities and became members of the urban elite.[43]

The rural middle class had previously benefitted from the expansion of political development following the overthrow of the monarchy in 1952. Nasser's efforts to mobilize the countryside paved the way for small landholders to compete for positions of political authority on the local, provincial, and ultimately national levels. Prior to the Nasser regime, a mercantile elite of absentee landowners held hereditary title to political representation.[44] Protective of their newly acquired political status and grateful to the regime for elevating them, the rural notables remained strong allies of the government until 1962, when Nasser granted the peasantry equal status in the ASU and national assembly.

Yet the regime and rural notables continued to share an affinity for culture, agricultural productivity, populism, and nationalism. Even the government's efforts to strengthen urban sectors did not disturb the farmers, as their own family members were often the recipients of the additional benefits. Nasser also successfully retained their support through a variety of practical and symbolic measures that pandered to rural values and protected their social and material status.[45]

Nasser's death and Sadat's subsequent accession to power interrupted the relative harmony between government policy and rural expectations. A certain disequilibrium in the relationship between government and farmer had already begun to emerge before September 1970. Sadat therefore stepped into the presidency at a delicate moment. The demands of an emerging power struggle immediately buffeted the new Egyptian president. By May 1971, Sadat had won the struggle. He purged the party stalwarts and relegated the ASU to a lesser role in the new governmental structure. He liberalized election laws to permit a wider variety of candidates to parliament. Competition among and between members of the rural middle class intensified as a result, eroding their unity and political power, while Sadat's haste to improve the economic investment climate increased the political power of the urban middle and upper classes. The relationship between the government and the rural middle class deteriorated further with the establishment of the <u>Minabar</u> in the fall of 1976.[46]

Changes in the government's approach to Islam accompanied the political, economic, and social reforms. Nasser had maintained strong rhetorical support for Islam after the fall of the monarchy, but imposed restrictions on religion similar to those applied to the rest of society. The Nasser regime tightened regulations governing the administration of mosques, the choice of religious officials, and the education of clerics. Certain religious practices -- the worship of saints, animism, and exhibitionism — were outlawed and clerical courts were abolished in the drive to secularize Islam. In a concerted move to weaken the institutional power of religion, Nasser approved the transfer of some functions and powers from the Ministry of Waqfs -- the Department of Religious Affairs — to other more centralized and loyal government organs. For example, land owned by Islamic orders were redistributed by the ministry of agrarian reform; the administration of clerical schools was shifted to the education ministry; and financial support for Al-Azhar University -- training grounds for the nation's clerics -- was now handled by the treasury ministry.[47]

Sadat encouraged a resurgence of Islam, both to stem the tide of secularism and to help in the de-Nasserization of Egyptian society. In the fall of 1977 he began to characterize the regime of Nasser as materialistic and atheistic, thus encouraging the revival of the Muslim Brotherhood as a viable political organization.[48] The Society of Muslim Brothers -- Muslim Brotherhood — had been outlawed in 1954 after conspiring to overthrow the government. The Brotherhood advocated a return to the fundamental precepts of Islam in order to counter corrupt Western values spreading through the Muslim community.[49]

Sadat ordered the release of one thousand members of the Brotherhood sent to jail in 1954, but prohibited the group from becoming a legal political group.[50] The Brotherhood eschewed the violent tactics they had previously espoused to achieve their goals. It encouraged the formation of militant or so-called "Mahdist" movements to spread fundamentalist views among the populace. The Mahdists, who numbered only a few thousand adherents, emphasized intervention by supernatural foes.[51]

Thus, by January 1977 Sadat had changed the balance of Egyptian politics, set his country on a new economic and social course, sought and achieved a degree of psychological redemption by going to war against Israel, and established himself as the dominant force in Egyptian and Arab politics. Yet despite his efforts the stability and well being of Egypt was far from achieved, as the food riots -- their cause and consequences -- demonstrated. This reality led Sadat to seek a dramatic solution to the central problem of the Middle East -- the Arab-Israeli conflict.

The Begin Regime

After nearly three decades of Labor party government, Menachem Begin and his followers in the Likud coalition were elected to office in the spring of 1977. Begin's elevation to the office of prime minister was, as one observer noted, "more than a change in government."[52] The election of Israel's perennial opposition leader confirmed a major shift in the country's socio-cultural makeup that became more pronounced after the October 1973 war.[53] The ethnic composition of the Israeli electorate had significantly changed by 1973. Nearly a majority of all Israelis were of Sephardim — Asian-African — origin, while Ashkenazim — European Jewry -- had dominated until then.[54] The median age of the Sephardic Jew living in Israel was considerably lower than his Ashkenaz counterpart -- 35.1 to 51.4.[55] Differences in place of origin and age mirrored economic and cultural distinctions and underscored the emergence of separate societies within Israel.

The Ashkenaz Jew's association with the land predated Israeli statehood. Successive waves of immigrants began to establish Jewish settlements in Palestine as early as 1905.[56] The majority of Sephardim arrived in Israel in the early 1950s, well after the Ashkenazim had established their dominance in the professions, the bureaucracy, and technical-managerial class. The Sephardim settled in new lands away from the urban areas. They populated the agricultural cooperatives and became recruits for the army. Those who entered the urban work force were semiskilled and found employment in nonprofessional areas. The benefits available in a rapidly developing society were therefore almost entirely reserved for second generation Ashkenazim who regarded themselves as heirs of the real pioneers.[57]

Social inequalities were accentuated by cultural conflicts among the three main Jewish groups residing in Israel — Ashkenazim of Central and Eastern Europe, Sephardim and certain East Europeans who resided in <u>shtetls</u> early in the century, and the Sabras or those born and raised in Israel. The assymetry among these cultural groups created tensions as each acted in accordance with its special identity.[58]

The state of Israel enjoyed spectacular growth in its formative period particularly in the half dozen years between its last two wars with Egypt. Jerusalem's gross national product grew by an average of 11 percent per year between 1967 and 1973. Real monthly per capita income rose steadily from 570 to 1,148 Israeli pounds during the same period. The economy managed this enormous increase in spite of a five-fold growth in population since 1948.[59]

The rate of capitalization nearly matched the rate of immigration through 1970, largely because of an inflow of wealth from abroad. West Germany, for example, provided nearly a billion and a half dollars to individuals and an equal amount in war reparations to Israel itself over a 15-year period. Worldwide Jewish financial support to the state of Israel added another one and a half billion dollars through 1969, the majority of which funded social and educational projects and assisted in providing immigration and housing services. West German reparations and funds provided by the United Jewish Appeal -- a U.S. fund raising institution of the World Zionist Organization -- offset nearly three-quarters of the state's budget deficit before 1973. Foreign loans and development bonds accounted for the remainder.[60]

Israel's increasing dependence on foreign resources was already overheating the economy by 1973. The conflict with Egypt in the fall of 1973 resulted in a massive program of defense spending, which soared to more than $2 billion by 1975. Worldwide inflation, spurred by drastic oil price increases, further exacerbated Israeli economic woes between 1974 and 1976. Israel's balance of payments deficits skyrocketed to between $3 and 4 billion in 1975-1976.[61]

The inflationary spiral hit the lower classes -- the Sephardim -- especially hard. Efforts to control inflation included measures to reduce the government subsidy program. The Sephardim accounted for only 7 percent of the nation's income and devoted between 51 and 59 percent of their wages to housing and food. The subsidies ensured that this economic burden would not increase. The upper classes earned approximately 38 percent of the national income and devoted only a third of their earnings to basic needs.[62] Yet the reduction of subsidies for the poor was not accompanied by similar measures affecting the middle classes or by wage limitations in the industrial or agricultural sectors.[63]

This basic inequity belied the myth of a unified, balanced, and egalitarian Israeli society even before the outbreak of war in October 1973. But the Egyptian attack across the Suez Canal shattered the nation's sense of security and its trust in its leaders, thus casting doubt on the viability of Israel's very political structure. The political elite had believed defense and foreign affairs to be beyond the pale of public inquiry or discussion. Yet the leadership of the dominant political party, the Israeli Labor Party (ILP), had utterly miscalculated.

The government of Golda Meir would probably have been forced to resign in the immediate aftermath of the war had the ILP and the opposition not agreed to hold new elections in December 1973.[64] A month of preparations for a national election hardly sufficed to find new and presumably more trust-worthy candidates, to alter party lists, or to restore confidence in discredited leaders who in any case had been overtaken by the evolution of Israeli society. Thus, despite Prime Minister Golda Meir's narrow election victory, the conditions for the fall of Labor and consequent elevation of Begin already existed.[65]

The ILP emerged from a coalition of labor and agrarian interests in the early 1930s. Its leadership then and later reflected the mainstream of Zionist thinking and catered to an expanding population by providing social, cultural, and educational services. The earliest immigrants had been exposed to various socialist philosophies in the last years before the triumph of Bolshevism in Russia. Some had even accepted Bolshevik doctrine before fleeing from its tyranny. But the notion of a strongly centralized state system that cared for its citizenry was central to the ideological framework inherited by the Israel Labor Party.[66]

The policy of Mamlachtiyut or etatism practiced by the first ILP prime minister, David Ben Gurion, resulted in the absorption by the state of pioneering and social services previously supplied by Histradrut -- the General Federation of Labor -- and the Kibbutz movement. Resort to nationalist symbols fundamentally weakened the ideological attraction of ILP services. The immigration of large numbers of Sephardim pressured the ILP to purge early ideological strains from its rhetoric and policy. The party had to come to terms with the increased diversity in Israeli society if it wished to remain successful at the polls. The Labor Party thus created political machines to dispense patronage in the large urban centers -- Tel Aviv, Haifa, and Jerusalem. Political bosses handed out jobs, housing, and offices, thus guaranteeing wide public support for ILP policies. Ideological incentives to mobilize the electorate all but disappeared.[67]

Debate within the ILP in 1958 and again in 1965 did little to reestablish democratic procedures, although party stalwarts Moshe Dayan, Shimon Peres, and David Ben Gurion led the effort to broaden and reform the ILP. Thus, in the years just prior to the 1973 war the Labor Party became even more centralized, increasingly subject to the whims of old guard politicians, and less responsive to the general population. National institutions such as the Histradrut or the Kibbutz collectives regarded their own previous emphasis on ideological purity as passe and instead opted for its share of spoils under the new machine politics.[68]

While the Labor Party became more corrupt and less dynamic, the opposition began to revive. The 1965 election process witnessed the emergence of a coalition of the right-wing Herut Party led by Begin and the former General Zionist wing of the Liberal Party. This union was known as Gahal and was the precursor of the Likud coalition that took power in May 1977.[69]

Golda Meir's fight to survive after the December 1973 elections suffered severe setbacks in the ensuing months. First a traditional coalition partner, the National Religious Party (NRP), decided to remain outside the cabinet; then Moshe Dayan and Shimon Peres refused government posts. Threats to form a minority government and the specter of renewed conflict with Syria convinced both the NRP and recalcitrant Dayan and Peres to join the cabinet in the end. Widespread criticism of his handling of the 1973 War, however, forced Minister of Defense Dayan to resign from office and eventually brought down the government in April 1974.[70]

Pinchas Sapir, the party's most powerful political boss, attempted to revive the flagging popular appeal of the Israel Labor Party by selecting former Army Chief of Staff and Ambassador to the United States Yitzhak Rabin to replace Meir as prime minister.[71] Rabin narrowly defeated Shimon Peres for the party leadership in a bitterly fought contest and went on to form a cabinet that would serve out the remaining three years of Meir's term.[72] As time wore on, jealousies and antagonisms among Rabin's rivals totally immobilized the government.   Challengers Shimon Peres and Yigal Allon had become defense minister and foreign minister respectively.[73]

Rabin brought many of the ILP's top leaders into government, thereby loosening the reins of party authority in major labor strongholds.[74]   He created further antagonism among important patrons by seeking to streamline the cabinet and to reduce the party's influence on the functioning of government.[75] In a bid to restore some semblance of party control, Meir and others formed a consultative body to the prime minister.   The effort quickly failed.   Meanwhile, Sapir died. His successors lacked stature and failed to stem the rapid decline of the party.   Key party posts remained vacant for long periods; when ultimately filled, weak and ineffective choices replaced skilled incumbents.[76]

Moreover, the Rabin government faced charges of widespread corruption in its last year in office.   Asher Yadlin — party nominee for governor of the Bank of Israel and director of Histradrut Health Services — was convicted of accepting bribes and making false income tax declarations. Minister of Housing Avraham Offer, who was implicated in the scandal but denied complicity, committed suicide six weeks before Yadlin was sentenced to five years in jail.[77]

The government, reeling from the charges of corruption, became a minority caretaker when it ejected the National Religious Party (NRP) from the coalition. The NRP had abstained in a vote of no-confidence called to protest the scheduling of a military ceremony on the eve of the Sabbath.[78]

The Rabin family itself would not escape the strange and ill-timed set of circumstances that ultimately led to the Labor Party's defeat.   Leah Rabin, the prime minister's wife, was charged with and later found guilty of minor foreign currency violations.[79] Yitzhak Rabin immediately tendered his resignation.   But because of a technicality that prevented him from stepping down from a caretaker government, he took an extended leave of absence instead.[80] The party immediately appointed Shimon Peres acting prime minister and subsequently chose him to stand as its candidate for the prime ministership.[81]

The composition of the Israeli electorate had changed substantially,   even since the 1973 national campaign.   A majority of Israelis were of Asian-African origin by 1976, and projected birth rates confirmed that the trend would continue in the future. While the voting population remained relatively static, the Sephardic voter was on the average much younger than his Ashkenazi counterpart.   The electorate as a whole was less well educated, and the average voter had become more conservative and highly suspicious of government promises. U.S. President Jimmy Carter's call for greater sympathy toward Palestinian rights did nothing to stop the Israeli drift to the right. Steady economic decline further alienated the voter from the party and policies that had dominated the country since statehood. Finally, Begin seemed to fill a need for a strong leader such as Israel had not had since David Ben Gurion.[82]

The parties that vied for power in the 1977 elections spanned the entire political spectrum, from ultra right wing to far left. The single new group to emerge in 1977 was called the Democratic Movement for Change (DMC). The DMC was formed from several protest groups disaffected by Labor's poor performance.[83] Led by former Army Chief of Staff and noted archaeologist Yigal Yadin, DMC supporters were largely urban university graduates above forty years of age with European or American backgrounds and relatively high income. These voters viewed economic matters and social distinctions as paramount. The DMC party platform emphasized hard work, increasing productivity, better labor-management relations, streamlining of government functions, changes in the electoral system, and narrowing of the social gap.[84]

The right-wing Likud coalition comprised several often disparate elements, including the Herut Party — organized out of the Irgun guerrilla organization of the early 1940s — led since its birth in 1948 by Menachem Begin, the Liberal Party under the leadership of Simcha Ehrlich, and La'am controlled by Yigal Hurvitz. Herut based its political views on the philosophy of Vladimir Jabotinsky, the founder of Revisionist Zionism. Jabotinsky advocated larger opportunities for private enterprise, efforts to reduce class differences, and, most important, retention of all the biblical lands of Israel and formation of a binational state. The nationalistic Herut Party upheld traditional Jewish religious values and in particular viewed historical bonds to the land of Israel as a moral imperative. Herut wanted to curb bureaucratic growth, the paternalism of the state, and preferential tax treatment of Histradrut. In order to safeguard the social and economic needs of the disadvantaged, Herut established in 1934 a trade union to compete with Histradrut. Although absorbed by Histradrut in 1963, the group has remained a troublesome faction. Herut supporters initially came from strongly nationalistic, middle- and working-class elements of the population. The party's early voters came from Eastern Europe, but Herut gradually grew popular among the less successful immigrants form Asia and Africa.[85]

The Liberals had many embodiments but derived from a faction of the general Zionist movement that represented the interests of the self—employed middle class and — like the Irgun — fought to expell the British from Palestine before independence. Liberal Party followers were generally middle class Israelis of European origin who espoused the virtues of private enterprise.[86]

La'am recruited its following mainly from former ILP supporters and members of the agricultural cooperative. It remained independent of the ILP after some of its most prominent young members — such as Dayan and Peres — rejoined the dominant party in 1969 as a result of poor success at the polls. The group's positions on domestic and foreign policy differed only slightly from those of the Liberal and Herut parties.[87]

In foreign policy, the Likud platform called for the retention of Judea and Samaria — the West Bank — and the Gaza Strip. It insisted on the rights of Jews to settle in any part of the territories and granted the Arabs the continued freedom to become Israeli citizens. It pledged to accept nothing less than secure and defensible borders in the Sinai and Golan Heights. Finally, it expressed disappointment in the step—by—step approach to negotiating peace in the Middle East and backed a comprehensive framework instead.

In domestic policy, it endorsed greater respect for traditional religious practice and education. It advocated compulsory arbitration in labor disputes and nationalization of public health services. And it proposed social and economic policies that sought to balance the demands of a free—market economy with the special needs of the lowest classes.[88]

The most significant of the smaller parties was the National Religious Party (NRP). Established in 1956 through a merger of two small religious parties, the NRP remained a coalition partner of the Israel Labor Party almost without pause until 1976, enabling successive ILP governments to stay in power. The NRP generally won 10 percent of the vote and succeeded in electing 11 or 12 of its members to the Knesset; the party had placed only 10 in the eighth Knesset as a result of its support for Golda Meir's unpopular government after the 1973 War. A leadership struggle in the party that began in 1970 and intensified under Rabin's prime ministership reflected the opposition of younger party members to any concessions regarding the future of the West Bank and Gaza Strip. The radical Gush Emunim organization, which advocated Israeli settlement and annexation of the West Bank territories, possessed great influence with the youth wing of the NRP. Rabin's decision to expell the NRP from his coalition in late 1976 freed its activist members to campaign in the 1977 election within an ideologically pure framework.[89]

In the May 17, 1977 election, Likud won 43 Knesset seats, up from 39 seats. Labor's share fell from 51 to 32 seats. The Democratic Movement for Change received 15 seats, the National Religious Party 12, and two smaller religious groups five. The larger of the latter two -- Aguda Israel -- advocated strict orthodoxy and accounted for four of the five seats. The stage was thus set for a coalition government under the leadership of Begin's Herut Party and including the NRP, Aguda Israel, and others.[90]

A unique combination of factors contributed to Likud's largely unexpected triumph. First, the DMC was a powerful and effective competitor for support among Labor's traditional constituency, the high-income urban professional. Second, the series of scandals that beset the government shortly before the election severely undermined its chances to restore the public trust in its competence lost during the 1973 war. Third, increased economic deprivation among the Sephardim and the growth of the Sephardic community as a proportion of the total Israeli population strengthened and expanded Likud's traditional constituency. Finally, continued Arab hostility toward Israel and evidence of U.S. support for a Palestinian entity on the West Bank increased the attractiveness of Likud's hardline, nationalist foreign policies.[91]

Menachem Begin, the tough, uncompromising leader of Herut and the Likud, suffered a heart attack during the campaign and remained immobile through the largest part of the election process. He rose from his bed, however, to debate Shimon Peres before a nationally televised audience. He acquitted himself well and projected an image of strength and conviction remeniscent of former Israeli leaders such as David Ben Gurion -- ironically Begin's archenemy for thirty years.[92]

Begin had established a party list prior to the election to determine the number of seats each Likud member would receive in the cabinet. He applied several immutable rules in devising the list:

o   The leaders of the Likud movement and its constituent groups were guaranteed a cabinet seat.

o   Each constituent group would receive a number of seats commensurate with its strength in the previous Knesset and estimated popularity.

o   And within that framework of proportional representation, Begin would attempt to fulfill the claims of subgroups and active party workers in order to prevent early disagreement, disaffection, or outright secession from the coalition.[93]   Thus the political balance if not the actual membership of the Likud cabinet was nearly preordained by pre-election maneuver and compromise.   The 43 seats won by the Likud Party were assigned in the following manner: Herut, twenty; Liberals, fourteen; La'am, eight; one undecided.[94]

The Begin cabinet was sworn in on June 20, 1977.   Begin, Minister of Defense Ezer Weizman, Minister of Agriculture Ariel Sharon, and Minister of Immigration David Levy, represented Herut in the cabinet.   Party leader and Minister of Finance Simcha Ehrlich, Minister of Construction Gideon Pat, and Minister of Energy Yitzhak Modai represented the Liberals. La'am leader Yigal Hurvitz became minister of health, completing the Likud block in the cabinet.   The NRP was represented by its head, Yosef Burg, as minister of interior and a leader of the youth faction, Zevulun Hammer, was appointed minister of education.   Moshe Dayan joined the cabinet as minister of foreign affairs despite the objections of Herut.   At the urging of Begin, however, Dayan resigned from the ILP and became an independent.[95]

In domestic matters, Herut and the Liberals differed substantially as each group served radically disparate constituencies.[96]   Cabinet unanimity on foreign policy matters was no less difficult to achieve.   For example, Dayan and Sharon disagreed over the settlements policy.   The former sought to retain territory principally as a bargaining chip, while the latter wished to settle and keep the land as a matter of principle.   Minister of Defense Weizman often sided with Dayan.   The Liberals remained noncommitial.   La'am and NRP members were violently nationalistic.[97]   These divisions within the cabinet would repeatedly assert themselves during the peace process with Egypt, forcing Begin to use all his political skills to achieve a settlement and playing a crucial role in determining the eventual parameters of peace.

18

1. Robert Springborg, "Patterns of Association in the Egyptian Political Elite" in George Lenczowski, ed. Political Elites in the Middle East (Washington: American Enterprise Institute for Public Policy Research, 1975), p. 92. See, also, Anwar el Sadat, In Search of Identity (New York: Harper and Row, 1977), p. 204–205; Leonard Binder, In a Moment of Enthusiasm: Political Power and the Second Stratum in Egypt (Chicago: University of Chicago Press, 1978), p. 383–396; Saad el Shazly, The Crossing of the Suez (San Francisco: American Mideast Research, 1980), p. 91–100; Raphael Israeli, The Public Diary of President Sadat: The Road to War (October 1970–October 1976) (Leiden: E. J. Brill, 1978), Volume 1, p. 47–72.

2. R. Michael Burrell and Abbas R. Kelidar, Egypt: The Dilemmas of a Nation — 1970–1977 (Beverly Hills: Sage Publications, 1977), p. 26–30; also, Raymond A. Hinnebusch, "Egypt Under Sadat: Elites, Power Structure and Political Change in a Post Populist State" in Social Problems, Volume 28, Number 4, April, 1981, p. 444, 453.

3. Burrell and Kelidar, Egypt: The Dilemmas of a Nation, p. 26–30. See also, Robert Springborg, "Patrimonialism and Policy–Making in Egypt: Nasser and Sadat and the Tenure Policy for Reclaimed Lands" in Middle Eastern Studies, Volume 15, Number 1, January 1979, p. 51–52.

4. Springborg, "Patrimonialism and Policy–Making in Egypt" in Middle Eastern Studies, January 1979, p. 52–53; also, Hinnebusch, "Egypt Under Sadat: Elites, Power Structure and Political Change..." Social Problems, April 1981, p. 445–446.

5. Ehud Yaari, "Sadat's Pyramid of Power" in The Jerusalem Quarterly, Number 14, Winter 980, p. 117–119.

6. Ibid., p. 118.

7. Sadat, In Search of Identity, p. 204.

8. Yaari, "Sadat's Pyramid of Power" in The Jerusalem Quarterly, Winter 1980, p. 110.

9. Springborg, "Patrimonialism and Policy-Making in Egypt" in Middle Eastern Studies, January 1979, p. 52–53; also, Hinnebusch, "Egypt Under Sadat: Elites, Power Structure and Political Change..." Social Problems, April 1981, p. 445–446.

10. Springborg, "Patterns of Association in Egyptian Political Elite" in Lenczowski, ed. Political Elites in the Middle East, p. 97–99.

11. Ibid., p. 99–104.

12. Springborg, "Sayed Bey Marei and Political Clientalism in Egypt" in Comparative Political Studies, Volume 12, Number 3, October 1979, p. 261.

13. Yaari, "Sadat's Pyramid of Power" in The Jerusalem Quarterly, Winter 1980, p. 112.

14. John Waterbury, Egypt: Burdens of the Past/Options for the Future (Bloomington: University of Indiana Press, 1978), p. 237.

15. Ibid., p. 250–251.

16. Munir K. Nasser, Press, Politics and Power: Egypt's Heikel and Al-Ahram (Ames: The Iowa State University Press, 1979), p. 89–102.

17. Waterbury, Egypt: Burdens of the Past/Options for the Future, p. 251.

18. Springborg, "Sayed Bey Marei and Political Clientalism in Egypt" in Comparative Political Studies, October 1979, p. 280.

19. Springborg, "Patterns of Association in the Egyptian Political Elite" in Lenczowski, ed. Political Elites in the Middle East, p. 104–105.

20. Burrell and Kelidar, Egypt: The Dilemmas of a Nation, p. 70; also, Hinnebusch, "Egypt Under Sadat: Elites, Power Structure and Political Change..." Social Problems, April 1981, p. 453–454.

20

21. Springborg, "Patterns of Association in the Egyptian Political Elite" in Lenczowski, ed. Political Elites in the Middle East, p. 99; also, see, Mark N. Cooper, "The Demilitarization of the Egyptian Cabinet" in International Journal of Middle East Studies, Volume 14 (1982), p. 203–225.

22. Yaari, "Sadat's Pyramid of Power" in The Jerusalem Quarterly, p. 113–114.

23. Ibid.; also, Hinnebusch, "Egypt Under Sadat: Elites, Power Structure and Political Change..." Social Problems, April 1981, p. 446.

24. Waterbury, Egypt: Burdens of the Past/Options for the Future, p. 251–253. See, also, Mark Cooper, The Transformation of Egypt (Baltimore: The Johns Hopkins University Press, 1982), p. 64–82.

25. Burrell and Kelidar, Egypt: The Dilemmas of a Nation, p. 30.

26. Waterbury, Egypt: Burdens of the Past/Options for the Future, p.251–253.

27. Burrell and Kelidar, Egypt: The Dilemmas of a Nation, p. 31–38. see, also, R. D. McLaurin, Mohammed Mughisuddin, Abraham R. Wagner, Foreign Policy Making in the Middle East (New York: Praeger, 1979), p. 42–45.

28. Burrell and Kelidar, Egypt" The Dilemmas of a Nation, p. 39.

29. Waterbury, Egypt: Burdens of the Past/Options for the Future, p. 202; also, Cooper, The Transformation of Egypt, p. 44–63.

30. Waterbury, Egypt: Burdens of the Past/Options for the Future, p. 202–205.

31. Ibid., p. 202.

32. Ibid.

33. Ibid., p. 221–232.

34. Ibid., p. 228.

35. Ibid., p. 231.

36. Ibid., p. 308–309.

37. Ibid., p. 314. For discussion of Egypt and the IMF, see, Ali E. Hillal Dessouki, "Policy Making in Egypt: A Case Study of the Open Door Economic Policy" in Social Problems, April 1981, p. 410–416.

38. New York Times, January 19, 1977.

39. New York Times, January 20, 1977.

40. Waterbury, Egypt: Burdens of the Past/Options for the Future, p. 315.

41. Ibid., p. 316.

42. Janet Abu–Lughod, "Rural Migration and Politics in Egypt" in Richard Antoun and Ilya Harik, ed. Rural Politics and Social Change in the Middle East (Bloomington: Indiana University Press, 1972), p. 329–331. See, also, Karima Korayem, "The Rural–Urban Income Gap in Egypt and Biased Agricultural Pricing Policy" in Social Problems, April 1981, p. 417–429.

43. Binder, In A Moment of Enthusiasm, p. 395–396.

44. Iliya F. Harik, "Mobilization Policy and Political Change in Rural Egypt" in Antoun and Harik, ed. Rural Politics and Social Change in the Middle East, p. 295–296.

45. Ibid., p. 302–310.

46. Binder, In A Moment of Enthusiasm, p. 395–396. See, also, Hinnebusch, "Egypt Under Sadat: Elites, Power Structure and Political Change..." Social Problems, April 1871, p. 445–451.

47. Monroe Berger, Islam in Egypt Today: Social and Political Aspects of Popular Religion (London: Cambridge University Press, 1970), p. 45–49.

48. Israel Altman, "Islamic Movements in Egypt" in The Jerusalem Quarterly, Number 10, Winter 1979, p. 97. See also, Saad Eddin Ibrahim, "Anatomy of Egypt's Militant Islamic Groups: Methodological Note and Preliminary Findings" in International Journal of Middle East Studies, Volume 12 (1980), p. 427; Gabriel R. Warburg, "Islam and Politics in Egypt: 1952–1980" Middle Eastern Studies, Volume 18, Number 2, April 1982, p. 131–157; Nazih N. M. Ayubi, "The Political Revival of Islam: The Case of Egypt" International Journal of Middle East Studies, Volume 12 (1980), p. 481–499; Fadwa El Guindi, "Is There an Islamic Alternative? The Case of Egypt's Contemporary Islamic Movement" International Insight, Volume 1, Number 6, July/August 1981, p. 19–24; Abd al–Monein Said Aly and Manfred W. Wenner, "Modern Islamic Reform Movements: The Muslim Brotherhood in Contemporary Egypt" in The Middle East Journal, Volume 36, Number 3, Summer 1982, p. 336–361.

49. Altman, "Islamic Movements in Egypt" in The Jerusalem Quarterly, Winter 1979, p. 90; Aly and Wenner, "Modern Islamic Reform Movements: The Muslim Brotherhood in Contemporary Egypt" The Middle East Journal, Summer 1982, p. 336–361.

50. Altman, "Islamic Movements in Egypt" in The Jerusalem Quarterly, Winter 1979, p. 92–93.

51. Ibid., p. 101–103.

52. Dan Horowitz, "More Than a Change in Government" in The Jerusalem Quarterly, Number 5, Fall 1977, p. 3–19.

53. Ibid.

54. Asher Arian, "The Electorate: Israel 1977" in Howard R. Penniman, ed. Israel at the Polls: The Knesset Elections of 1977 (Washington: American Enterprise Institute for Public Policy Research, 1979), p. 83.

55. Ibid., p. 84.

56. Daniel J. Elazar, "Israel's Compound Polity" in Penniman ed. Israel at the Polls, p. 4–5.

57. Ibid., p. 24.

58. Ibid., p. 24–30.

59. Richard F. Nyrop, ed. Israel: A Country Study (Washington: The American University, 1978), p. 179; Harold I. Greenberg and Samuel Nadler, Poverty in Israel: Economic Realities and the Promise of Social Justice (New York: Praeger, 1977), p. 23.

60. Nyrop, Israel: A Country Study, p. 218–219.

61. Ann Crittenden, "Israel's Economic Plight" in Foreign Affairs, Volume 57, Number 5, Summer 1979, p. 1005.

62. Greenberg and Nadler, Poverty in Israel, p. 73–82.

63. Ibid., p. 57–69.

64. Myron J. Aronoff, "The Decline of the Israeli Labor Party: Causes and Significance" in Penniman, ed. Israel at the Polls, p. 136.

65. Ibid., p. 133.

66. Ibid., p. 117–118.

67. Ibid., p. 119–120.

68. Ibid., p. 124.

69. Benjamin Akzin, "The Likud" in Penniman, ed. Israel at the Polls, p. 95–96.

70. Nathan Yani, Party Leadership: Maintenance and Change (Ramat Gan: Turtledove Publishing, 1981), p. 53–54.

71. Ibid., p. 54–58.

72. Aronoff, "The Decline of the Israeli Labor Party" in Penniman, Israel at the Polls, p. 137.

73. Ibid.

74. Ibid., p. 141.

24

75. Ibid., p. 141–142.

76. Ibid., p. 142.

77. Ibid., p. 143.

78. Ibid.

79. Ibid., p. 144. See, also, Marie Brenner, "The Very Strange Life of the Yitzhak Rabins" in New York, February 13, 1978, p. 50–56.

80. Aronoff, "The Decline of the Israeli Labor Party" in Penniman, ed. Israel at the Polls, p. 144.

81. Ibid.

82. Arian, "The Electorate: Israel 1977" in Penniman, ed. Israel at the Polls, p. 59–67.

83. Efraim Torgovnik, "A Movement for Change in a Stable System" in Penniman, ed. Israel at the Polls, p. 147–164.

84. Ibid., p. 156–158. See, also, Eli Eyal, "The Democratic Movement for Change: Origins and Perspectives" in Middle East Review, Volume 10, Number 1, Fall 1977, p. 54–59.

85. Akzin, "The Likud" in Penniman, ed. Israel at the Polls, p. 92–95.

86. Ibid., p. 95–96.

87. Ibid., p. 98.

88. Ibid., p. 104–106.

89. Elyakim Rubinstein, "The Lesser Parties in the Israeli Elections of 1977" in Penniman, ed. Israel at the Polls, p. 177–180. See also, Gary S. Schiff, Tradition and Politics: The Religious Parties of Israel (Detroit: Wayne State University Press, 1977), p. 89–125.

90. Akzin, "The Likud" in Penniman, ed. Israel at the Polls, p. 110–111.

91. Arian, "The Electorate: Israel 1977" in Penniman, ed. Israel at the Polls, p. 88. See, also, Don Peretz, "The Earthquake: Israel's Ninth Knesset Elections" in The Middle East Journal, Summer 1977, p. 251–266; New York Times, September 6, 1977; New York Times, June 4, 1977.

92. Akzin, "The Likud" in Penniman, ed. Israel at the Polls, p. 107–110.

93. Ibid.

94. Ibid., p. 112–113.

95. For discussion of Dayan appointment see, Moshe Dayan, Breakthrough: A Personal Account of the Egypt–Israel Peace Negotiations (London: Weidenfeld and Nicholson, 1981), p. 1–7; also, New York Times, June 15, 1977; "Interview with Dayan" in Washington Post, May 26, 1977; Washington Post, May 27, 1977; New York Times, May 27, 1977.

96. Akzin, "The Likud" in Penniman, ed. Israel at the Polls, p. 105, 114.

97. Ibid., p. 94, 104, 114.

1
The Struggle
for a Geneva Conference

The Motives

Egypt and Israel shared a common desire for peace at the start of 1977. Yet the separate paths each chose to achieve that goal resulted from dissimilar motives.

Egyptian President Anwar Sadat had by mid–December 1976 abandoned Kissinger's step–by–step approach to peace negotiations and successfully sponsored a United Nations resolution calling for talks to resume in Geneva no later than 1 March 1977.[1] He also called for a Palestinian presence at the conference. Sadat later emphasized that the "core" and "crux of the problem" continued to be the Palestinian situation. He said the "Palestinians must have their state" and indicated that Egypt would press for creation of a Palestinian entity on the West Bank of the Jordan and in the Gaza Strip, with a corridor linking the two territories. The Palestinian entity would, however, be linked in some manner to Jordan.[2]

Sadat's empathy for the Palestinians was actually a hollow gesture. His endorsement of Palestinian statehood resulted not from a heartfelt belief in their cause but from fears that a continued impasse would jeopardize attempts to secure a return of the Sinai. Egypt had restored its honor with the 1973 Suez Canal crossing, but even that partial success had worn thin by January 1977. Reestablishment of sovereignty over the Sinai would boost Egyptian military morale, reduce the cost of maintaining a large standing army, and reduce the competition among advisers who, depending on their ideology, viewed rapprochement with Israel as either desirable or disastrous. In short, reacquisition of the Sinai would achieve large political gains at a time of declining economic fortunes.

Lower military expenditures would allow Sadat to channel additional resources to the urban poor, partially mitigating the ill–effects of excessively rapid development. The Egyptian president would then be in an excellent position to balance the needs of an army tied in large part to the rural middle class with the conflicting but equally important needs of an urban peasantry willing to seek alliance with radical religious sects who could topple the regime.

Sadat's effort to accommodate Palestinian demands for statehood at a Geneva–style, comprehensive peace conference was an effort to recover the lost territories quickly and under multilateral auspices. Kissinger's step–by–step strategy after nearly four years of bargaining had gained Sadat only a separation of combatants and small slices of land. The Palestinians –– once uncontrollable, leaderless, and hopelessly radicalized –– had moderated their tone and appeared to have found a natural leader in Yasir Arafat. Sadat would not demand a totally independent Palestine but one constrained through some form of relationship with Jordan. Palestinian representation at Geneva could be as part of an all–Arab delegation. Even a partial success at a new Geneva Conference would lead to an end to hostilities between Arab and Jew and pave the way for the return of the Sinai to Egypt –– or so Sadat reasoned.[3]

The Israelis, however, were conditioned by experience to view the dynamics of Geneva from a different perspective. Prime Minister Yitzhak Rabin favored a new international conference to deal with the issues still outstanding. His concept of the new Geneva negotiations was patterned after the recently successful European Security Conference in Helsinki, but with an important difference. The Helsinki meeting had ratified existing boundaries; a Geneva meeting, in Rabin's view, could consider negotiation of new frontiers. Israel was determined –– at whatever type of conference that might be called –– to require recognition of its legal and moral right to exist. Failure to obtain that singularly important concession had caused Israel to boycott several previous conferences. Israel had always insisted, as it would under the Rabin plan, that all essentials of cooperation with a neighboring state –– trade, technological assistance, and human coexistence –– must be on the conference agenda. Rabin blocked any representation of the Palestinian Liberation Organization (PLO) by restricting attendance at the meeting to "heads of sovereign governments."[4]

The earlier step–by–step negotiating strategy had served Israeli interests well. Partial withdrawals from captured territory could be exchanged for substantive Arab retreat from a formal state of war. Furthermore, Israel could obtain complete recognition and full relations –– including an exchange of ambassadors, lifting of trade restrictions, and extension of oil lease arrangements -- incrementally through staged evacuation of the occupied lands.[5]

There were other problems, however. Most proposals for a general settlement threatened Israeli sensibilities and perceived security needs by explicitly calling for Palestinian self-determination. Israeli leaders had refused to attend a Geneva-style conference for fear of being forced into an unacceptable solution of the Palestinian impasse. Measures to provide for territorial adjustment in the West Bank, such as the Allon Plan, were advanced only within the context of Jordanian sovereignty.[6]

Rabin's acceptance of a comprehensive framework seems all the more curious unless viewed as a by-product of the volatile Israeli political scene during the winter of 1976. The National Religious Party (NRP), the Israeli Labor Party's (ILP) traditional coalition partner, had stiffened its position toward the West Bank and stubbornly refused to consider even minor concessions to Jordan. A mixture of younger NRP members and other more radical -- but orthodox religious -- elements even urged outright annexation of the territory to accommodate a planned expansion of Jewish settlements. Rabin's overall political weakness enhanced the ability of the NRP, minority party, to exert heavy influence on Israel's foreign policy. In addition, Rabin had been outflanked by rival party leader Yigal Allon who, as foreign minister, articulated a plan of self-rule for Palestinians in the West Bank and Gaza Strip, linked to Israeli military administration and Jordanian political federation. Shimon Peres, the more serious contender for party leadership, favored more Israeli settlements in the West Bank and a total ban on any talks with the PLO. As defense minister in the Rabin cabinet, Peres had tried unsuccessfully to sponsor municipal elections in administered Arab territories -- hoping thereby to drive a wedge between local Palestinian officials and the PLO.[7]

It was to ensure his own political survival that Rabin sought a middle-of-the-road negotiation posture. A pragmatic yet principled stance -- equidistant between the positions of Peres and Allon -- could earn Rabin renomination as prime minister. Increased U.S. financial and material support obtained as a result of firm but flexible bargaining could reassure a divided electorate of Rabin's effectiveness. The Israeli prime minister had committed a serious gaffe by seeming to endorse incumbent President Gerald Ford prior to the 1976

U.S. election. The newly elected U.S. president, Jimmy Carter, was known to favor a solution to the impasse along the lines suggested in a December 1975 Brookings Report,[8] and a demonstration of reasonableness by Rabin would probably erase any lingering ill-effects of his impolitic endorsement of Ford. In any event, the struggle to achieve a reputation for moderation was joined with Egypt, as the focus for settlement of the Arab–Israeli conflict shifted from the Middle East to Washington.

Washington Meetings: First Rounds

The Brookings Report offered the Carter administration a welcome opportunity to design its own policy.[9] Zbigniew Brezinski and William Quandt were members of the Brookings study group and each was to play a key role in developing Carter's Middle East strategy — the former as National Security Council (NSC) adviser, the latter as senior Middle East Director for the NSC.[10]

Middle East policy making in the U.S. government had been the special province of Henry Kissinger during the Nixon and Ford administrations. Despite Kissinger's penchant for close and detailed supervision of foreign policy making, he had organized a particularly able group of assistants at both the NSC and Department of State to pursue a settlement of the Arab–Israeli conflict. Carter chose to retain most of the Kissinger team. Quandt had served for two years as a junior White House staff member in the early 1970s. Assistant Secretary of State for the Near East and South Asia Alfred Atherton also remained and would, before the end of 1977, emerge as a special presidential assistant, shuttling between Cairo and Jerusalem as Kissinger had in 1975. Quandt's former superior at the NSC, Harold Saunders, became Director of the Bureau of Intelligence and Research at the state department and later succeeded Atherton as Assistant Secretary for the Near East and South Asia. Leslie Janka, a former NSC press aide of Kissinger, remained the ranking head for Middle East matters in the Defense Department's Office of International Security Affairs.

The drafting of papers on the Arab–Israeli conflict —— unlike other maiden attempts at foreign policy making — became a smooth operation during the Carter administration. This efficiency was not surprising because Quandt, Saunders, Atherton, and Janka had worked together during the Kissinger era, spoke the same bureaucratic language, and to a certain extent viewed the Middle East through similar lenses.[11]

Such effective management assured the administration of at least modest success in its effort to achieve some progress toward peace before the end of 1977. Carter sought to hasten the process by sending Secretary of State Vance to the Middle East in mid–February to solicit advice from local officials.[12] Meanwhile, the administration worked to construct a balanced peace proposal to present to a succession of Middle East statesmen visiting Washington during March and April. Significant progress toward the convening of a new Geneva Conference would be unlikely until after the May 17 Israeli elections, but valuable insights concerning the minimum demands of the parties involved could be gained in the interim. The idea of granting PLO representation as part of an all–Arab delegation appeared to be gaining nearly universal acceptance.[13] The Brookings Report had spoken of "comprehensive" peace, but that term was defined narrowly in one capital and broadly in another. Moreover, the staged withdrawal envisioned for Israel in the Brookings study could occur only after several prerequisities had been met. To detail the ultimate objective, the administration seemed to assume, would be the easiest step toward an accommodation between Arabs and Israelis.[14]

The Rabin Visit — March 1977

Rabin underscored the vast differences that separated Arab and Israeli notions of a final peace during a visit to the White House in early March. In the view of Rabin and Vance the Arab position amounted to an offer to end hostilities in exchange for the return of the occupied territories. Such a tradeoff did not suffice for the Israelis. Rabin sought a comprehensive peace treaty that ensured open borders, cultural exchanges, and diplomatic relations. He still considered a Geneva–style conference a desirable objective. Staged Israeli withdrawal from occupied territory was also possible if accompanied by Arab actions to grant Jerusalem permanent status.

Rabin's political insecurity prevented him from being too specific on final borders. A territorial compromise with Jordan, which would include some degree of cooperation in civil matters, was advanced as a likely Labor Party response to a peace proposal. But Rabin was required to point out that the opposition Likud party would oppose adamantly any withdrawal from occupied lands.

Neither the Israeli government nor its opposition would accept either the establishment of a Palestinian state on the West Bank or direct negotiations with the PLO. Palestinian representatives, however, might be included in a Jordanian delegation to a Geneva Conference. Rabin held to his earlier insistence that only sovereign states would be allowed to participate in discussions. Israel opposed the proposal for a single united Arab delegation favored by the more radical Arab states.

Carter's preference for a separate Palestinian entity, direct talks with the PLO, and a substantial return of territory occupied by Israel clearly irritated Rabin. The Israeli prime minister expected Washington to urge a Geneva Conference, but he did not anticipate Carter's apparent desire to spell out in advance the entire scenario for settlement. Even more unsettling was Carter's decision to make the plan public, thus informing Arab and Israeli audiences of the ill-fated success of the visit. Rabin had hoped for a visible confluence of views with Washington to enhance his attractiveness to party and nation. Now, he would have to return to Jerusalem amidst a barrage of criticism that Israel might have to return to the Rogers Plan and pre–June 1967 borders. The Israeli press characterized Rabin's trip a failure despite the prime minister's willingness to accept the popularly held view of a future peace with the Arabs.[15]

The Sadat Visit — April 1977

Anwar Sadat visited Washington one month later. Egypt's President had just finished hosting the 13th session of the Palestine National Council. This grand strategy meeting of the Palestinian leadership failed either to resolve local leadership conflicts or to forge a general agreement on how to achieve statehood on the West Bank. Sadat's orchestration a few days earlier of a Cairo–based discussion between Jordan's King Hussein and PLO leader Arafat had also failed to achieve federation between the guerrilla movement and Amman.[16]

Sadat's own domestic position had eroded as a result of the January food riots. He faced strident criticism from the left, as the belief spread that the January uprising was a populist revolt. Sadat had acknowledged that rapid growth in food technology and more housing for the urban poor were essential to curb internal insecurity.[17]

The appearance of progress toward a peace treaty was therefore critical to Sadat. But the Egyptian leader could produce nothing more than the hope that the occupied territories might be recovered. First, the PLO would not abandon its charter -- and that was a sine qua non for Israeli withdrawal from the Sinai. Second, a PLO federation with Jordan was unlikely, and might lead to an independent Palestinian state on the West Bank — a development unacceptable to Cairo and Amman as well as to Tel Aviv.

Sadat therefore temporized in his meetings with Carter. He believed that delay would earn him gratitude in Cairo, among the Palestinian leadership, and in other Arab capitals for driving a tough bargain with Israel's American patron. In reality, Sadat knew he could not get Arab moderates to join a three-party agreement at Geneva in the spring of 1977 or at any other time. So he stalled. He pressed for detailed preparations for a Geneva conference before the end of 1977 and for dialogue between the United States and the PLO. He cited the centrality of the Palestinian problem, hinting that Jordan was a key to its solution, and asserted that Egypt would not yield on its claim to the whole Sinai.[18] Thus, Sadat avoided the controversial issue of full ties with Israel while catering to Palestinian desires for a homeland and enticing his domestic audience with the prospect of obtaining the return of the Sinai. Each element of his negotiating posture satisfied at least one of Egypt's uncertain allies, and overall would assure Sadat's domestic safety for a time.

Carter nevertheless managed to wring some small concessions from the Egyptian president. Normalization of relations with Israel, Sadat agreed, would occur within five years of signing an agreement, and certain interim steps could take place sooner. Demilitarized zones could be established on a reciprocal basis following agreement between the parties on the nature of a peace.[19] Rabin's April 8 withdrawal as head of the Labor Party -- after a scandal had broken out concerning violations of Israeli currency laws by his wife -- cast a pall over the Carter-Sadat talks.

The Hussein Visit -- April 1977

Jordan's King Hussein was the final Middle East visitor to the White House in the spring of 1977. His formula for a successful peace conference involved bringing a pan—Arab delegation to Geneva to meet with the Israelis. The PLO could be part of a single Arab delegation, but Hussein believed Palestinians not connected with the umbrella organization should also participate. He vowed to respect any decision agreeable to the Palestinian people, including affiliation of a Palestinian entity with Jordan. Israel would be required, however, to relinquish all occupied territory, including the West Bank.[20]

Hussein's proposal to include Palestinians from outside the PLO introduced a new element in the discussions. It was entirely consistent with Jordanian domestic needs. The PLO had been a source of great discomfort for Hussein almost since its founding. The 1948 Arab defeat by Israel sent hundreds of thousands of Palestinians fleeing into Jordan, where they were treated as second—class citizens. PLO commanders sought to organize the rootless masses and on several occasions posed a severe threat to Hussein's rule. In late 1970, he tried to eliminate the cream of the PLO leadership in a forest preserve outside Amman. The PLO members who escaped fled into Lebanon and later formed the core of Arafat's present—day commandos.

The nearly one million Palestinians who remained in Jordan were herded into camps, and key troublemakers were expelled. Some Palestinians were invited eventually to join in expanding the nation's economic base. By 1977, sound business management and the effective removal of potential guerrilla leaders had created a degree of stability unmatched in Jordan's less than 60—year history.[21] Hussein feared that if a separate Palestinian entity under PLO leadership was established, he would be unable to assure Jordan's border security and his hold on the crown. Palestinian henchmen had murdered Hussein's grandfather, Abdullah, the first King of Jordan and son of the venerable Arab Sheikh who negotiated with the British in 1916 for Arab independence.

At a Geneva Conference, Palestinian representation independent of the PLO would lessen the threat to Hussein and permit moderate Palestinian leaders to emerge. However, the action could also trigger a serious struggle within the Palestinian movement and lead to further radicalization, guerrilla warfare, and bloodshed. But Hussein was bargaining for time and seeking to retain his kingdom. Some Israelis, if asked, would point to Jordan's controversial beginning — as a set of parallel lines drawn on a map in 1922 by Colonial Affairs Administrator Winston Churchill to fulfill a commitment to Abdullah's father -- and suggest that a Palestinian state already existed -- Jordan.[22] Hussein wished to ensure that view never gained credibility.

The period immediately prior to Menachem Begin's election in Israel saw considerable diplomatic maneuvering but little progress toward a peace conference. Syrian President Hafiz al-Assad moderated his earlier intransigence and accepted the need for demilitarized zones provided they were narrow and drawn on both sides. But Assad also held firm to the establishment of a Palestinian homeland, no doubt hoping to begin filling the West Bank with thousands of refugees who continued to cause instability both in Syria and neighboring Lebanon. The Saudis remained convinced the PLO would accept Israel's right to exist if it would lead to the formation of a Palestinian state in the West Bank and Gaza. In Israel, however, the election campaign was in full swing and serious dialogue.

The Begin Shock

Menachem Begin's surprise election victory had a cataclysmic effect on the peace negotiations. In separate statements issued within days of the May 17, 1977 vote, Begin said he would never relinquish "Judea and Samaria" (the West Bank) or allow Israel to return to its pre-1967 borders.[23] He also indicated he favored an expansion of Jewish settlements in the West Bank and would not participate in any Geneva Conference that included PLO representation.[24]

Begin adopted that uncompromising attitude for at least four reasons. First, his position reflected strong convictions articulated over three decades of service to his party and nation. As the political heir to Jabotinsky, Begin subscribed to the Revisionist Zionist tenet that the territorial and political integrity of Palestine is indivisible. Jabotinsky advocated Israeli rule over all of mandated Palestine. His dream was shattered in 1922 by the establishment of a Jordanian Kingdom on the east bank. Thereafter, he supported Jewish control over all biblical areas from the Mediterranean to the western banks of the Jordan. The population could be binational -- i.e., composed of both Jews and Arabs. The establishment of Jewish settlements on the West Bank was thus in accord with Begin's historical vision of a sovereign people predestined to occupy at least the western portion of Palestine. Begin regarded the PLO both as alien and as an enemy of society. He argued that under his policies, Arabs could live in peace so long as the land remained under Jewish control.

Second, Begin wished to halt U.S. efforts to convene a Geneva Conference in 1977. An international meeting to seek solutions to the Arab-Israeli conflict would conform with Begin's strategic view. He believed, however, that substantive discussions on such matters as the future status of the West Bank, PLO participation in the conference, and new Israeli borders were matters for private negotiation with a U.S. president. He considered public pronouncements from the White House or deliberate disclosure of a specific U.S. peace plan violations of the special relationship between Washington and Jerusalem.

Third, the most efficacious means to secure an equitable settlement, in Begin's view, was through long, arduous negotiations between Jews and Arabs. The United States would obviously be the mediator. But Carter's decision to advance his preferred solutions might permit the Arabs to regain what they had lost through war and violence. Israel's refusal to accommodate its views to matters it had not formally agreed to labeled Jerusalem as "obstreperous" and "unyielding" and led to public censure at the United Nations and elsewhere.

Fourth, Begin wished to assure his political supporters and potential coalition partners that he would remain faithful to his principles. To form a government, he would have to attract competent men from other parties whose constituencies adamantly opposed compromise on the West Bank, revised borders, or recognition of the PLO. Nevertheless, his selection of Moshe Dayan as foreign minister reflected a willingness to rely on experience in dealing with U.S. and Arab representatives. The appointment added a significant measure of continuity with the Rabin government and displayed an understanding that tactical compromise could gain for Begin the strategic results he intended.[25]

Dayan's view of the peace process was less rigid and more pragmatic than that of Begin. The new foreign minister was convinced of the need to retain the West Bank to assure Israel's security. He maintained that the West Bank should be linked to the economy and society of Israel in order to reduce the dependence of the area's inhabitants on the PLO or other Middle East states. Dayan's preference for functional West Bank integration with Israel did not include outright annexation of the land. In fact, he won a substantial concession from Begin before joining the cabinet: Future annexation of Judea and Samaria would be contingent on popular acceptance among West Bank Palestinians of the measure. West Bank Arabs, in Dayan's view, would be eligible for citizenship — the exact nature of which was not defined. The other occupied territories — the Sinai, Gaza Strip, and the Golan Heights — could be traded for final peace acceptable to Israel, including defensible borders. He regarded settlements in the West Bank as justifiable and approved of joint tenancy to permit Arab and Jew the experience of living side by side. The Arab people in Judea and Samaria could be attached to Jordan in some manner so long as the territory remained in Israeli hands.

Dayan also opposed negotiations with the PLO and creation of a Palestinian state. In his view, the Palestinians were citizens of Jordan, their capital was Amman, and they had relinquished any rights to an independent existence when they merged with Jordan in 1947. Finally, Dayan argued that since Israel was at war with Jordan and not the Palestinians, it could negotiate only with King Hussein.[26]

Sadat

Sadat's public response to the election of Begin as Israel's prime minister was muted. It mattered little, he said, since all Israeli leaders "adopt the same line."[27] However, Sadat's actions spoke otherwise. He went to Riyadh, Saudi Arabia, to discuss the Israeli elections with King Khalid and Syrian President Assad. Saudi Deputy Prime Minister Fahd was to visit Carter soon, and the three undoubtedly wished to coordinate strategy for the upcoming Washington meeting.

The Egyptian President convinced his hosts that the United States would before mid-summer advance a plan or a series of suggestions calling for Israeli withdrawal from the occupied territories, with minor adjustments for border security, promoting some form of Palestinian presence at a Geneva Conference, and defining the status of refugees in the West Bank. Despite Begin's prior position on these matters, Sadat believed the U.S. government could force compromise. He pointed to the 1973–1974 Sinai disengagement talks when the United States had prevailed over Israeli objections. This time, Sadat reasoned, it could be easier. Begin's brusque manner and obstinate views encouraged little sympathy from the rest of the world. The best Arab tactic, therefore, was to be patient, and Israel would have to yield captured territory because of, rather than in spite of, Begin's hawkishness.

Sadat may not have fully believed his own publicly articulated views. He certainly had little choice but to hope the United States would force Israel to come to terms. He could tell a restless domestic audience that close and effective ties between Cairo and Washington could produce more attractive peace terms. An upbeat attitude could produce at least the appearance of continued success.

The Carter–Begin Talks — July 1977

Preliminaries

Preparations for a meeting with Carter in Washington began almost immediately after Begin's election. The U.S. State Department sharply rejected the notion that any Israeli-occupied territory, including the West Bank, was automatically excluded from the negotiation agenda. Vice President Walter Mondale, long a supporter of Israel, reiterated the administration position on borders, a full peace, and a Palestinian homeland. In a statement only one week prior to the scheduled meeting with Begin, Carter stressed his personal preference for a link between a Palestinian entity and Jordan. Days earlier, Egypt and Jordan had urged much the same thing. Finally, just four days before the White House meeting, Yasir Arafat suggested that the PLO was prepared to settle for a state in the West Bank and Gaza Strip. The PLO, he added, could co-exist with Israel. However, radical Palestinians still threatened to assassinate any Arab leader who agreed to sign a peace agreement with Israel. Sadat ignored the warning and announced on the eve of the Carter–Begin talks that he would accept Israel as a complete Middle East partner once a peace treaty was signed.[28]

Saudi Arabia apparently had a hand in orchestrating a more moderate Arab tone before the Carter–Begin talks. Prince Fahd met with Carter at the White House in late May and presumably conveyed to him the results of the tripartite meeting in Riyadh. Earlier, Washington made public urgent reminders that Israel was bound by the provisions of UN Resolutions 242 and 338. Carter continued his tough line toward Israel following Fahd's visit, and Riyadh agreed three days before Begin's arrival in Washington to finance Egypt's military development until 1982.[29] The Saudis also may have persuaded Arafat to tone down his militant talk. In any case, the stage was set for a critical dialogue between the United States and Israel on the possibility of a Geneva Conference in 1977.

Begin and Dayan arrived in Washington on July 19, 1977 for two days of talks. Begin quickly conceded that a Geneva–style conference to resolve outstanding Arab and Israeli differences could take place by October 10. He had earlier told a Congressional delegation visiting Israel that observance of the Jewish New Year and Day of Atonement in early fall prevented a meeting before that date. Egypt announced its acceptance of the same time frame on July 5.

Begin and Dayan also introduced several proposals concerning negotiating procedures at a Geneva conference, which had been a formidable barrier to improved U.S.–Israeli relations. First, a Geneva conference sponsored by the United States and the Soviet Union would be convened on the basis of UN Resolutions 242 and 338 but without prior conditions. Second, an initial session in which all parties would publicly present their positions, would be followed by the formation of mixed commissions. The mixed commissions — Egypt and Israel, Jordan and Israel, Syria and Israel, and Lebanon and Israel — would negotiate bilateral peace arrangements between Israel and its neighbors, including the diplomatic and economic aspects of normalization. The commissions would also define final borders. Third, should the Arab nations insist on PLO participation — totally unacceptable to Israel — Begin and Dayan would insist on one or two other options. One would involve the use of American diplomacy to establish the mixed commissions through negotiations with the Arab states. The other option focused on proximity talks in New York, as promoted by the United States in 1972.[30]

The Struggle At Home

The substantive portion of the Begin–Dayan plan, hidden from public view during the meetings with Carter, emerged from two months of domestic bargaining preceding Begin's first visit. The leadership of the Herut faction within the Likud did not expect the May 17 election results. Herut's executive command held a long debate over the election arithmetic and the development of a coalition strategy that would produce a functioning cabinet in the shortest possible time. Doctrinal purity appealed to most of the Herut inner circle and dictated a strong effort to draw the religious parties into a coalition. The National Religious Party (NRP) and the smaller Aguda Israel Party together commanded 18 seats in the Knesset (NRP 12; Aguda Israel 4). Ariel Sharon, hero of the 1973 military victory on the East Bank of the Suez Canal, agreed on May 30 to deliver the Shlomozion's two seats to the Likud. The Likud's 43 seats, Sharon's two seats, and the religious parties' 16 seats, would give Begin a bare majority of 61 in the 120-seat Parliament.

The Democratic Movement for Change (DMC) had 15 seats in the new Knesset and could give Begin a wide government majority. A cabinet backed by 76 votes in the Knesset would free Begin from internal restrictions during a period of anticipated difficulties with the United States and Arab nations.

But the DMC opposed Begin's selection of Dayan as foreign minister.[31] The Likud's Liberal faction was also unhappy over the Dayan nomination. Each group had its own preferred nominee. But Begin had not consulted the DMC on the appointment, leading the party to believe the prime minister considered the DMC only marginal to the governing process. Begin compromised, however, and postponed the formal appointment of Dayan until after he became prime minister.[32]

The DMC still refused to join the government until October, however, because of other more critical factors. The party had campaigned on several immutable promises, including a pledge to "explore all possible arrangements to assure the security of the state."[33] DMC leader Yigal Yadin said during the election campaign that "the desire for peace demanded territorial concessions."[34] But Begin had already asserted that his government would not yield any land. By mid-June, however, he would omit from his foreign policy program any reference to the inviolability of Judea and Samaria, emphasizing instead that their annexation would be prohibited during peace negotiations. The DMC in late May was still fearful of compromising its principles and disappointing the party faithful, so it temporized. Another cause for the DMC decision to reject a coalition with Likud was its expectation that deepening economic chaos and a likely confrontation with the United States would cause Begin's government to fall. Thus, the DMC voted on June 13 to remain outside the coalition.

Four days earlier -- on June 9 -- the religious parties had agreed to join a Begin government. The NRP favored the appointment of Dayan. Like Begin, it apparently believed that despite mixed reviews of Dayan's 1973 performance as minister of defense, his international reputation would serve the government well. The NRP also favored additional West Bank settlements. Aguda Israel, however, governed by a council of 13 sages ranging in age from 65 to 80, placed several demands on the coalition as its price for support. Begin would have to urge repeal of liberalized abortion laws, exempt women from military service for religious reasons, curb routine autopsies, and limit the issuance of work permits during the Sabbath.[35]

Formation of the Likud government on June 20 had a serious impact on the peace process. Begin had only a slight majority in the Knesset, although his popularity in the country was at its zenith. The nature of the coalition put a premium on views considered anathema in the Arab world. DMC opposition to additional settlements in the West Bank and support for territorial adjustments as part of the peace process had been neatly ignored. The religious parties' rejection of terri-torial compromise in the West Bank, recognition of the PLO, and return to pre-1967 borders permitted Begin to promote the illusion that he represented a unified Israel. Although Begin's internal base of support was uncomfortably narrow, he would be able to present Carter a set of rigid principles.[36]

Only a sound defeat in the Histradrut elections on June 21 gave pause to Begin's preparations for his mid-July visit to the United States. Some 58 percent of the Israeli adult population -- representing 80 percent of the nation's salaried workers -- voted in the Histradrut balloting. Enterprises owned by Histradrut accounted for one quarter of Israel's gross national product. The voting, therefore, represented the first test of popular reaction to Begin's government. Nearly 57 percent of the Histradrut workers chose candidates tied to the Israel Labor Party, thus seriously weakening the Likud with its lower income supporters.

Dayan's contribution to Israel's July 1977 peace proposals were crucial. His diplomatic foes had long regarded the new foreign minister as a creative negotiator. Dayan would not disappoint his admirers. For example, he encouraged Begin to accept Arab autonomy on the West Bank under Israeli military control. Retention of the West Bank was essential to Dayan for security purposes, not as a matter of faith.[37] In that regard, his views differed from those of Agriculture Minister Sharon and Education Minister Hammer. But Minister of Defense Ezer Weizman -- an ex-brother-in-law -- supported Dayan; together they would create conditions for future Israeli compromises.[38]

Just one week before Begin's visit to the United States, the Gush Emunim (Bloc of the Faithful), an orthodox religious pressure group, reminded Begin of his commitment to defend the right of Jewish citizens to settle anywhere in the biblical lands of Israel. Begin agreed to the establishment of seven new settlements in the West Bank as part of an overall plan to develop five additional towns, eventually adding 150,000 Jewish residents. This policy complicated negotiations in Washington, but inside Israel it served to vindicate the views of Sharon and Hammer. Politically, Dayan remained virtually isolated until Yadin and his DMC joined the cabinet near the end of the year.

The core of the Israeli plan presented to Carter focused on a functional separation of issues. Begin and Dayan addressed U.S. concerns by separating such topics as troop withdrawals, demilitarized zones, and border delimitations from the central matters of Palestinian rights and overall diplomatic and economic relations. Egyptian negotiations on the Sinai would not depend on events in the Golan Heights or elsewhere. Similarly, Jordan would be asked to deal bilaterally with Israel on the West Bank. The explosive Palestinian question would be handled separately between the Israelis and an all-Arab delegation.

Dayan feared that discussion of contentious matters with a combined Arab delegation would at best be convoluted, but he may also have reasoned that the Israeli cabinet would be just as rigid. So as not to appear inflexible, Dayan included in the Israeli plan a reference to Arabs and Israelis living side by side on the West Bank of the Jordan River and enjoying independence in civil and administrative matters. Security, however, would remain in the hands of the Israeli Army. Begin brushed aside U.S. opposition to new settlements in the West Bank.[39]

A test of confidence was no longer critical to the new Israeli leadership. Previous Labor governments had followed the practice of coordinating its policies with the United States. Thus, the two sides would seek to negotiate common positions on important issues. But American insistence on a Palestinian homeland, Begin's own hardline views, and the nature of coalition politics in Israel created an opportunity for Begin to declare at the end of his Washington visit that he and Carter had "agreed to disagree."[40]

Nevertheless, Israel's reported willingness to withdraw from the Sinai and Golan Heights, and its flexibility on the West Bank, put the burden on the United States and moderate Arabs to maintain the peace momentum. A rupture in the peace process would thus be considered as much an Arab responsibility as an Israeli one. Begin could also claim that he had avoided a confrontation with the U.S. government without sacrificing essential principles. The argument would play well in Jerusalem and Tel Aviv — for a time.

Confrontation

A week after the Begin–Carter talks, Jordan's King Hussein and Syria's President Assad rejected Israel's peace plan out of hand. In Cairo, however, the mood was less pessimistic as Sadat prepared alternative suggestions for Vance, who was visiting Middle East capitals for the second time in six months in an effort to arrange a Geneva Conference before the end of the year.

Vance's arrival in Cairo on August 1 followed a sharp U.S. condemnation of Israel's recognition of three previously illegal West Bank settlements as permanent, legal entities. In announcing the decision to reverse the Rabin government's policy, Begin disclosed that Israel had made no promises to Carter regarding the settlements. The United States insisted that the creation of new West Bank settlements "is contrary to international law and presents an obstacle to peace."[41]

Cairo showed patience in the matter as the Egyptians were more concerned to discuss a compromise in the PLO's position on representation at Geneva. Sadat had talked with Arafat several times during the Egyptian–Libyan border clashes in July. One formula they reportedly agreed on called for using West Bank Palestinians as surrogates for the PLO within a Jordanian or unified Arab delegation. Another plan would grant the PLO observer status at Geneva.[42]

Egypt may have relaxed its suspicion of Israeli intentions following an unprecedented warning from Jerusalem that Libya was behind an attempt to overthrow Sadat.[43] Details of the exchange of information remain unclear, but the relationship between key members of the two security services was apparently sufficient to establish a longer–term link between Dayan and

Egyptian Deputy Prime Minister Hassan al-Tuhamy. Nevertheless, Sadat was leery of Begin's peace plan. He feared that Israel's prime minister wanted either to postpone the Geneva talks indefinitely or to divide the Arab leadership by creating procedural entanglements.

Vance submitted proposals to Sadat that called for a five-year, phased Israeli withdrawal from the Sinai, linked to a gradual transition to full diplomatic relations. A referendum to determine the area's future would follow an indefinite period of joint Israeli-Jordanian trusteeship of the West Bank.[44] Vance's suggestions took into account many Israeli concerns regarding an equitable agreement but not those of the PLO, Jordan, Syria, or others in the Arab world. Sadat there-fore argued -- much as Dayan had a month earlier -- for a separation of the more contentious political issues from the less sensitive territorial ones. He also refused to accept a drawn-out, phased Israeli withdrawal from the Sinai. Sadat's controlled press had revealed that six months was Egypt's limit for obtaining the desert lands.

Egypt insisted on certain guidelines, calling for -- among other things -- total Israeli withdrawal from captured lands; Israeli recognition of Palestinian rights, including self-determination and establishment of a Palestinian state; and the right of all nations in the region to enjoy peace within secure and internationally supervised borders. Within those guidelines, two types of guarantees would exist: The United States and the USSR — as co-chairmen of the Geneva Conference — would have to arrange for the demilitarization of sensitive areas and the establishment of a political structure to enforce a state of peace.[45]

Sadat called for new meetings in the United States in September between the Arab and Israeli foreign ministers to restore momentum to the peace process. Begin quickly accepted, but the PLO had to be reassured that the talks would not preclude their attendance at a Geneva Conference. Egypt issued a clarification that its proposal for a foreign ministers' meeting was intended to reflect intensified consultations between U.S. and Arab representatives on the one hand and between the United States and Israel on the other.

Sadat evidently sought to keep alive the prospects for a peaceful solution to the Arab-Israeli conflict. He continued to view success in the peace process as essential to the preservation of his regime. Recent violence, spurred by restiveness among Egypt's ultraconservative right, had created severe unease among Sadat's entourage.

The lifting of political restraints on the Muslim Brotherhood in the summer of 1976 energized ultraconservative sentiment through mid–1977. Reforms were sought, not only in religious values but in education and social policies as well. Memorization of the Koran was advanced as a central task of primary schools. The kidnap and murder in early July of a former government minister of religious affairs –– for opposition to fundamentalist practices –– by members of a fanatical religious group motivated Sadat to seek urgent action. The terrorists were immediately arraigned, tried, and executed.

Government actions to curb violence nevertheless betrayed serious anxieties. The rural notables had begun to express discontent as their wealth and influence dwindled and extremist activity increased. The urban elite and the military might be persuaded to move against the regime in the event of chaos generated either by further internal disorder or by Egyptian isolation from the Arab world. Nevertheless, the masses yearned for economic security and a return to fundamentalist values. A return of the Sinai and new Western investment and aid would help bolster Sadat's position. A peace agreement that brought Egypt these benefits would allow him to procure new weapons and otherwise satisfy the demands and needs of the military, mollify the rural middle class, and reduce the progressive polarization between poor and poorer. The left would be isolated for lack of an effective platform, and the right encouraged by restraints on secularism.

The Egyptian president received no help from other Arab leaders in his quest for domestic tranquility. Assad and Hussein had both told Vance in early August that Egypt's proposal for a meeting of foreign ministers would be counterproductive. Assad characterized U.S. suggestions as "inappropriate" for improving the chances for peace. Hussein acknowledged the usefulness of America's role in the peace process but said he believed a difficult period remained before tangible progress could be achieved. The Jordanian monarch appeared pleased, however, by the formulation of guidelines prior to convening the conference.

Arafat remained tentative. He first hinted that the PLO might accept UN Resolution 242, but he later said it would be necessary to change the wording of the resolution so that it would pledge to respect the rights of "Palestinians" rather than "refugees." The PLO would regard a resolution amended in this manner as a basis for attending a Geneva Conference –– a de facto recognition of Israel.

Begin believed he had persuaded Carter to avoid imposing substantive pre-conditions on the conference but rather to allow the parties an opportunity to establish face–to–face contact. The Israeli prime minister was thus dismayed in late July when he learned that Vance would bring to the Middle East specific U.S. proposals for a Geneva Conference.

Vance was greeted in Jerusalem on August 10 with a reaffirmation of Israel's refusal to withdraw from the West Bank, permit establishment of a Palestinian state, or recognize the PLO, even if the organization accepted UN Resolution 242. Begin and Dayan reiterated their support for the pre–Geneva ministerial meeting in New York suggested by Sadat.

Pre–Geneva Talks –– September 1977

Sadat's proposal for a New York meeting was intended to prevent the PLO from disrupting the Geneva Conference itself and to facilitate direct Egyptian–Israeli discussions. The Egyptian president appreciated the Israeli warning of the Libyan plot and was further encouraged by Romanian reports of Begin's willingness to meet Egyptian leaders and negotiate without preconditions. Begin had seemed somewhat flexible during a seven–hour meeting with Romanian President Ceausescu in August. The Begin–Ceausescu meeting apparently convinced Sadat that direct Egyptian–Israeli talks could be productive.[46] Egypt was perplexed, however, by U.S. ambivalence. Discussions with Vance in early August persuaded Sadat that Washington was eager for a Geneva–style meeting, but the United States appeared unenthusiastic over the prospect of bilateral negotiations between Cairo and Jerusalem.

The U.S. State Department had, in fact, on September 12, reminded its Middle East allies that Palestinian participation at the Geneva Conference was essential. The PLO Central Council meeting in Damascus on August 25–26 rejected Carter's call for recognition of UN Resolution 242, but the possibility of Palestinian representation in either a Jordanian or all–Arab delegation still seemed viable.

Washington was sensitive over the precariousness of its own position in the Middle East and concerned that comprehensive peace negotiations might fail. Arab League members ––

Syria, Jordan, and Saudi Arabia among them — had in early September severely criticized Israel's expansionist policies. The 21-member organization urged the creation of a Palestinian state and promised to work for a new UN resolution condemning Israeli settlements on the West Bank.

Israel had approved construction at three new locations on August 17, bringing to six the number of new Jewish settlements in the West Bank since Begin's election. Israel countered U.S. criticism by stating that the Rabin government had approved the new settlements and that Begin was merely implementing the policy. An earlier cabinet decision to raise services in the West Bank and Gaza Strip to the level enjoyed by Israeli citizens also drew sharp protests. Publication in the Israeli press on September 1 of Sharon's intention to settle two million Jews in a security belt extending from the Golan Heights to the Sinai was seen as proof that Jerusalem would soon "annex" the occupied lands.

Sadat shared Carter's disapproval and the Arab League's dislike of Israeli actions, but the threat of internal dissent spurred him to seek a forum outside of Geneva to achieve Israeli moderation. Nearly 60 members of the radical religious sect that had participated in the July murder of Sadat's former Minister of Waqfs had been caught and charged with treason. But the crackdown was certain to strengthen the resistance of rural notables and their military allies angered by government liberalization moves. Tangible results in the peace negotiations would blunt any attempt by these groups to join forces and threaten the government.

Sadat searched for a method to break the deadlock and decided in mid-September to send Deputy Prime Minister Tuhamy to Rabat for a secret meeting with Dayan.[47] Tuhamy's selection for the mission underscored Sadat's relative isolation from his foreign policy advisers as well as his determination to maintain his urban support. Tuhamy had been a low-ranking member of the Free Officer Corps, although he had participated with Nasser in an abortive attempt to assassinate Farouk's Army Chief of Staff. He served in diplomatic posts from 1961 to 1967 and was appointed a presidential adviser in the waning years of Nasser's regime. Sadat retained Tuhamy and gave him the post of Secretary General of the Islamic Conference in 1973 and later, the honorary titles of deputy prime minister and lieutenant general.[48] Tuhamy's role as Egypt's overseer of Islamic proselytism in the mid-1970s offered Sadat a loyal, competent, and knowledgeable negotiator who would be trusted by the nation's fundamentalists. Tuhamy could help persuade the urban poor and the clerical community that bilateral ties with Israel, and concomitant sacrifice of PLO aspirations, were not heretical and could smooth the way to an improved existence for all Egyptians. Moreover, Tuhamy could negotiate without having to appease single-issue constituencies. Also influencing the selection of Tuhamy was the fact that the Egyptian Foreign Office seemed committed to Palestinian aspirations and was certain to be highly suspicious of any Israeli proposals affecting the Palestinians.

Moroccan King Hassan had earlier received former Israeli Prime Minister Rabin in an effort to seek a solution to the Arab-Israeli conflict. That effort ended when a planned meeting between Rabin and Saudi Prime Minister Fahd in October 1976 was cancelled due to the Lebanese crisis.[49] On September 17, 1977, Tuhamy and Dayan met secretly for seven hours at one of Hassan's palaces in Rabat. Dayan had changed planes in Paris while supposedly en route to the foreign ministers' talks in New York. (He removed his famous eye patch in favor of sunglasses to avoid recognition.)

Dayan began the meeting with a proposal for direct talks between Begin and Sadat. Tuhamy responded with a question on Israel's willingness to withdraw from the Sinai. Dayan replied that Israeli withdrawal from the Sinai could only be the result of discussions, not a pre-condition. The talks turned to more peripheral matters, and the negotiators concluded on a positive note. Each believed that the other's nation would be receptive to further official discussions at a higher level. Dayan returned to Jerusalem and reported to Begin on the conversations. Tuhamy was concerned over the session. He feared that public speculation over Dayan's movements might result in disclosure of the secret meeting and threaten new Egyptian initiatives. In any case, Egyptian-Israeli direct contacts had been initiated on the eve of the scheduled foreign ministers talks.[50]

Thus, two seemingly disconnected events preceeded Dayan's visit to the United States. The first was the mysterious break in his journey to New York and later return to Jerusalem. The second was the sudden public discussion of an Israeli draft treaty that could serve as a basis for the New York talks. Begin had revealed in an Israeli radio interview in early September that Israel's plan would include proposals for diplomatic relations and trade ties with the Arab nations and would specify the territories Israel was prepared to surrender in exchange for peace -- but those specifics could be realized only through bargaining between the various parties involved. Israel again ruled out Palestinian statehood in the West Bank, but the talks would include arrangements involving the status of refugees and compensation for lost lands.

Dayan amplified Begin's remarks a week before resuming his trip to the United States. He said that the solution to the Palestinian problem lay in the grant of rights to the refugees by their countries of exile. Jerusalem would be willing to grant either Israeli or Jordanian citizenship to the 300,000 Gaza Strip residents. The 700,000 residents of the West Bank, however, were in a separate category, since most of them had lived in the area even before the establishment of Israel. West Bankers would be granted a substantial measure of autonomy, with Israel maintaining security. Dayan would depend on the cooperation of moderate West Bank mayors, religious leaders, lawyers, educators, and businessmen to implement arrangements for self-government -- but without the PLO's participation. West Bank ministries for commerce, industry, health, and education could be established. Israel would retain the right to purchase vacant lands on the West Bank, and travel restrictions affecting both Israelis and Arabs would be eliminated. A common market economy among Israel, Jordan, and the West Bank was a further possibility.

Negotiations with Palestinians to amend the agreement could take place anywhere but Geneva, which would be reserved as the site for ratification of a general peace agreement. Israel therefore continued to reject proposals for Palestinian representation at Geneva, except as part of another nation's delegation.

Israel's insistence on defining the status of refugees in the West Bank and elsewhere was an effort to invest UN Resolution 242 with legitimacy. The resolution, under broad Arab attack, mentioned "refugees" rather than "Palestinians." A plan for limited self-government in the West Bank appealed to Begin's Talmudic and juridical mind without compromising his Jabotinsky-inspired principles. Such a plan, if implemented, would preserve the security of Israel and undercut any ultra-nationalist sentiment to annex the disputed territories. Sharon and others preferred a less generous treatment of West Bank Arabs, but the compromise permitted Jerusalem to appear flexible without inviting its own demise as a nation. The meeting between Dayan and Tuhamy also confirmed that Egypt's leaders were interested in recovering the Sinai and less committed than before to the fortunes of the PLO.

The convening of a Geneva Conference in 1977, however, remained of critical importance to the United States. Carter therefore arranged for Dayan and Egyptian Foreign Minister Ismail Fahmy to meet at the White House prior to scheduled discussions in New York. Dayan was apparently persuaded during initial talks with Carter and later meetings with Vance in New York that the Palestinians must, at the least, be represented in Geneva as part of an all-Arab delegation.[51]

A compromise formula approved by the Israeli cabinet on September 25 called for the establishment of a unified Arab delegation, which would include Palestinians -- referred to in Israel as "Arabs of Eretz Yisrael." The Palestinians selected, however, could not be known members of the PLO, nor could they participate as a separate entity in an opening session of the conference. Israel would not conduct negotiations with an all-Arab delegation at the ceremonial opening and would bargain substantively only with separate Middle East states in later sessions. In return for Israel's acceptance of the Geneva representation formula Washington grudgingly agreed to veto any attempt by UN members to alter Resolution 242.

Nevertheless, Fahmy continued to assert that some form of PLO presence would be required at Geneva and that a Palestinian state ultimately must be created on the West Bank. Palestinians should choose their own delegates to the conference, he added, thus totally rejecting the conditions imposed by Israel for convening the Geneva Conference.

Fahmy may have exceeded Sadat's instructions. Sadat clearly had sent him to New York to revitalize the peace negotiations. President Carter and other interested leaders now would be reminded of the many unresolved issues that prevented a return of the territory occupied by Israel. Nevertheless, the Tuhamy-Dayan meeting — possibly unknown to Fahmy — and Sadat's own predilection toward the dramatic combined to provide a new opportunity for progress. Dayan had been receptive to proposals for return of the Sinai, and PLO intransigence now appeared to be the major obstacle. Therefore, it seemed prudent to allow the United States to urge an Israeli compromise while Egypt prepared itself for swifter action. But Fahmy would not mute his obvious distaste for Dayan's tactics.

Fahmy, a veteran diplomat, had artfully represented Egyptian interests during and following the October 1973 War. His apparent success in dealing with U.S. Secretary of State

Kissinger enabled him to force the removal of rival Presidential Adviser Hafiz Isma'il in 1974. Fahmy was critical of the second Sinai disengagement agreement in 1975 and predicted it would isolate Egypt from the rest of the Arab world. He therefore found himself repeatedly used to allay Syrian and Palestinian criticism of Sadat's peace efforts. Fahmy also supported the convening of a Geneva Conference, expecting that the participation of Palestinians, under whatever guise, would guarantee an acceptable result. Fahmy had served as an intermediary between U.S. and PLO officials.[52] In this role, he probably followed guidelines established in Cairo prior to the Tuhamy–Dayan discussions.

Fahmy was obviously not an apologist for the Soviet Union. He had been suspended from his position as Under Secretary of the Foreign Ministry for four months in early 1972 after having sharply criticized Soviet policy toward the Arabs. Yet Sadat had sent him to Moscow in June 1977 to seek rescheduling of Cairo's huge debt and the possible purchase of additional spare parts for his rapidly rusting Soviet–equipped military machine.[53] The trip was an abysmal failure, but the cordiality of his reception in Moscow may have persuaded the self–assured Fahmy that Palestinian –– and therefore all Arabic –– interests could best be served by inviting Moscow to play a more active role in the upcoming conference. In any case, an apparent impasse had developed.

NOTES

1. See, Washington Post, December 12, 1976.

2. For discussion, see, New York Times, April 5, 1977; Al Ahram, April 6, 1977 contained in Foreign Broadcast Information Service, Middle East and North Africa, April 7, 1977, hereinafter referred to as FBIS; Raphael Israeli, The Public Diary of President Sadat: The Road of Pragmatism (June 1975–October 1976) (Leiden, E. J. Brill, 1979), 111, p. 1366; New York Times, April 7, 1977; "Interview with Egypt's President" Business Week, April 4, 1977, p. 99; Newsweek, December 13, 1976, p. 44.

3. Israeli, The Public Diary of President Sadat: The Road of Pragmatism, 111, p. 1292, 1310.

4. See, Newsweek, December 13, 1976, p. 43; New York Times, December 6, 1976.

5. See, "Interview with Rabin" Newsweek, December 20, 1976, p. 47.

6. Yitzhak Rabin, The Rabin Memoirs (Boston: Little, Brown and Company, 1979), p. 293–294; see, also, Shlomo Aronson, Conflict and Bargaining in the Middle East: An Israeli Perspective (Baltimore: The Johns Hopkins University Press, 1978), p. 329.

7. Aronson, Conflict and Bargaining in the Middle East, p. 320–330.

8. See, Ibid., p. 331–333, for discussion of Brookings report from Israel's point of view; also Aronson, "Israel View of the Brookings Report" in Middle East Review, Volume 10, Number 1, Fall 1977, p. 19–26.

9. The full title of the 1975 "Brookings Report" was Toward Peace in the Middle East—Report of Study Group. A member of the study group has written that the report itself was vague on key issues because of differing views of many of the participants. The study was noteworthy for shifting the focus of the search for peace in the Middle East by calling for a "comprehensive" settlement instead of Kissinger's step–by–step approach. It called for a settlement based on normalization and phased territorial withdrawal. For discussions see, Steven L. Spiegel, "The Carter Approach to the Arab–Israeli Dispute" in Haim Shaked and Itamar Rabinovich, ed., The Middle East and the United States: Perceptions and Policies (New Brunswick: Transaction Books, 1980), p. 102–103.

10. Brezinski and Quandt had authored works asserting that American and Middle East interests would be better served by movement toward a comprehensive agreement and away from a step–by–step solution. See, Zbigniew Brezinski, Francois Duchene, and Kiichi Saeki, "Peace in an International Framework" in Foreign Policy, Number 19, Summer 1975, p. 3–17; William Quandt, Decade of Decisions: American Policy Toward the Arab–Israeli Conflict, 1967–1976 (Berkely: University of California Press, 1977), p. 290–300.

11. Kissinger's policies in the Middle East revolved around Egypt and a continuing effort to keep the Soviets out of the area. Brezinski, however, was to concentrate on luring Saudi Arabia into a settlement, thus assuring the U.S. of an uninterrupted flow of oil. Consequently, while policy channels remained smooth priorities were constantly at issue. For discussion, see, Spiegel, "The Carter Approach to the Arab-Israeli Dispute" in Shaked and Rabinovich, ed., The Middle East and the United States, p. 101–102.

12. See, Morton Kondracke, "A Medieval Maze" in New Republic, March 5, 1977 for discussion of the Vance trip; little flexibility was demonstrated by any of the parties involved and mutual suspicions and antagonisms persisted.

13. Alan Dowty, "Current Perceptions of the Conflict: Cairo, Damascus, Amman" in Middle East Review, Volume 10, Number 1, Fall 1977, p. 30.

14. Morton Kondracke, "Is '77 the Year" in New Republic, February 12, 1977; also, Abraham Ben-Zvi, "Full Circle on the Road to Peace? American Preconceptions of Peace in the Middle East: 1973–1978" in Middle East Review, Volume 11, Number 2, Winter 1978–79, p. 54.

15. Rabin, The Rabin Memoirs, p. 292–300; see, also, Jimmy Carter, Keeping Faith: Memoirs of a President (New York: Bantam Books, 1982), p. 279–281.

16. See, "How to Welcome President Sadat" editorial, New Republic, April 8, 1977, p. 6, for discussion of Cairo based meetings.

17. John Waterbury, Egypt: Burdens of the Past/Options for the Future (Bloomington: University of Indiana Press, 1978), p. 315–316.

18. See, Washington Post, April 7, 1977; New York Times, April 7, 9, 1977; Carter, Keeping Faith, p. 282–284.

19. New York Times, April 8, 1977; Carter, Keeping Faith, p. 283.

20. New York Times, April 28, 1977; Carter, Keeping Faith, p. 285.

21. For discussion of Jordanian history and preferences concerning national identity, see, Adam M. Garfinkle, "Negotiating by Proxy: Jordanian Foreign Policy and U.S. Options in the Middle East" in Orbis, Volume 24, Number 4, Winter 1981, p. 849–857.

22. See, Ariel Sharon's views regarding Jordan in Ranan R. Lurie, "Israel's General Sharon: As Tough as Ever" Playboy Magazine, March 1978, p. 43.

23. Washington Post, May 19, 1977.

24. Newsweek, May 30, 1977, p. 36–37.

25. Amos Perlmutter, "Begin's Strategy and Dayan's Tactics: The Conduct of Israeli Foreign Policy" in Foreign Affairs, January 1978, p. 359–361, 363–365; also, Erich and Rael Jean Isaac, "The Impact of Jabotinski on Likud's Policies" in Middle East Review, Volume 10, Number 1, Fall 1977, p. 31–42.

26. Perlmutter, "Begin's Strategy and Dayan's Tactics" Foreign Affairs, January 1978, p. 364–366; also, Perlmutter, "Cleavage in Israel" in Foreign Policy, Number 27, Summer 1977, p. 149–150. For Dayan's views as articulated to Begin by letter on June 24, 1977, see, Moshe Dayan, Breakthrough: A Personal Account of the Egypt-Israeli Peace Negotiations (London: Weidenfeld and Nicholson, 1981), p. 11–16.

27. New York Times, May 21, 1977.

28. New York Times, June 19, July 2, July 7, July 16, July 17, 1977; Washington Post July 14, 1977.

29. New York Times, May 27, 1977; Washington Post, July 17, 1977; See also, Jake Wien, Saudi-Egyptian Relations: The Political and Military Dimensions of Saudi Financial Flows to Egypt (Santa Monica: The Rand Corporation) P-6327, p. 52–73 for discussion of saudi military assistance to Egypt.

30. Perlmutter, "Begin's Strategy and Dayan's Tactics" in Foreign Affairs, January 1978, p. 366–367.

31. Washington Post, May 21, 1977.

32. Washington Post, May 30, 1977.

33. Efraim Torgovnik, "A Moment for Change in a Stable System" in Howard R. Penniman, ed. Israel at the Polls: The Knesset Elections of 1977 (Washington: American Enterprise Institute for Public Policy Research, 1979), p. 161.

34. Ibid.

35. Washington Post, June 11, 1977.

36. Bernard Reich, "Israel's Foreign Policy and the 1977 Parliamentary Elections" in Penniman, ed. Israel at the Polls, p. 268–270.

37. Perlmutter, "Begin's Strategy and Dayan's Tactics," in Foreign Affairs, January 1978, p. 366.

38. Ezer Weizman, The Battle for Peace (New York: Bantam Books, 1981), p. 114–115.

39. Perlmutter, "Begin's Strategy and Dayan's Tactics" in Foreign Affairs, January 1978, p. 367.

40. New York Times, July 21, 1977.

41. Washington Post, July 29, 1977.

42. New York Times, July 31, 1977.

43. Interview with Yehiel Kadishai (Bureau Chief to Prime Minister Begin) Jerusalem, August 22, 1981. Israeli and Egyptian intelligence chiefs met secretly in Casablanca Morocco during July 1977 to discuss the Libyan plots against Egypt. See, Howard Sachar, Egypt and Israel (New York: Richard Marek, 1981), p. 20.

44. Al Ahram, August 3, 1977 contained in FBIS, Middle East and North Africa, August 3, 1977, D–8–9.

45. See, Washington Post, August 3, 1977, also, FBIS, Middle East and North Africa, August 4, 1977, D-1, D-3.

46. The meeting had been arranged during a discussion between the Romanian Ambassador to Israel and Begin at a July 4, 1977 reception in US Ambassador Lewis's residence. See, Eitan Haber, Zeev Schiff and Ehud Yaari, The Year of the Dove (New York: Bantam Books, 1979), p. 3–5; Dayan, Breakthrough, p. 47; Sachar, Egypt and Israel, p. 258–259. Sayed Marei, Egypt's Speaker of the People's Assembly, father-in-law of Sadat's daughter and the Egyptian President's personal adviser also met secretly with Begin in Romania during the Ceausescu discussions. See, Robert Springborg, Family, Power and Politics in Egypt: Sayed Bey Marei—His Clan, Clients and Cohorts (Philadelphia: University of Pennsylvania Press, 1982), p. 241; also David Hirst and Irene Beeson, Sadat (London: Faber and Faber, 1981), p. 285; also Uzi Benziman, Prime Minister Under Siege (Jerusalem: Adam Publishers, 1981) translated from the Hebrew by Mordecai Schreiber, p. 10; also New York Times, November 19, 1977; also Washington Post, November 17, 1977.

47. Dayan, Breakthrough, p. 41–42.

48. Biographical details are drawn from P. J. Vatikiotis, Nasser and His Generation (New York: St. Martin's Press, 1978), p. 49, 94, 124, 308–309; also R. Hrair Dekejian, Patterns of Political Leadership, Egypt, Israel, Lebanon (Albany: State University of New York Press, 1975), p. 178, 222.

49. Rabin, The Rabin Memoirs, p. 320–321; also, Haber, Schiff and Yaari, The Year of the Dove, p. 9–10.

50. Dayan, Breakthrough, p. 44–35; also Haber, Schiff and Yaari, The Year of the Dove, p. 10–13.

51. New York Times, September 21, 1977; Washington Post, September 24, 1977.

52. Mark Bruzonsky, "Interview with Ismail Fahmy" in The Middle East, July 1979, p. 54.

53.   New York Times, June 12, 1977; see, Robert O. Freedman, Soviet Policy Toward the Middle East Since 1970, Revised Edition (New York: Praeger, 1978), p. 288–289.

2
The Soviet-American Communique

In separate statements issued simultaneously in New York and Moscow on October 1, 1977, the United States and the Soviet Union pledged to reconvene the suspended 1973 Geneva Conference — of which they were co-chairman — "not later than December 1977" for the purpose of negotiating a "comprehensive" peace in the Middle East. They undertook to resolve outstanding issues such as

> . . . withdrawal of Israeli armed forces from territories occupied in the 1967 conflict; the resolution of the Palestinian question, including insuring the legitimate rights of the Palestinian people; termination of the state of war and establishment of normal peaceful relations on the basis of mutual recognition of the principles of sovereignty, territorial integrity and political independence.[1]

The superpowers further declared their willingness to serve as guarantors of the settlement, subject of course to their national constitutional processes. Such assurances would not preclude other supranational efforts to ensure security in the border areas such as stationing United Nations troops or observers there. Finally, the conference would be composed of "representatives of all the parties involved in the conflict, including those of the Palestinian people."[2]

The Soviet-American statement was greeted in most Arab capitals with surprise and in Israel with indignation. What were the intentions of the authors? What implications did Soviet-American ties have for the major parties to the agreement? And what direct impact did the joint statement have on the future of the Middle East peace process?

The Soviet-American View

Moscow had resented its exclusion from the peace process after Kissinger launched his 1973 effort to settle the Arab-Israeli conflict. The Soviet leadership sought to establish its presence in the Middle East through largesse — arms, diplomatic support or initiative and monetary assistance. The Kremlin had labored for decades to establish itself as a super-power but received recognition of its status only in a series of arms control agreements with the United States. Kissinger's decision to freeze the Soviet Union out of the Arab-Israeli peace process was therefore an affront to Moscow's claim of parity with Washington in global matters.

In addition, Soviet military planners probably encouraged the collective leadership to focus on the strategically significant Middle East. The area remained an important point of egress for waterborne access to the West as well as a buffer against land incursions from the territory of hostile neighbors. Soviet military control of the oil fields in the Persian Gulf would place pressure on Western Europe and significantly retard an increasingly dependent United States economy. Furthermore, the demands of East European industrialization and rising consumer needs at home would eventually strain the Soviet Union's own immense petroleum resources.

Moscow's repeated calls for resumption of the Geneva Conference thus sprang from several motives. First, a recon-vened international meeting to settle the conflict in the Middle East under the cochairmanship of the Soviet Union would remind the world of its superpower status. Second, the Soviet Union's enhanced position would underscore its potential ability to help the Arabs regain their lost territories. Soviet leaders continued to smart from Kissinger's oft-repeated assertion that while the United States could obtain an equitable peace for nations of the Middle East, the Kremlin could offer only "more war" for the Arab states.[3] Third, the United States would be exposed as an apologist for and protector of Israeli intransigence if, as expected, the conference revealed, Jerusalem's unwillingness to allow the return of conquered Arab territory. Fourth, agreement at Geneva to redefine the status of Palestinians from "refugees" to a people with defined rights in the area, would be a victory for the Soviet Union and its sponsorship of Palestinian state-hood. Finally, Soviet military influence in the region would

gain credibility if supported by a strong and successful
diplomatic effort to ensure the "just" rights of Arabs
throughout the Middle East.[4]

Despite Moscow's careful preparation for a recovered
Geneva Conference, its influence in the Middle East remained
marginal through mid-summer 1977. The Kremlin continued to
criticize Israel for refusing to relinquish captured Arab
territory but chose not to insist on the elimination of the
Jewish state from the area.[5] The Soviet Union had disapproved
of Syrian intervention in the Lebanese civil war and remained
indifferent to the PLO's fortunes in the same conflict.
Successive visits by Arafat and Assad to Moscow in April 1977
allowed the parties to paper over their previous differences.
But the Soviet leaders refused to lessen their commitment to a
Geneva Conference or their support of an Israeli state confined
to its pre-1967 borders with some minor adjustments. The
Libyan and Iraqi presidents had earlier failed in separate
attempts to budge the Kremlin from its pursuit of these two
controversial goals. Moscow viewed support for an Israeli
state, promotion of a revitalized Geneva Conference, and
control of the fractious PLO as means to improve its bilateral
ties with the United States.[6]

U.S.-Soviet relations remained in disrepair. The U.S.
commitment to human rights and substantial disagreements in
arms control negotiations stood in the way of significant
accommodation between the two superpowers. Nevertheless, Arab
dissatisfaction with both the status quo and with positions
offered by mediators stirred Washington and Moscow to review
their posture in the Middle East.

The failure of Secretary of State Cyrus Vance's trip to
the Middle East in August 1977 provided the occasion for Moscow
and Washington to join in an urgent effort to reconvene the
Geneva Conference. The near-unanimous Arab rejection of the
American proposals apparently persuaded Vance that the Kremlin
alone held the key to moderating extremist Arab views such as
those held by Syria and the PLO.[7] The Soviet formula for
achieving a settlement in the Middle East was far more reasonable than those of the less moderate nations of the region.
Washington may have reasoned that improved Soviet relations
with these Arab states and an increased flow of Russian arms
and other support would incline the recipients to support
another concerted attempt at peace negotiations.

The Soviet proposal resembled the U.S.-sponsored package
in important ways. Both favored the withdrawal of Israel to

its pre—1967 borders; only the details of the frontiers remained in doubt. Both insisted on universal recognition of Israel's right to exist. Both proposed demilitarized zones in border areas and elimination of restrictive practices, such as Egypt's obstruction of Israeli use of the Straits of Tiran.[8] Moscow and Washington disagreed, however,on the eventual terms of interstate relations in the area. The United States and Israel insisted on full cultural, economic, and diplomatic ties between the protagonists, while the Kremlin did not. And the American and Russian conceptions of a Palestinian territorial entity diverged although Moscow, like Washington, did not define the entity's links to Jordan.

The two sides had considerable confidence that they could eliminate some of the disparities in their positions. This had not always been the case. American officials tended to believe that the proper balance of U.S.—Soviet relations in the Middle East lay somewhere between cooperation and conflict, depending on the issue and circumstances. Even during the Nixon and Ford administrations, National Security Council officials held competing views. One group argued that Moscow benefitted from a continuing high state of tension in the area and therefore did not want peace. Others believed the Soviet Union feared wider international conflict and preferred to settle regional quarrels. Kissinger chose to accept the first hypothesis, while the Carter administration opted for the second.[9]

A general improvement in other bilateral superpower negotiations, such as the SALT II talks, in August and September 1977, fueled the rising expectations of U.S.—Soviet accommodation in the Middle East. Through a judicious use of inducements and threats, the U.S. State Department had begun by mid—September to move both Israel and the Arab states toward acceptance of some form of Palestinian presence at a forth-coming Geneva Conference. But the Palestinians themselves balked at their indefinite status, and the 21—member Arab League threatened to seek UN involvement in the matter.[10] Neither unofficial Egyptian and Israeli talks nor more formal bargaining in the United Nations had produced a satisfactory solution to the developing impasse on the Palestinian issue. In fact, the positions put forward by Egyptian Foreign Minister Fahmy in New York appeared out of tandem with those being advanced in Morocco by the Cairo government.[11] Israel was quietly reaping benefits from the Arab divisions by remaining out of the fray and staying just beyond the pale of U.S. pressure. The constant buffeting and seesawing convinced

Washington that to sponsor a Geneva Conference alone to settle the ills of the Middle East by year's end was an exercise in futility.[12]

Resuscitating a direct and complementary Geneva role for Moscow could earn Washington increased flexibility in the peace process. Soviet military and financial assistance to Arab clients in Damascus and to the PLO at base camps in Lebanon were expected to provide Moscow with sufficient leverage to ensure progress at Geneva.[13] Moreover, the Soviet Union was a cosponsor of the suspended Geneva Conference and would eventually be required to address diplomatically the issues arising from that aborted meeting. A joint superpower effort could serve as a warning to Middle East states sympathetic to the United States that American patience was being sorely tested and that time was fast yielding to practicalities.[14]

Israeli Response

The Soviet-American communique drew an immediate and sharp reaction from all segments of Israeli society. This response occurred even though Israel's government was beleaguered and its leader — fatigued and hospitalized — the object of ridicule from an opposition party claiming that his foreign policy had failed. Acting Prime Minister and Minister of Finance Simcha Ehrlich conveyed the government's formal comment, stating that Jerusalem rejected the declaration "with both hands."[15] Shadow government leaders Peres, Rabin, and Allon considered the joint statement "unprecedented, unnecessary, ill-timed, and ill-phrased."[16] Foreign Minister Dayan, in New York since September 21 to work out a formula for new Geneva talks with U.S. and Egyptian representatives, was no less disturbed by the superpower communique.[17]

Israelis considered the Soviet-American statement an obvious effort to impose a settlement that would entail the establishment of a separate Palestinian state under PLO control. Furthermore, Jerusalem regarded the communique as a direct violation of the September 1, 1975 U.S.-Israeli Memorandum of Agreement. That document — negotiated as part of the 1975 Sinai II accord by Kissinger — pledged support for UN Resolutions 242 and 338 and stipulated that the parties would consult fully on strategy for a Geneva Peace Conference and on the question of PLO representation.[18]

Dayan previously had recommended a solution to the vexing problem of seating Palestinians at Geneva. It had been sanctioned by the full Israeli cabinet on September 25 but was roundly condemned by most Arab nations, including Jordan and Egypt. The Israeli proposal envisioned the participation of "Palestinians" who had no ties to the PLO as part of an all-Arab delegation but prohibited them from bargaining on substantive issues.[19]

The Israeli foreign minister was able to regain the initiative and lessen the import of the Soviet–American statement within days of its issuance. He met with President Carter and Secretary of State Vance in New York on October 4–5 to resolve bilateral differences over the meaning of the superpower communique. The U.S.–Israeli discussions, apparently held in an atmosphere of discord, produced a "working paper" designed to nudge the parties toward resumption of a Geneva Conference.

The document, subsequently circulated privately, provided: that a unified delegation including "Palestinian Arabs" would represent the Arabs at Geneva; that bilateral working groups to negotiate peace treaties would be formed upon completion of the opening session and would be composed of Egypt and Israel, Jordan and Israel, Syria and Israel and Lebanon and Israel; that issues relating to the West Bank and Gaza Strip would be "discussed" in a group consisting of Israel, Jordan, Egypt, and the Palestinian Arabs; that Arab and Jewish refugee problems would also be discussed "in accordance with terms to be agreed upon;" that the agreed basis for negotiations would be UN Security Council Resolutions 242 and 338; and that terms previously accepted at the December 1973 Geneva meeting would remain in force "except as may be agreed by the parties."[20]

Washington was already sensitive to the perceptions that the joint superpower statement was disadvantageous to Israel and chose immediately after the meeting with Dayan to reassure the public by publicizing the last point of the working paper. The United States also issued a press notice underscoring that the joint U.S.–USSR statement of October 1, 1977 was not a "prerequisite for the reconvening and conduct of the Geneva meeting."[21]

Although purportedly a product of "brutal" American pressure,[22] the working paper itself was in fact consistent with long-held Israeli government policy. First, the agreement contained no mention of even low-level PLO representation on a unified Arab delegation at Geneva. The paper referred instead to the presence at Geneva of "Palestinian Arabs," a term formulated by Begin himself. The Israeli prime minister intended both to establish the legitimacy of "Palestinians" unconnected to the PLO and to provide a historical link to the concept of "Palestinian Jews." Second, the document omitted any reference to consideration of a Palestinian entity at the conference. The stipulation that UN Resolutions 242 and 338 would govern the parties' actions at Geneva prohibited discussion of a Palestinian state — the UN measures referred only to "refugees." Third, "Palestinian Arabs" would participate at Geneva only in substantive negotiations relating to the West Bank and Gaza Strip. The Geneva meeting would therefore not establish a precedent legitimizing a formal Palestinian representation able to operate independently on general issues. Finally, even matters relating to the West Bank and Gaza Strip were to be "discussed" rather than "negotiated" at the forthcoming international conference.

Dayan's skill as a negotiator and the general esteem in which he was held by his adversaries permitted him sufficient latitude to forge a document that endorsed many of the policies espoused by Israel. This was done despite the U.S. commitment to its recent undertaking with Moscow and its determination to obtain a form of PLO representation at Geneva. In addition, a reasonable working relationship between Dayan and Begin brought a measure of clarity and strength to Jerusalem's position on the PLO and was a crucial element in bolstering the Jewish position in talks over the working paper. Both Israeli leaders rejected the notion of negotiating with the PLO, even if the organization chose to strike from its charter clauses calling for the annihilation of the Jewish state or to accept the language of UN Resolution 242 that prescribes recognition of Israel's right to exist. Dayan and Begin reasoned that discussions with the PLO would serve no other purpose than to establish a Palestinian state ruled by Arafat on the West Bank and in the Gaza Strip. The prospect of Palestinian statehood under any condition was totally unacceptable to either the Israeli foreign minister or prime minister. Both believed that a West Bank state for the Palestinians would become a "dagger struck at the heart of Israel" and that its establishment would introduce the Soviet Union into the area in an active military role. Thus, the two Israeli leaders viewed the Soviet-American statement as creating conditions for international conflict and the elimination of the state of Israel.[23]

Serious and widespread fears in Jerusalem that the new Soviet–American connection would lead to Israel's destruction had the unintended effect of narrowing internal divisions and solidifying Begin's rule. Those fears played a major role in convincing the Democratic Movement for Change (DMC) to join the prime minister's government. Despite Begin's concerted effort to attract the faction's support, Yadin and the DMC had chosen to remain outside the government. The Israeli prime minister went so far as to refuse to fill several cabinet posts, preferring to lure the DMC with anticipated ministerial representation.

Throughout the summer and early fall of 1977, however, Yadin continued to emphasize philosophical and practical differences with the Begin government. The DMC had campaigned on a platform of change, and Yadin held fast to those principles. For example, the DMC favored changes in the electoral system that would substitute direct district elections to the Knesset for the existing nationwide system of proportional representation. The National Religious Party (NRP) — a member of Begin's Likud coalition — strongly opposed any such changes because its electoral strength resided in demography rather than geography. More crucial, Yadin disagreed with Begin's refusal to deal with the PLO. During the election campaign the former Army Chief of Staff had claimed indifference to what type of regime ruled east of the Jordan River. And he was willing to negotiate with the PLO and Jordan over the future of the West Bank provided he could extract sensible security arrangements from them.

Although sharp differences in perception and commitment about the future of Israel persisted, Begin and Yadin continued to negotiate throughout the summer. The selection in June of Dayan as foreign minister dashed Yadin's apparent desire to determine the outcome of the captured territories. Moreover, shrewd bargaining by Begin to draw the NRP, Schlomozion, and Auguda Israel parties into a coalition provided the prime minister with a narrow majority in the Knesset. The ideological purity advanced mainly by "Young Turks" within the NRP and Likud, who viewed Begin's election as a mandate for a strong nationalistic policy on the West Bank, was thus protected. But more important, Yadin's earlier assumption that Likud would be unable to form a government without the participation of the DMC proved false. He could now merely supply Begin with the security of a larger plurality in Israel's Parliament; in exchange, the prime minister offered the DMC ministerial representation. Yadin, proud and principled, refused the offer, and talks with Begin were adjourned in September 1977.

In early October, Begin informed Yadin that he would offer the portfolios previously reserved for DMC members to others. Within several weeks, members of the DMC persuaded Yadin to cave in and join the government. Many DMC members reportedly believed that their advanced age precluded their participation in subsequent cabinets. Perhaps more significant, Yadin had visited the United States in October to assess American support for a toughened U.S. Middle East policy. He expressed fears during and after the visit that the United States and Israel were on a collision course and claimed that several well-connected American Jews had urged him to moderate the extremist leanings of the Likud government by joining the cabinet.

In any event, at the end of October the Likud and DMC parties announced complete agreement on key principles regarding a Middle East settlement: Israel would not deal with the PLO, it would not accept a Palestinian state In the occupied territories, and it would not return to its 1967 borders. Only two points of disagreement remained: The DMC would favor territorial compromise on all fronts, and it would continue to oppose the Begin government's policy of establishing settlements on the West Bank. With this solid compromise in hand, Begin offered Yadin the post of deputy prime minister, and two other DMC stalwarts received minor cabinet positions.[24]

Although the political pragmatism of DMC leaders undoubtedly helped produce the compromise struck by Begin and Yadin, the perceived threat to Israel's security posed by the Soviet–American communique of October 1, 1977 clearly provided the excuse if not the cause for the reconciliation. Thus, at the precise moment when it appeared that Israeli leaders would be indecisive and divided over a proper reaction to U.S. government pressure, Jerusalem became more united and stronger than at any time since Begin's election.

The View from Cairo

Anwar Sadat viewed the Soviet–American statement with a mixture of contempt and confusion. The Egyptian leader had steadily moved away from Moscow since the expulsion of Soviet military advisers from Egypt in July 1972. Sadat abrogated the

1971 Egyptian–Soviet Treaty of Friendship and Cooperation in March 1976. He subsequently turned to France and the People's Republic of China for modest arms acquisitions. In the summer of 1977, Egypt stopped exporting cotton to the Soviet Union. At the end of September, Sadat postponed repayment of $4 billion owed Moscow for military equipment provided during the preceding two decades. More serious, the Egyptian president accused the Soviet Union of helping stir up dissent in Egypt.[25]

Cairo's shift away from Moscow occurred at a time when the enmity between Sadat and Libyan leader Muamar Qhadaffi — an ally of the Soviet Union — was escalating sharply. Religious zealots opposed to the regime had kidnaped and murdered a prominent Islamic scholar in early July 1977, and a government crackdown had revealed Libyan support for the perpetrators. Sadat and Qhadaffi detested one another, the result of a long-simmering dispute over Egyptian government efforts to de-Nasserize Egypt and a belief in Tripoli that Cairo was too secularist and tolerant of Israeli domination over Arab occupied territories. Sadat, for his part, resisted the more obvious terrorist schemes that sprang from Qhadaffi's radical notions and was suspicious of the Libyan leader's apparent loyalty to and ties with the Soviet Union.

Sadat had already begun to purge leftists popularly and mistakenly believed to have fomented rebellion at the time of the January 1977 food riots. In April 1977 the Egyptian president even purged the leftists' most conspicuous and articulate spokesman, longtime Nasser confidant Mohammed Heikal. Heikal had maintained ties to Qhadaffi, and it was widely believed that the Libyan colonel stimulated, and perhaps financed, the former editor of Al-Ahram's vilifications of Sadat's government.[26] Likewise, many in Cairo believed that the more recent surge of dissidence from the right had been hatched in Tripoli with the connivance of the Soviet Union.[27] Qhadaffi hardly needed encouragement to underwrite a campaign of fundamentalism in Egypt. And although the Soviets would seem to be strange bedfellows for Moslem fundamentalists they may have chosen to play the right against the left in an effort to unseat their Egyptian adversary.

Sadat drifted toward a broader conflict with Libya in late July. Cairo believed that with Soviet help Qhadaffi might successfully bring down friendly neighboring regimes and encircle Egypt. Libya threatened both the Sudan and Chad. A Qhadaffi-inspired replacement for Sudanese President Nimeri could close Egypt's lifeline, the Nile River.

Just days prior to the July mini—war in Libya, Sadat revealed details of a new agreement with Saudi Arabia in which Riyadh undertook to pay for all Egyptian armed force development costs through 1981. The noticeable improvement in Egyptian—Saudi relations since 1973 had depended on Sadat's commitment to Arab solidarity and the expulsion of the large Soviet military presence from Egypt. Riyadh sought to preserve stability in the region and maintain its traditional values. The Saudi monarchy believed that the Soviet Union's hegemonic desires, fashioned by its messianic atheistic philosophy, seriously threatened Riyadh's guardianship of Muslim virtue and sanctity.

Saudi financial assistance was crucial to Egypt's economic and military development, particularly in light of the tepid Western response to Egyptian entreaties for large—scale investment. The Saudis had provided aid to rebuild Egyptian localities laid waste during the 1973 war and had supplied the funds necessary to cover annual budget deficits caused by food and fuel subsidies. Newly—promised Saudi assistance to purchase weapons further reassured Sadat that domestic tranquility could be preserved for a time. A restive Egyptian military would use Saudi money to replace worn Russian equipment that Egypt could no longer maintain or repair since the eviction of the Soviets. More important, the Saudi largess would permit Cairo to flex its military muscles against neighboring Libya and other Red Sea states under Soviet tutelage —— such as Ethiopia and South Yemen. In this latter effort, Riyadh would be an eager but silent partner.[28]

In the summer of 1977, the United States was moving quickly to fill a military gap created by the declining Egyptian—Soviet relationship. The Carter administration sanctioned two American firms —— General Electric and Lockheed —— to rehabilitate Egypt's fleet of MiG—21 aircraft. In late July the United States reportedly also considered furnishing 12 pilotless reconnaissance drone aircraft and six sophisticated reconnaissance cameras for installment in existing Egyptian-owned winged vehicles at a cost of $37 million. In addition, as part of the assistance program Egyptian military officers would be trained at U.S. military staff institutions.[29]

Massive American economic assistance also began to flow into Egypt following the downturn in ties between Cairo and Moscow. The United States was busily engaged in projects as diverse as building a cement factory and supplying tallow for soap. The nearly $1 billion aid program, however, was still in its infancy. The summer of 1977 witnessed a marked improvement in the emerging U.S.–Egyptian economic relationship, in part because the Cairo government devoted significant efforts to long–range planning.[30]

Thus, by the close of September 1977 Sadat had labored hard to eliminate Soviet radical presence in Egypt and at key strategic locations in the Middle East. He had turned away from Moscow and toward the West for his military and economic needs. He had strengthened ties with the United States and Saudi Arabia. He had even prepared to challenge Soviet–supported nations -- such as Libya -- in an effort to reduce Moscow's influence in the region.

At home, Sadat had changed the direction of economic planning to entice still greater Western investment. He had deftly parried threats from the left and right by isolating his detractors and undermining their legitimacy. Nevertheless, his rivals' association with Libya, and perhaps with Communists directed from Moscow, seemed to pose deeper, long term dangers. The beleaguered Egyptian leader believed that the West, United States in particular, would assist him if only he demonstrated fidelity to the cause of freedom. Under these circumstances, Sadat may have finally believed that an American invitation for the Soviet Union to cosponsor a new Geneva Conference was the least satisfactory way to reward a potential ally; in fact it amounted to placing the proverbial fox in the chicken coop. American officials commenting on the Soviet–U.S. statement claimed that Sadat regarded the superpower initiative as a "masterstroke." The evidence does not support that conclusion.[31]

October Moves

In the first weeks of October 1977, Sadat moved with vigor to negate the impact of the Soviet–American statement. He hurriedly convened a National Security Council (NSC) meeting in Cairo within hours of being notified that the superpowers would issue a communique. Those who attended the NSC meeting — all senior Egyptian officials -- debated the merits of the Soviet–American statement during a six–hour marathon session. Sadat emerged from the meeting with an apparent mandate to mobilize support against the joint communique in the Arab world, in Western Europe, and in the United States. He quickly dispatched Vice President Mubarak to Saudi Arabia, Syria, Jordan,

Iraq, Iran, and lesser Persian Gulf kingdoms and urged Assembly Speaker Marei to accept a standing invitation to Scandinavia. The Egyptian president sent a special envoy to New York with a carefully guarded message to be given Foreign Minister Fahmy for delivery to President Carter.[32]

The identity of the emissary bound for the United States was not publicly revealed, but it may have been Deputy Prime Minister Tuhamy. Tuhamy's secret meeting with Israeli Foreign Minister Dayan in Morocco a month earlier had helped gauge the extent of possible agreement between Cairo and Jerusalem at a reconvened Geneva Conference. But the Soviet–American statement upset all calculations.

For example, in Morocco Tuhamy had insisted on an Israeli commitment to withdraw from the occupied territories and had expressed optimism about containing Palestinian extremism, provided the Soviet Union was prevented from playing a role in the area. Tuhamy confidently informed Dayan that Egypt and Jordan could counter Communist influence within the Palestinian movement but asserted that Cairo wished no contact with the Russians, even one to establish peace in the area. Under the Egyptian proposals, the West Bank could be linked to Jordan. Saudi Arabia and Egypt would underwrite a campaign to restrict Palestinian excesses there and in the Gaza Strip, and the two Arab powers would maintain King Hussein on the throne in Amman. UN or U.S. supervision could enforce international guarantees to preserve peace and stability in the area, but the Soviets would be barred from participation. Had Dayan been prepared to reach agreement on Tuhamy's proposals in September, Egypt would have proceeded to Geneva to sign a complete peace agreement. In the absence of such an arrangement, Tuhamy preferred that peace documents be prepared, studied, shown to the United States, and reviewed in a future meeting between the same representatives. The subsequent working session with Dayan, scheduled for mid–October, would constitute the beginning of official Cairo–Jerusalem relations. Finally, the Egyptian deputy premier indicated that Cairo wanted a "complete package deal...not a partial arrangement, not in public, and not at Geneva, but there, between our two sides."[33]

The second meeting with Dayan did not materialize until after Sadat's journey to Jerusalem. But the object of the September discussions in Morocco, Sadat told Dayan in June 1979, was to "ensure that...Egypt and Israel would reach some kind of agreement before the conference convened so that it would not end in failure."[34] Sadat believed the Soviet-

American statement promised exactly what he wished to avoid: A long, drawn out, inconsequential Geneva meeting that would settle little. Sadat also thought Moscow's presence at Geneva would encourage PLO bellicosity and dash Egyptian dreams of restoring sovereignty over the Sinai.

Thus, in early October Sadat probably began to look for ways to torpedo the Geneva Conference. For that eventuality would permit Sadat to resume his search for a modus vivendi with Israel that might lead to a return of the Sinai. Tuhamy underscored how critical the Sinai was to Sadat when he stated to Dayan in September that "Israel's withdrawal (from the administered territories) was the basic problem. Its solution was the key to peace, for involved in it were the questions of sovereignty, of national honor, and of Sadat's own continuance in office."[35]

The Egyptian president met separately with PLO leader Yasir Arafat and opposition leader Mustafa Kamil Murad on October 3 and 4 to review Cairo's intentions toward the Soviet-American statement. Details of the discussions have remained obscure. But statements issued in New York, Beirut, and Paris by Foreign Minister Fahmy beginning on October 7, 1977 provided solid evidence of Egypt's campaign to undermine Arab support for the joint statement. Fahmy initially accused Moscow of retreating from its support of the 1974 Rabat Conference resolution declaring the PLO the sole legitimate spokesman for the Palestinians. The Egyptian foreign minister further pointed to the change in the Kremlin's position on the occupied territories: An earlier Soviet commitment to require Israel to return "all the occupied territories" merely became a call on Jerusalem to withdraw "from occupied territories." Moscow's new stance, according to the Egyptians, would leave each of the Arab states to wonder whether it would be one of the favored countries that regained sovereignty over its former land. Finally, Fahmy noted that the superpower communique committed the parties to normalization — a step considered by many as an infringment on the national rights of Arab states to establish external political relations with countries of their own choosing.[36]

Briefing Murad was an unusual step for Sadat. The leader of the Liberal Socialist Party had been a lesser member of the Free Officers group -- headed by Nasser and Sadat — that had overthrown King Farouk in 1952. However, he remained loyal to Nasser's philosophy for just a short period, preferring instead to become scion of the right, an economist, and a successful cotton broker. In 1977 Murad advocated a return to capitalism, liberalization of import policies, reform of the currency system, opening of independent banks, and a return of light industry to private ownership. He was less sympathetic to the ⌐⌐⌐ ⌐⌐⌐⌐ strongly opposed to Soviet advances in the Middle East and intrusion in Egyptian internal affairs.[37]

In order to enlist Murad in the anti-soviet but pro—PLO cause, Sadat had to be careful not to invite suspicion that Egypt's rural population would benefit from the move at the expense of others in Egyptian society. The right derives its strength from protecting the urban poor, advancing fundamentalist precepts, and assuring an expansion of the money supply.[38] The economic demands of that program required improved ties to the West. The PLO, however, is an eastern convenience, and its support lies mainly in the Egyptian countryside. Thus, Sadat could orchestrate a public media campaign in support of PLO rights only within a context that would capture wide acclaim among anti-Soviet elements of the population without at the same time incurring the mistaken wrath of those who feared a renewed governmental alliance with the rural middle class.

In his meetings with Arafat, Sadat intended to convince the PLO leader that Moscow, in league with Washington, had already decided to disregard the Rabat Conference formula. Sadat informed Arafat of the September 30 Egyptian NSC discussion and asked the PLO leader to visit Cairo again upon Mubarak's return from his tour of Arab capitals. The Egyptian vice president's three-day tour apparently resulted in a unified and fully coordinated stand on three points: The Arabs would continue to support the PLO as the sole representative of the Palestinian people; they would hold Israel responsible for the failure to reconvene the Geneva conference should Jerusalem refuse to meet with Palestinians or withdraw from the occupied territories; and the Arab states would coordinate their strategies despite their differences over tactics.[39]

Mubarak's trip sensitized Arab leaders to the necessity of regaining their Israeli-held lands without superpower intervention. Each Arab state had its own perceptions of how best to achieve the task. Syria, for example, had endorsed the call to reconvene the Geneva Conference and was prepared to negotiate with the Israelis there. But Damascus believed a carrot and stick policy would best ensure Israeli withdrawal from the conquered lands. The carrot -- recognition of Israel as a sovereign and legitimate state -- would be offered in exchange for Israeli agreement to return to its pre-1967 territorial lines. The stick -- a continuing, effective, and credible threat to utilize force -- would guarantee Israeli compliance with Arab strategic goals.[40]

The Saudis, however, were more patient and believed U.S. persuasion and the specter of a unified Arab world would dampen Israel's appetite for ruling captured territory. Moreover, Riyadh was uncomfortable with the prospect of a renewed Soviet presence in the area and probably looked to the demonstrated military prowess of Egypt to restrain radicalism.[41]

However distinct their motives might have been, Major General Naji Jamil, Syria's Deputy Defense Minister, and Prince Abdullah, Saudi Arabia's National Guard leader and Deputy Prime Minister, went to Cairo in October 1977, presumably to discuss strengthened ties. Jamil and Abdullah also possessed important credentials as contacts of their respective governments with the PLO, and both had negotiated with the movement in Lebanon and elsewhere. Jamil's visit was unannounced, short, and may have served to clarify the method and timing of future military coordination if Arab-Israeli discussions continued to deteriorate. Abdullah, however, stayed in the Egyptian capital for five days and met with Mubarak and Prime Minister Mamduh Salim. They undoubtedly discussed a variety of topics, but the questions of how to proceed militarily and politically to negate the effects of the Soviet-American statement and of how to dislodge Israel from the occupied territories held center stage.[42] Meanwhile, Arafat had shuttled between Cairo and Damascus and may have received a different view of Soviet intentions from the Syrians.

Anwar Sadat had accomplished much in the two weeks since the Soviet-American initiative was announced. He had convinced his closest advisers of the grave consequences that would befall Egypt if the superpower statement was used by Moscow to expand its activities in the area. He had sent emissaries to convey the same message to his allies in th Arab world. More important, these states -- Syria, Saudi Arabia, and others -- had or would soon look to Cairo as the leader of the Arab world. The military strength of Egypt was in decline but no coalition of Arab states could hope to launch a successful attack against Israel without Cairo's active involvement. Therefore neighboring Arab states heeded Egyptian counsel, whether for peace or war. Anwar Sadat was now able to "do battle" with Moscow, and even his friend Jimmy Carter, in order to erase the threat to stability in Egypt and the Middle East region.

On October 13 Sadat received President Carter's reply to his protest of the Soviet–American statement; the response was disappointing to him.[43] A second Egyptian NSC meeting was convened on October 15. Recently returned from Damascus, Arafat held long meetings with Sadat and Fahmy on the 17th and 18th. Cairo also announced on October 18 that Sadat would go to Eastern Europe. His meeting with Romanian leader Nicolae Ceausescu at the end of the month would be influential in Sadat's decision to go to Jerusalem. Finally, in an October 19 address to the People's Assembly Fahmy laid out in detail the official government position on reconvening the Geneva Conference and on efforts by the superpowers to impose their will on the conferees. Fahmy reiterated the PLO right to speak on behalf of all Palestinians but affirmed that Egypt had agreed to a U.S. formula whereby Palestinian representatives would be members of an all–Arab delegation at the opening of a Geneva Conference; subcommittees would discuss individual substantive matters including the Palestinian issue.

Fahmy also indicated that Egypt and the PLO were studying the U.S.–Israeli working paper issued on October 4 and 5. The matter had in fact been discussed during the Sadat–Arafat meeting two days earlier, and the PLO leader had shown some flexibility toward the document. Nevertheless, he had requested certain clarifications and amendments including a demand that the PLO be designated a conference participant. The Egyptian government's harshest rhetoric, however, was reserved for the Soviet–American communique. Fahmy noted:

> Any arrangements agreed upon by the two superpowers express only their own views, because they are achieved on the basis of their interests and outlook. We, however, have our own interests and outlook. Whatever weight and importance the views of the two superpowers have on the international level, they cannot themselves decide our fate and influence our rights. Therefore, we do not take their decisions and statements as self–evident, as though they contain the seven pillars of wisdom, but we take them for information only.[44]

The die was now cast. Negotiations continued with the United States, Syria, the PLO, Jordan, and Saudi Arabia over technical modifications to the American–Israeli working paper. But Fahmy, who presided over these legalisms, was frozen out of participation in Sadat's more basic, strategic decisions about what Egypt should do next.[45] The Egyptian president had resolved to make a dramatic -- almost incredible -- gesture in order to wrest the Sinai from Israeli control. He would travel to Jerusalem and confront the "enemy" in its own backyard. But he needed reassurance that the new Israeli leadership would in fact receive him cordially.

A six-day itinerary was quickly established for Sadat to visit Romania, Iran, and Saudi Arabia at the end of October. Ceausescu and the Shah of Iran had separately received Begin and Dayan in August, and Cairo probably thought these leaders could provide valuable insight into the intentions of Israeli officials toward the peace process. The Shah had cautioned Dayan to avoid at all costs the establishment of a Palestinian state, because no one could ensure that Arafat's eventual successors would turn out to be either moderate or reasonable.[46] The stop in Saudi Arabia would permit Sadat to tighten Egyptian-Saudi relations and to preserve the illusion of consultation with the "bankers" of the area. Moreover, a visit to Teheran alone would slight Riyadh, and Cairo wanted to protect Saudi Arabia's position as a Gulf power.[47]

Ceausescu provided Sadat with just the proper amount of assurance about Begin to encourage the risky Jerusalem gambit. Sadat was a bold man who had deftly established his rule over Egypt by undertaking dramatic moves. He had also displayed guile in excluding the Soviets from the Arab-Israeli conflict and shifting his country's allegiance toward the United States. The Egyptian president had altered Western opinion of Arabs by waging a political war in the Sinai in October 1973. He had for a time unified the Arab world behind his leadership. To achieve peace with Israel, obtain the return of the Sinai, and above all dodge the slings and arrows of Arab radicals certain to follow a journey to Jerusalem, Sadat needed a strong partner able to withstand both domestic and international pressure. The Egyptian president sought Ceausescu's opinion of Begin's sincerity and ability to take strong measures. Sadat received positive responses to both questions.[48] The Egyptian president was finally ready to go to Jerusalem.

NOTES

1. New York Times, October 2, 1977.

2. Ibid.

3. Henry A. Kissinger, Years of Upheaval (Boston: Little, Brown and Company, 1982), p. 200.

4. For a contrary view of Soviet intentions and expectations in the Middle East as a result of Geneva, see, U.S. Congress, Hearings, Subcommittee on Europe and the Middle East, Committee on International Relations, House of Representatives, 95th Congress, First Session. The Soviet Union: Internal Dynamics of Foreign Policy, Present and Future (Washington: US Government Printing Office, 1978), p. 304–305. Attitudes expressed are contained in a statement and response by Marshall Shulman, Special Adviser to the Secretary of State on Soviet Affairs, recorded on October 26, 1977.

5. Robert O. Freedman, Soviet Policy Toward the Middle East Since 1970, Revised Edition (New York: Praeger, 1978), p. 279–280.

6. U.S. Congress, The Soviet Union: Internal Dynamics of Foreign Policy, p. 304–305.

7. Ibid., p. 304.

8. Freedman, Soviet Policy Toward the Middle East Since 1970, Revised Edition, p. 304.

9. William Quandt, Decade of Decisions: American Policy Toward the Arab–Israeli Conflict, 1967–1976 (Berkely: University of California Press, 1977), p. 86–87.

10. Time, September 19, 1977, p. 51.

11. See, New York Times, September 23, 1977, for statement in which Fahmy continued to set two conditions for Israeli compliance prior to settlement: (1) total withdrawal from all captured territories, and (2) agreement on statehood for Palestinians. Conversations between Dayan and Tuhamy in Morocco days earlier revealed an Egyptian willingness to

restrain Palestinian extremism under some sort of Cairo–Riyadh guarantee. See, Moshe Dayan, Breakthrough: A Personal Account of the Egypt–Israeli Peace Negotiations (London: Weidenfeld and Nicholson, 1981), p. 47. Thus Fahmy's call for unlimited Palestinian statehood was hardly consistent with Tuhamy's assurances that palestinians would be shackled in the West Bank.

12. See, transcript of Zbigniew Brezinski interview on Issues and Answers, December 11, 1977, for implied admission of ineffective US effort to draw parties to a Geneva Conference.

13. See, US Congress, The Soviet Union: Internal Dynamics of Foreign Policy, p. 304.

14. Transcript, Brezinski Interview, Issues and Answers, December 11, 1977, p. 2.

15. Washington Post, October 3, 1977; New York Times, October 3, 1977.

16. Ibid.

17. Washington Post, October 4, 1977; New York Times, October 4, 1977; Dayan, Breakthrough, p. 65–66.

18. Raymond Cohen, "Israel and the Soviet–American State-ment of October 1, 1977" in Orbis, Fall, 1978, p. 626–627.

19. New York Times, September 28, 1977.

20. See, Dayan, Breakthrough, p. 66–72 for discussion of meeting from Israeli perspective; for text of "working paper," see Ibid., p. 71–72; for discussion of "working paper" from the American view, see Jimmy Carter, Keeping Faith: Memoirs of a President (New York: Bantam Books, 1982), p. 294–295.

21. Washington Post, October 6, 1977.

22. The term "brutal" to describe Carter's pressure tactics against Israel was conveyed to newsmen by Dayan after Israel accepted the "working paper." See, Washington Post, October 14, 1977. Vance responded publicly on the 13th and

rejected the notion. See, Washington Post, October 14, 1977. Dayan retreated from the charge on the 15th. See, Washington Post, October 16, 1977. Dayan's memoirs reveal a sharp series of exchanges between the President and the Israeli Foreign Minister but do not substantiate the "brutal" accusation. See, Dayan, Breakthrough, p. 66–72.

23. Dayan, Breakthrough, p. 71–72; see, also, Amos Perlmutter, "Begin's Strategy and Dayan's Tactics "The Conduct of Israeli Foreign Policy" in Foreign Affairs, January 1978, p. 362–366.

24. Efriam Torgovnik, "A Movement for Change in a Stable System" in Howard R. Penniman, ed. Israel at the Polls: The Knesset Elections of 1977 (Washington: American Enterprise Institute for Public Policy Research, 1979), p. 165–169; also, Washington Post, October 20, 22 1977.

25. See, Raphael Israeli, The Public Diary of President Sadat: The Road of Pragmatism (June 1976–October 1976) (Leiden: E. J. Brill, 1979), 111, p. 1189–1190.

26. Munir K. Nasser, Press, Politics and Power: Egypt's Heikal and Al Ahram (Ames: The Iowa State University Press, 1979), p. 100–102; also, see, Washington Post, May 9, 1977.

27. Washington Post, August 1, 1977; also, Assem Abdul Moshen, "Cairo: Dispute Precipitated by Moscow to Pressure Egypt" Middle East, September 1977, p. 36–40.

28. Jake Wien, Saudi–Egyptian Relations: The Political and Military Dimensions of Saudi Financial Flows to Egypt (Santa Monica: The Rand Corporation) P-6327, p. 31–33, 52–53.

29. See, Washington Post, July 31, 1977; Washington Post, September 8, 1977; Washington Post, September 16, 1977; New York Times, July 27, 1977; New York Times, September 16, 1977.

30. Anwar Sadat restructured his cabinet on October 26 replacing old–line economic advisers with seven new ministers while stressing streamlined planning. Dr. el–Qaissuni, a strong proponent of Western economic investment in Egypt was therefore strengthened by the moves. See, New York Times, October 27, 1977.

31. Anwar Sadat was reported to have told US Ambassador Eilts that the Soviet–American statement was a "masterstroke." Interview with William Quandt, Washington, D.C. September 25, 1981. Mr. Eilts has further indicated in a letter to the editor that Sadat was pleased with the joint statement largely due to its implications in fostering a reconvened Geneva Conference. Eilts cites Fahmy's full knowledge and endorsement of the communique, as evidence of Cairo's approval. Moreover, the U.S. Ambassador quotes Sadat as saying that the action was a "brilliant maneuver." He concludes by noting that while there was some concern in Washington and Cairo that the Soviet Union might utilize Geneva for its own purposes, the risks were manageable to both parties. This author's views are contrary and are substantiated in this and further sections of the book. For Eilts views, see, Herman Eilts, "The Syrians Have Been their Own Worst Enemies" Editorial Column, New York Times, January 12, 1982.

32. See, FBIS, Middle East and North Africa, October 3, 1977, D–2–D–6; October 4, 1977, D–4.

33. Dayan, Breakthrough, p. 47–48.

34. Ibid., p. 88.

35. Ibid., p. 47.

36. FBIS, Middle East and North Africa, October 3, 1977, D–1; October 5, 1977, D–3; October 7, 1977, D–1; October 11, 1977, D–3.

37. R. Michael Burrell and Abbas R. Kelidar, Egypt: The Dilemmas of a Nation 1970–1977 (Beverly Hills: Sage Publications, 1977), p. 38.

38. John Waterbury, Egypt: Burdens of the Past/Options for the Future (Bloomington: University of Indiana Press, 1978), p. 242.

39. FBIS, Middle East and North Africa, October 11, 1977, D–15.

40. A. I. Dawisha, "Syria and the Sadat Initiative," The World Today, Volume 34, Number 5, May 1978, p. 196.

41. Tamar Yegnes, "Saudi Arabia and the Peace Process" in The Jerusalem Quarterly, Number 18, Winter 1981, p. 196.

42. FBIS, Middle East and North Africa, October 11, 1977, D-15; October 12, 1977, D-10-11; October 13, 1977, D-2-3.

43. Ibid., October 18, 1977, D-1. Earlier Sadat offered the view to the United States that a five-power conference composed of heads of governments from America, Britain, France, the PRC and the Soviet Union could precede a Geneva meeting. The Egyptian president probably believed that such an august group could design a peace program that would include restoration of the Sinai without the promise of a Palestinian veto. Nevertheless, Carter himself rejected the notion and the October 14 U.S. reply may have contained that explicit statement. See Ibid., December 30, 1977, D-7 for discussion of five-power meetings. Also, Anwar Sadat, In Search of Identity (New York: Harper and Row, 1977), p. 306-307. President Carter mentions his negative reply to Sadat but places the matter in the context of a telephone conversation on November 2. The formal written US response, however, may have been delivered earlier. See, Carter, Keeping Faith, p. 296.

44. FBIS, Middle East and North Africa, October 20, 1977, D-5; for earlier Fahmy statements cited, see, Ibid., October 18, 1977, D-1-2, 7.

45. Tuhamy revealed to Dayan during their first meeting in Morocco on September 17, 1977 that only Mubarak and he among Sadat's advisers were aware of the secret contacts with Israel. See, Dayan, Breakthrough, p. 45. Fahmy was similarly excluded from Sadat's private plans for breaking the Geneva logjam during visits to Romania, Iran, and Saudi Arabia. Sadat was queried why he did not reveal his intentions regarding the Jerusalem initiative to King Khalid during the late October visit. His response is curious yet informative. He replied that he did not wish to embarass Khalid or other Arab leaders. Sadat also may not have wished to allow Fahmy knowledge of the impending move and thus be placed in a position to be pressured for its cancellation. See, FBIS, Middle East and North Africa, December 30, 1977, D-8.

46. Dayan, Breakthrough, p. 33.

47. Wein, Saudi–Egyptian Relations, Rand P–6327, p. 29–34.

48. Sadat, In Search of Identity, p. 306.

3
Sadat's Visit to Jerusalem

November Preparations

President Sadat returned to Cairo on November 3, 1977. Arrangements were begun immediately for the journey to Jerusalem, although few of Sadat's advisers knew of the planned visit. The Egyptian NSC had met three weeks earlier on October 15 and discussed a visit to Israel, but the participants had believed the matter to be exploratory. The intention to visit Jerusalem would remain a closely guarded secret for several days.

Important leaders in the military and technological sectors would be informed of the delicate subject but not necessarily consulted. In foreign policy Sadat was first among equals, and his NSC contained the leaders of all critical elements of Egyptian society. Therefore, Sadat needed only to gain the tacit approval of that group to embark on foreign policy ventures.

The army — potentially the gravest internal threat to Sadat's rule — had long been depoliticized. Its size, sophistication, and receptiveness to command contributed to its general passivity toward most political matters.[1] Sadat probably also believed that a direct approach to Jerusalem for peace would appeal to the Egyptian army, which in a period of continued hostility with Israel and spiraling inflation was burdened daily by long duty and uncertain pay.

The Egyptian NSC was composed of Vice President Hosni Mubarak, People's Assembly Speaker Sayed Marei, Prime Minister Mamduh Salim, General Secretary of the Arab Socialist Union Mustapha Khalil, Minister of War and Deputy Prime Minister Muhammad Abd el–Ghani Gamassy, Director of the General Intelligence Department of the Ministry of Interior Kamal Hassan Ali, and Sadat. Other members of Sadat's entourage, such as Tuhamy and Osman Ahmad Osman, a family friend, also had influence on general foreign policy matters. Boutrus Ghali and Usama al–Baz administered the Foreign Office, and Hasan Kamil presided over the president's office. Each of these individuals played a significant role in the drive to achieve peace with Israel; some eventually became casualties of the effort. In November 1977 none of these officials represented a threat or could diminish Sadat's authority over foreign affairs. Certain members of the NSC, however, retained important influence on the forthcoming Jerusalem visit.

Gamassy had been Army Chief of Staff during the October War and masterminded Egypt's crossing of the Suez Canal. He had fought the Israelis in several major conflicts and respected their military prowess. Although he was deeply suspicious of Israeli intentions, he desired to reduce the chances that Egypt's youth would have to fight another war and feared Israel's alleged nuclear capacity. Gamassy had also negotiated the disengagement of forces after the 1973 war and believed that personal contact could help resolve differences. He did not enjoy great popularity with his troops but commanded respect for his professionalism.[2] Gamassy favored the trip to Jerusalem, provided Israel reciprocated with equal gestures of good will and ultimately substantive concessions.

Vice President Mubarak, a former commander of the Air Force, was mostly confined to the role of diplomatic messenger during the fall of 1977. Yet he had begun to establish important relations with junior officers worried about the country's future military–industrial capacity and external arms sources. Mubarak championed those slighted by Gamassy's plans to equip the Egyptian Navy with helicopters at the expense of the Air Force. He criticized Gamassy's efforts to acquire U.S. weapons and unwillingness to assist African neighbors in need of defense.[3] The rivalry between Mubarak and Gamassy permitted Sadat to make new peace overtures more freely, as neither official possessed the independence or following to unify the military.

Intensification of the competition between Mubarak and Gamassy may have persuaded Sadat not to include both on the delegation to Jerusalem. Intelligence chief Kamal Hassan Ali represented the military during the visit. Ali had commanded Egypt's armored forces before moving to the Ministry of Interior in 1975. Although once an assistant to Gamassy, General Ali probably believed an alliance with Mubarak would best assure his future. Or perhaps Gamassy's opposition to challenging Libya militarily soured Ali. In any case, the intelligence chief favored the November 1977 peace initiative, and his reputation as a resourceful and popular military leader undoubtedly enhanced Sadat's standing with the army's rank and file.[4]

Party General Secretary Mustapha Khalil, who was added to the Jerusalem party at his own request, ably represented Egypt's industrial and technological sectors. A professional economist and engineer, Khalil was educated at Harvard University, taught at the University of Illinois and Ain Shams University in Cairo, and held several cabinet posts under Nasser. He was Deputy Prime Minister for Communication and, later, for Industry, Mineral Wealth and Electricity.

A disagreement with Nasser confidant Ali Sabri over the party's proper role in the industrialization of Egypt resulted in Khalil's removal. Shortly before Nasser's death, Khalil became head of the board of trustees of the Radio and Television union. Soon after Sadat took power, Khalil became Director of Research of the Arab International Bank, Chairman of the Engineer's Syndicate, member of the economic, planning and budget committee of the People's Assembly, and Secretary General of the Arab Socialist Union.[5]

The addition of Khalil to the Jerusalem delegation reflected the potential importance peace with Israel could have on Egypt's technocratic elite. Egypt was already producing engineers at a rate far out of proportion to the country's needs. The majority of these graduates were rapidly assuming significant management roles throughout Egyptian society.[6] As the head of the engineers syndicate, Khalil wished to preserve and advance their position in the country.

Improved relations with Israel would undoubtedly enhance relations with the West. But a separate peace with Jerusalem could only enrage the Arab world, drying up needed subsidies from oil-rich Arab countries and eliminating access to important creditors such as Saudi Arabia. These considerations tempered Khalil's enthusiasm for the visit as he recognized that the benefits of the move would be counterbalanced by Egypt's subsequent isolation from the Arab world.

The civilian technocracy and the military were the main power centers in Egypt after the presidency. Sadat preferred to avoid an alliance between the two that could limit his ability to maneuver. This desire may in part explain the decision to leave Gamassy in Cairo, as the minister of war was known to be on good terms with Khalil.[7]

Sadat invited his old friend and shrewd business companion Osman Ahmad Osman to join the delegation to Jerusalem. Sadat had married his two daughters to the sons of important members of the Egyptian elite. Osman's eldest son was the husband of the Egyptian president's youngest daughter. Osman headed the largest construction firm in the Arab world and was a prominent member of the business community in Egypt. Among many projects, he built the Aswan Dam. He was the epitome of the wealthy urban conservative and functioned as liaison and voice for Sadat with that important social group. Osman served in 1973 and 1974 as Minister of Reconstruction and Housing, but charges of corruption forced him to resign. Nevertheless, he remained an important and close economic adviser to Sadat, often providing advice contrary to that of Khalil.[8]

Sadat's eldest daughter married the son of Sayed Marei, a perennial member of the elite, who had served in Egyptian governments even before Nasser acceded to power. Marei, a member of the Ancien Regime, was minister of agriculture in an early Nasser cabinet, an agronomist by trade, and successively presidential adviser and Speaker of the People's Assembly under Sadat. Like Osman, Marei was an important link to the urban right and often foreshadowed swings in Sadat's moods and policies.[9] In November 1977 the speaker remained at home in favor of Osman, as Sadat probably preferred to offer the left fewer targets in its anticipated campaign against the visit to Jerusalem.

The foreign office opposed the Jerusalem gambit, unless the move was certain to yield an immediate return of the occupied territories and establishment of a Palestinian state in the West Bank. The foreign office and its leaders were fooled completely by the propaganda mill that Sadat had carefully constructed to bludgeon the Soviet-American statement and prepare for a unilateral gesture toward Israel. Fahmy resigned soon after the Jerusalem visit became public; his participation in the visits to Eastern Europe and the Persian Gulf had helped maintain confidence in the Arab world that Sadat would observe well-established Muslim concerns.

Fahmy's chief administrative officer and immediate successor, Boutrus Ghali, was an academic with an international reputation in the fields of law and politics. Ghali had achieved graduate degrees in public and international law from the University of Paris. He had served as editor-in-chief of a popular Egyptian political science quarterly, as director of al-Ahram's Center for Political and Strategic Studies, and as head of the political science department at Cairo University. A coptic Christian, Ghali married the daughter of a Romanian Jew; she converted to the coptic faith after their marriage.

Ghali was a pan–Arabist who believed that Egyptian moves to improve relations with the Israelis would seriously erode Egypt's position within the Arab world if Sadat failed to achieve considerable success in retrieving occupied lands and solving the Palestinian impasse.[10] A junior foreign affairs officer of some promise, Usama al–Baz, also served on the delegation. Al–Baz had risen in the service to become Fahmy's eminence grise; he soon deserted the foreign minister and joined Mubarak's camp when Fahmi began to fall out of grace with Sadat. Al–Baz would become the drafter of Egypt's official positions established during the Cairo–Jerusalem negotiations.[11] A certain degree of antagonism would arise between Ghali and al–Baz. But initially at least the two reinforced each other's views that Sadat should under no circumstances conclude a separate agreement with Israel.

Two presidential advisers, Tuhamy and Hasan Kamil, brought balance and experience in foreign affairs to the negotiating table in Jerusalem. More than any other Egyptian official Tuhamy had been privy to Sadat's thinking regarding bilateral negotiations with Israel. He had already met with Dayan in Morocco and was part of the delegation that greeted Sadat in Cairo when the president returned from Eastern Europe. Thus, Tuhamy would play a crucial role in providing insight into both the Egyptian president's thoughts and Israel's perceptions of the visit.

Kamil had served ably as ambassador in three posts and for a short period as an under secretary in the Ministry of Foreign Affairs before becoming chief of administrative services in the presidential office. He led the advance team that prepared Sadat's arrival in Jerusalem. He was a valued and trustworthy personal adviser to Sadat and possessed no agenda of his own to affect his counsel.[12]

Sadat was therefore served in Jerusalem and after by a team of men that shared neither his perspective nor his breadth of vision. Those who supported the move were wary of Israeli intentions. Some worried more about personal gain and promises of alliance with others. A few opposed the adventure altogether and served on the delegation merely to avoid the consequences of refusing.

The Egyptian president, ever the consummate politician, carefully balanced every adviser opposed to his plans with one loyal to his views. He knew that Khalil, in league with Gamassy, would seek to gain at the expense of Mubarak and that Ghali and al–Baz would attempt to block any option untenable to

Egypt's technocrats. But in November 1977 Sadat needed Khalil's talents, expertise, and popularity with the Egyptian elite and thus preferred to include Khalil on the negotiating team. Osman, Marei, Tuhamy, and Kamil remained the real eyes and ears of the Egyptian president. In time, an alliance between Mubarak and Ali would seek to redesign Sadat's plans and programs. The Jerusalem visit would, however, be cast as the work of a talented and united group seeking to bring prosperity and peace to the Egyptian masses.

Sadat announced his decision to go to Jerusalem on November 9 in an address to the opening session of the People's Assembly. The speech itself was a long, rambling discourse on the benefits to the individual of government-sponsored programs. Near the end of the speech, the president reviewed the external situation and his attempts to produce peace in the area. He dwelt on personal efforts to revive the Geneva Conference and lauded President Carter's devotion to the just cause of the Palestinian people. Sadat revealed the efforts of the past weeks to achieve Arab coordination. He reiterated his commitment to go to Geneva, although he cautioned such a meeting should be held only after careful preparations. Finally, in a flourish, Sadat revealed to an astonished audience that he was even ready to go to the "Knesset itself" if such an act would contribute to peace.[13]

Sadat had scheduled his announcement for November 7, but a flurry of last-minute consultations with King Hussein and Arafat in Cairo -- and internal dissension over the decision -- postponed the statement for two days. The Jordanian King traveled to Riyadh on November 5 before meeting with Sadat the following day. Arafat arrived in the Egyptian capital on the 7th and remained for the address to the People's Assembly.

Sadat may have informed the two Arab leaders in Cairo of his intended visit to Jerusalem. If the Egyptian president did indeed consult Hussein and Arafat, he most likely presented the move as one sure to elicit an Israeli rejection. Such a reaction, he could have pointed out, would reveal to the world Israel's determination to avoid peace with its neighbors. A round of meetings among Fahmy, Marei, and Arafat on November 8 could have been orchestrated to remove any lingering doubt that the bold gesture would work.

A three-hour Egyptian NSC meeting on November 5 probably provided Sadat the first occasion to declare formally his readiness to travel to Jerusalem and appear before the Knesset. The length of the meeting and the two-day delay in the public announcement before the People's Assembly suggest that the NSC meeting was acrimonious.

Sadat may have privately expected an immediate and favorable Israeli reply to his offer. Instead, Begin did not extend the official invitation -- conveyed through U.S. channels -- until November 15.[14] Meanwhile, the meeting of Arab foreign ministers convened in Tunis to prepare for a more formal Arab summit, and Fahmy represented Egypt. He maintained publicly that no Middle East solution was possible without PLO participation.

Arafat went to Damascus before returning to Lebanon to meet with senior Palestinian officials. The United States continued to seek ways to include Palestinian representatives in a Geneva Conference and simultaneously avoid formal PLO participation. Sadat proposed the establishment of a new "working committee" to ensure an adequately prepared Geneva Conference; the Israelis, however, rejected the move as unnecessary.

The Israeli Perspective

The Israeli Government was as unprepared as the Egyptian people for Sadat's proposal to address the Knesset. Many Israelis were indifferent to the gesture but others were wary. Israeli military intelligence officers had earlier consulted the nation's oriental affairs scholars to determine if Egyptian officials might possibly modify their refusal to accept the existence of the Jewish state; a September 1977 report circulated within the Ministry of Defense concluded that Cairo's ruling circles would not.[15]

The deployment of a significant portion of Egypt's land forces near the Suez Canal in October in response to a large-scale Israeli military training exercise renewed Jerusalem's fears that a conflict with Cairo might break out in the winter. Army Chief of Staff Mordecai Gur even accused the Egyptian government of preparing for war despite Sadat's offer to visit Jerusalem. Gur was castigated and later removed from office for the remark, but the statement reflected the deep suspicion of Egyptian military intentions that pervaded the senior echelons of the Israeli Defense Forces. Director of Military Intelligence Shlomo Gazit regarded the proposal to address the Knesset as sincere but believed that the speech would contain far-reaching demands. The Israeli military establishment therefore approached Sadat's bold plan gingerly.[16]

Foreign Minister Dayan also worried that Sadat's visit to Jerusalem would place unprecedented burdens on Israel to respond with measures it wanted to avoid. He was particularly anxious about the steady barrage by the Egyptian media designed to force Israel to vacate the occupied territories and recognize Palestinian rights immediately. Dayan was also troubled by Sadat's efforts to coordinate Egyptian positions with those of Syria and the PLO.[17]

After initial skepticism, it was Begin who first recognized the historic import of a speech by the president of Egypt to the Parliament of Israel. Begin may have first believed that Sadat intended to exploit the visit to Jerusalem to pressure Israel at Geneva. Upon deeper reflection, however, the Israeli prime minister decided that a serious attempt to achieve peace might result from a visit to Jerusalem by Sadat.[18] After three decades of searing Arab hostility, Begin could not simply dismiss the opportunity to welcome the Arabs' leading spokesman to Israel, regardless of Sadat's motivation.

The glare of worldwide publicity, intensified by the instantaneous global communications, placed enormous pressure on both leaders to attempt the gamble. In addition, Israeli military intelligence officials advised Begin to invite Sadat. They believed that the Jewish state would lose credibility within the international community if, having long complained that there existed no one to talk to in the Arab world, Jerusalem refused Sadat's offer.[19]

The Visit

The Egyptian Boeing 707 carrying Sadat and his aides landed at Ben Gurion Airport shortly before 8:00 p.m. on November 19, 1977. It was an event nearly unequaled in the annals of recorded history. The majesty and ceremony that followed during the 36-hour visit, however, masked the unease of the Egyptian party as it began a dialogue with senior Israeli officials.

Dayan and Boutrus Ghali shared their views during the 30-minute ride from the airport to Jerusalem. Ghali stressed that Egypt would not enter into a separate peace with Israel and that forthcoming discussions would have to deal with the Palestinians and Jordan. Dayan responded that although he was aware of Sadat's increasing isolation, Jordan and the Palestinians would most likely stay away from the conference table. Cairo would have to sign a peace treaty alone with Israel, Dayan pointed out, if the Egyptians wished to settle the conflict.

Ghali conveyed his displeasure with the Israeli foreign minister's assessment, having apparently misinterpreted it as Dayan's personal desire. Dayan also told Ghali that Israel regarded the PLO as an unfit negotiating partner. The warning found its mark, as Sadat did not mention the organization in the following day's speech to the Knesset.[20]

Sadat and Begin talked briefly in Jerusalem's King David Hotel soon after the Egyptian's arrival. Sadat emphasized that he had not come to Jerusalem to establish a separate peace and reiterated his desire to discuss the Palestinian issue. Begin expressed his wish for a return visit to Cairo, but Sadat remained noncommittal. The Israeli prime minister, however, did indicate during this initial meeting his willingness to return the Sinai to Egyptian sovereignty. Disillusionment would arise later in Sadat's mind over that commitment, which Begin understood to mean returning sovereignty without handing over all the land. Sadat attempted to lessen Begin's concern over the future of the Sinai by promising to demilitarize the area east of the Gidi and Milta passes.[21]

A more formal session took place at lunch in Jerusalem the next day, November 20. Sadat, Khalil, and Ghali represented Egypt; Begin, Dayan, and Yadin represented Israel. Khalil began by reminding his hosts that Egypt did not seek a separate peace. He also deflected a suggestion by Begin to establish a hot line between Cairo and Jerusalem, as such a move would be tantamount to establishing formal relations between the two countries. Sadat wished to discuss substantive measures but agreed that the schedule of Muslim festivities arranged by Cairo allowed precious little time to air opposing views.

The Egyptian president emphasized that the two governments should arrive in Geneva with an "agreed programme" and urged the participants to turn their energies toward that objective. When pressed, however, to state who he believed should take part in the "programme," Sadat remained evasive. He inferred that it did not matter who participated in the Geneva Conference: Those who wanted to come could; the others might just as well stay away.

Dayan wondered what purpose a conference would serve if all contentious matters were settled in prior meetings. Would

Geneva therefore "...simply set the formal seal on an agreement that would already have been reached, or was it to negotiate with those Arab leaders who refused to take part in the preliminary discussion?"[22] The luncheon concluded without much progress.

A hush filled the packed Knesset chamber as Sadat nervously strode to the rostrum and began to deliver his carefully crafted speech later that afternoon. A traditional Muslim blessing blended well with calls for dedication to peace and eradication of war. Sadat recalled early efforts to establish relations with the State of Israel but placed greater emphasis on the future. He asserted that he would not sign a separate peace with Israel, or arrange further interim agreements, or even bargain over Arab lands. But he promised that if Israel merely agreed to live within its borders, the Arabs would never again go to war against the Jewish state. Sadat underscored Arab insistence on Israel's total withdrawal from the territories occupied since 1967, including East Jerusalem. Finally, he reiterated that the "heart of the struggle" remained the Palestinian problem and that only recognition of the Palestinians' right to a state or some other national entity would constitute a first step toward peace.

The Egyptian president concluded the speech by restating principles that he believed would have to govern any peace agreement signed in Geneva: Return of all occupied Arab lands; recognition of the Palestinian right to an independent national entity; acceptance of the basic right of all countries in the region to live in peace under reasonable guarantees; agreement by these nations to observe the terms of the UN charter by resolving conflict through peaceful means; and termination of the state of war dominating the area.[23]

Begin's response was anticlimactic. He reviewed Israel's views on what its permanent boundaries should be but urged his guest not to rule out negotiations on any subject. The Israeli prime minister emphasized that Jerusalem regarded all matters as open to discussion. Although he ignored the Palestinian issue completely, Begin did promise that Moslems and Christians would continue to enjoy unlimited access to their holiest places in Jerusalem in perpetuity, thus underlining Israel's intention to retain control over the entire city.

He reiterated Israel's willingness to attend a Geneva Conference but reminded his guests that he would only negotiate on the basis of UN Resolutions 242 and 338. Peace had to be complete, he asserted, and the initial clause of any treaty would have to declare the end of the state of belligerency. Talks could begin with Egypt that very day in Jerusalem, or the next day in Cairo, or anywhere else, Begin concluded.[24] Israeli opposition leader Shimon Peres ended the special gathering with a short statement. The 800-seat auditorium was electric with excitement as Sadat left the chamber. He then met briefly with Defense Minister Ezer Weizman and Begin in the Israeli prime minister's office.[25] Weizman had been injured in an automobile accident days before Sadat's journey to Jerusalem and was confined to a hospital bed when the Egyptian president arrived. The effort to attend the Knesset session had been painful for Weizman, and Sadat appreciated the gesture. Weizman had been mentioned frequently as a possible successor to Begin, who was in poor health, and Sadat probably wished to scrutinize the hawkish defense minister.

Hours later, Sadat, the fourteen members of his party, and an equal number of Israelis attended a banquet hosted by Begin at the King David Hotel. The mood was glum. Although Weizman attempted to introduce some liveliness, even he had been sobered by the Egyptian president's remarks to the Knesset. The Israeli defense minister had passed a note to Begin during the speech in which he stated his belief that Israel would now have to prepare for war.

The Egyptian president expressed disappointment, particularly with Begin's speech. Dayan reminded Sadat that the Egyptians could not expect an immediate Israeli approval to everything in the Egyptian president's address. Cairo and Jerusalem held very different views on many subjects but, Dayan pointed out, Begin had assured that all matters would remain open to discussion.

Sadat noted that talks could continue in Morocco or possibly Romania but that a visit by Begin to address the People's Assembly in Cairo would not be possible as long as Israel occupied the Sinai. Egypt's president could, however, invite the Israeli prime minister to Ismailia and convene a parliamentary meeting there. Others at the table sought to introduce light conversation, but awkward reminders of the wars between Egypt and Israel and the casualties suffered, including relatives of those assembled, foiled the attempt. The dinner ended with an apparent agreement over the wording of the next day's joint communique.[26]

Begin and Sadat met privately after the banquet, presumably to arrange future joint discussions. The two leaders agreed that the link between Tuhamy and Dayan would remain active and that Weizman and Gamassy would meet in the near future.[27] While these discussions took place, Weizman, Yadin, Khalil, and Ghali met in a nearby room of the King David Hotel. The encounter produced a mixture of reminiscences of Cairo during a bygone era and of serious exchanges about the security concerns of each side. The Israeli defense minister offered a short review of how narrow the Jewish state's military perimeter was. Khalil retorted that Israel had nothing to fear from Cairo as the Egyptian state had no final military solution to impose on Israel.

The participants jousted over the effects on their countries of previous wars, as the Egyptians estimated that that their nation had lost between 80,000 and 100,000 men in the four conflicts. Khalil and Ghali wondered whether the previous month's training exercise forshadowed a fifth war, and the Israelis began to understand the significance that miscalculation could have on relations between two neighboring states. Khalil pointedly reminded Weizman that Israel's security concerns meant nothing, because Jerusalem possessed a nuclear capability. The conversations continued late into the night.[28]

Early the following morning, November 21, Khalil invited Weizman to meet with Sadat. Khalil had evidently portrayed the Israeli defense minister in a favorable light, perhaps as someone who appeared to be reasonable and who could presumably reflect the real security interests of the Israeli military. Sadat -- bracketed by Khalil, Ghali, and Osman -- opened the talk with a brief restatement of the themes in his speech to the Knesset. Weizman led the Egyptian president to the window and asked how the streets of Jerusalem below could be redivided. Sadat reiterated that Arab soil was sacred and that he would not be able to look a single Egyptian in the face again if he allowed Israel to remain in the occupied lands. Sadat then spoke about Soviet expansionism before returning to the discussion at hand: The senseless killing had to end. He recognized that Egypt and Israel had fundamental differences but noted that he had come to Jerusalem to resolve them.

The Israeli defense minister reminded the Egyptians of Israel's vulnerabilities, which he had described the night before. Weizman examined the October troop movements on both sides, but Sadat limited his response. The Egyptian president was obviously engaged in a broader, more far-reaching analysis of how to achieve peace in the area. Sadat guessed correctly that Israeli leaders worried about his longevity. The Egyptian president noted that he could be counted on to keep his word and asserted that a successor would commit political suicide if he advanced against Israel after signature of a peace agreement. The two leaders parted with only faint hints that the climate for future meetings had been improved.[29]

That afternoon the two sides held a joint press conference. Begin and Sadat deflected questions regarding a return visit to Cairo by the Israeli prime minister but agreed that a serious and direct dialogue had begun and would continue. Both leaders stressed their pledge to avoid war between their countries. They differed on the meaning, not the principle, of security. Reconvening a Geneva Conference remained a distant goal of both parties. Sadat pointed to his strained relations with the Soviet Union and reminded his listeners that Moscow could obstruct any efforts to achieve success at such a conference.[30]

Ghali and Dayan reviewed the visit on their way to the airport immediately after the press conference. Ghali criticized an article that had appeared that morning in the Egyptian daily Al-Ahram calling upon Israel to respond to Sadat's initiative by withdrawing from the occupied territories unilaterally and agreeing to the establishment of a Palestinian state. Ghali informed Dayan that the newspaper comment did not represent the views of Sadat's delegation in Israel. Those conclusions would depend in great part on the nature of future Egyptian-Israeli discussions. The Egyptian official stated that the talks should continue in private, not through public pronouncements, and stressed that Jerusalem had to understand that Cairo regarded the Palestinian problem as the primary issue separating Egypt and Israel.

Dayan, feeling a sense of deja vu, attempted to persuade Ghali that the two sides should discuss first the future state of bilateral relations. Ghali stubbornly insisted, however, that Egypt could consider only a comprehensive arrangement that included all the Arab states and the Palestinians. Dayan retorted that the Syrians, Palestinians, and Jordanians would most likely refuse to join the discussions. Ghali revealed he had not even read the U.S.-Israeli working paper of October 4-5, believing — as did Sadat — that the Jerusalem visit would open a new era.

The two officials discussed Jerusalem. Dayan suggested that perhaps the parties should concentrate on the status of the holy places instead of sovereignty. Surprisingly, Ghali agreed but admitted that Egypt might find it impossible to persuade the Saudis to accept that view.

The Israeli foreign minister then reiterated that Egypt could achieve positive results more quickly if it confined its efforts to those areas where it possessed independent authority to act. Responding to the cue, Ghali asserted that Sadat wished to achieve independence for the Gaza Strip. Dayan regarded that objective as foolish, noting that Gazans found employment in Israel and that the territory possessed neither an industrial base nor markets for its farm produce. He complained that Egyptian officials often failed to understand the economic realities of the areas in question. When the two officials parted, they expressed hope that joint consultations between Egypt and Israel would in fact continue.[31]

The Visit — An Assessment

Sadat's journey to Jerusalem achieved many of its goals, advanced others, and, perhaps most important, began the dialogue that would eventually culminate in a peace treaty between Egypt and Israel. Begin offered to return the Sinai to Egypt — a primary objective of the visit — in his first encounter with Sadat. The Egyptians also obtained Israel's tacit agreement that a Geneva Conference represented a suitable forum for ratifying agreements rather than for negotiating them. Egyptian representatives convinced their Israeli counterparts that Moscow and the PLO could and probably would employ obstructionist tactics at Geneva. Thus, the two recognized that they would have to prepare the ground carefully for peace and security between Egypt and Israel to flourish.

At the same time, Sadat and his entire entourage stressed continually that Egypt could not accept a separate peace between Cairo and Jerusalem. At each juncture, whether in less formal meetings between second echelon officials or at sessions attended by Sadat and Begin, the Egyptians underscored this point. Sadat's advisers may well have made constant repetition of that point a quid pro quo for joining the delegation. Ghali and Khalil voiced other concerns as well: The Palestinian issue remained the key to establishing a comprehensive peace; and Jerusalem's nuclear capability made Israeli security concerns inconsequential.

Both sides wished to avoid dealing with the PLO. Cairo disliked Arafat's propinquity to Moscow, and Jerusalem viewed the organization as its sworn enemy. But each side approached the Palestinian issue from the perspective of its own requirements. The Egyptians saw the matter as central to retaining and widening links with their Arab neighbors and patrons. Israeli officials assigned importance to the issue insofar as it affected the character of the future status of Judea and Samaria.

Despite Egyptian concern about Israel's ability to manufacture nuclear weapons, each side adopted a more cautious attitude toward the other's military activities. The prospect of going to war because of an accident or malfunction became very real in the light of the direct conversations in Jerusalem about recent training exercises and troop movements. Although the Egyptian delegation to Israel would not even consider establishing a hot line between the two countries, they agreed to communicate through European governments to defuse potential crises.

Central, however, to all the public and private meetings between Israelis and Egyptians was the mutual belief that the visit would fundamentally change the nature of relations between Cairo and Jerusalem. The two former adversaries were determined never again to go to war. Sadat wanted to convince not only his own supporters but more especially enlightened Israelis of his vision of total peace. Begin seemed to move along the perimeter of this vision by agreeing to discuss every subject, including Jerusalem, and to continue the dialogue despite real differences of opinion between the two countries over key issues.

The behavior of the two leaders at the several meetings satisfied their respective domestic constituencies and most important advisers. The visit was a test of Sadat's ability to elicit meaningful responses from the Israeli leadership without sacrificing pan-Arabism or his commitments as spokesman of the Arab world. The Egyptian president never deviated from his position that Egypt would not undertake separate arrangements or abandon major Arab demands. And he wisely protected the interests both of the right and the urban poor in Egypt. He continued to move away from Nasserism by stressing strong religious themes and, with Begin's support, opposing an ill-prepared Geneva Conference under the strong influence of Moscow and the PLO.

The resignation and public disavowal of two of Sadat's important foreign policy advisers prior to the journey dealt a blow to national honor and prestige. But the eager participation of Ghali and Khalil in the discussions and their apparent success in establishing favorable relations with important Israelis softened the impact of the defections. It remained to be seen whether Cairo's vast media apparatus could convert the masses in Egypt and their willing allies in other important Arab capitals to Sadat's bold course. However, the promise of further contacts with Israel, including a possible meeting in Ismailia, had not diminished Sadat's popularity with the Egyptian public.

In Israel, Begin had bolstered his narrow majority when Yigal Yadin's Democratic Movement for Change joined the prime minister's coalition in the weeks preceding the Egyptian visit. And the visit increased the willingness of Yadin and Dayan to undertake new efforts to draw Egypt into peace arrangements. Begin's forthcoming approach throughout Sadat's stay comforted those who sought real compromise and facilitated future discussions. The Israeli prime minister dangled the Sinai as bait before his Egyptian guests but retained the right to use it to obtain a real peace, including recognition, exchange of ambassadors, open and secure borders, trade, and travel.

Egypt's guidelines concerning Judea, Samaria, and Palestinian rights were so vague that the religious parties and other nationalist elements in Israel could pose nothing more than broad objections. And the clamor of an Israeli population yearning for peace after four wars and thousands of casualties was more than Begin could ignore, however nationalistic, cynical, and unyielding he might be.

NOTES

1. See, Ehud Yaari, "Sadat's Pyramid of Power" in The Jerusalem Quarterly, Winter 1980, p. 113-114.

2. Ibid., p. 116.

3. Ibid.

4. See, Eitan Haber, Zeev Schiff and Ehud Yaari, The Year of the Dove (New York: Bantam Books, 1979), p. 6.

5. See Khalil biographic data in New York Times, December 1, 1978.

6. See, Clement Henry Moore, Images of Development: Egyptian Engineers in Search of Industry (Cambridge: MIT Press, 1980), p. 3–10.

7. Yaari, "Sadat's Pyramid of Power" in The Jerusalem Quarterly, Winter 1980, p. 117.

8. Earl L. Sullivan, "The U.S. and Egypt: The Potential Crisis" in Worldview, December 1979, p. 18.

9. See, Robert Springborg, Family Power and Politics in Egypt––Sayed Bey Marei––His Clan, Clients and Cohorts (Philadelphia: University of Pennsylvania Press, 1982), p. 121–141.

10. Haber, Schiff and Yaari, The Year of the Dove, p. 57–58.

11. Ibid., p. 258.

12. Ibid., p. 53.

13. See, Foreign Broadcast Information Service, Middle East and North Africa, November 10, 1977, D-20.

14. See, Moshe Dayan, Breakthrough: A Personal Account of the Egypt–Israel Peace Negotiations (London: Weidenfeld and Nicholson, 1981), p. 75.

15. Ezer Weizman, The Battle for Peace (New York: Bantam Books, 1981), p. 19.

16. Ibid., p. 20–29.

17. Dayan, Breakthrough, p. 76.

18. Weizman, The Battle for Peace, p. 37.

19. Ibid., p. 25.

20. Dayan, Breakthrough, p. 77–78.

21. Haber, Schiff and Yaari, The Year of the Dove, p. 63–64.

22. Dayan, Breakthrough, p. 79–80.

23. See, Transcript, New York Times, November 21, 1977.

24. Ibid.

25. Weizman, The Battle for Peace, p. 34–35.

26. Ibid., p. 56–59; Dayan, Breakthrough, p. 83–84; Haber, Schiff and Yaari, The Year of the Dove, p. 71–73.

27. Haber, Schiff and Yaari, The Year of the Dove, p. 97; Dayan, Breakthrough, p. 83–84.

28. Weizman, The Battle for Peace, p. 59–61; Haber, Schiff and Yaari, The Year of the Dove, p. 73.

29. Weizman, The Battle for Peace, p. 64–70.

30. New York Times, Transcript, November 22, 1977.

31. Dayan, Breakthrough, p. 84–86.

4
The Triangular Relationship

The View from Cairo, November 1977

Sadat returned home from Jerusalem to a hero's welcome, but the reception disguised official nervousness over the task of maintaining momentum in the peace process. The Egyptian president's historic visit had superseded the Soviet-American call for a Geneva meeting. But the Arab world opposed Sadat's journey nearly unanimously, and Moscow's support of radical Moslem states threatened to isolate Cairo in the region.

Sadat therefore devised a move designed simultaneously to split the temporary Soviet-American alliance, induce Washington to join Cairo and Jerusalem in advancing their peace initiative, and restore Egyptian leadership among moderate Arab nations. Egypt decided to hold its own international meeting to remove procedural obstacles to peace as a prelude to Geneva. Washington hesitated, while Jerusalem quickly accepted the invitation to the conference.

Soviet, Syrian, and PLO refusal to attend was virtually assured, however, by the tone and substance of Sadat's address to the People's Assembly announcing the conference. He castigated the Soviet Union for promoting conflict in the Middle East and stimulating division among Cairo, Damascus, and the Palestinians over the peace process. Sadat also omitted any mention of the PLO in his 80-minute speech, although he did reiterate his desire to protect the legitimate rights of the Palestinian people. Finally, he defended his visit to Jerusalem as the most promising method of convincing the world of the Arabs' peaceful intentions.[1]

The timing of the announcement — four days after returning from Jerusalem — suggests Cairo may have prepared the move well in advance as a means to force the Arabs either to adopt Egypt's position in its entirety or to reject it outright. The Egyptians could attribute rejection to Soviet mischief and thus attract direct U.S. involvement on the side of America's clients and friends in the area. Sudan — a treaty ally of Egypt since October -- had already endorsed Sadat's diplomacy. Morocco continued to provide the venue for secret meetings between Dayan and Tuhamy. The shah of Iran would not commit himself publicly but privately applauded Sadat's gesture as a viable measure to prevent PLO obstruction of peace efforts.[2] Sadat therefore appeared to act in tandem with prominent American allies who could be expected to encourage active U.S. support for a policy designed to restrict radicalism and promote peace in the area.

The Arab Rejectionist Front

Several Arab states angry about the visit to Jerusalem met in Tripoli the first week of December and decided to freeze diplomatic relations with Egypt. The five so-called "rejectionist" states -- Algeria, Libya, Syria, South Yemen, and Iraq -- did not follow Baghdad's call for harsher measures, including economic and trade sanctions. Nevertheless, Sadat responded to the political boycott by throwing out of Egypt the official representatives of the five radical states.[3] The severance of relations with Damascus in particular dashed any serious hope that discussions could lead to a rapid settlement of the Arab-Israeli conflict. The PLO and Jordan restrained their criticism of Sadat, but neither was willing to challenge the militants by attending the Cairo meeting.

Sadat may have privately welcomed the outcome of the Tripoli meeting, believing that it revealed the Soviet Union's nefarious influence in the region. Moscow responded to Sadat's visit to Jerusalem by launching strong propaganda attacks against Egypt's solitary diplomacy. Soviet representatives soon toned down the barrage and adopted a more neutral stance.[4] But the stridency of Soviet clients in the area and Moscow's apparent realization that a Geneva-style settlement with direct involvement of both superpowers had become unlikely attenuated Soviet ambivalence.

Sadat wanted the meeting in Cairo to permit Egypt to regain the Sinai without bending either to the Arab states' single-issue desires or to the will of the Soviet Union. He would offer Israel full peace -- including trade and recognition -- in exchange for territory. The conference would seek agreement on the broad issues, leaving the details to another negotiation. Thus, only bilateral talks between Damascus and Jerusalem could determine the final status of the

Golan Heights, but the principle of Israeli withdrawal and Syrian sovereignty over the area would be affirmed at the Cairo meeting. According to this Egyptian view, an Arab summit could legitimize specific agreements, and Washington would become guarantor of the peace. The Palestinians and Syria, Sadat thought, would ultimately join the discussions once the facts of peace became evident. Sadat was convinced that the five elements outlined in his Knesset speech offered the basis for a settlement. An Israeli decision to relinquish the occupied territory was the essential first step.[5]

Egypt set the Cairo meeting for December 14. Aside from Egypt, only Israel, the UN, and the United States agreed to attend. Sadat believed that Washington continued to hold "99 percent of the cards," a view that softened the blow of Arab rejectionism, and that Moscow was behind the intransigence of the other Arab states. Nevertheless, the Egyptian Foreign Office took pains to underscore that Syria and the PLO could reverse their decision not to attend the Cairo meeting at any time.[6]

The New Neighbors

Sadat invited Israel to the Cairo Conference both to underscore his commitment to the peace process and to remind Jerusalem that renewed pressure to yield territory and satisfy other major Arab aims would be applied. An apparent willingness among leading Israeli citizens to reconsider long-held positions had encouraged the Egyptian foreign office. In the wake of Sadat's visit, Dayan and others had suggested a public review of the government's posture toward the occupied territories, including the West Bank.[7] The Egyptians may have calculated that an Israeli delegation would be more flexible and more willing to compromise under the glare of the publicity certain to surround the Cairo meeting.

The Israeli government's eager acceptance of Sadat's offer to attend the conference convinced Cairo officials that progress could be achieved. Israeli presence at the meeting would assure U.S. participation, and Sadat regarded American support as crucial to regaining the Sinai and achieving agreement on other contentious bilateral issues with Jerusalem. American involvement would also internationalize the Cairo Conference and broaden its perspective and agenda. The Egyptian president believed that Israeli agreement to the principles of a broad Arab—Israeli peace would belie radical claims that Cairo wanted to conclude a separate peace with Jerusalem. Only then could Sadat meet with Begin in Ismailia.

The View From Jerusalem, December 1977

Anwar Sadat's voyage to Jerusalem did not jolt the Arab world only. The visit produced a consensus in Israel to reexamine relations with Egypt. For the first time, Jerusalem recognized that total security for one nation required total insecurity for another. The absence of a single Middle Eastern nation willing to talk with Israel directly accounted for Jerusalem's hitherto narrow view of security. But now the Jewish state would have to negotiate with Egyptians in Cairo and security issues would be high on the agenda. Israel agreed to Sadat's request to maintain the secret Dayan—Tuhamy link in Morocco in part because the Israeli foreign minister believed it could serve to clarify Egyptian attitudes toward these issues.

Dayan expected the discussions begun with Tuhamy in mid-September to be followed by a second meeting within two weeks.[8] Sadat's obsession with the Soviet—American statement, however, postponed resumption of the talks. The Egyptian president's visit to Jerusalem should have eliminated the necessity to hold the talks in secret. But the rage of Arab radicals over Sadat's journey and the convening of the Cairo Conference required that substantive Egyptian—Israeli contacts be resumed cautiously.

The second round of discussions took place in Moroccan King Hassan's palatial Marrakech retreat on December 2 and 3, 1977, and focused initially on a handwritten position paper drawn up by the Israeli foreign minister. The document contained several proposals to ensure demilitarization of the Sinai following Israeli withdrawal. Begin and Sadat had already agreed in Jerusalem to place the Straits of Tiran under international supervision and to disarm the whole of Sinai east of the Gidi and Mitla passes.

Israel's foreign minister now recommended that the two sides agree either to joint patrols or to the stationing of UN forces in the eastern Sinai to ensure that the areas remained demilitarized. Dayan preferred joint monitoring. But in either case Israel intended to withdraw entirely from all parts of the Sinai except those where circumstances required special arrangements. Jerusalem also wanted the port and airfields of Sharm el-Sheikh and east of El Arish to be off limits to all except civilians, administered by Israel under UN supervision, and open to all nations. Israeli settlements located in the Sinai would remain under Dayan's proposal, and lightly armed Israeli police forces would defend them. Although local Egyptian forces could administer Bedouin areas, Jerusalem would possess the right to enter the area without obstruction.[9]

Tuhamy rejected out of hand combined patrols of the demilitarized areas, continued existence of Israeli settlements in the Sinai, and any Israeli military presence in the Straits of Tiran. He insisted that Israel would have to return the whole area to Egyptian sovereignty and control. The Egyptian deputy prime minister brought to the meeting a handwritten four-point document summarizing Cairo's bargaining posture. First, the return of all occupied territory and establishment of an independent status for the Palestinians would necessarily be the final objective of any peace agreement between the Arab states and Israel. Second, U.S. or International forces would ensure compliance with security guarantees provided to Israel in the Sinai and elsewhere. Third, the agreement would contain provisions dealing with eventual settlement in the West Bank, Gaza Strip, and Golan Heights and establishing free passage through the Straits of Tiran. The return of the Sinai, however, was the most significant matter to be resolved during the bilateral discussions between Cairo and Jerusalem, and Egypt wanted a written agreement governing "every square yard" of that territory. Finally, Cairo wanted guidelines established for covert and open contacts between Egypt and Israel during the negotiations. Each side for example, agreed separately that a representative of the other could be based in their respective American embassies.[10]

The two officials differed substantially in several areas. Dayan's principal assumption revolved around the notion of a "full peace" between Egypt and Israel — one that would include diplomatic and cultural relations, open borders, trade, and tourism. He insisted that the two sides must seek to establish peace quickly, perhaps in two or three months. More crucial, Dayan did not believe that agreement between Egypt and Israel should depend upon similar arrangements with other Arab states.

For his part, Tuhamy expressed the Egyptian view that only a sufficiently broad peace treaty would attract leading Arab actors. He adamantly refused to envisage a separate agreement. When pressed to assess the unanimous refusal of other Arab states to attend the Cairo Conference, Tuhamy observed that Egypt might lower the level of participation at the meeting as a result. In that event, private, high–level contacts such as those in Marrakech could be expanded. The two officials apparently did agree that active U.S. participation was a key to a successful outcome in the negotiations, although at one point Tuhamy suggested that the talks with Dayan should remain a secret from Washington.

Although neither diplomat was empowered to speak authoritatively for his government, Israel's foreign minister conveyed a clearer impression of what might be expected from Israel during the give and take of diplomacy. He noted, for example, that he had advanced his position paper to obtain an unofficial Egyptian response. Should the response reveal substantial common ground a more formal government–wide endorsement would follow, according to Dayan; should Cairo react negatively, however, the proposals would be shelved.[11]

Dayan came away from the meeting with the impression that Tuhamy possessed little of the independence, self–confidence, and authority of their initial meeting. The Egyptian deputy prime minister's manner appeared to reflect Cairo's nervousness about the steps it had chosen to take. Sadat's growing isolation in the Arab world had created confusion within Egypt's ruling circles. Tuhamy's statement that the Cairo Conference might be downgraded demonstrated how tentatively the Egyptians approached Israeli–Egyptian relations. Nevertheless, the Marrakech meeting added momentum to the process and permitted both sides to gauge more accurately each other's negotiating posture as the time for face–to–face contacts drew near.

Begin had announced the Israeli delegation to the Cairo meeting on November 27, nearly a week before the Dayan–Tuhamy conversations. Eliahu Ben–Elissar, director general of the prime minister's office, and Meir Rosenne, legal adviser to the Israeli foreign ministry, would represent Jerusalem at the start of the Cairo talks. Major General Avraham Tamir, the head of the planning branch of the general staff in Israel's Defense Forces, would join the group later.

Ben–Elissar, a former intelligence officer, was a close advisor of Begin and previously served as spokesman for the Likud leader while still in opposition. Rosenne commanded a great deal of respect and had the confidence of Dayan. He could be expected to provide technical expertise on contentious legal matters. Tamir would provide the military knowledge to define and assess the strategic importance of border demarcations.

Ben-Elissar was a curious choice to head Israel's delegation to the Cairo Conference, even though he possessed impressive credentials. He had led the Israeli team that received Egypt's advance party preceding Sadat's trip to Jerusalem. Ben-Elissar held graduate degrees in political science from the Universities of Paris and Geneva and had served in diplomatic posts in Paris, Ethiopia, and Kenya. Most important, the dapper 45-year-old official was a favorite of Begin.[12] Nevertheless, Ben-Elissar was not the foreign minister and was unfamiliar with Egyptian negotiators and negotiating positions.

Begin had always demanded and received the strictest loyalty from his subordinates. His relationship with Dayan — never warm — was correct, and the two shared similar convictions. Begin appointed Dayan foreign minister in part to project an image of respectability and moderation among international statesmen. The Sadat visit, however, offered Begin new challenges and a world stage. The prime minister viewed Dayan's public calls for the Israeli government to revise its policies toward the occupied territories, including the West Bank, as nothing short of heresy. Begin was placing the final touches on an autonomy scheme for Palestinians in Judea and Samaria and considered Dayan's comments as damaging to that process. Finally — perhaps most crucial — Begin's party and the handful of other Knesset members dubious about the possibility of peace with Egypt did not trust the foreign minister. Begin might therefore have lost future votes and tarnished his image with right-wing constituents had he appointed Dayan to lead the delegation.[13]

Dayan, who learned of the prime minister's choice while on an official visit to West Germany, may have insisted that Rosenne be added to the party in order to protect the foreign minister's prerogatives. Dayan demanded that Ben-Elissar be prohibited from negotiating on matters relating to the Palestinian problem, territorial compromise, or a reconvened Geneva Conference.[14] With those restrictions, only one issue — the text of an Israeli-Egyptian peace treaty — would remain for discussion, and Rosenne would be better prepared than Ben-Elissar to handle its intricacies.

Begin's surprise decision to name Ben-Elissar reportedly angered Sadat, who viewed the move as a deliberate attempt to spoil the conference and retard the peace process.[15] And the perception that the Cairo meeting had run into trouble increased the credibility of Egyptians opposed to Sadat's peace initiative. The Egyptian president called for an immediate resumption of the Dayan–Tuhamy negotiations in Morocco. He probably wanted to reconfirm that Israel remained serious about its earlier commitment to relinquish control of the Sinai. Tuhamy's noticeable reticence at the December meeting probably resulted from strict instructions to listen and report on Israeli government plans. The warning that the Cairo Conference might be downgraded reflected Sadat's unhappiness with Begin's appointments.

Washington: First Stirrings

Sadat's historic journey to Jerusalem left American officials confused and groping for a policy. Before Sadat's stunning move, Middle East specialists in Washington had devoted all their energy to resurrecting the Geneva Conference and establishing a framework for comprehensive peace. Secretary of State Cyrus Vance had tried to stimulate radical Arab support for a Geneva meeting by inviting Moscow to participate. But his effort had attracted only a lukewarm response and, more important, had produced elaborate and separate agendas in Cairo and Jerusalem. Sadat and Begin, in fact, had decided not to inform the United States about the secret Tuhamy–Dayan discussions in September.[16] American insistence on resuscitating the Geneva Conference with Soviet backing convinced Sadat in October not to tell Washington of his intention to visit the Knesset. Sadat's initiative came as a complete surprise to U.S. decision makers.[17]

Thus, the United States could hardly ignore Sadat's call for official American attendance at the December 1977 Cairo Preparatory Conference if Washington wished to become an effective mediator in future Middle East diplomacy. Yet important voices within the U.S. State Department counseled delay as senior advisers sought to shift American policy toward accommodation with allies in the Arabian Gulf and Fertile Crescent. Vance and other State Department officials cautioned that a highly visible conference in Cairo lacking the partici- pation of key Arab leaders would mean little and could contribute significantly to the further isolation of Egypt in the Middle East.[18] These officials apparently argued that Washington should seek postponement of the Cairo meeting to allow time to convince Riyadh — and possibly Amman or the PLO — to abandon its tacit support for the rejectionists. The United States would also woo the Soviets and Syria during the projected hiatus.[19]

Traditional American policy toward the Middle East was based on general support for the stated aspirations of the majority of Arab nations.[20] Arab demands for the return of all captured lands and the establishment of a Palestinian state remained clear Arab goals even after Sadat's visit to Jerusalem.[21] Washington feared that the Middle East would again explode into conflict — whether through Soviet manipulation or the unrelieved buildup of local tensions — and threaten the flow of oil to the West.[22] There existed no assurance that a positive solution to so complicated a tangle would result from Sadat's solitary initiative.

White House officials were less committed than the State Department to Arab aspirations. But Sadat's bold and seemingly sincere gesture toward peace attracted them. They recommended a quick U.S. embrace of Egypt's decision to sponsor the meeting, despite the tepid international response.[23] President Carter first chose to accept the State Department's counsel.[24] But negative decisions in Moscow, Damascus, and Riyadh stymied this choice. In addition, Sadat would agree to delay the conference by only a few days. Washington finally decided to attend.

Meanwhile, Carter dispatched Vance to the Middle East on December 9 to ascertain Sadat's immediate plans and perhaps to press for a program that could win broad support within the Arab word. If unable to achieve support for such a program, Vance was to seek assurances from Israel that it conceived of peace with Egypt within a general framework.[25]

The hastily organized Vance itinerary included stops in Cairo, Jerusalem, Amman, Beirut, Damascus, and Riyadh. The American secretary of state told Israeli officials he felt elated about the future following initial talks in Cairo. He emphasized that Sadat wished to conclude a peace agreement but only one within a sufficiently wide framework to prevent the total loss of support from Arab states. An agreed formula for peace with Egypt as well as with other Arab nations would be necessary. The negotiations would also have to deal with the Palestinian issue. Vance suggested that the parties might include in the agreement a "declaration of principles" governing the Palestinian problem. Such a document could help shield Sadat from domestic and external criticism and provide him with flexibility needed to negotiate a bilateral peace treaty.[26]

Dayan told Vance of his earlier talks with Tuhamy. After an embarrassed silence, the American guests assured him that they regarded the Israeli proposal offered on December 2–3 in Morocco as an acceptable basis for negotiations. The Israeli foreign minister, perhaps more so than his colleagues, was encouraged by Vance's description of the Egyptian position and regarded the proposal for a "declaration of principles" toward the Palestinian issue as an "understandable necessity." No one — least of all the Jordanians — had empowered Sadat to negotiate on behalf of the Palestinians. Negotiations on the Sinai, however, could be bilateral, detailed, and comprehensive. Sadat's insistence that a firm link would have to exist between any Egyptian–Israeli agreement on the Sinai and an eventual resolution of the Palestinian impasse would threaten discussions until the signing of the treaty in March 1979.[27]

The common view that it was Sadat who proposed the declaration of principles in early December 1977, however, was not plausible. Only shortly before the Egyptian president had responded to Arab criticism of his peace moves in extremely harsh tones. He countered the measured disapproval of the rejectionists with a sharp rebuke; Sadat's detractors merely cooled relations while the Egyptian president ended them. He followed the move with bitter verbal attacks on the character of the Arab leadership arrayed against him — a strategy hardly designed to encourage Muslim support for his program. Sadat belittled the leadership of the PLO and tied them and Assad to the Soviets, whose diplomats he expelled from Egypt. By quickly announcing the Cairo Conference without notifying even the Saudis beforehand, Sadat signaled that he would neither consult other Arab states nor moderate his views. For the Egyptian president to insist on a peace formula designed to attract the support of the very Arab neighbors he had earlier labeled as enemies would seem a sharp contradiction.

Vance, not Sadat, proposed the declaration of principles during his visit to the Middle East and convinced Sadat that such a proclamation would help build bridges to the Arab world.[28] Sadat's closest advisers, already quite nervous about Egyptian policies undoubtedly backed the American secretary of state's argument. The declaration of principles would also help Washington repair the damage already inflicted on its relations with Arab allies. Whether Sadat agreed to adopt the proposal as his own is unknown. Nevertheless, in

Jerusalem Vance promoted the idea as Sadat's. The American secretary of state wanted the proposal to become an essential ingredient of future Egyptian–Israeli negotiations and provide Washington with leverage to entice key Arab nations into the peace process. He clearly believed he would advance this purpose by identifying the statement of principles with Sadat. Vance's subsequent visits to Amman, Beirut, Damascus, and Riyadh, however, netted Washington no new participants for the Cairo Preparatory Conference or converts to Egypt's peace efforts.

The U.S. Delegation

Alfred (Roy) Atherton Jr., then assistant secretary of state for Near Eastern and South Asian Affairs (NEA), led America's delegation to the Cairo Preparatory Conference. Atherton had served with distinction in a number of bureaucratic positions within NEA. He was known for his self-effacing manner and ability to work as a team–player. The Carter White House appreciated those qualities, particularly after Sadat's several surprise moves had so severely damaged Washington's carefully constructed Middle East policies. Carter and Vance obviously desired a respite to reconstruct what remained of their Middle East program, which aimed to resolve the Arab–Israeli conflict and guarantee a secure flow of oil from the Persian Gulf.[29]

Atherton was thus the ideal selection for an assignment that required a delicate combination of tact, loyalty to superiors, and intimate knowledge of opposing personalities and their differing views. The assistant secretary believed his task would be taxing and perhaps long. He recognized almost immediately that his effort would center on two major goals: to interpret and refine discreetly suggestions put forward by Egypt and Israel and to mark time while Washington redesigned its shattered policy.[30] The conferees remained suspicious of each other's motives and reticent to offer major proposals. Nevertheless, Atherton put his patient, deliberate style to good use and helped the parties narrow their obvious antagonisms. Although the conference achieved only modest progress, the experience gained negotiating with one another would later prove critical during joint meetings at Ismailia, Leeds, and Camp David.

America's Posture

The Carter administration had placed the contentious North–South relationship at the center of its foreign policy structure.[31] Prior to the Carter presidency discussions among the wealthy, industrialized nations of the North over policy toward the South were often strained, sometimes even acrimonious. At the beginning of 1977, the new administration sought to alter that pattern. The most crucial and problematic issue confronting the West was the status of relations with the oil–producing nations in the Persian Gulf, in particular Saudi Arabia. Washington regarded Saudi Arabia –– with its huge oil reserves, heavy investments in the West, and financial leadership of the Arab world –– as one of the keys to resolving the impasse between rich and poor countries.

For that reason and to reduce the vulnerability of the increasingly energy–dependent West, Washington's Middle East policy sought to ensure that any general peace settlement would take into account Riyadh's political preferences. Jimmy Carter's persistent and very personal involvement in negotiations over the Palestinian issue resulted, therefore, in part from his desire to maintain credibility in Riyadh. Washington believed the moderate Arab states would support any satisfactory arrangement the Saudis concluded with Israel.[32]

Sadat's surprise visit to Jerusalem and his open break with Syria and the PLO destroyed Washington's plans. Riyadh sought to develop a consensus among Arab leaders favoring establishment of a Palestinian state in the West Bank. Sadat's actions appeared to preclude such an outcome. Washington insisted on a firm link between Israeli return of the Sinai and a settlement in the West Bank and Gaza strip. The United States evidently believed that such a link would attract Saudi support despite Riyadh's preference for immediate Palestinian statehood. The Carter administration had not made up its mind about whether to support PLO representation in the peace process but did favor inclusion of Palestinians unconnected to the terrorist organization.[33]

A set of competing factors thus complicated the American perspective on the emerging Egyptian–Israeli relationship. Washington wanted Cairo and Jerusalem to resolve their fundamental differences but did not support Sadat's attempts to bludgeon other Arabs into supporting his peace moves.[34] Cairo's self–imposed isolation from its neighbors and its over–

identification with the United States had already set back Washington's efforts to ingratiate itself with Saudi Arabia and other Arab moderates.

It could be argued that a U.S. decision to force the parties to link the Sinai pullout to a Palestinian settlement in the West Bank would reverse Washington's declining fortunes with the Arabs. In any case, Washington felt it could not permit signature of a separate Egypt–Israeli Peace Treaty.[35] For a bilateral arrangement that ignored the Palestinian problem would anger the Saudis, who might even provoke an Arab oil embargo in response. American decision makers, therefore, decided to push hard for a linkage between bilateral and Palestinian–related issues in the hope of reversing the increasing vulnerability of America's position in the Middle East.[36]

False Start in Cairo

The Cairo Preparatory Conference convened on December 14, 1977, at the luxurious, picturesque Mena House Hotel next to the Pyramids. Eliahu Ben–Elissar and Ismet Abd–el Meguid, the chief Israeli and Egyptian representatives, each put forth proposals. Neither country's plan was acceptable to the other or even sufficiently detailed to merit a reasonable response. The Israeli plan, for example, failed to address borders, buffer zones, demilitarized areas, or Sinai settlements. It dealt only with bilateral diplomatic relations, cultural exchanges, and transit rights in the Suez Canal and adjacent waterways. It ignored completely the Palestinian issue, which was a central feature of the Egyptian program. Cairo also called for Israeli withdrawal from all occupied territories and designated the PLO to represent the Palestinians in the negotiations.[37]

Both sides seemed to recognize that the import of their initial proposals was more theatrical than real, and neither was disappointed by the inevitable rejection of its plan. Ben–Elissar –– a courteous and polished man –– almost immediately established himself as a more credible choice than most had expected despite his relative lack of familiarity with previous Israeli–Egyptian negotiations. The Israeli representative quickly established a relaxed, friendly rapport with his opposite in the Egyptian delegation. Meguid –– then Egypt's permanent representative to the UN and previously director of the cultural exchange department in the foreign ministry, ambassador to France, and minister of state for cabinet affairs — was careful not to stray too far from Egyptian Foreign Office positions during informal talks with Bel–Elissar.

Although the conferees made little progress on political issues, military officials at the conference cautiously proceeded to discuss options for withdrawal from the Sinai and even drew preliminary evacuation lines. The Egyptian military wanted quick, tangible results and called for specific plans for Israeli withdrawal. The Egyptian officers were not prepared, however, to relinquish any territory or to accept anything short of full sovereignty over the area. Egyptian preoccupation with indivisible sovereignty and Israeli concern with protecting its security would envelop all future discussions.[38]

Begin's Autonomy Plan

Menachem Begin based his autonomy plan for Judea, Samaria, and the Gaza District on the concepts of his mentor, Vladimir Jabotinsky.[39] Jabotinsky's political activism conflicted with the tenets of modern zionism. He preferred to establish a state in Palestine on both sides of the Jordan River but protected by a militant Jewish defense force.[40] Yet the Israeli prime minister's interpretation of autonomy as applying to Arab cultural but not territorial rights parted from Jabotinsky's earliest teachings. In 1906 at Helsingfors, Finland, Jabotinsky sponsored a program emphasizing settlement in Palestine over the objections of others who sought cultural autonomy only for Jews within a Russian state system. This debate occurred as the participants struggled to present a list of candidates for the DUMA (parliament) during a period of limited relaxation in Russian autocratic rule. Nevertheless, pogroms against Russia's large Jewish population were increasing, and Jabotinsky regarded assimilation or even cultural autonomy an inadequate solution. In his view, the only real choice available to European Jews was emigration to the historic and biblical lands, and therefore territorial independence.[41]

Begin altered Jabotinsky's 1906 definition of autonomy as he searched in December 1977 for a viable program to satisfy Palestinian demands without sacrificing his conception of national security. He had as early as 1975 suggested that

Israel grant its Arab minority cultural autonomy. The future Israeli prime minister defined the concept as the right to educate children in one's own language and according to one's own traditions and religious customs.[42] The term eventually found its way into the Likud Party's 1977 platform; the relevant portion read that a Begin–led government would "...guarantee to the Arab nation in the land of Israel a cultural autonomy, a fostering of the values of their national culture, their religion, and heritage."[43]

In time, Begin undoubtedly would have instituted a measure of self–government for the West Bank.[44] However, the spectacular success and challenge created by Sadat's visit to Jerusalem forced the Israeli prime minister to confront the issue quickly. Early in his administration, Begin boasted of his ability to undertake serious and far–reaching steps toward peace while protecting Israeli interests. Together with Dayan, he presented a set of proposals in July and September 1977 that would have provided the inhabitants of the West Bank with independent authority over civil and administrative matters and left responsibility for security in the hands of the Israeli military. The subsequent struggle to reconvene a Geneva Conference, however, sidetracked that effort.

In mid–December, Begin faced the central task of meeting Egypt's demand for the return of the Sinai and ensuring Israeli–Egyptian normalization without sacrificing Israel's broad security requirements. The difficult relationship between sovereignty and security was at the heart of the Middle East conflict and the Israeli prime minister could hardly resolve the problem by simply amending Jabotinsky's pronouncements on autonomy. Begin could not afford to repudiate tenets crucial to a Likud Party constituency composed of disgruntled settlers, rightists, and religious zealots or to contradict principles carefully articulated for a generation to audiences large and small throughout Israel. Hence the prime minister chose to offer a limited form of Palestinian self–government in the West Bank in exchange for peace in the Middle East.[45]

Begin's plan would preserve the right of Israeli citizens to reside and acquire land in the biblical areas, subject only to normal restrictions that apply to purchases. Israeli law would apply in Judea, Samaria, and the Gaza Strip, although Jerusalem agreed to review the arrangement in five years and to consider the proposals of other claimants. Arabs settling in the biblical lands could choose either Jordanian or Israeli citizenship. Those who opted for Jordanian citizenship would vote in Jordanian elections and could run for seats in Jordan's representative assembly. All would enjoy freedom of movement and the opportunity to do business inside Israel. The local inhabitants would freely elect an eleven-member administrative council to administer the area from either Bethlehem or Ramallah.

A joint Israeli-Jordanian committee would regulate the return of refugees. The Israeli government would retain exclusive authority over defense and foreign policy. Begin's autonomy proposal sought to shift the focus of Palestinian leadership from the PLO to local Palestinians in the West Bank and to attract Jordanian participation without granting Amman too strong a role in the area. The local inhabitants would not be allowed to raise an army or establish the symbols of independence, such as a national anthem, a flag, or currency.[46]

Begin envisaged a two-stage settlement in the Sinai that would include adequate compensation for Israel. An initial withdrawal line would stretch from El Arish on the Mediterranean to Ras Muhammad on the Red Sea. According to this plan, Israel would maintain control of Sharm el-Sheikh in order to ensure free passage through the Gulf of Eilat.

The second stage of the evacuation would be more difficult. Egypt would initially have the right to rule over the whole peninsula to the previous international border but would not receive full sovereignty immediately. For example, Jerusalem would insist on retaining the Rafah settlements and three Israeli-built military airports in the Sinai until the year 2001. Two of the facilities would be handed over to civilians, and the third would remain under Israeli control, although within an area supervised by the United Nations. A defense force composed of local settlers would protect the Israeli settlements in the Rafah salient and the airports. The first stage would be completed within three-to-five years, and the overall agreement would be reviewed in 2001.[47]

Begin Visits Washington

Begin considered Washington less committed to its alliance with Israel than most thought it was, despite the charge of many critics that America acted as "Israel's attorney."[48] Nevertheless, the collapse of efforts to reconvene the Geneva conference -- a direct result of Sadat's visit to Jerusalem --

had placed the United States into the middle of increasingly intense negotiations between Jerusalem and Cairo. America's role as amicus curiae in the peace process dictated that the Israeli prime minister should unveil his autonomy proposal to Carter at the White House. It would provide good theater and remind listeners that Begin could also contribute to peace significantly.[49]

Preparations for the meeting in Washington had begun during Vance's December 10 encounter with Begin in Jerusalem.[50] During the following few days, Israel played a carefully contrived cat and mouse game with the American press to heighten interest in the Israeli peace plan.[51] Finally, on December 16, the Israeli prime minister presented to Carter in the White House his proposed solution to the Palestinian problem and his plan for the return of the Sinai to Egypt.

The Carter White House did not look forward to Begin's visit.[52] Earlier discussions in Jerusalem had failed to reveal any new proposal on the Palestinian issue, and the United States was unprepared for what the press heralded as an important peace overture. Carter listened intently as Begin furnished the details of his plan. The presentation of the Sinai proposal went well as the Carter administration had already learned of the major points during exchanges in Israel and elsewhere. Carter and his advisers, however, closely questioned Begin on the Palestinian self-rule plan. The Americans expressed concern over the location of Israel's defense forces in the West Bank and Gaza territories, the future status of the settlements there, choice of citizenship for the inhabitants of the areas, and their right to vote and be represented in national parliaments.[53] At the conclusion of the discussion, Begin asked Carter to evaluate the proposal.[54]

Carter's response would later create a serious rift between Washington and Jerusalem. The American president told Begin that he regarded the autonomy program favorably. But Carter intended the comment to encourage Begin to refine the plan taking into account the doubts raised during their meeting.[55]

The Israeli prime minister was consciously seeking external support, however limited, for a proposal expected to receive extensive and perhaps harsh criticism at home. Seven hours of review by the Israeli cabinet preceded Begin's arrival in Washington, but the prime minister had offered the ministers only an oral outline of the peace plan. Even then, the cabinet's assessment was mixed and Army Chief of Staff Mordecai Gur expressed strong reservations.[56]

Nevertheless, Carter telephoned Sadat from the White House to recommend careful Egyptian consideration of the plan.[57] Israel's prime minister had advised the U.S. president that he could officially offer the proposal only after approval by the cabinet and Knesset. Carter probably omitted that condition from his conversation with Sadat, preferring not to encumber the peace process at that point. Furthermore, the U.S. government may have expected that a face-to-face meeting between Begin and Sadat would lead to Israeli acceptance of amendments necessary to satisfy moderate Arab leaders. Sadat had already called publicly for a meeting with Begin to be convened shortly in Egypt.[58]

Begin returned to Israel on December 18 satisfied with the results of his Washington trip. The prime minister apparently believed he had gained the Carter administration's support for a program of limited autonomy in Judea, Samaria, and the Gaza Strip.[59] An enthusiastic reception by a few of Israel's Congressional supporters prior to Begin's departure from Washington reinforced the misperception.

Weizman-Gamassy: First Rounds

Between Begin's visits with Carter in Washington and Sadat at Ismailia, defense chiefs Weizman and el-Gamassy met for consultations in Egypt. Begin and Sadat had agreed in Jerusalem to the meeting, as each wanted to learn more about the other's future military plans. Weizman arrived in Cairo on December 20 aboard an American DC-9 in order to maintain secrecy and because no direct air link existed between the Israeli and Egyptian capitals.[60]

Weizman's arrival in Egypt gave Sadat an opportunity to respond personally to Dayan's draft proposals for a Sinai settlement earlier provided to Tuhamy in Morocco. The Israeli defense minister was met at Cairo International Airport by Gamassy and quickly ferried to Ismailia for a private encounter with Sadat. The meeting was held in a relaxed, friendly atmosphere. Sadat, however, described Egypt's position toward prospective relations with Israel in candid terms.

He wished to conclude a peace pact, complete with full diplomatic recognition and normalization, early. He was prepared to begin the process with the establishment of a civilian air route linking Cairo with Tel Aviv. He would appoint an Ambassador to Jerusalem in return for Begin's agreement in principle to withdraw from all occupied territories and resolve the Palestinian problem. Sadat waved off any mention of the Israeli prime minister's domestic constraints or the belief that Jordan and Syria would find it difficult to conclude similar agreements with Jerusalem. Most crucial, the Egyptian president emphasized that he could not permit the Rafah settlements to remain under Israeli control and that any peace arrangement between Cairo and Jersualem would have to be viewed as the first step toward accords with other Arab nations, not as a separate peace.[61]

Gamassy then took Weizman to the Janklis Estate near Alexandria for lunch. Israel's defense minister, joined by General Shlomo Gazit, chief of Israeli intelligence, and General Herzl Shapir, head of the southern command, opened the conversation by proposing establishment of a telephone link between opposing armies in the Sinai to avoid future misunderstanding.

Gamassy and his aides brushed aside the suggestion, choosing instead to concentrate on matters already broached by Sadat. To no avail Weizman attempted to deflect discussion of a full peace. Gamassy did not allow the Israelis to draw him into an extended debate over Israeli security needs and warned that Egypt could not accept Dayan's proposal to alter the border in the Sinai. An Egyptian decision to permit Israel to retain the Rafah Settlements and either or both of the major airfields, even in exchange for territory, according to Gamassy, would be tantamount in the eyes of many to abetting Israeli expansionism and annexation of Egyptian land. The Egyptian asserted, however, that Cairo would agree to pare down its Army and redeploy it away from Israel following the signature of a peace treaty.

Gamassy then amended a promise made by Sadat during conversations with Begin in Jerusalem. The Egyptian Army and Air Force, he said, would seek to station forces and aircraft east of the Mitla and Gidi passes in the vicinity of El Arish as a matter of "prestige and honor." The Egyptian war minister dismissed Sadat's commitment not to do so with the comment that the president was "not a military man." Further, he informed the Israeli delegation that under no circumstances would Egypt agree to reduce its forces along the Suez Canal or to demilitarize the area altogether. He told Weizman that "not even the President could explain [such an agreement] to Parliament."

Finally, although Egypt would go along with UN supervision of settlements in the Rafah salient, an Egyptian governor would rule those near Sharm el Sheikh. Cairo wanted all bilateral negotiations completed by October 1978 when the 1973 interim agreement expired.[62]

Next morning, Weizman and his party were escorted once again to Ismailia to meet with Sadat. This time, the Egyptian president, in the presence of Vice President Hosni Mubarak, was curt and pointed in his remarks. He told his guests that the two sides could look forward to a complete peace treaty, but only if Israel consented to return the entire Sinai. Not a single Israeli settlement or any vestige of its defense forces could stay. Civilian airfields could remain, but only under Egyptian sovereignty. In addition, Egyptian troops would take up positions east of the Suez Canal. United Nations forces would not be required either at Sharm el Sheikh or at the international border. Egyptian forces would patrol their side of the line, and the peace treaty would be sufficient to ensure mutual compliance.[63]

Sadat's behavior disconcerted Weizman. The Israeli defense minister had not expected Egypt to leave the Rafah settlements in Israeli hands. But loss of the airfields at Etam and Etzion without suitable replacements and Sadat's renege on his pledge not to station forces east of the Gidi and Milta passes raised significant questions.[64]

The abrupt change in Sadat's demeanor during Weizman's 30-hour stay in Egypt betrayed the president's anxiety that peace with Israel might elude his grasp, as Israel's seeming lack of enthusiasm only added fuel to rivalries among his aides. Vice President Hosni Mubarak appeared the firmest of those opposed to the nascent Egyptian-Israeli peace. He had been excluded from the Egyptian delegation that carried peace proposals to Jerusalem in November. Although Gamassy also stayed behind, his position as leader of the army and the respect he enjoyed within the ranks demanded that Sadat consult him regularly on matters relating to peace with Israel. In addition, Sadat could more easily satisfy the desire of Gamassy and the army to obtain American equipment, as conventional weapons for ground forces were relatively cheap. The Mubarak-dominated Air Force, however, would require highly specialized, sophisticated gear that was both expensive and difficult to bring on line quickly. Washington had also backed Gamassy in his continuing effort to restrain the Egyptian Air Force's desire to punish Libyan leader Muammar Qhaddafi.[65]

Mustapha Khalil's deep fear of a nuclear crisis with Israel matched Gamassy's known views. This convergence placed the army in tacit alliance with the Egyptian technocracy in support of a limited arrangement with Israel, further strengthening Gamassy's hand. Egypt remained dependent on large quantities of foreign aid, which only the West could supply. To acquire such aid at needed levels and to revive the non-military domestic economy, Egypt had to achieve a respite from conflict with Israel.

Perhaps more than the demands of the Mubarak-Gamassy power struggle, Egypt's growing isolation from the Arab world, in particular from moderate nations such as Saudi Arabia, soured Mubarak toward the peace process. He had not only acted as a presidential emissary to these countries but had invested a great deal of energy in efforts to construct an industrial and military relationship between Egypt and Saudi Arabia. Gamassy, who remained in control of military industry, had stymied the effort; the peace process ended it. Mubarak did not yet possess a network of clients that would provide him the political power to exert strong influence on the Egyptian president. But the next meeting between Sadat and Begin would confirm that the foreign office was his willing ally.

Weizman had not grasped the domestic reasons behind Sadat's behavior. But he pondered his own role in the peace process as he returned to Tel Aviv. He realized that he did not know the full substance of either Begin's autonomy proposal or Dayan's earlier discussions in Morocco with Tuhamy. The sudden appearance in Ismailia of U.S. Ambassador to Egypt Herman Eilts probably related to Begin's autonomy plan, delivered to Washington the previous week. That plan and the proposal delivered to Tuhamy in early December by Dayan probably helped spark Sadat's ire.

Both plans envisaged a drawn-out peace process — measured in years — and sought to separate the Sinai and West Bank from all other issues. Sadat, however, required that all bilateral and multilateral issues be linked in order to decrease his political vulnerability at home. He also wanted to negotiate a peace treaty quickly, before domestic and international pressures forced him into an indefensible posture.[66]

Meanwhile, in Jerusalem, Begin was similarly beset by harsh domestic criticism. Many in the Israeli cabinet believed his autonomy proposal would inexorably lead to a Palestinian state. Weizman's account of his meeting with Sadat did little to rebut that claim. Hours of debate thus led to a series of amendments that radically altered the plan presented to Carter.

The amended plan would preserve Israeli government responsibility for law and order in the West Bank, place limits on the number of refugees allowed to return, alter the procedures to regulate access to the territories, restrict acquisition of land to Israeli citizens, require that all legislative decisions of the committee of eleven be unanimous, and link the entire plan to the achievement of peace with Egypt. Additional settlements in the Rafah salient, moreover, would remain under Israeli administration by law.[67]

Thus, differences over the details of the Sinai withdrawal and the nature of Palestinian rule in the West Bank increased sharply on the eve of the Christmas meeting in Ismailia between Begin and Sadat. Most important, domestic imperatives that neither Sadat nor Begin championed or entirely sympathized with had dictated the change.

The Ismailia Conference

Begin -- accompanied by Dayan, Weizman, Gazit, Shapir, Attorney General Aharon Barak, and an assortment of other aides -- arrived at Abu Sweir air base near Ismailia on Christmas Sunday to present peace proposals to Sadat. The reception was noticeably chilly as Vice President Mubarak greeted the delegation and led a short motorcade to the Egyptian president's villa on the banks of the Suez Canal.[68]

After a brief ceremony to swear in new Foreign Minister Mohammed Ibrahim Kamel — a long-time Sadat friend and former Ambassador to Bonn — Sadat and Begin retired to an anteroom for a private twenty-two minute discussion. Begin then gleefully announced that the two sides had agreed to set up separate political and military committees.[69]

Sadat welcomed his guests officially, and Begin responded with a recitation of the momentous historical events that had preceded the current search for peace. The Israeli prime minister proceeded to deliver an hour-long monologue describing in detail his peace plan. The mood of Begin's listeners alternated among boredom, impatience, chagrin, and discomfort. The Israeli leader emphasized that Israel viewed retention of its settlements at Rafah and near Sharm el Sheikh as necessary.

Begin reserved his most confident remarks for his autonomy plan. He reminded those present of Israel's natural and biblical rights to the land but carefully assured them that the issue of sovereignty would remain open. He placed his offer of administrative autonomy for the Palestinians into the context of Israel's vulnerable security -- an emotional issue in Israel. He asked the Egyptians to realize how difficult and far reaching the plan was, pointing to the extraordinary and vocal criticism of the proposal by right-wing constituents in Israel. Finally, Begin asserted that both American and British leaders had pronounced the autonomy program as fair and equitable.[70]

Sadat replied quietly that Egypt had committed itself at the Rabat Conference of 1974 to seek full Israeli withdrawal from the occupied territories and resolution of the Palestinian problem in all its aspects. He asserted that although the recently formed political and military committees would negotiate the details, Israel would have to agree to withdraw to its 1967 borders and grant the Palestinian people self-determination. A joint declaration of principles along these lines would, according to Sadat, bolster the Cairo Conference and revive the broader peace process. Sadat described his visit to Jerusalem as an effort to "get at the essential problems," and suggested that the declaration of principles should contain only substantive matters, not procedural details. The Egyptian president then suggested that the meeting adjourn until late afternoon, at which time the two sides would discuss the proposed declaration.[71]

Dayan told the Egyptians that he opposed full discussion of the Palestinian issue at Ismailia. He wished the political committee to handle the matter. Sadat, however, reiterated that the committee could debate security arrangements in the West Bank or withdrawal on the Golan Heights but that agreement on general principles should be reached at Ismailia. The committees themselves would only begin their work after completion of the declaration of principles.

The Israelis disregarded the veiled ultimatum, as Weizman questioned the need for Egypt to maintain forces east of the Gidi and Mitla passes. A discussion ensued over force requirements in the Sinai during the transition to peace, including the Israeli determination to hold the airfields. Sadat appeared ready for compromise, indicating that the cost of maintaining unnecessary forces in the Sinai would be burdensome and that he therefore regarded a brigade-size force as sufficient. Lunch and a tour around Ismailia led by Sadat himself followed the tension-filled morning session.[72]

The afternoon session began with a summary of the earlier meeting but quickly focused on a formula by Begin to resolve the impasse over the Palestinian issue within the framework of a declaration of principles. The Israeli proposal resembled a portion of the working paper Dayan gave Vance and Carter in New York in October. It stated that:

> The issues of the West Bank and Gaza will be discussed in a working group consisting of the representatives of Israel, Egypt, Jordan, and Palestinian Arabs, with the aim of finding a just solution to the Palestinian problem.[73]

Sadat warmed to the notion, but Egyptian Foreign Office officials dissuaded him from accepting it.[74]

Most officials in the Egyptian Foreign Office opposed improving ties with Israel. The foreign affairs ministry lacked a leader in December 1977. Boutrus Ghali, who temporarily became foreign minister following the resignations of Fahmy and Riad, was a Coptic Christian and therefore unacceptable as a permanent replacement. Ghali's successor, Kamel, was sworn in at the start of the Ismailia Conference and was entirely unfamiliar with the technical details of the peace process. Meguid, head of the Egyptian delegation to the Cairo Conference and a seasoned diplomat, judged proposals for Palestinian self-rule from the standpoint of traditional Arab positions. Ghali doubted Israel's commitment to peace and was a committed pan-Arabist. The final foreign office representative at the Ismailia conference was in many ways the most interesting and least known. Usama al-Baz served as Fahmy's office director from 1974 until the latter's resignation before Sadat's visit to Jerusalem. His outstanding skills in foreign affairs landed him a spot on the delegation to Jerusalem. He allied himself to Vice President Mubarak and became director of political affairs in Mubarak's office days before the Ismailia conference.

At the time of the Ismailia conference the power struggle between Mubarak and Gamassy was in full swing. Gamassy supported peace with Israel if it promised to eliminate the risk of nuclear war in the Middle East[75] permanently and to improve the lot of Egypt's military and civilians alike. Mubarak naturally sought to prevent Gamassy's positions from succeeding or gaining support among the leaderless foreign ministry officials. The vice president could count on Al-Baz to protect his interest during the conference.

Sadat formally opened the evening session with a statement that reflected foreign ministry views. He frankly admitted that he could not survive politically if he allowed Israel to retain settlements in the Sinai. He also pointed out that Egypt intended to remain part of the Arab world and that neither a separate peace with Israel nor an Egyptian posture contradicting the Rabat Conference declaration would ensure that objective. But a declaration of principles such as the one outlined during the morning session, he claimed, could encourage moderate Arab nations such as Saudi Arabia and Jordan to adopt a more favorable view of the peace process. The Egyptian president reiterated that full diplomatic relations between Egypt and Israel, including economic ties, trade, and complete normalization, would follow approval of the declaration immediately.[76]

Begin's response evoked memories of the past but also hinted at complications for the future. The Israeli prime minister suggested that he was prepared to leave for Damascus immediately to meet with Assad. Jerusalem could not negotiate, however, with a party that refused to appear at a conference table. The implication was clear: Israel's firm stand against dealing with the PLO and the categorical refusal of Syria and Jordan to join in the talks made a separate peace between Cairo and Jerusalem unavoidable. But Egypt and Israel, said Begin, should not permit the Ismailia Conference to fail. Begin then proposed his draft declaration of principles that addressed the need to find a just solution to the Palestinian issue and assigned the task to a working group consisting of Egypt, Israel, Jordan, and a representative of the Palestinian Arabs.[77]

Sadat appeared ready to discuss Israel's proposal but was interrupted by Meguid, al-Baz, and Boutrus Ghali: "It's unacceptable, totally unacceptable,"[78] they shouted. Begin countered by inquiring whether the Egyptians really favored a Palestinian state dominated by Arafat. Sadat stated that his goal was to achieve Palestinian self-determination, not a PLO-operated enclave. The Egyptian president repeated that he needed to produce a document acceptable to the Arab world. Recognition of Sadat as the leader of the Arabs was in Israel's interest, he reminded Begin. Should he fail to produce an acceptable declaration of prinicples, according to Sadat, "they are going to stone me."[79]

After the Egyptian president completed his remarks, Meguid read aloud a declaration of principles drafted by the foreign office. It contained nearly all of the points most offensive to Begin. The statement called for Israeli withdrawal from the Sinai, the Golan Heights, the West Bank, and the Gaza Strip as provided for in UN Resolution 242 and its preamble, which precluded acquisition of land by force. The proposal also stipulated settlement of the Palestinian issue in all its aspects on the basis of self-determination through talks among Egypt, Jordan, Israel, and representatives of the Palestinian people.[80] A heated discussion ensued.

The Egyptian president, under obvious duress, attempted to stop the bickering among his advisers and between the two delegations. He proposed that a smaller group from both sides reformulate the language pertaining to Israeli withdrawal from the occupied territories. He granted that Arafat should not be allowed to participate in future discussions and instead endorsed some form of joint Jordanian-Palestinian representation. He insisted, however, that the principle of Palestinian self-determination could not be dropped. Once again he asserted that he must obtain a "declaration of principles which will enable me to face my opponents in the rejectionist front and in the Arab world."[81]

Begin requested a short intermission for consultation. He then revealed that he could not accept Sadat's reasoning or formulation of Palestinian self-determination. Dayan observed that approval of Sadat's statement would lead to an "attack in stages on Israel."[82]

The hour was late and the conferees exhausted. The proceedings adjourned after 10 p.m. with agreement to meet again in the morning. The original agenda had called for the Israeli delegation to return to Tel Aviv on Christmas morning. The two sides did reach preliminary agreement on the nature of peaceful relations between Cairo and Jerusalem prior to adjournment. A mixed group of Israeli and Egyptian foreign ministry representatives attempted to negotiate a joint communique during meetings through the night. They failed, and the two sides tentatively agreed that each would issue its own statement.[83]

The facial expressions of the members of both delegations at breakfast were sullen. Dissension broke out among Begin's senior advisers over the advisability of issuing a joint declaration. The Israeli prime minister quieted his most recalcitrant associates and advised that he would pursue the matter with Sadat and that if he failed to reach an agreement the conference would conclude without a communique.[84]

The final session of the Ismailia Conference began cordially with a paragraph by paragraph review of an Israeli draft declaration. Sadat summarily approved each point until the Palestinian issue arose. At that stage, Begin suggested that the two sides announce that no agreement was reached only on the Palestinian issue. Instead each side would declare its preference -- Egypt, a Palestinian state; and Israel, autonomy in "Judea, Samaria, and the Gaza District."

Sadat listened carefully and, surprised by the mention of a Palestinian state, nodded approval. Meguid once again interrupted, stating that such an outcome was "unthinkable."[85] He emphasized that Egypt could not accept a declaration that did not deal with the Palestinians. Suddenly, Meguid turned to Sadat and said: "You are risking your position, it is impossible! This would be a statement of surrender."[86] Ghali seconded Meguid's statement, while Mubarak remained silent. Begin angrily noted that a final communique need not be issued, thus permitting each side to cast its own version of events.

Sadat, sorely disappointed, confided that a communique that omitted the Palestinian issue would be "enfeebling" to Egypt. The Egyptian president agreed that an announcement could be made listing the points of agreement and those that remained at issue. He also suggested that the announcement state that the Cairo Conference would continue. Begin offered and the two sides accepted an alternate proposal: Egypt and Israel concurred that efforts to reach a comprehensive peace settlement would continue based on Security Council Resolution 242 and 338, and that the political committee would hold further discussions on the Palestinian issue. The venue remained unspecified.[87]

At a joint press conference, Begin invited the United States and the United Nations to become full partners in the negotiations.[88] The Israeli delegation departed at mid-day, ending a frustrating 30-hour struggle to achieve peace. Begin dismissed charges that a less painful result at the conference might have been possible had the participants taken more time. "The minimum condition in Ismailia," asserted the prime minister; "was a retreat on all frontiers and a declaration on the Palestinian issue. We could not accept that."[89]

The Relationship Between Sadat and Begin

The Ismailia Conference provided the first opportunity for a meeting between the Egyptian and Israeli leaders after the Egyptian president's historic trip to Jerusalem. It was also their first encounter in Egypt. Sadat had no desire to make this visit resplendent for Begin and his entourage. He was troubled by Israel's lack of flexibility on the issues of sovereignty over the Sinai and of Palestinian self-determination on the West Bank and Gaza Strip. Sadat could not survive politically unless he restored complete Egyptian sovereignty over the entire Sinai, and he had earlier attempted to convey that view to Weizman.

The Palestinian issue was not as crucial to his political fate, but it too posed serious problems. He desired neither a Palestinian state dominated by the PLO nor the open-ended and transparent attempt to preserve Israeli control contained in Begin's autonomy proposal. Sadat probably reasoned that a statement of principles would only commit the parties to whatever course later proved acceptable after deliberate negotiations. The declaration would, he believed, enhance Egypt's position in the Arab world and relieve the anxieties of Egyptian political elites concerning the nation's future. Suspicion among Egyptians of Israel's motives still lingered. An accommodation by Begin to new realities would dispel those doubts.

Begin's belief that Washington favored his autonomy plan had already given him considerable satisfaction. He therefore approached the Ismailia trip with little trepidation. The timidity of Egypt's official reception disappointed him, but he refused to be ruffled. Begin believed Sadat's visit to Jerusalem showed raw courage, and he expected to face a statesman at Ismailia. Begin would present a proposal that he considered both reasonable and far reaching.

Begin capitalized from the start of the meetings on his personal relationship with the Egyptian president and on Sadat's determination to avoid a deadlocked conference. They immediately agreed to convene political and military committees, to continue the talks after the conference, thus establishing important links for the future. But the Israeli prime minister committed a serious error by delivering a pedantic speech and laboring through the text of his autonomy proposal. Begin was also poorly prepared for Sadat's argument in favor of a declaration of principles or for the strength and determination of the Egyptian president's advisers in advancing that cause.

However, neither their regard for one another nor their realization that they shared a common destiny suffered irreparable harm, as most commentators would later claim. Sadat and Begin were less antagonistic toward one another during the meetings than their advisers toward their respective leader or among themselves. The specifics of each side's official position produced strain, but Sadat remained the courteous host. Neither leader wished to be blamed for obstructing the peace process or charged with violating the larger principle of. peace. Thus, throughout the conference and specifically at the end of the two-day marathon session when both leaders were exhausted and frustrated, Sadat reminded Begin that his power to compromise, like the Israeli prime minister's, was limited by domestic forces. He mentioned in particular the Egyptian foreign office.

The meeting revealed the core issues that would divide Egyptian and Israeli officials until the conclusion of Camp David in the fall of 1978. Egypt, in keeping with the grand vision of its president, desired agreement only on broad out-lines. Israel wanted clear, specific pronouncements that would protect its interests during implementation of the treaty. Begin was not only steeped in the minutiae of the law, he was also an accomplished negotiator determined to secure for his nation an agreement that would entail the minimum possible sacrifice and risk.

In the end both Sadat and Begin may have held inflated expectations of success at the conference and unrealistic views of their ability to influence one another. Both were experienced and wary politicians who had survived beyond the expectations of their adversaries. Sadat had to satisfy too many other domestic and foreign actors. The Israeli prime minister was too confident that the Egyptians would regard his proposal as a major concession. Begin expected that the Egyptian elites would be far more solicitous over his domestic situation and personal historical commitment than he himself would be over Sadat's internal constraints. Finally, neither leader had yet recognized the limitations on his ability to persuade the other to alter favored positions. This myopia would produce, in time, a more central role for the United States.

The Political and Military Committees

Begin's signal achievement at Ismailia was to convince Sadat to establish political and military committees to resolve matters under dispute. The political committee would meet in Jerusalem, and the military committee in Cairo. The parties sought thereby to separate the more manageable, technical details of the Sinai withdrawal from the contentious issues of principle surrounding the future of the West Bank and Gaza Strip.

The Israeli prime minister's success in achieving agreement at the outset to establish the committees gave the parties a safety valve in case the conference collapsed. Selection of Jerusalem as the seat of the political committee could be interpreted by Israel as tacit recognition of the Israeli capital. The two countries would engage in bilateral negotiations -- Israel's desire from the start -- without unilateral pretense. Nevertheless, by calling for UN and American participation in future political talks, Begin acknowledged the difficulties ahead.

Sadat at one point in the conference threatened to delay establishment of the committees if the two sides failed to reach agreement on a declaration of principles. He probably backed down when he realized that the Israelis -- determined to prevail in their attempt not to adopt any formula that might later lead to a Palestinian state in the West Bank -- would call the bluff.

The private accord between the two leaders clearly troubled Egyptian foreign office officials, and they would seek to undermine the political committee. The military committee had begun to take shape in Jerusalem, at the Cairo Conference, and during the Weizman–Gamassy tete–a–tete. A formula now existed to preserve the dialogue while each side reviewed the situation.

NOTES

1. New York Times, November 27, 1977.

2. Moshe Dayan, Breakthrough: A Personal Account of the Egypt–Israel Peace Negotiations (London: Weidenfeld and Nicholson, 1981), p. 106–107.

3. Washington Post, December 2, 6, 1977.

4. New York Times, November 24, 1977.

5. Washington Post, December 4, 1977.

6. Ibid., December 7, 1977.

7. Ibid., November 24, 1977; December 9, 1977.

8. Dayan, Breakthrough, p. 52.

9. Ibid., p. 92–93.

10. Ibid., p. 94–96.

11. Ibid., p. 92–96.

12. See biographic data on Ben–Elisar in New York Times, November 29, 1977.

13. Washington Post, November 24, 1977.

14. See, Eitan Haber, Zeev Schiff and Ehud Yaari, The Year of the Dove (New York: Bantam Books, 1979), p. 88.

15. Ibid.

16. Tuhamy requested that Dayan refrain from informing the U.S. of their secret conversations during initial meetings in Morocco in mid–September 1977. See, Dayan, Breakthrough, p. 47. Dayan may have revealed certain facts regarding the meeting during a convoluted discussion with Vance in New York in early October 1977. However the U.S. remained officially uninformed about the event during and immediately after the Dayan–Tuhamy conversations. Interview with Harold Saunders (U.S. Assistant Secretary of State for Near East) Washington, D.C. September 3, 1981.

17. Interview with Alfred Atherton, Cairo Egypt, August 18, 1981.

18. New York Times, December 1, 1977; Washington Post, December 2, 1977; Newsweek, December 12, 1977, p. 52.

130

19. <u>Newsweek</u>, December 12, 1977, p. 52.

20. See, Bernard Reich, "United States Interests in the Middle East" in Haim Shaked and Itamar Rabinovich, <u>The Middle East and the United States</u> (New Brunswick: Transaction BOoks, 1980), p. 78.

21. <u>Time</u>, December 12, 1977, p. 38–45; <u>Newsweek</u>, December 12, 1977, p. 59–62; <u>The Economist</u>, December 3, 1977, p. 17–18.

22. See, Steven Spiegel, "The Carter Approach to the Israeli Dispute" in Shaked and Rabinovich, <u>The Middle East and the United States</u>, p. 110.

23. <u>Newsweek</u>, December 12, 1977, p. 51.

24. <u>Ibid</u>.

25. Dayan, <u>Breakthrough</u>, p. 98.

26. <u>Ibid</u>.

27. <u>Ibid</u>., p. 98–99.

28. Telephone interview with Cyrus Vance, March 3, 1983.

29. See, Spiegel, "The Carter Approach to the Arab-Israeli Dispute" in Shaked and Rabinovich, <u>The Middle East and the United States</u>, p. 109.

30. <u>Interview with Alfred Atherton</u>, Cairo Egypt, August 18, 1981.

31. See, Spiegel, "The Carter Approach to the Arab-Israeli Dispute" in Shaked and Rabinovich, <u>The Middle East and the United States</u>, p. 94–95.

32. <u>Ibid</u>., p. 101–102, 109–110.

33. See, Interview with Zbigniew Brezinski, Transcript, <u>Issues and Answers</u> December 11, 1977, p. 1; also, <u>New York Times</u>, December 12, 1977.

34. Spiegel, "The Carter Approach to the Arab–Israeli Dispute" in Shaked and Rabinovich, The Middle East and the United States, p. 111.

35. Ibid., p. 108–110.

36. Ibid., p. 111.

37. Dayan, Breakthrough, p. 99–100.

38. Haber, Schiff and Yaari, The Year of the Dove, p. 106.

39. Interview with Yiehel Kadishai, Jerusalem Israel, August 23, 1981.

40. Joseph Schechtman, Rebel and Statesman: The Vladimir Jabotinsky Story, Fighter and Prophet (New York: Thomas Yoseloff, Inc., 1956) Volume 2, p. 258.

41. See, Uri Avnery, "Menachem Begin: The Reality" Worldview, May 1978, p. 13; also, Joseph Schechtman, Rebel and Statesman: The Vladimir Jabotinsky Story, The Early Years (New York: Thomas Yoseloff, Inc., 1966) Volume 1, p. 83–125.

42. Haber, Schiff and Yaari, The Year of the Dove, p. 106.

43. Ibid., p. 106–107.

44. Begin could have chosen to blend a self–government scheme with the Labor Government's previous administrative efforts. A self–administration plan for the West Bank was drawn by the Israeli Defense Forces (IDF) Planning Division under direction of General Tamir in 1975–6. The IDF Planning Division document, though, called for self–administration in the West Bank taking place as part of a broad reform program established under a decentralized system of government in Israel. Preparatory to the creation of a secondary district organization, however, military government would be eliminated in the occupied lands. The self–governing authority would be prohibited from making laws, raising military forces, or establishing its own currency in order to prevent the birth of a Palestinian state. The Tamir plan, moreover, was conceived

132

within a framework of Israeli–Jordanian political and economic cooperation in the West Bank and Gaza Strip. For discussion, see, Uzi Benziman, Prime Minister Under Siege (Jerusalem: Adam Publishers, 1981), Translated from the Hebrew by Mordecai Schreiber, p. 70–74.

45. Haber, Schiff and Yaari, The Year of the Dove, p. 107–108.

46. Ibid.

47. Ibid.

48. Rowland Evans and Robert Novak, "No Longer Israel's Attorney" Washington Post, December 19, 1977.

49. Dayan, Breakthrough, p. 101.

50. Interview with William Quandt, Washington, D.C. September 23, 1981.

51. See, New York Times, Interview with Menachem Begin, December 14, 1977.

52. Interview with William Quandt, Washinton D.C. September 23, 1981.

53. Haber, Schiff and Yaari, The Year of the Dove, p. 110–111.

54. Ibid., p. 111.

55. Interview with William Quandt, Washington D.C. September 23, 1981.

56. Haber, Schiff and Yaari, The Year of the Dove, p. 109–110.

57. Time, December 26, 1977, p. 23.

58. Time, December 26, 1977, p. 23.

59. Ezer Weizman, The Battle for Peace (New York: Bantam Books, 1981), p. 120.

60. Haber, Schiff and Yaari, _The Year of the Dove_, p. 97.

61. Weizman, _The Battle for Peace_, p. 91–92.

62. _Ibid._, p. 96–101.

63. _Ibid._, p. 103–106.

64. _Ibid._, p. 117.

65. Following Sadat's death on October 6, 1981, it became known that the Carter Administration was pressured by Egyptian officials to support a military operation against Libya during 1977. _Washington Post_, October 7, 1981.

66. Weizman, _The Battle for Peace_, p. 116–117.

67. Haber, Schiff and Yaari, _The Year of the Dove_, p. 111–112.

68. Weizman, _The Battle for Peace_, p. 123–124.

69. Haber, Schiff and Yaari, _The Year of the Dove_, p. 116; Dayan, _Breakthrough_, p. 102–103; Weizman, _The Battle for Peace_, p. 126.

70. Weizman, _The Battle for Peace_, p. 128–132.

71. _Ibid._, p. 132.

72. _Ibid._, p. 132–133.

73. Haber, Schiff and Yaari, _The Year of the Dove_, p. 123.

74. _Ibid._

75. For discussion of Gamassy's views on nuclear fears, see, Weizman, _The Battle for Peace_, p. 109–110.

76. Haber, Schiff and Yaari, _The Year of the Dove_, p. 124–126.

77. _Ibid._, p. 126–127.

78. _Ibid._, p. 127.

79. _Ibid._, p. 128.

80. _Ibid._, p. 128–129.

81. _Ibid._, p. 131.

82. _Ibid._

83. _Ibid._, p. 132.

84. _Ibid._, p. 133.

85. _Ibid._, p. 134.

86. _Ibid._

87. _Ibid._, p. 135.

88. _Ibid._

89. _Ibid._, p. 137.

5
The Triangular Relationship Deepens

Cairo and Jerusalem: Mixed Responses

Domestic support for the peace process ebbed in Israel and Egypt in the days immediately following adjournment of the Ismailia conference. Both leaders were under seige by cabinet ministers, members of parliament, and segments of the general electorate for either granting too much or too little in negotiations over the Palestinian issue, the West Bank and Gaza Strip, and the Sinai. Neither Begin nor Sadat fully deserved the charges, but the perceptions nevertheless existed and threatened to undermine the popularity, if not the survival in power, of both.

Begin, for example, had earned an approval rating above 75 percent before meeting with Sadat in Egypt in late December 1977.[1] But a nagging belief in some Israeli quarters that autonomy would produce a Palestinian state spoiled his return to Jerusalem.[2] An even larger number of Israelis was convinced that the government would soon end the policy of establishing settlements throughout the biblical lands of Israel — a bedrock of Zionist doctrine for half a century.[3] The Knesset resolved the first concern temporarily on December 28 when it voted by a narrow margin to approve Begin's autonomy plan; one-third of the members abstained. The second issue — settlements — became the subject of intense debate in Israel, the United States, Western Europe, and the Arab world both before and after the Egyptian-Israeli treaty was signed in March 1979.

The right of Jews to establish residence anywhere in the biblical lands was a central tenet of Zionism prior to the birth of Israel and remained a paramount goal of Israelis after its founding. The notion derived less from biblical dictates than from a practical Zionist commitment to the land. In time, the settlements became a symbol of security. Hostile neighbors would be unable to strike at Israel's heartland and threaten the majority of its population without first overrunning settlements strategically located near the borders of those countries. The settlements would also provide early warning of any ground attack, giving Israel a possibly critical margin of safety.[4]

Labor Party governments approved the original, crucial network of settlements, and Labor groups constructed and populated it prior to Begin's election in 1977.[5] Dayan, a stalwart Labourite in the aftermath of the 1967 Six-Day War, created in particular the settlements in the Rafah salient.[6] He also regarded Israeli possession of Sharm el-Sheikh without peace as preferable to peace without Sharm el-Sheikh.[7] The Likud Party and its component elements had settled few of the existing camps in the Sinai or the West Bank.[8]

Thus when the Likud government came to power, it was neither responsible nor traditionally committed to preserving the settlements. Under the circumstances, it appeared especially incongruous for Ariel Sharon, then minister of agriculture and head of the cabinet committee on settlements, to propose in early January 1978 swift creation of dummy settlements in the Sinai.[9]

Sharon was a complicated man with strong ties to the land. He spent his early youth as a farm boy, a tiller of the soil on an isolated agricultural cooperative near Tel Aviv. A brilliant soldier, paratroop commander, and military strategist and the hero of the 1973 war, Sharon initially entered politics as a Liberal Party candidate within the Likud bloc after the Yom Kippur War. He soon resigned his Knesset seat either from boredom or disappointment at not receiving a major government post in Golda Meir's short-lived postwar grand coalition. He then advised the government of former Prime Minister Rabin on military matters before stepping down to prepare for the 1977 elections. This time Sharon organized his own party, Shlomo Tzion — Peace of Zion. He courted the left and supporters of the peace movement, whom he believed to be crucial to victory.

Shlomo Tzion won only two seats in the 1977 election, and it might not have received any without a large turnout from Sharon's former comrades-in-arms. Nevertheless, Sharon's decision to align himself with Begin provided the Israeli prime minister with the margin necessary to form a government. Sharon quickly converted the agriculture ministry into an effective vehicle for aggressively enlarging Israel's presence in the West Bank. His actions attracted renewed support from the Israeli right -- old members of the Herut Party and newer voices from the Gush Emunim and its followers.

The country remained sharply divided between right and left, between those who favored annexation of occupied land and those who believed that territorial compromise would in the end ensure peace. But support for increasing Israel's security at any price was growing steadily. Sharon was searching for a trend he could manipulate to advance his political career. To champion the right of settlers to expand in the Sinai would obviously serve his purposes. It could help Sharon secure a base of support, and perhaps Begin's endorsement as successor to the prime ministership, by strengthening his links to the Israeli right during the difficult struggle for peace with Egypt.[10]

Cairo and Washington criticized sharply but privately the Israeli cabinet's January approval of Sharon's plan to erect waterdrilling derricks and to place empty, rusted buses along imaginary defense positions in the Sinai. Bedouins observed the work and reported progress to Egyptian intelligence, and U.S. satellites photographed the effort. Jerusalem intended the gambit either to lead to Egyptian acquiescence to further Israeli colonialization of the area or provide a bargaining chip in future negotiations over the fate of the settlements in the Rafah salient and Sharm el-Sheikh.[11] These objectives, however, were blocked when Israeli radio revealed the operation.[12] Sadat and Carter openly denounced the act.[13] Jerusalem reacted quickly by strengthening the Rafah settlements on January 8.[14]

Meanwhile, in Cairo, Sadat was grappling with vocal criticism of the Ismailia Conference. Israeli reluctance to concede the whole Sinai or offer substantial compromise on the Palestinian issue fueled fanaticism in Egypt. The Muslim Brotherhood and its more activist offshoots had been implicated already in plots to overthrow Sadat's regime during the last months of 1977.[15] And the Brotherhood won an overwhelming mandate in student elections in Egyptian universities on the final day of the Ismailia meeting.[16]

Army officers and members of the Egyptian bourgeoisie feared that the religious right would gain inordinate influence among enlisted men and in the state bureaucracy.[17] Infitah, Sadat's policy to encourage free-enterprise, had not yet provided the margin of economic progress that would limit the ability of Muslim fundamentalists to exploit successfully the urban poor. Furthermore, peace prospects were not promising enough to satisfy the restive military whose support Sadat needed to assuage the concerns of rural Egyptians disturbed by the growth of the urban aristocracy.

To counter these pressures, Sadat encouraged the resurgence of the Wafd Party, which he had attacked bitterly in the summer of 1977. The party, Egypt's most nationalistic, supported constitutionally guaranteed civil liberties, a form of presidential rule that eschewed the autocratic tendencies of Nasser, and a limited Egyptian role in the Arab world rather than the interventionist one that fostered a military expedition into Yemen in the early 1960s. The Wafdist political platform had also always emphasized Egyptian patriotism and unity of the Nile Valley. The Wafd Party leadership thus viewed Sadat's attempt to regain the Sinai and the negotiation of a peace treaty with Sudan as attractive measures.[18]

The Nasserites could be relied upon to oppose strongly the return of the Wafdists. But there existed only a small number of Nasser loyalists, and they possessed no significant following. Sadat's economic recovery program sought in part to undermine what base they did have. The program's attention to rural problems -- including health care, nutrition, housing, and employment -- placed Sadat's regime firmly behind Wafdist objectives and interests. In addition, Sadat and the Wafd Party shared a desire to generate public backing for individual freedoms and initiatives.[19] Thus, Sadat's regime had dismantled the centralized planning and collectivization that characterized agricultural development a decade earlier.

Sadat's moves to secularize Egyptian society and to rehabilitate the Wafd Party underscored the delicacy of his political position and had serious implications for Egypt's relations with its Arab neighbors. For example, fundamentalist opposition to Sadat's internal development program and to his search for peace with Israel stood in the way of close ties with Saudi Arabia. Sadat perceived Riyadh as a possible source of moral if not financial support for fundamentalism in Egypt.[20] Saudi Arabian refusal to respond positively to Western enticement to join in the peace process gave Cairo a pretext to cool relations with Riyadh.

Sadat's domestic difficulties, however, were a secondary concern of key Egyptian elites. Foreign office officials were determined to reestablish Egyptian leadership and respect in the Arab world. Cairo could not achieve that goal without Saudi Arabia. Mubarak had devoted much of his time and energy to completing a network of allies devoted to introducing greater flexibility in Sadat's program. Thus, Usama al-Baz was co-opted as a political adviser and could be expected to cooperate with the foreign office in seeking to improve Egypt's posture among Arab states, particularly with Saudi Arabia. Kamel Hasan Ali, also allied with Mubarak, would become defense minister in October 1978 after Gamassy, the vice-president's adversary, was removed. Minister of Interior Nabawi Isma'il completed the triumvirate and together with Ali provided Mubarak with the latest and most complete information available on internal disorder and on the extent of domestic support for or opposition to an Egyptian-Israeli treaty. Mubarak carefully screened the flow of intelligence to Sadat, ensuring that it reinforced the vice-president's preferrences.

Compromise and Deadlock

The political and military committees established at the Ismailia meeting were scheduled to meet in early 1978. The military group convened on January 11 at Tahara Palace on the outskirts of Cairo. When Weizman arrived in Cairo to join the talks, he was first taken to Aswan for a private meeting with Sadat. The Egyptian president, flanked by Gamassy and Mubarak, reiterated his nation's commitment to regain from Israel the entire Sinai, including the settlements and airfields. To no avail, Israel's defense minister explained the security concerns behind Israel's desire to maintain at least temporary control of Rafah, Etam, and Etzion.[21]

After the meeting, Weizman and Gamassy went to a suburb of Cairo, where they and their aides began the first of several heated discussions on Israeli withdrawal from the Sinai. The conferees did not adopt a fixed agenda or choose a permanent chairman.

The two sides discussed the settlements and airfields but made no progress toward an agreement. They broached proposals for demilitarized zones and joint inspection procedures with greater success. The Israelis wished to ensure that Egypt would never again use the Sinai as a springboard to launch an attack against Israel. A sufficiently wide demilitarized zone would provide early warning in the event of a future Egyptian offensive. And Egyptian forces would have to move across a broad expanse of empty desert without proper logistical support. To establish the necessary infrastructure prior to such an operation would require violation of the Egyptian–Israeli agreement to demilitarize portions of the Sinai. Remembering the poor performance of UN constabulary forces in the Sinai prior to the 1967 war, Jerusalem also insisted on establishment of mixed Egyptian–Israeli units to monitor the peace.[22]

The Egyptian military sought limitation of forces on both sides of the border. Buffer zones and demilitarized areas would, in Cairo's view, make such an initiative possible. But Weizman refused to accept more than the principle of joint demilitarization. He wondered aloud which Israeli site the Egyptians would want demilitarized — "Beersheba?" Gamassy and his advisers appeared to comprehend Weizman's reference to Israel's severe territorial limitations and left discussion of the details of military arrangements to another meeting.[23]

Weizman and Gamassy held their second meeting in Cairo near the end of the month. Israel stated its intention to retain control of three early-warning stations in the Sinai capable of detecting Egyptian troop movements west of the Suez Canal. Israeli military intelligence preferred to keep the sites indefinitely but would settle for a minimum of fifteen years. Gamassy believed that technological advances would outpace the stations' utility but could not agree to combined Israeli control. At most, Egypt would agree to allow the United States or another third party to operate the facilities. Sharp differences remained over a variety of important territorial and military issues at the end of the January discussions.[24]

An even less satisfying beginning to the meetings of the political committee in Jerusalem punctuated the lack of substantial progress in the military talks. An acrimonious debate over the agenda threatened to abort the opening of the political discussions. The Egyptian government demanded that Israel agree in advance of the negotiations to withdraw from the occupied territories and grant the Palestinians the right to establish an independent state. However, the Egyptians yielded to a compromise formula proposed by Vance. The three-item agenda would contain: a declaration of intent to govern discussions for comprehensive peace in the area; guidelines for negotiations over Judea, Samaria, and the Gaza Strip; and an endorsement of UN Resolution 242 as a basis for peace treaties between Israel and its neighbors. The first and second items would not impose any preconditions for Israeli withdrawal from the occupied lands and settlement of the Palestinian problem.[25]

The Egyptian delegation, led by Kamel and consisting of Meguid, Boutrus Ghali, and al-Baz, arrived in Jerusalem on January 15. The American team headed by Vance followed on the 16th. The meetings began on January 17 in the morning. The conference's first agenda item quickly became the object of dispute. The Egyptian delegation complained that Vance's declaration of intent did not commit Israel specifically to withdraw from the Sinai, the Golan Heights, and the West Bank and Gaza Strip or to recognize the Palestinian right to self-determination.[26]

Israel was represented on the Political Committee by a delegation headed by Dayan and Attorney General Aharon Barak. Jerusalem based its position toward withdrawal from the occupied territories on the wording of UN Resolution 242. Israel would agree only to discuss the resettlement of "refugees" — a euphemism for Palestinians — and establishment of administrative autonomy for the Arab inhabitants of "Judea, Samaria, and the Gaza District."[27]

After the Egyptian and Israeli negotiations failed to narrow their wide differences, the U.S. delegation offered compromise language. Vance's team proposed four drafts and either the Israelis or the Egyptians or both rejected each one. Kamel then abruptly left the talks before the parties could consider a fifth suggestion.[28]

The Egyptian government's decision to break off the political committee meetings reportedly resulted from an after-dinner remark by Begin that offended Kamel. The Israeli prime minister had earlier agreed to refrain from issuing polemical statements. In a public declaration at the Jerusalem airport upon arriving on the 15th, Kamel reiterated Egypt's demands and reasserted its devotion to peace. On January 18, at the end of a dinner in honor of the Egyptian delegation, Begin responded by listing the Egyptian conditions that Israel could not accept as part of a peace treaty — the redivision of Jerusalem, establishment of a Palestinian state, and return to the pre-1967 borders. He then apparently offended Kamel by referring to the senior Egyptian diplomat as "my young man." The Egyptians considered Begin's tone as abrasive and the remark itself as derisive.[29]

Within hours of the dinner statement, Sadat was reportedly informed of the faux pas and of Begin's violation of the promise not to make impolitic statements. The Egyptian president allegedly ordered the delegation to return to Cairo immediately. An official statement asserted that Sadat ordered

Kamel to leave Jerusalem when it became apparent that Israel sought "partial solutions" rather than a clear comprehensive peace in the Middle East. Some also believed Sadat seized the opportunity provided by Begin's remark to interrupt a cycle of negotiations he considered stuck on marginal issues.[30] More likely, however, internal Egyptian politics dictated the move.

During the first weeks of January Sadat's political situation improved, as he began to isolate the religious right and ignite nationalist sentiments through the return of the Wafd Party. But his ability to prevail over recalcitrant foreign affairs advisers remained uncertain. In general, Sadat's only loyalists were contemporaries like Tuhamy or relatives like Marei and Osman. The members of the national security council were mostly either sychophants or powerful and ambitious men becoming less responsive to Sadat's will. Of the latter, the most important was Mubarak, who could count on the support of Ali and Kamel. Prime Minister Salim was committed to Sadat but had little influence. Although inscrutable, Gamassy backed the peace effort viscerally. Finally, Khalil was both independent and respected, and even the president of Egypt could not intimidate him easily.

Mubarak trusted the Saudis to create the necessary bridges to the Arab world should the Egyptian–Israeli peace process founder. Riyadh would later unsuccessfully promote with the Kuwaitis and others the idea of holding an Arab summit conference to entice Egypt back into the fold.[31] Harsh criticism in the Egyptian press of Jerusalem's bargaining tactics and Egypt's decision to leave the political committee discussions convinced the Saudis that Sadat's peace initiative was after all designed only to expose Israeli intransigence.[32]

The Egyptian vice president had sought a central role in coordinating the negotiations of the political committee even before they were broken off. He had participated with his chief adversary, Gamassy, in a meeting to plan strategy for the dialogue with Israel.[33] Additional discussions with U.S. Ambassador Herman Eilts, who was attempting in vain to elicit Egyptian approval of Israeli proposals and American amendments, had also enlarged the vice-president's expertise on the peace process.[34] Finally, a leading performance in the January 15 NSC meeting, called to refine Egypt's position for the political talks, solidified Mubarak's influence on the deliberations.[35] Sadat assigned Mubarak and Salim the task of receiving, analyzing, and processing information relating to the talks in Jerusalem.[36] And Usama al-Baz, Mubarak's political adviser, continued to play a crucial role in the political committee meetings.

In the aftermath of the breakdown of the political committee talks, Mubarak chaired a 90-minute meeting in Cairo on January 22 to review the state of the negotiations with Israel.[37] Following the sessions, he embarked on a five-day visit to several Arab capitals, including Riyadh, to brief them on the peace process and to coordinate future moves.[38] Marei and Ashraf Marwan, a son-in-law of former President Nasser and chairman of the Arab Industrial Organization,[39] had previously performed this role of emissary to Saudi Arabia and other Arab states. Mubarak would eventually engineer Marwan's fall from power in October 1978.

The United States Becomes Mediator

The lack of progress toward a settlement at Ismailia spurred the U.S. government to adopt the role of mediator at the beginning of 1978. Washington continued to believe that the more moderate Arab states might under the right circumstances join the peace process and help produce a Geneva-style comprehensive agreement and that the Soviet Union would force its radical allies — such as Syria — to support it.[40]

Former National Security Advisor Zbigniew Brezinski spoke of a peace process composed of three concentric circles. The first would encompass the existing dialogue between Cairo and Jerusalem with Washington offering its good offices. The second would include the moderate Arabs such as Jordan, Saudi Arabia, and Palestinians not linked to the PLO. The third would envelop the Soviet Union and Syria and would take place in Geneva.[41]

In the last weeks of 1977, the Carter administration remained publicly optimistic over the prospects for success in the Egyptian–Israeli discussions. Privately, however, the White House feared an impasse. After the deadlock at Ismailia, the American government began to grope for any way of attracting Arab support for Sadat's peace initiative. Phillip Habib, then undersecretary of state for political affairs, had gone to Moscow in early December but could not persuade the Kremlin to induce Damascus to soften its opposition to the Egyptian–Israeli peace negotiations. That failure may have convinced U.S. policy makers that the lack of Soviet cooperation reflected the Kremlin's inability to influence the Assad government. Even if Damascus had wished to join the peace process, serious internal instability in Syria would have prevented it from doing so. For Assad's minority Alawite government needed the Israeli threat to justify its brutal repression at home. Moscow's consistent refusal to support Syria's long-standing call for the destruction of Israel also undermined Soviet influence. Finally, Assad regarded the Kremlin's signature on the Soviet-American statement of October 1, 1977 as perfidious.[42]

Carter therefore appealed directly to Assad to join the peace process. He indicated that Syria should participate in negotiations over the Golan Heights but did not invite Damascus to take part in discussions over the West Bank and Gaza Strip.[43] In essence, Carter wished to promote Arab support for Sadat's initiative but to avoid seriously damaging the Egyptian-Israeli peace process should the Arabs refuse to endorse it. The American president offered to meet with his Syrian counterpart during a projected world tour. Assad turned down the offer.

Carter planned to embark on a nine-day, seven nation visit at the end of December. The four-continent odyssey had originally been scheduled for November but was postponed when the president's energy bill ran into trouble in Congress. Due to further rescheduling, the journey was split into two, with the second part delayed until March.[44] The new itinerary required that the Carter entourage rest between its departure from Poland on December 31 and arrival in India on January 1. Iran seemed the most appropriate choice for the one and a half-day stop. Since Shah Mohammed Reza Pahlevi had recently visited Washington, no substantial policy differences existed between he and Carter, promising that the stop would be both restful and social.[45]

The shah, however, had other plans. A presidential visit to Teheran would provide him a clear opportunity to demonstrate his importance in the area and to assert a role in the Middle East peace process. He therefore sought -- and received -- Carter's agreement to invite Jordan's King Hussein to Teheran. The resulting encounter failed to soften Hussein's determination not to participate in the Egyptian-Israeli peace process.[46]

But prior to these setbacks with Assad and Hussein, Carter himself made a statement in Washington on December 29 that seriously undermined America's role as mediator. In his

nationally televised year-end assessment of his administration's progress, Carter informed the world that although he
opposed the creation of an independent Palestinian state, he
nevertheless favored a "homeland or an entity wherein the
Palestinians can live in peace."[47]

By announcing his opposition to the formation of a
Palestinian state only a few days after the deadlock at
Ismailia, Carter wished to encourage the Israelis to moderate
their stances in subsequent meetings with the Egyptians. The
Knesset had only narrowly approved Begin's plan for Palestinian
self-rule on the West Bank and Gaza Strip, and the immoderate
remarks of Egyptian officials at the Christmas meetings between
Begin and Sadat did little to inspire Israeli confidence in the
prospects for peace. If he could induce Jerusalem to become
more reasonable and to show greater willingness to compromise,
Carter believed he would satisfy Egyptian desires and attract
wider Arab support for the peace process.

Carter's initiative did not work as intended. His
statement placed Sadat in an uncomfortable and exposed
position. Egyptian officials had restrained Sadat's apparent
eagerness to achieve peace with Israel at nearly any price.
Vice-President Mubarak and his widening circle of allies
insisted that any agreement should include an equitable
arrangement for the Palestinians and thus reduce Egypt's
isolation in the Arab world. The Wafd Party had not yet
achieved full strength, and a public campaign to stir patriotic
sentiment over the expected return of the Sinai had not yet
begun. Neither the Saudis nor the Jordanians had indicated
clear support for Sadat's peace initiative. Their silence
boded ill for a quick settlement, but Sadat hoped that they
would in the end go along with his initiative if it remained
sufficiently ambiguous to allow for various interpretations and
preserve the prospect of further change. Sadat therefore began
to frame all references to the Palestinians in an equivocal
manner, hoping thereby to thaw frozen Arab positions. For
example, Sadat employed "Palestinian self-determination" as one
such ambiguous reference.[48]

Consequently, Sadat publicly reproached Carter on December
30 for his unfortunate and ill-timed remark. The White House
attempted to soothe Sadat's ruffled feelings, but to no avail.
The Egyptian president evidently wished to meet with Carter to
save face and bolster his sagging position at home and abroad.
Carter relented and announced on January 1 from Teheran that he
would visit Sadat at Aswan briefly after meeting in Riyadh with

the Saudi leadership on January 3 and 4.

Carter's visit to Saudi Arabia failed to produce a promise of support for Sadat's peace effort. Indeed, two influential members of the Saudi Royal family -- Deputy Prime Minister Abdullah and Foreign Minister Saud al-Faisal -- reiterated publicly during the presidential visit their support for the establishment of a Palestinian state.[49] The Saudis had been ambivalent about Sadat's peace initiative since its very inception in November. Saudi policy rested on two central objectives: preservation of regional stability and maintenance of the monarchy. A Saudi endorsement of Sadat's peace effort might worsen relations with Damascus and Baghdad. Such a trend would increase tensions in the Gulf area and destroy Saudi efforts begun in 1976 to nurture internal and external security relations with Iraq. Further deterioration in relations with South and North Yemen, Bahrain, and Kuwait might also result. And most crucial, threats to internal stability from the significant Palestinian presence in Saudi Arabia would increase.[50]

Nevertheless, Riyadh did not condemn Sadat's peace move immediately. The Saudis probably considered the initiative a temporary expedient unlikely to achieve success or lead to the signature of a separate agreement between Egypt and Israel. According to this view, Saudi Arabia could revive Arab solidarity by helping Cairo return to the fold after the failure of Sadat's gambit.

The meeting at Aswan between Carter and Sadat on the morning of January 4 lasted less than an hour and took place in a hastily prepared VIP lounge in an old terminal building of the airport. Carter sought answers to three questions: what Sadat expected to achieve from the forthcoming military and political talks; what positions the Egyptian president would advance during the next full round of bilateral negotiations with Israel; and what were Egypt's specific objections to Begin's autonomy plan for the West Bank and Gaza Strip.[51] Carter received few specific responses, and he did not press Sadat to provide them. In part, their meeting was too short to expect significant results. But Carter also realized that the Egyptian president needed to be appeased and reassured and thus chose not to press hard.

Nevertheless, the two leaders issued a declaration that would guide all future peace discussions. Its three principal elements stated that: Peace would include establishment of normal relations between the parties and reflect more than

simply an end to belligerency; Israeli withdrawal from
territories occupied in 1967 would take place in accord with UN
Resolutions 242 and 338; and the Palestinian problem would be
resolved in all its aspects, including recognition of the
legitimate rights of the Palestinian people to participate in
the determination of their own future.[52]

Israel reacted to the Aswan declaration with apprehension
and misgivings. Not only could the statement be interpreted as
supporting the establishment of a Palestinian state, but
Carter's visit to Aswan demonstrated that the vicissitudes of
Sadat's political position had a profound impact on American
policy. Nevertheless, Dayan recognized the constructive side
of the declaration. It contained the three principles at the
heart of the search for peace and did so in a manner that
differed substantially from the rigid language of UN Resolution
242. It stipulated that Israel would withdraw from occupied
territories -- not the territories -- in exchange for full
normalization, not simply an end to belligerency, and within
the context of a settlement of the Palestinian problem.[53]

The Palestinian issue remained at the heart of the
differences between Israel and Egypt. Begin rejected outright
Carter's effort to include the notion of Palestinian self-
determination in the declaration. Israelis tended to view
"self-determination" as a euphemism for statehood. Moreover,
any indication that Begin accepted new, controversial wording
on the meaning of Palestinian rights would be self-destructive,
as domestic support for his autonomy plan remained shallow and
disappointment with the failure at Ismailia deep.

The American suggestion that the declaration support
Palestinian "participation in the determination of their own
future" was a novel way of bridging the semantic barriers
errected by both Cairo and Jerusalem. Although the wording did
not entirely satisfy either side, it went part of the way
toward the Egyptian position and avoided terminology considered
anathema by the Israelis. Thus, the Carter administration had
inaugurated the new year demonstrating the flair, technical
skill, and balance necessary to succeed as a mediator in
structuring peace in the Middle East. In the ensuing months
American attempts to secure an Egyptian-Israeli peace treaty
would swing from frustration to elation, from perspicacity to
obtuseness. Those efforts would earn Carter both praise and
rue from supporters and detractors alike. But none would be
more grateful than Sadat.

Sadat Visits Washington

Washington viewed the breakup of the political committee meeting in Jerusalem on January 18 with a mixture of regret and bafflement. Vance had already resolved many of the quarrelsome issues that had obstructed adoption of a declaration of principles and succeeded in narrowing disagreement on others. Both Israel and Egypt had approved five of seven paragraphs in a draft Egyptian–Israeli settlement prior to suspension of the talks. Yet according to one account of a January 20 meeting in Cairo between Sadat and Vance, the Egyptian president did not even know how much progress had been achieved. Sadat may have been feigning ignorance. More likely, however, his surprise at learning of the extent of the progress reflected his isolation from daily events and indicated that Mubarak's working group had chosen to portray the discussions in Jerusalem in a most disparaging manner.

In the midst of the confusion surrounding the abrupt termination of the political committee meeting and following an Egyptian request for arms from Washington, Carter invited Sadat to Camp David for private talks. The White House evidently wanted assurances from Sadat that he really desired direct and sustained negotiations with Israel. Sadat's sudden public appeal for the United States to lift its arms embargo and supply Egypt with a quantity and quality of weapons comparable to those provided Israel was intended to pacify his discontented military. His peace initiative had thus far brought neither peace nor even a relaxation of Israel's military posture, and many in the Egyptian Army had begun to view the process with suspicion.

Prior to his trip to Washington, Sadat dispatched key aides to important world capitals for consultations. Marei went to Washington to prepare for the Camp David meetings and to alert Congress of the importance of approving military aid to Egypt. Kamel flew to Western Europe to seek the assistance of West Germany, France, and Great Britain in opposing Israeli dismissal of legitimate Palestinian rights. Mubarak explained Egypt's toughened policy toward Israel to key Arab nations, including Saudi Arabia. Cairo promoted this broad diplomatic effort as an attempt to secure universal support for Egyptian peace plans. But in truth it reflected Sadat's inability to gain necessary Israeli compromise on the Palestinian issue. Only the United States possessed the power to pressure Jerusalem on that very delicate matter.

The usual high drama and formality surrounded Sadat's arrival in Washington on February 3 but he was soon whisked away to Camp David for more informal talks with Carter. The American president nearly always succeeded in cowing the opposition, persuading the faithless, or encouraging dispirited supporters in open, direct, one–on–one exchanges in private surroundings. The rustic solitude of Camp David thus provided a fitting locus for his special brand of personal diplomacy.

Sadat needed to achieve at least the appearance of progress on the Palestinian issue. The struggle to achieve self–determination for the Palestinians would undoubtedly receive a boost from wider Arab participation in the peace process. Thus, Sadat wanted Carter to devote increased efforts to drawing Hussein into the peace process and to press Israel to compromise in the negotiations over the Sinai.

Sadat approved Carter's suggestion that Atherton undertake an intensive shuttle between Cairo and Jerusalem to nail down an agreement on a declaration of principles. Meanwhile, the United States would step up its criticism of Israeli settlement policies and adopt a broad interpretation of UN Resolution 242. The American president would also seek to assure Egyptian domestic tranquility by asking Congress to approve the supply of F–5 fighter planes to Egypt. The White House believed that these steps would restrain Sadat's mercurial behavior and assure careful and proper bilateral coordination on future peace moves. It also anticipated that the U.S. willingness to chastise Israel publicly might soften Arab resistance — particularly in Amman — to the peace process.

The Carter administration chose not to restrain Sadat from delivering a harsh attack against Israeli inflexibility in a speech before the National Press Club, even though Vance reviewed the remarks beforehand. Carter apparently preferred to rely on Sadat's oratory in seeking to alter Jerusalem's posture rather than on the unpredictable and politically risky alternative of threatening to reduce American assistance to Israel. Sadat ended his visit with a virtuoso performance on Capital Hill that could only enhance the Carter administration's effort to gain approval of a Middle East arms package that included the sale of F5s to Egypt.[54]

The six-day U.S. trip netted Sadat a degree of success — at least in appearance — that had of late eluded him in Egypt. Israel's reluctance to compromise on the Sinai, its attitude toward settlements, and its delusion that it could create a solution that would satisfy Palestinian needs in the West Bank and Gaza Strip bedeviled the Egyptian leader. He suffered criticism from a restive Egyptian public and a dimunition of authority with anxious domestic elites who wished to control future negotiations with Israel.

Only Carter appeared to bolster Sadat's position. The U.S. president publicly affirmed the necessity to solve the Palestinian problem. He reiterated his view stated in the Aswan declaration that the Palestinians might participate in the determination of their own future. But Carter went beyond the Aswan formula in a February 8 White House statement. He interpreted UN Resolution 242 as requiring the withdrawal of Israeli forces from all fronts. He thus implied that Jerusalem would eventually have to withdraw from the West Bank. The American leader also issued a sharp reminder that Israeli settlements in the occupied territories violated international law and represented an obstacle to peace.[55]

Sadat and Carter hoped the Atherton shuttle would convince dissidents in Egypt that the U.S. commitment to the preservation of Egyptian interests was genuine and likely to yield positive results in the negotiations over the Sinai and the Palestinian issue. Finally, the promise of U.S. arms for Egypt and the obvious amity between the U.S. and Egyptian presidents suggested a solid bilateral relationship that could only result in tangible security advantages for Cairo.

Dayan Visits Washington

American policy in February 1978 revolved around an effort to draw Jordan into the peace process. Atherton met with King Hussein immediately following the collapse of the political committee talks. Washington was seeking to break the deadlock and wanted to know Jordan's conditions for entering the negotiations. Hussein apparently told Atherton that the cost would be modest: a declaration of vague principles providing for Israeli withdrawal from the West Bank and a statement of Palestinian rights. Jordan also warned that it would not join the negotiations unless convinced that Israel intended to negotiate peace seriously.[56]

Hussein remained wary of Sadat's peace initiative and subsequent moves to resolve the Palestinian issue. Recent U.S. and Egyptian moves to discredit the PLO leadership and to preclude permanent Israeli occupation of the West Bank encouraged him. But he doubted the ability of Washington or Cairo to carry out their good intentions.

In Hussein's view the Carter administration had botched its promise to impose a comprehensive solution on Israel and had imprudently invited increased Soviet meddling in the area when it agreed to the October 1, 1977 superpower communique. Most damaging from the Jordanian perspective, however, Washington had become an advocate of PLO participation in peace talks. The Jordanian monarch — who lost the West Bank in the 1967 war, rules over a nation over half Palestinian, and expelled the PLO from Jordan after a brutal civil war in 1970 — still chafed at the implications of the 1974 Rabat Declaration that made the PLO the sole legitimate representative of the Palestinian people. If he decided to participate in negotiations, he would have to do so as head of a confrontation state not, as the arbiter of Palestinian fortunes.[57]

U.S. and Egyptian attempts to involve Hussein in the peace process thus met with a great deal of circumspection. He favored Egypt's efforts to achieve agreement on a declaration of principles that would create strong ties between the West Bank and Jordan. But Israel's refusal to accept such a formula at Ismailia precluded Jordanian involvement in the negotiations. For without a binding set of principles regulating relations between Palestinians outside Jordan and the Hashemite Kingdom, the PLO would continue to dominate affairs on the West Bank and threaten Hussein's rule.

Under the circumstances, Hussein refrained from denouncing Sadat's peace efforts and instead nurtured American and Egyptian attempts to involve him in the process. This policy preserved Jordan's moderate image and its central role in the search for peace. The policy also ensured that in order to achieve Jordanian participation Washington would find it necessary to press for larger Israeli concessions on the problems of the West Bank and settlements. As one observer noted, "Hussein set out to harvest the benefits of Jordan's position as a 'swing state' without necessarily swinging..."[58]

Washington did not even suspect Hussein's machinations. He was both cordial and receptive to American courting during his brief encounter with Carter in Teheran. He took reasonable, moderate positions during the discussions with Atherton in Amman on January 27 and 28. Sadat himself asserted at Camp David in early February that Hussein would join the peace process if Israel agreed to a declaration of principles that included guidelines for Israeli withdrawal from the West Bank.

Jordan's leader believed that a flexible stance would contrast sharply with Israel's utterly negative position and convince Washington to adjust its policies in the direction of Arab interests. Carter's February 8 statement that UN Resolution 242 required Israel to withdraw from all the occupied territories aimed in part at luring Jordan into the stalled negotiations.[59]

On February 9, however, the king announced that a simple declaration of principles would no longer suffice. Israel would now have to agree in advance to withdraw totally to its 1967 borders and to support Palestinian self-determination in the evacuated territories. He also asserted that UN Resolutions 242 and 338 no longer fulfilled Jordanian requirements and that the Palestinian refugees would have to be repatriated and compensated. If Israel refused to accept his terms, Hussein warned, the Arabs would establish an all-Arab force to whittle Israel down to its proper size.[60]

Meanwhile, Dayan was touring the United States to counter the Jewish community's criticism of Jerusalem's settlements policy. The Carter administration had been waging a tough campaign against the establishment of new Israeli settlements in the West Bank. The president held official briefings for Jewish-American leaders and swayed many to oppose publicly the actions of the Israeli government.[61]

Few understood that the controversial settlements program represented a compromise designed to placate domestic hardliners without prompting an overly severe international reaction. In the wake of the uproar that followed public revelation that Sharon intended to erect dummy settlements in the Sinai, Israel strengthened settlements in the Rafah Salient but did not add new ones. The Israeli cabinet approved twenty additional settlements, however, for the West Bank. This combination of restraint and continued activity reflected Begin's desire to maintain the support of his party's most dogmatic members and carry out his own beliefs without disrupting relations with Sadat and Carter. The Israeli prime minister sought to belie Egyptian charges of duplicity and to reduce Carter's ire by refusing to establish new settlements in the Sinai and by adding only housing facilities to non-civilian settlements there. The radical Gush Emunim, however, undermined even this compromise by creating its own new settlement in the West Bank.[62]

Begin's refusal to oppose strongly all attempts to circumvent the compromise reflected his reticence to battle Sharon, reformers within the Herut Party, Gush Emunim zealots, and elements of the NRP and DMC. The Knesset had barely approved the Israeli prime minister's choice for minister-without-portfolio on January 8. The government won only limited support for its plan for Palestinian self-rule from Begin's Herut wing of the Likud coalition on the 9th. On the same day, pessimistic forecasts of steady inflation during the coming years were released.[63] Begin's public approval rating fell substantially from a high of 78.3 percent in December 1977 to 68.4 percent during the first month of 1978.[64]

These domestic problems and doubts about the new relationship with Egypt helped produce a tough Israeli response to recent Egyptian and American assertions. On February 13, just three days before Dayan's White House visit, the Israeli cabinet issued a statement regretting and protesting American accusations that the creation of settlements violated international law and harmed the search for peace. The cabinet also expressed its belief that Vance's proposal that the West Bank become a Palestinian homeland linked with Jordan would likely result in the establishment of a PLO-controlled state determined to eliminate Israel. The government statement concluded with a warning that

> No political aim of any kind can move Israel to place almost her entire civilian population within firing range of the enemy, and her very existence in direct danger.[65]

Faced with both Jordanian and Israeli resistance to his policies, Carter invited the touring Israeli foreign minister to the White House. Vance, Brezinski, Atherton and Israeli Ambassador to the United States Simcha Dinitz joined Carter and Dayan in the February 16 meeting. Despite Hussein's improvident remarks of February 9, U.S. policy makers wished to discuss ways of involving Jordan in future bargaining between Israel and Egypt.[66]

The U.S. participants described Sadat as frustrated and disappointed at the lack of progress in the negotiations. They warned that the Egyptian president's political standing at home had eroded and that he would probably be able to continue negotiations with Israel for only a few weeks unless Hussein joined the process. Even then, they claimed, Sadat's position would remain tenuous. The Americans argued, therefore, that the parties must produce a declaration of principles. The document would have to include an Israeli agreement to withdraw from the West Bank. Carter emphasized that previous Israeli governments had agreed to UN Resolution 242, which required Israel to withdraw from all occupied territories including the West Bank.[67]

Dayan responded that Israel had no desire to rule Palestinian Arabs but would not evacuate Jewish military forces and civilian settlements from the West Bank and Gaza Strip under pressure. Jerusalem did not agree that UN Resolution 242, he continued, applied to all fronts. Dayan assured his hosts that Israel would consider any legitimate Egyptian proposal. For example, he said Israel would discuss Egyptian demands that it withdraw from the West Bank, but it would not agree to do so unilaterally prior to negotiations as Sadat wished. [68]

The Israeli foreign minister was convinced Jordan would not join the negotiations. Hussein did not believe he possessed a mandate to speak for the Palestinian Arabs or to offer the refugees a choice between Israeli and Jordanian citizenship. Dayan's conviction derived in large measure from a secret meeting with Hussein in London on August 22–23, 1977. During their initial encounter, Hussein remained subdued, withdrawn, and monosyllabic and seemed concerned exclusively with administering his own kingdom. Dayan also found the Jordanian leader neither able nor willing to struggle with other Arab nations or the PLO over his role vis–a–vis the West Bank and the Palestinian refugees.

A second meeting revealed equal indifference to the fate of the Palestinians and the future of the West Bank. The king reiterated that he felt no obligation to act on behalf of the Palestinians. He reminded Dayan that he no longer represented the Palestinians but made clear that he would do so if asked to by the Palestinians and other Arabs. The king cautioned that he would oppose any attempt to divide the West Bank between Jordan and Israel. No Arab leader, he said, could accept the separation of a single Palestinian village from the rest of its people.

Hussein also believed that not a single Arab living in the West Bank or Gaza Strip would willingly accept Israeli citizenship. The only solution, he suggested, was for Israel to return to its pre–1967 border. Hussein could not concede any portion of the West Bank or East Jerusalem. He did not preclude Israeli access to these areas, but insisted that all territory captured in the 1967 war be returned to Jordanian sovereignty.

Finally, Hussein did not deny that a PLO state would threaten his country's interests and the security of his throne. But the Jordanian leader would take no action, direct or indirect, to steer the Palestinians future. They could do as they wished. He would not represent them. The Rabat Declaration of 1974 had taken that duty out of his hands.[69] These two meetings convinced Dayan that the negotiations should not depend on Jordan.

Carter ended the meeting with Dayan by offering his assessment of the state of Egyptian–Israeli relations. He believed Egypt and Israel would likely achieve a peace treaty if each side exhibited greater flexibility. Any agreement on the West Bank and Gaza Strip, Carter asserted, should last for a period of five years and remain within the spirit of Begin's autonomy plan. At the end of the five–year period, he suggested, Palestinian Arabs should be free to choose one of three options: linkage with Jordan or Israel or maintenance of the status quo.

The United States believed that the Palestinians must inevitably opt for some form of association with Jordan. Carter probably recognized the difficulty of convincing Hussein to join the peace talks, but believed that it could be done if the Egyptians and Israelis demonstrated a willingness to compromise.

The American president reiterated that he considered Israel's settlements program unacceptable, particularly in the Sinai. Work to improve or expand the sites, he stressed, would have to end. Israel would have to provide a clear commitment to leave the West Bank, according to Carter, or the entire peace process could collapse. The assessment was bleak.[70]

Begin was coming to Washington in March, a visit that would help determine whether or not the negotiations would succeed. Meanwhile, Atherton would attempt to keep the Egyptian–Israeli talks alive by undertaking a limited shuttle effort.

Begin Visits Washington

The one month interval between Dayan's and Begin's visits to the White House merely sharpened U.S.–Israeli discord. In

Cyprus, Palestinian gunmen assassinated Yusef el-Sabeh — a
confidant of Sadat and editor of the noted Egyptian daily, Al-
Ahram — in a Nicosia hotel lobby on February 18.[71] The attack
reminded the Israelis of their vulnerability and in part
prompted Begin to reaffirm his government's strong opposition
to Carter's interpretation of UN Resolution 242 on March 4.

On March 11, a band of Palestinian guerrillas attacked a
bus load of vacationing Israelis, killing 30. Jerusalem
responded by launching a week-long military operation in a six-
mile belt of southern Lebanon aimed at eliminating all
terrorist bases in the area.[72] The belligerents declared a
truce, and UN troops replaced the Israeli defense forces in
southern Lebanon only a day before Begin's trip to Washington.

Meanwhile, the Carter administration was fighting for
Congressional approval of a $4.8 billion Middle East arms
package. It included the supply of 50 F-5s to Egypt, 50 F-15s
to Saudi Arabia, and a mix of 90 F-15s and F-16s to Israel.
Vance announced the sale on February 14. Ten days later he
warned that Congress had to vote on the package as a whole,
that the Carter administration would cancel the entire request
if Congress separated or blocked the Egyptian and Saudi
portions.[73]

The shape and content of the sale reflected both Carter's
desire to maintain a balanced position among the parties and
reward allies in the Middle East as well as to place a ceiling
on American global arms transfers. Israel and Saudi Arabia
wanted to modernize their air forces and made requests that
alone placed severe strains on Carter's new policy. But Carter
also wanted to reward Sadat for his peace efforts and decided
in December 1977 to provide Egypt with advanced fighter
aircraft.

The meetings between Carter and Sadat at Camp David on
February 4 and 5, 1978 added momentum to the arms package.
Carter increased substantially the number of F-15s for Saudi
Arabia over the number discussed during the Ford administration
and, to remain within tolerable limits, decreased the number
promised Israel by former Secretary of State Henry Kissinger.[74]
On March 8, Weizman delivered an Israeli request for additional
American weapons designed to maintain Israel's military
advantage in the area despite the sale of highly-advanced
American planes to the Arabs. The Carter administration
remained non-committal.[75]

The debate over the arms sale consumed Washington.
Israel's supporters feared that the sale of sophisticated

aircraft to Saudi Arabia in particular could upset the balance of power and establish a dangerous precedent. Others, including staunch allies of Israel, argued that to refuse the request would signal the moderate Arab states that Washington was incapable of balance and insincere in its professions of friendship. Such a perception would, they claimed, encourage Arab radicalism, set back the peace process, and severely damage U.S. interests in the area.[76]

In the midst of this highly-charged atmosphere, Begin arrived in Washington on March 22 for two days of intensive discussions over the future of the Israeli-Egyptian peace process. The Israeli delegation included Dayan, Barak, Rosenne, Dinitz, Eliakim Rubinstein -- bureau chief for the foreign ministry -- and various other advisers from Jerusalem and the israeli Embassy in Washington. The American delegation featured Mondale, Vance, Brezinski, and an assortment of aides.

Carter began the initial meeting on the morning of March 22 with a statement deploring the March 11 terrorist attack and noting that such violent acts were intended to block peace negotiations. He then reviewed the progress of Arab-Israeli talks and asked Begin to assess the future. The Israeli prime minister complained about what he viewed as Egypt's obstructive behavior since the Ismailia Conference. During the conference itself, mutual respect reigned and an agreement was within reach, according to the Israeli leader. Since that date, he complained, Cairo's insistence on total Israeli withdrawal from the territories captured in the 1967 war and its call for Palestinian self-determination had hindered the process. Begin expressed Israel's belief that Palestinian self-determination would inevitably produce a Palestinian state. "We shall never agree to it," he vowed.[77]

Carter insisted that Sadat was willing to settle for less than total Israeli withdrawal from all the occupied territories and the establishment of a Palestinian state in the West Bank. The deadlock, he asserted, resulted from the failure to agree on a declaration of principles. Israel wanted the declaration to be based on UN Resolution 242. Egypt wished it to include a greater array of commitments than the UN resolution.

The United States offered a compromise the language of which would allow each side some leeway to interpret the declaration as it wished.[78] Although Carter's proposal amounted to an attempt to disguise practical distinctions with semantics, the American commitment to Israel's future security remained firm and specific. Carter believed the parties could reach a solution in the West Bank that for "some interim period" allowed Israel to maintain a military presence there and included the establishment of electronic monitoring facilities and buffer zones patrolled by UN troops. Carter also thought the military issues on the West Bank could be resolved separately from the broader political matters and agreed with Sadat that new settlements in the Sinai harmed the peace process.[79]

The president and Dayan argued over Sadat's apparent willingness to accept less than total Israeli withdrawal from occupied territories. The Israeli foreign minister wondered whether Sadat's stand meant Egypt would accept broader adjustments in the Sinai as well, remarking that consistency would require such a concession. Vance replied that Sadat's position did not apply to the Sinai, and Carter noted that Egypt intended to place Egyptian units east of the Milta passes.[80]

Begin asked why Sadat had not informed the Israeli government directly if in fact he no longer demanded a complete withdrawal to the 1967 borders or creation of a Palestinian state.[81] Carter responded that both he and the Egyptian president worried that Israel statements appeared to imply that UN Resolution 242 did not apply to the West Bank and Gaza Strip. Barak expressed the Israeli view that Begin's proposal for Palestinian self-rule fulfilled the spirit and letter of the UN resolution. Dayan agreed, pointing out that under the autonomy plan Israel would dismantle the military government in the West Bank and Gaza Strip and therefore remove some forces. He asserted that UN Resolution 242 did not require Israeli withdrawal on all three fronts in any case.[82]

Carter expressed the view that Jerusalem's position contradicted commitments made by previous Israeli governments. Begin and Dayan denied the claim, pointing to a Labor Party formula that designated the Jordan River as Israel's security border and excluded any military retreat from that line. Dayan, a military man, maintained that only one question really mattered: "Who will decide if a hostile force has crossed the Jordan and who will prevent such a force from doing so?"[83] Dayan believed that the era of barbed wire fences, mines, and UN sentries had ended and that Arabs and Jews could monitor their own security arrangements without neutral forces between.[84]

The U.S. president returned briefly to the settlements issue, characterizing it as the most difficult problem to solve in the negotiations over the Sinai, before changing directions again. He asked whether Israel would consider withdrawing its defense forces to camps in the West Bank. Begin responded that it might accept such an arrangement, but only within the context of his self-rule plan.[85]

The first day of discussions ended with a debate on the relevance of UN Resolution 242 to the West Bank. Brezinski began by stating that the autonomy plan could be interpreted as a pretext for perpetuating Israeli domination of the area. He indicated that the proposal could produce a solution if it fulfilled the principles of UN Resolution 242 and committed Israel to eventual withdrawal.

Begin retorted that Washington had favored the plan the previous December and asserted that it should therefore have the same attitude in March. Carter interposed that he was concerned with what would happen at the end of the proposed five-year autonomy period. "Will the inhabitants," he asked, "be given the freedom to determine their status?" The Israeli prime minister replied that given the PLO's aggressive policy toward Israel, a plebiscite appeared too dangerous. Carter responded directly that to preclude self-determination for the inhabitants of the West Bank and Gaza Strip would spell the end of the peace negotiations, even if Israel intended to conclude only a separate peace with Egypt. Dayan favored an Israeli pullback in the West Bank but not permanent abandonment of control over the territories.[86]

Brezinski rebuked the Israelis sharply, asserting that Israel's intentions reminded him of South Africa's treatment of Botswana. Begin and Dayan haughtily rejected the comparison, and the foreign minister emphasized that even under present circumstances the Palestinian inhabitants of the West Bank possessed the option of choosing Jordanian, Israeli, or local citizenship. Carter pointed out that Washington, Cairo, and Jerusalem had the power to prevent the creation of a Palestinian state. Begin expressed his respect for U.S. power but maintained that the formidable influence of the PLO in the West Bank would preclude a fair and just election and instead guarantee the emergence of a Palestinian state. A plebiscite in the West Bank would, according to Begin, constitute both a psychological and physical threat to the very existence of Israel.[87]

Carter ended the first session on an angry note. He decried Israel's desire to maintain its political domination of the West Bank and Gaza Strip as a key obstacle to peace and expressed the hope that the Begin government would eventually see fit to exchange political control for adequate security arrangements. In an attempt to soften the outburst, Carter gave Jerusalem credit for its willingness to withdraw from the Sinai.[88]

The second day of meetings was equally tense, Carter began by pointing out that the administration would soon report the status of the peace process to the House International Relations Committee and Senate Foreign Relations Committee. He then described the U.S. position: Washington would not press for total Israeli withdrawal from the West Bank but would support maintenance of some Israeli military outposts in the area; it would not support the birth of a radical Palestinian state in the West Bank; it would oppose the establishment of any new Israeli settlements in the occupied territories and expansion of those already in existence.[89]

Carter followed the recitation of America's position with a set of statements that described his understanding of Jerusalem's position. He pointed to Begin and asserted

> You said: The settlements in Sinai will not be abandoned. You said: The settlement activity will not be halted. Israel is not prepared to undertake a political withdrawal from the West Bank. Israel says that Resolution 242 is not applicable to the West Bank. You said: Israel is not willing to accord the inhabitants of the West Bank the right of self-determination.[90]

The U.S. president concluded his peroration by claiming that if Israel did not alter its entirely negative posture progress toward a peace treaty would not be possible.[91]

Begin responded slowly and with force that Israel advocated a more positive policy than the one described by Carter. For example, he reminded the Americans that Jerusalem had offered to negotiate directly with all its neighbors on the basis of UN Resolution 242. Israel had already offered Egypt far-reaching proposals, he continued, regarding the Sinai and the West Bank, which the White House had described in December 1977 as a "fair basis for negotiations." The Israeli position envisaged a full withdrawal from the Sinai. It left the question of sovereignty in "Judea and Samaria" open to future negotiations. It called for Palestinian self-rule under a plan that allowed Israel to protect its security.

The Israeli prime minister also took issue with Carter's portrayal of his settlements policy. Jews would retain inherent rights to settle in "Judea and Samaria," but all settlement would be carefully regulated by the Israeli government and no new settlements would be established in the Sinai. Begin concluded by urging Carter to present the Israeli position before the Congress in a fair and positive manner.[92]

Carter promised to provide a fair assessment of Israel's posture that afternoon but again expressed his disagreement with Israel's stand that UN Resolution 242 did not apply to the West Bank. He asked Begin why he would not simply state that Israel would negotiate over the West Bank on the basis of UN Resolution 242, leaving the actual details of the solution for the talks. Sadat, he pointed out, was as sensitive about that as Israel was over retaining the "wailing wall." And Israel's unwillingness to remove its settlements in the Sinai was tantamount to refusing to withdraw from the entire peninsula.

The U.S. president asserted that he had sought a compromise solution by suggesting that Egypt place the Sinai settlements under UN jurisdiction. Sadat rejected the proposal. Begin exclaimed that he and Sadat had never discussed any such option, that the Egyptian leader had demanded rather briskly that they be dismantled. Nevertheless, the Israeli prime minister altered his belief that the sole aim of Egyptian demands for full withdrawal from the West Bank and self-determination for the Palestinian people was to create a Palestinian state.[93]

Vance interjected that he had expected the Aswan declaration, which acknowledged the right of Palestinians to participate in the determination of their own future, to provide an acceptable formula for resolving the matter. The U.S. secretary of state also did not regard the Egyptian call for self-determination as a thinly-disguised demand for the formation of a Palestinian state.

The president acknowledged that Israeli plans to withdraw from the Sinai, grant the Palestinians self-rule in the West Bank and Gaza, and adopt a declaration of principles were "courageous and noble" gestures. But the fact remained that the talks in Jerusalem had broken down, and the parties would have to find a common language to reignite the process.

Carter wondered aloud whether the two sides would agree to an American proposal stating that Egypt would not demand establishment of a Palestinian state and in exchange Israel would withdraw from the West Bank with some modifications to the 1967 border. The American leader indicated that his greatest experience in office was when Sadat and Begin had held direct talks without U.S. participation. Begin asked Carter to inform the Congress of that fact. The president responded that he would.[94]

Dayan then turned the discussion to the specifics of Israel's plan for Palestinian self-rule. The Israeli foreign minister noted that the autonomy plan would free the Palestinian Arabs from Israeli army supervision and from the political control of Jerusalem. Israel, he said, did not wish to grant the Arabs control over Jewish settlements in Judea, Samaria, and the Gaza Strip, nor did it desire to maintain its rule over the Arabs. Palestinian Arabs should administer their own affairs. Nevertheless, the Israeli Army must retain the right, Dayan stressed, to enter a town that served as a base for terrorist actions.

The history of Lebanon in the previous decade or of the Gaza Strip under Egyptian control before 1967 gave Israelis little confidence that guerrillas would unilaterally disarm or be restrained adequately without direct Israeli involvement. Who would defend Jewish citizens in the area from attack, Dayan wondered, if Israeli Defense Forces could not maintain security?[95]

Dayan believed that the right of Palestinian Arabs to determine their own future was not the central issue but simply a means to accomplish the goal of Palestinian self-rule. Israel objected to a referendum on the question, for it would only encourage the birth of a radical, PLO-dominated state. Dayan pointed out that the Arab inhabitants of the area could at any time choose Jordanian or Israeli citizenship or local status under the autonomy plan. And Jerusalem did not impede the links between Jordan and the West Bank and Gaza Strip. But practical economic circumstances would greatly influence the final status of the territories. Dayan believed the inhabitants of the area, for example, would not wish to sacrifice their employment or opportunity to market produce in Israel. Thus, the Israeli foreign minister believed that day-to-day experiences during the five-year autonomy period would reveal the best status for the Arab inhabitants of the area. Israel would confine its activities there to maintaining the civilian settlements and assuring their protection. Jerusalem, Dayan repeated, had no desire to exert political control over the Palestinian Arabs.[96]

Carter responded favorably to Dayan's description of Israeli views. He believed that Israel's stated intention to withdraw its military from the Arab population centers and its assurance that it desired no political control over the Palestinians would encourage Sadat. The president and his secretary of state asked Dayan and Barak to remain in Washington to compose a statement that might produce agreement with Egypt. Begin offered no immediate response. But later, after Vance and Dayan failed to narrow the differences between Egyptian–U.S. and Israeli drafts of a declaration of intentions toward the Palestinian issue, Begin told Dayan he would oppose further bilateral discussions. The Israeli foreign minister returned to Tel Aviv with the remainder of the Israeli delegation.[97] Carter appeared as promised before the House and Senate committees on the afternoon of March 23, 1978, and publicly chastised Israel for closing off even the smallest openings toward peace.[98]

Carter regarded the impasse in the negotiations as the result of Israeli insensitivity to Egypt's difficulties with its neighbors. He believed that positive Israeli movement toward accepting a declaration of principles would satisfy moderate Arab states and elicit their support for the peace effort. The hardening of Jordan's position and Saudi Arabia's ambivalence toward the peace process had disappointed the president. But he maintained his faith that if Israel altered its views, Arab opposition to Egypt's gambit would soften. Although pressing Israel to moderate its posture might strain bilateral relations, increases in U.S. military aid to Israel could relieve the tension. Carter knew, however, no one could purchase a Middle East peace, that any solution would have to enjoy the complete and enthusiastic support of Israel.

The American president probably expected his threat to attack Israeli intransigence before Congress to have a larger impact on Begin. Respect and support for Israel had always been high on Capital Hill. But Begin's reputation as an imprudent and unwise leader who insisted on a settlements program opposed by the majority of world jewry tarnished that image among key congressional supporters. Carter intended to soil Begin's reputation further and perhaps nudge the prime minister's government a step closer to its fall. The American president underestimated the extent of internal Israeli support for a tough posture toward the Arabs and overestimated the disaffection of American Jews with Begin's regime.

The Carter administration's strategy of packaging aircraft sales to Middle East nations made ample geopolitical sense. But at a time when many in Washington believed that Israel's considerable military advantage was slipping, it became an ill-timed maneuver to pressure Israel for concessions in the peace talks. Begin's visit to Washington did, however, play a vital role in moving the dialogue to specifics. And Dayan's concluding observations convinced Carter that the Israeli foreign minister's unique flexibility and presence would play a crucial role in later discussions.

In Israeli eyes, the talks marked a new low in White House regard for Israel's security needs. The Israelis had sought to persuade Carter that the complex practical and emotional web that enveloped the Middle East conflict could only be unravelled with care, prudence, and patience. For confidence and trust between Arabs and Israelis would only grow with time, and quick solutions would therefore be unrealistic, even dangerous. The Israelis pointed out that their country, like all others, had the right to protect its citizens and calm the fears of a nation that had waged four wars against terrible odds in thirty years. Dayan observed that the Arabs did have the right to decide their own future but not to determine Israel's.[99]

Begin left Washington believing that his meticulous arguments had fallen on deaf ears.[100] To the prime minister, Carter had moved away from his role as mediator and become an apologist for Egyptian views. A laager mentality had begun to dominate Israel's view of the peace process. The downturn in Israeli relations with Egypt and the United States, however, did not meet only regret in Israel. Serious questions about the nature of peace were being raised daily within the military security establishment and among those on the far right who zealously maintained the right of Israelis to settle where they wished in the biblical lands.[101]

Dayan Returns -- April 1978

Atherton's shuttle between Cairo and Jerusalem to negotiate a declaration of principles was fated to fail in the aftermath of the Carter-Begin meetings. Egypt's reluctance to grant Israel concessions increased in light of Carter's declared intention to press Jerusalem for a commitment to withdraw eventually from the West Bank. Similarly, the Begin government believed that if it modified even slightly its opposition to Sadat's views, it would encourage the perception that Israel had bowed to American pressure. Perhaps more important, nothing had happened to convince either leader's domestic contituencies to abandon their serious doubts about the peace process or reverse their strong commitment to deeply-entrenched national principles.

Under the circumstances, Atherton returned home in April, and the United States invited Dayan to come to Washington for additional talks. Before leaving Israel, Dayan emphasized that he would only discuss the tangible aspects of peace and would not review an endless series of drafts of a declaration of intentions. The Israeli foreign minister arrived on April 26.[102]

Although disillusioned with the results of the Carter-Begin talks, Dayan did not believe Israel should seek to squeeze the United States out of further negotiations, as advocated by some of his colleagues. Some in the Israeli cabinet, including Weizman and perhaps Begin himself, suspected that Egypt was waiting for American pressure to produce results that Cairo could not achieve on its own at the bargaining table. Dayan disagreed. He believed only the United States could convince Egypt to modify extreme positions that threatened to cause a permanent impasse in the talks.[103]

Dayan also discerned nuances in the U.S. position outlined during the meetings in March that seemed to presage future success in the peace effort. For example, the American stance toward Israeli withdrawal from the West Bank envisaged a pullback from Arab population centers, redeployment of Israeli troops along the Jordan River, and maintenance of defensive positions in the territory -- hardly the same as total, unconditional withdrawal. American policy makers also had not flatly rejected an Israeli suggestion that the Palestinians participate in the determination of their future within a framework established in discussions between Cairo, Amman, and Jerusalem.[104]

Atherton began the April 26 meeting at the state department with a review of his latest conversations with Sadat. The Egyptian president's concern about his exposed position in the Arab world remained deep as a result of the lack of progress in negotiations with Israel. He would not enter into practical arrangements over the Sinai until Egypt and Israel reached a satisfactory agreement on the Palestinian issue. But if Hussein and the Palestinians continued to refuse to join the talks, Sadat would discuss the future of the West Bank and Gaza Strip for them.

The Egyptian leader agreed that some Israeli forces could remain in the West Bank and that minor border changes could be made. He demanded self-determination for the Palestinians but within a West Bank and Gaza Strip linked to Jordan, not an independent state. Most important, in Sadat's opinion, the territories would have to remain Arab. He wanted Israel to announce quickly that it agreed to withdraw from the West Bank and Gaza Strip, making only slight border rectifications and preserving limited defense forces in the area.[105]

Dayan responded to Atherton's summary of Sadat's position by carefully reviewing Israel's stance. He was encouraged by the Egyptian readiness to discuss the West Bank issue even without the direct participation of Jordan or the Palestinians. But he noted that if Cairo insisted on an Israeli commitment in advance to grant Arab sovereignty over "Judea, Samaria, and the Gaza District" after the five-year transition period, the two sides would not reach agreement regardless of border modifications or security arrangements. Instead, the negotiations should concentrate on relations between Arabs and Israelis in the area during the transition period. Dayan further argued that conclusion of a peace treaty with Egypt and establishment of normal relations between the two countries could enhance mutual confidence and accelerate any timetable for resolving the Palestinian issue. For example, Israel might abolish its military government in the territories without a formal agreement with Palestinian Arabs.[106]

But Israel would not agree to limit its ability to maintain security in the West Bank or Gaza Strip. Jerusalem would also reject any solution that might require Israeli defense forces to leave the West Bank at the end of the five-year period. Dayan told his hosts that Israel's recent military operation in southern Lebanon, designed to put an end to terrorist incursions into Israel, demonstrated the impracticality of removing its army from the West Bank. Thus, Israel would never give up the right to conduct reconnaissance patrols and enter the territories freely. He stressed that Israel did not wish to interfere with the daily lives of the Arab inhabitants of the area but to maintain access to those territories for Jews and ensure Israeli security. Dayan regarded it as unrealistic to expect Arabs from the West Bank and Gaza Strip to have unlimited access to Israel, while Jews were barred from those territories. Israel would also insist on the right of Jews to acquire land and establish settlements anywhere in the territories. Arab–Israeli differences on this issue, according to Dayan, could only be resolved through direct, frank talks between Cairo and Jerusalem.

The question of sovereignty over the West Bank and Gaza Strip would remain open throughout the transition period. The territories would neither belong to Israel nor to any Arab state or entity during the five years. The inhabitants of the area would administer their own affairs under the self–rule scheme and presumably experience the realities of autonomy. At the end of the five years, the final status of the area would be determined in negotiations involving all claimants.[107]

Vance acknowledged that Washington had earlier favored the Israeli autonomy plan as a basis for an interim solution but asserted that material changes were required to guarantee its viability. For example, the proposed Arab administrative council would only have responsibility over Arab residents in the area, not over Israeli settlements. Egypt would not accept that provision. The Americans also wanted to know more about the practical and legislative arrangements in the West Bank and Gaza Strip under Israel's plan. Dayan carefully avoided providing specific answers, stating that those details would have to wait for Egyptian–Israeli negotiations.[108]

But Dayan did point to the refugee problem to illustrate Israel's contention that a general principle could not adequately resolve the West Bank problem. Dayan observed that Jerusalem would accept the return of some Palestinian refugees displaced in 1967. But any suggestion that refugee camps from Lebanon should relocate in the West Bank would meet with total Israeli rejection.[109]

Vance returned to the question of sovereignty over the West Bank at the end of the transition period. He warned that the Arab–Israeli talks would collapse if the parties could not resolve the question right away. Vance wanted to know whether Israel would state categorically that the question of sovereignty would be conclusively resolved through negotiations at the end of the five–year period. Dayan asserted that Israel would agree only to discuss, not decide, the issue at that time. The U.S. secretary of state admitted that his concern about this issue derived from Sadat's demand to know the final status of the West Bank and Gaza Strip after the transition. Dayan asserted that if Sadat expected the Israelis to hand over the territories to Arab sovereignty at the end of five years, the Egyptian would be disappointed.[110]

The Americans did not allow Dayan's negative responses to deter them and during successive meetings reexamined the essence of Israel's position on the post–transition status of the territories. The visit ended with an American request for formal answers to two questions: Was Israel prepared to commit itself to resolving the sovereignty issue after five years, and if so, how would the solution be found?[111]

Dayan agreed to convey the questions to his government but complained about the manner in which the talks had proceeded. First, he said, his hosts would ask a question, and he would respond. The U.S. participants would repeat the query, and he would explain his answer. The American team would ask again. Dayan regarded the questioning as interrogation and not simply an attempt to elicit information. To the Israeli foreign minister, Vance was acting as Sadat's attorney. Dayan warned that this abominable practice had to end. He asserted that the Egyptians should be forced to submit their proposals as Israel had already done.[112]

The Israeli foreign minister met briefly with Begin on April 30 in New York and passed on the American questions. The prime minister had come to America to preside over a massive rally commemorating the thirtieth anniversary of the founding of the state of Israel. Carter celebrated the occasion with a lavish banquet and other festivities. During the visit, Begin waved all attempts to elicit answers to the American questions and announced that Israel would respond in a few weeks after the cabinet had sufficient time to review the matter.[113]

The Israeli government had hardly broached the subject of future sovereignty over the territories when U.S. Ambassador Samuel Lewis delivered to Dayan a draft of Washington's preferred responses to its questions. Dayan remonstrated that despite its superpower status, the United States had far exceeded its prerogatives.[114]

On June 18, the Israelis gave Washington their reply. It was based largely on a memorandum presented to the Israeli cabinet by Dayan. The Israeli position stressed two points: Five years after the start of administrative autonomy in Judea, Samaria and the Gaza Strip, the nature of future relations between the parties would be considered and agreed upon at the request of any of the parties; and an agreement would be reached through negotiations between the parties. Representatives of the Palestinian residents of the territories elected under the provisions of administrative autonomy would participate in those negotiations.[115]

In the spring of 1978 the U.S. government feared that the peace process was quickly unraveling. American pressure had neither moved the parties to compromise nor attracted moderate Arab nations, such as Jordan and Saudi Arabia, to join in the talks. Atherton's shuttle mission had failed, and Israeli resistance to Egypt's demand for a declaration of principles had solidified. Carter and Vance employed a variety of methods to achieve Israeli restraint to no avail. The Americans had tried persuasion. They relied on the logic of their position and on the fear that bilateral negotiations between Cairo and Jerusalem might fail. Unable to alter Israel's negativism substantially through persuasion led the United States to use veiled threats. Finally, Washington launched a campaign to separate the most flexible member of the Israeli bargaining team — Dayan — from his more irascible colleagues and penetrate Israel's solid shield in that manner.

American negotiators sympathized with Sadat's fragile position in the Arab world and recognized the merits of his position. Washington believed that if only Jerusalem agreed to return the territories to Arab control at the end of the transition period, Cairo could restore its status in the Arab world, and the United States could establish productive relationships with moderate states of the region, including Saudi Arabia. Washington and Cairo could prevent the creation of a Palestinian state. Sadat was even willing to accept a modification of the 1967 border in the West Bank and allow Israel to retain security outposts there.

The Carter administration, however, totally misunderstood the Israeli perception, which explained Jerusalem's rejection of the American–Egyptian posture. Israeli experience, not Washington's view or Cairo's needs, determined policy in Jerusalem. Dayan, for example, believed that the moment Israel announced that final sovereignty would be determined in five years, the transition period would become "pointless."[116] In Dayan's opinion, instead of a half–decade to allow a new pattern of relations and cooperation to develop, a period of constant struggle over the sovereignty decision would result from the declaration. The Israelis were persuaded that if allowed to run their course under the autonomy, economic realities — thousands of Palestinians enjoying either employment or markets in Jewish–run towns — would remain the most significant factor determining what citizenship the Palestinians chose. The Begin government tended to discount nationalism as a determinant of future relations with the Palestinians.[117]

Jerusalem wished to assure that its view of the future of the occupied territories would prevail. The operation into Lebanon and the events leading up to it had deepened Jerusalem's conviction that to turn over the West Bank to Arab control would spell the end of the state of Israel. Finally, although the Israeli government remained generally insensitive to Sadat's exposed position in the Arab world and his difficult domestic situation, it did not discount the Egyptian leader's private claims that his public commitment to the Palestinians was flexible.

The Messenger

Ezer Weizman caught glimpses of Sadat's psyche and intentions toward Jerusalem during two conversations with the Egyptian president.

On February 27 Sadat withdrew special privileges granted to the Palestinians in reaction to the murder of prominent Egyptian journalist Yussef el-Sabeh in Cyprus. On March 15 he issued a harsh condemnation of the Palestinian attack against a bus carrying civilians inside Israeli territory four days before. He was the only Arab leader to do so. The Egyptian president also refused to break off peace negotiations with Israel after the Israeli invasion of Lebanon. On March 27, the first day of an Arab League Council meeting held in Cairo to discuss the Lebanese crisis, Weizman received an invitation to visit Egypt. The first meeting took place outside Cairo in Sadat's residence on March 30-31, 1978.

The Weizman-Sadat talks would take place in the shadow of growing domestic difficulties in both Cairo and Jerusalem. Seasonal fluctuations in the prices of basic commodities had kindled discontent in Egypt. The Egyptian government's subsidy programs helped keep the unrest under control but increased budget deficits eroded the country's ability to attract economic assistance from abroad. The International Monetary Fund (IMF) would not approve long-term investment in Egypt without basic economic reforms.[118]

A growing upper middle class that benefited from Sadat's infitah policy helped fuel further inflation, as it consumed large quantities of imported delicacies and locally grown vegetables. The prices of these products rose rapidly, and new black markets began to appear.[119] The gap between rich and poor widened. The peace process failed to yield even the smallest improvement in the lives of Egypt's impoverished masses.

The government, therefore, began to turn to the rural areas and an accelerated "green revolution" to stave off a possible urban revolution. Yet increasing food output through recovery of desolate wastelands was a chancy and long-term project unlikely to improve the government's popularity rapidly.[120]

Meanwhile, the extreme right in Israel dominated the opposition to the government's peace program. Its members fought the military to establish unauthorized settlements in the Sinai and the West Bank.[121] Sympathetic ministers disrupted cabinet sessions and embarrassed the nation.[122] In response, Begin began to toughen his speeches, statements and policies.

A new movement on the left — the so-called "Peace Now" movement — joined the chorus of criticism. Marches and demonstrations buffeted the Israeli prime minister from both ends of the political spectrum.[123] Begin's margin of popularity, which had recently declined, threatened to plummet.[124]

Yigal Yadin's Democratic Movement for Change (DMC) had maintained its support for the government's peace program in the wake of Ismailia. But Begin's obvious turn to the right and the extremism of the Likud Party's natural constituency troubled DMC supporters who had more in common with the Peace Now movement than with Begin. The opportunity to exert some leadership in the movement for peace if he sided with his partisans tempted Yadin, then still deputy prime minister in Begin's government.[125] The Israeli government found that it could neither control this political ferment nor mobilize it behind the peace process.

Sadat presided over a meeting of the Egyptian NSC in Abedin Palace on March 25, prior to Weizman's arrival in Cairo. The session reviewed five interrelated topics: the situation in the Middle East in light of recent exchanges between Sadat and the leaders of Arab countries, the nonaligned states, and other nations; a report by the Egyptian foreign minister on the recent Begin–Carter meetings, supplemented with comments from the U.S. Ambassador to Cairo and the Egyptian Ambassador to Washington; the Israeli invasion of Lebanon; messages received from Kings Hussein, Hassan, and Khalid; and the Palestinian problem. Mubarak, Salim, Marei, Khalil, Gamassy, Ismail, Kamel, and Ali attended the meeting.[126]

There exists no direct evidence of what happened during the discussions. But the NSC did defer final decisions on the future of the peace process with Israel and on Egypt's stance toward the Palestinian cause.[127] It opted instead to invite Weizman to Cairo for private conversations. Thus, the meeting gave Sadat, who had grown impatient with the PLO and seemed ready to abandon his support for the organization, increased latitude to seek a compromise with Israel.

The invitation to Weizman was a bid by Sadat to recapture the spirit of compromise at a time when support for peace with Israel among Egypt's elite groups had become brittle and economic conditions had deteriorated severely. The discussions in Cairo began on a cordial note. Sadat reminded his guest of the broad opposition within Egyptian ruling circles and among key Arab states to the Israeli defense minister's visit.[128] Weizman accompanied by Barak responded that Begin also had to cope with intense domestic pressure to abandon the peace effort. He assured Sadat that agreement on Israeli withdrawal from the Sinai was certain but warned that Israel would not concede its right to maintain a presence in the West Bank and Gaza Strip. Jerusalem, he said, would postpone its claim to sovereignty in "Judea and Samaria" and would expect Jordan to do the same. Although some Israelis and Arabs would inevitably judge any solution as unacceptable, according to Weizman, the problem of "Judea and Samaria" should not constitute an obstacle to a peace treaty between Cairo and Jerusalem.[129]

Sadat objected strenuously and responded that:

> Even if we resolve the problem of the Sinai, without solving the Palestinian problem, there is no peace. I understand your concern over the West Bank and I know Israel has a security problem there, that it's a matter of life and death for her. But without solving the Palestinian problem, there will be no peace. A separate agreement with Egypt will not bring peace.[130]

Weizman asserted that he understood the importance of the Palestinian problem to Egypt. But he indicated that a first agreement -- an Egyptian-Israeli treaty -- could promote peace. The Israeli defense minister informed Sadat that,

> You have to decide whether you're going for the whole
> game or only part of it. If the Palestinian problem
> has to be solved, then the autonomy plan we've
> proposed may solve it. Our proposal guarantees them
> self-rule. They can find some link to Jordan; If
> Jordan consents to a separate peace with us, that
> would greatly encourage Israeli willingness on the
> subject. You must understand our insecurity. The
> average Israeli doesn't feel safe. An agreement with
> Egypt will contribute to his sense of well-being.[131]

The Egyptian president noted that a separate peace would only
lend credence to Soviet claims that Egypt wished to desert the
remaining Arab states in favor of a secret arrangement with
Washington and Jerusalem. That result "...will serve no one,
neither me nor you."[132]

Weizman asked Sadat to present his own solution. The
Egyptian president asserted that he and Begin had begun to
establish a reasonable basis for peace and friendship In the
region at Ismailia. But he was disappointed in the Israeli
prime minister. Begin could not resist making public
statements about the negotiations and conveying its substance
to the press. Only Egypt had offered Israel friendship.
Israel would have to show its good will by helping resolve the
Palestinian problem. Sadat observed that,

> I must tell my people that I have induced the
> Israelis to withdraw from the West Bank. I have
> excluded the PLO from my lexicon. By their own
> behavior, they have excluded themselves from the
> negotiations. But I can say this only to you -- not
> to Begin because the next day Begin would announce:
> 'Sadat has excluded the PLO.' I have to be able to
> tell the Arabs: 'The Arabs of the West Bank and Gaza
> will be able to shape their future, and the Israelis
> will leave.' I don't care whether Hussein comes in
> or not. The West Bank and Gaza should be
> demilitarized. Any solution must guarantee your
> security. We shall try to find a suitable
> formula.[133]

Weizman asked who would rule in "Judea, Samaria and Gaza." "If
Jordan enters into the negotiations," Sadat answered, "Jordan,
the representatives of the local population, and you."[134] The

Israeli defense minister understood Sadat's response as excluding the establishment of a Palestinian state. The Egyptian president assured his guest that he would support maintaining a small number of military strong points in the West Bank and Gaza Strip guarded by Israeli forces and would oppose a Palestinian state. Weizman summarized: "There will be no sovereignty over Judea and Samaria. Neither Israeli nor Jordanian. And there won't be an independent state, either."[135]

The Israeli defense minister then raised the question of settlements. He stated that they must remain in the West Bank. He himself grew up in a farming community. The Weizman family had its roots in Israel for a hundred years. The healthy Jew, according to the traditional view, lived on the soil. No Israeli government could survive after uprooting a settler from the land. Jews, asserted Weizman, must be permitted to reside in "Judea and Samaria," and the army would have to protect them.[136]

Sadat replied that Israel would have to return to its pre-1967 borders, with the West Bank linked to Jordan and the Gaza Strip to Egypt. In either case, he assured Weizman, Israeli troops could assume an active role in protecting its citizens' security -- "The Palestinian state can wait."[137] Egypt wished to free Israel, Sadat continued, of the responsibility of guarding the settlers through some type of joint administration. But he informed his guest that Israel must announce its intention to withdraw from the occupied territories as soon as the parties resolved the security issues.[138]

Weizman countered that Israel would not even consider total withdrawal from the West Bank. Sadat noted plaintively that "it's enough if you say you are willing to withdraw."[139] Weizman wished to know once again who would possess the central administrative authority in "Judea and Samaria." Sadat again assured the Israeli defense minister that Egypt would not support a Palestinian state. An elected legislative and executive council with Jordanian and Israeli representation could administer the area. But if the Jordanian monarch refused to join in the proposed arrangement, Egypt would take its place. Barak asked whether the council would possess the power to pass laws banning Jewish settlement in the area. Sadat responded that,

Israel and Egypt will have the power of veto over any law. If an Arab is willing to sell his land to you, I have no objections. But you must proclaim your willingness to withdraw. As to the question of sovereignty -- that will remain open. It won't be mine, and it won't be yours.[140]

Weizman asked what the Egyptian president expected of an Arab's daily existence in "Judea and Samaria." Sadat responded,

I agree to freedom of movement -- of people and merchandise -- between the West Bank and Gaza and Israel. If the Arabs want to work in Israel -- let them! The problem is how it will look to the world. It must be seen that you have withdrawn. After your declaration of a full withdrawal, I promise that we shall solve everything.[141]

The Israeli defense minister pointed out the resemblance between the two countries' proposals and wondered why Sadat considered Israel's unacceptable. Sadat noted that "your proposal implies a continuation of the occupation. It makes the occupation official."[142] But Weizman indicated that Israel had specifically declared that it would withdraw its military administration. The Egyptian president carefully replied that,

No one will believe you. But when I come along together with you and say that this will be the arrangement, everyone in the Arab world will believe you. You must proclaim your withdrawal. If Hussein doesn't come to negotiate -- you don't withdraw! When you do withdraw, it will be to military strong points.[143]

Sadat concluded the day's conversation by asserting that he no longer wished to engage in personal negotiations with Begin or Dayan. He regarded both as offensive and too indiscrete. The process, he said, called for trust, courtesy, and sensitive discussions.[144]

That evening Weizman, Barak, Khalil, Gamassy, and Boutrus Ghali blended social chatter and semiofficial business at a soiree held in Tahara Palace in the fashionable Helipolis suburb of Cairo. Barak and Gamassy retired to discuss the terms and venue of future secret discussions. They did not exclude American involvement. The talks would aim to work out the details of a solution for the West Bank and Gaza Strip and of the bilateral relationship between Cairo and Jerusalem.[145]

Israeli and Egyptian negotiators would initial documents at the conclusion of the secret talks. The first paper would contain the details of a settlement for the West Bank and Gaza Strip, including a declaration of intent. According to Weizman, Egypt would then insist that Israel proclaim its willingness to withdraw from the territories, remaining only in specific military positions for security purposes. These positions could include settlements along the Jordan River or the tops of mountain ridges overlooking, for example, Nablus.

Sadat believed that the Israeli declaration would allow him to announce that the two sides had completed a statement of intent, according to Weizman, and to issue invitations to interested Arab states to enter negotiations with Israel. The Egyptian president would then wait several weeks and, even if other Arabs refused to join the peace process, then sign the second paper initialed at the end of the secret talks -- a peace agreement with Israel including the return of the Sinai. Should Jordan enter the negotiations, Hussein would deal with "Judea, Samaria, and Gaza." If it refused to participate, Sadat would stand in Hussein's place and sign an agreement covering the West Bank and Gaza Strip.

Weizman also claims Sadat agreed that existing Israeli settlements in the West Bank and Gaza Strip could remain but that in the future Jews could only establish themselves there by purchasing private lands. The right of Jews to purchase state lands would be determined in negotiations. Israeli defense forces would retain a free hand in responding to terrorist activity in the territories. Egypt would have sovereignty over the settlements in the Sinai, and their inhabitants would become Egyptian citizens, losing protection of the Israeli Army. Presumably few settlers would remain in the Sinai under those conditions.[146]

As Ezer Weizman prepared to return to Israel early in the morning of March 31, smug in the belief that Cairo and Jerusalem had moved closer to peace, Sadat summoned him for an unscheduled meeting.

The Egyptian president appeared tense. He asserted that in the aftermath of Begin's visit to Washington Carter had asked whether Egypt would insist on the creation of a Palestinian state in the West Bank. After careful consideration, Sadat informed Weizman, the Egyptian president had decided to offer the generous proposal presented the day before. Nevertheless, a confrontation with Palestinian representatives from the Gaza Strip on the evening of March 30 had convinced Sadat to retract his plan. The Egyptian president explained that the Gazans had rejected his ideas.

> They want self-determination. At this point Palestinian support is important to us. In view of their opposition, I cannot say that my plan of yesterday is still in force. We have a problem. I know my limitations, and I will stick to it. Now in view of the opposition of the Palestinians, I don't know if I can stick to it. Therefore, I return to the position existing before yesterday: Begin must display flexibility. I don't demand a Palestinian state -- only a link with Jordan. A link with Jordan implies that there is no Palestinian state. That was my view before the peace initiative. That is my view now. There will be a plebiscite.[147]

Weizman interrupted, attempting to return to the previous day's discussions:

> A plebiscite is unacceptable to us. Let us go back to our talk yesterday and my proposal that we conclude a peace treaty with Egypt as the first stage. You are a courageous man. You expelled the Russians, you launched the peace initiative, and you should have the courage to bring it to a conclusion.[148]

The plea fell on inattentive ears, and Weizman returned to Israel dejected and confused.[149]

Although Sadat may well have encountered stiff resistance during a meeting with Palestinians from the Gaza Strip, other pressures probably also contributed to Sadat's overnight reversal. Mubarak and Gamassy remained arch rivals within the military establishment. Sadat had chosen the war minister to deliver the essence of a peace proposal to Weizman on the evening of March 30, a decision that probably annoyed Mubarak. But more important, the generous terms offered Israel could only set back the vice president's efforts to repair Egyptian ties to the Arab world. Mubarak believed that pressure on

Jerusalem to accept a Palestinian entity in the West Bank would help improve those ties.

Sadat's March 30 offer for the first time excluded the possibility of forming a Palestinian state and committed Egypt to enforce that restriction if Jordan did not join the process. Under those circumstances Cairo would become more isolated in the Arab world and risk formal and permanent ostracism. That prospect probably convinced Kamel and other foreign office officials to press Sadat to put aside his latest peace proposal. That same day, the Egyptian foreign minister publicly praised Sadat's wisdom for rejecting Israeli demands on the West Bank and Gaza Strip. Kamel noted that 300 officers and men had petitioned Begin to offer Egypt better terms, ones consistent with the theme that "peace is better than the occupation of territory."[150]

The Israeli peace movement had struck a responsive chord in Egypt and had convinced many that strengthened presidential resolve could produce more palatable terms. The majority of Sadat's close advisers, themselves fearful of the consequences of deeper isolation from the Arab world, probably agreed with that view.

Meeting in Austria — July 1978

Ezer Weizman's second meeting with Sadat occurred in mid-July 1978 at a vacation retreat near Salzburg, Austria, and followed months of political ferment in both Cairo and Jerusalem. The Egyptian government ritually blamed the turmoil in Egypt on the new Wafd Party and on the left, which daily called attention to the regime's faltering policies.[151] Sadat had revived the Wafdists earlier in the year to become the vanguard of a political liberalization effort and to provide an alternative to the increasingly popular Muslim fundamentalists. Sadat both welcomed and expected Wafdist support for his peace efforts, but the decline in the economic conditions of the Egyptian people and the growth in appeal of the Wafd Party offset the benefits. The Wafdists had drawn some of their new membership from the Marxist community in Egypt, and the government thus found it easy to link them with the left — a permanent and vulnerable target for the regime.[152]

Sadat had long identified Mohammed Heikel, former editor of Al-Ahram and a close aide of Nasser, as leader of the leftists, a term often used interchangeably with "Nasserists."

Heikel was purged in April 1977 and remained mostly in foreign capitals. From there, he issued lengthy broadsides against Sadat's handling of the economy and relations with the Arab world.[153] In late April 1978, Heikel carried his campaign to Cairo and urged Sadat to renounce peace with Israel.[154] Two dozen members of the foreign relations committee of Egypt's Parliament nearly attacked Boutrus Ghali during his testimony over the status of talks with Jerusalem only days after Heikel's statements to a leftist weekly.[155]

Burgeoning dissent against Sadat's economic and foreign policies prompted the government to adopt strong measures in mid–May. Sadat removed a key economic adviser in charge of seeking foreign assistance, Deputy Prime Minister for Financial and Economic Affairs Dr. Abdel Moneim el–Qaissouny. El–Qaissouny favored trimming subsidies on basic commodities as a necessary step toward balancing the budget and satisfying Egypt's international investors. By ousting el–Qaissouny the regime intended to signal greater government attention to the needs of the urban poor. More important, Sadat ordered the suppression of leftist editorial criticism and held a national referendum to endorse further repressive measures against allegedly extreme challengers.[156]

The official results of the May 21 referendum showed Sadat receiving 98 percent of the vote, although most estimate that only about 30 percent of Egypt's population went to the polls. With this questionable mandate in hand, Sadat launched a wide crackdown on individuals and groups accused of domestic opposition. The measures included the recall and investigation of some 30 Egyptian journalists stationed in foreign countries for writing what the government regarded as slanderous articles against the Sadat regime. The government later barred Heikel and others from traveling abroad. It arrested and jailed several dozen other individuals -- including many known Communists.[157] Sadat ordered the Wafd Party disbanded, and Egypt's small leftist organization -- the National Unionist Progressive Party (NUPP) -- suspended activity following new government–imposed restrictions on political dissent. NUPP's weekly publication - Al Ahaly -- closed, and the government confiscated previous editions criticizing the regime.[158]

Sadat responded to domestic and foreign disapproval of his crackdown by claiming he only wished to rescue an imperiled democracy. Sadat's moves aimed to create popular will and acclaim for improved relations with Jerusalem. Instead, his severe measures cost him crucial support among the country's intellectuals, the very people who had persuaded him in the mid-1970's to seek peace with Israel.[159] In addition, former Egyptian Army Chief of Staff General Saad Shazli began in late June to attack Sadat's dictatorial methods and ridicule his programs from exile in Portugal.[160] Cairo feared the effect the attack might have on an already restive Egyptian military.

Begin also faced growing domestic opposition to his program of peace with Egypt. The prime minister had suffered stinging political defeats -- first, the selection of Labor Knesset member Yitzhak Navon as the next president of Israel and, second, the decline of Yadin's influence within the DMC.

Yadin was losing control of his party to a faction seeking either a greater commitment to peace with Cairo or withdrawal from the government coalition.[161] In August, the DMC split apart, reducing Begin's majority in the Knesset.[162] Massive protests in Tel Aviv and Jerusalem, estimated to include between 40,000 and 100,000 marchers against the government's hard line approach to the peace process triggered the split. Supporters of Begin's peace policy organized counter demonstrations, but failed to match his opponents' turnout.[163] Moreover, open quarreling among Israeli cabinet officials created a circus-like atmosphere in mid-June around government deliberations on long-term Israeli intentions in the West Bank.[164]

A leadership void in Begin's own Herut Party, caused when many of its members assumed senior government posts, added special poignancy to the cabinet crisis. Since Begin had become prime minister, the party had turned back thousands of new applications, as its leaders wanted to restrict membership in order to preserve the party's ideological purity. Yet despite this boost in popularity, many old-line party leaders relinquished their political duties to enter the government, leaving behind a serious power vacuum. As a result, the more ideological, narrowly based party members such as Geula Cohen and Yitzhak Shamir gained greater voice in party councils. Both were militantly opposed to peace with Egypt -- they would later vote against the peace treaty negotiated by Begin and Sadat. In the early summer of 1978, they possessed significant influence within Herut and therefore on Begin himself.[165]

Weizman, who joined Herut late in his career and rose quickly to become Begin's campaign manager in the successful 1977 election campaign, was viewed with mixed feelings by others in the right-wing party. Many members of Herut were suspicious of his contacts with Sadat. The addition of Barak to the March 30 meeting with the Egyptian president aimed in large measure to defuse their concern.[166] In presenting his views during cabinet sessions called to interpret moves by Sadat, Weizman often sought to enlist the support of Dayan -- his ex-brother in law -- a tactic that only earned him greater mistrust among the Herut party faithful. Many party members openly hated Dayan, as they considered him responsible for leading Israel to the brink of defeat in the 1973 war.[167]

On June 16, the cabinet easily defeated a formula sponsored by Weizman with lukewarm support from Dayan and Yadin that envisaged a moderate solution on the West Bank after the five years of Palestinian self rule.[168] Pressure from Begin and a number of Herut back-benchers stiffened the resolve of most ministers in the face of threats from Weizman that he would resign if the proposal was defeated. Weizman's bluff lacked credibility, because he knew that he would possess little influence on the peace process out of office and would lose the ability to meet with Sadat. Yadin was quickly losing control of the DMC and as a result had lost much of his power with Begin. Dayan, either out of conviction or to avoid increasing his vulnerability within the coalition, did not press hard for Weizman's plan and instead offered his own compromise. Thus, the defense minister's influence and effectiveness as a spokesman for Israeli policy toward the peace process appeared uncertain on the eve of his meeting with Sadat in Austria.

Weizman and Sadat met on July 13 in venerable Foschel Castle overlooking Salzburg. Sadat arranged for the session in order to assure that contacts with Israel continued following the expected failure of a meeting between the Egyptian and Israeli foreign ministers scheduled to convene in London a few days later. Sadat asserted that the stalled negotiations had placed two critical deadlines in jeopardy: the mandate for UN peace-keeping operations in the Sinai, negotiated after the 1973 war, would run out in October, and the first anniversary of his historic visit to Jerusalem the following month could pass without progress. Egypt and Israel would have to make a joint decision to extend the UN operation. Sadat jokingly warned that he might resign from office if the peace talks did not achieve progress by fall, although he confided that his countrymen would not permit him to do so.[169]

Sadat then turned to more serious matters, informing Weizman that Israel would have to make a gesture toward peace.

He wanted Jerusalem to restore El Arish and Mount Sinai to Egyptian control immediately. Egypt would supply the two enclaves by air. If Israel agreed to this request, Sadat planned to fly to St. Catherine's monastery at the foot of Mt. Sinai following Ramadan in August and, accompanied by a single clergyman, lay the foundation for a mosque, a synagogue, and a church. Sadat wished to use the return of El-Arish for similarly symbolic purposes. He would designate the Mediterranean town as a center for future peace talks and invite the leaders of Syria and Saudi Arabia to take part there.[170]

The Israeli and Egyptian officials then moved on to other matters. Weizman chided Sadat for seeking to undermine Jerusalem's official positions on peace by inviting opposition leader Shimon Peres for a meeting. Peres had agreed to visit the Egyptian president. Although he did not approve, Begin did nothing to block the encounter. Thus, Sadat and Peres had held talks near Vienna earlier in the week.[171] Weizman reminded the Egyptian leader that the party in power set government policy. A majority of Israeli voters, Weizman warned, would oppose sharply any effort to split the nation. Sadat could only deepen widespread Israeli suspicion of his motives by resorting to such tactics.[172] Sadat denied that he met with Peres in order to create dissension in Israel. He noted, however, that he would only meet with Begin to sign an Egyptian-Israeli peace treaty. Sadat once again refused to meet with Dayan. The Egyptian leader expressed the hope that Weizman would continue to serve as the messenger between the two sides.[173]

Weizman and Sadat then returned to their previous discussions over the details of Israeli withdrawal from the West Bank, Gaza Strip, and the Sinai. Sadat continued to insist that Israel must leave all three areas after establishing adequate security arrangements. Joint patrols would ensure internal security after Israeli withdrawal. Sadat expected the Jordanians to join in the policing. He renewed his pledge to take responsibility for the West Bank and Gaza Strip if Jordan refused. The Egyptian leader also called for a plebiscite in the territories, denying that the move would lead to a Palestinian state. Sadat believed Arafat would lose his leadership post to more moderate leaders if peace were established.[174]

Sadat then introduced the subject of Jerusalem's future status. The Egyptian president thought there should be two municipalities in the holy city, one Arab and the other Jewish.

A joint council would oversee both. He did not know, however, whether Hussein would agree with his view that Jerusalem should not be repartitioned. But he believed the parties could discuss the matter later.[175]

The meeting reverted to the subject of the Sinai, and Weizman again expressed the Israeli desire to retain the Rafah settlements and a single airfield. Sadat refused to budge on the Rafah salient but did promise to allow Israel to maintain control of the air facilities for two years, after which they would be converted to civilian use. He asserted that Egypt would confine its military presence in the area to a brigade instead of the division Gamassy had earlier suggested.[176] Sadat stressed that the United States must become an active participant in the peace process. He told Weizman,

> Without the United States, we will not be able to reconstruct our country. We need them — and so do you. They will foot the bill for the peace agreement.[177]

Sadat ended the talks with a detailed sketch of the Soviet threat to Egypt's neighbors and described his vision of future relations between their two nations, including the sale of Sinai oil to Jerusalem. A gracious social discussion with Jihan Sadat concluded the visit, and Israel's defense minister returned to Tel Aviv the following day.[178]

The meetings with Weizman were initially intended to provide Sadat with private channels to convey his views to Israel even if they differed with positions presented by Egyptian foreign office officials. During his November 1977 visit to Jerusalem Sadat was attracted to Weizman. The Israeli defense minister was a military man, and Sadat knew that guns rather than butter determined affairs of state in the Middle East. For those reasons, he chose Weizman as his negotiating partner.

The first meeting with Weizman failed to produce a joint Egyptian-Israeli view of peace that would be practical, acceptable to both parties, and likely to improve the Egyptian public's economic well-being rapidly. Mubarak's presence at the meeting and the opposition of other high Egyptian officials helped foil Sadat's plans. The vice president did not attend the second encounter in Austria. To avoid even a hint of favoritism that Mubarak would try to exploit, Gamassy also did not participate. Rather, Jihan Sadat would become her husband's single most influential confidante and begin to assume the role that would earn Sadat wide-spread criticism in the future.[179]

Sadat had only modest expectations of what the meetings could produce, realizing that he might not be able to achieve support for any far-reaching decisions at that time. He merely wanted the meeting in Salzburg to provide some continuity, no matter what happened at the forthcoming London foreign ministers meeting.

But Sadat misjudged his chosen negotiating partner. Weizman's position in the Israeli hierarchy had plummeted. He was disdained by the Herut party faithful, ignored by Begin and the cabinet, and criticized by the general public for his fits and outbursts. And the perceived coziness of his relationship with Egypt's president tarnished his reputation among the more nationalistic Israelis. His show of personal vanity in claiming that only he understood Sadat undermined his rapidly declining support among the military. The left and supporters of the Peace Now movement similarly distrusted him.

The talks with Sadat did not succeed in reducing the natural antagonisms between the two old enemies or in clarifying the motives behind Sadat's new peace moves. Jerusalem never gave the repeated sharp reversals in Egyptian policy proper or careful consideration. Had it done so, it would have discovered sharp rifts between Egypt's president and his foreign policy elite. Thus, the parties merely limped from conference to conference without recording any progress.

The Leeds Conference

After Ismailia, U.S. state department and NSC officials formulated proposals for a new policy toward the Arab-Israeli conflict.[180] Bursts of dialogue between Cairo and Jerusalem in the first months of 1978 precluded a direct, active American role in the peace process. The Egyptian and Israeli inability to reach agreement on a declaration of principles and the resulting stalemate, however, encouraged U.S. policy makers to consider imposing a solution on Sadat and Begin.

Jerusalem had consistently argued that Cairo could not simply reject the Israeli self-rule plan without offering a reasonable alternative. The White House apparently encouraged Sadat to design his own solution to the Palestinian issue and to put it forth at a foreign ministers conference rescheduled for the following month. Carter made this suggestion during an impromptu White House meeting with Marei and al–Baz and in a formal message to Sadat on June 22–23.[181]

In Cairo, Sadat reviewed the matter with Mubarak and Kamel on June 23.[182] The Egyptian president probably preferred to avoid producing an Egyptian plan out of fear that it would lock Egypt into defending Palestinian interests and thus paralyze the peace process. Al–Baz had already told Carter in Washington that a detailed Egyptian proposal for the West Bank and Gaza Strip would be difficult to devise because Egypt possessed no mandate to speak for the Palestinians.[183] Mubarak and his political adviser favored a positive resolution of the Palestinian issue as a way to build bridges to the Arab world and allay fears that Cairo would agree to a separate peace with Jerusalem. But neither official nor even the foreign office believed themselves able or qualified to devise specific treaty arrangements protecting Palestinian rights.

Thus, Kamel merely dusted off previous Egyptian positions. A Cairo radio report blandly noted that new proposals would revive calls for Jordanian control of the West Bank and Egyptian control of the Gaza Strip.[184] The Israeli cabinet swiftly condemned the statement on June 25. Washington contended that Jerusalem had opposed a proposal prior even to its presentation. The Israeli prime minister acknowledged that Egypt had not proposed a peace plan but asserted that Jerusalem could not accept any preconditions to talks.[185]

Carter decided to put an end to the verbal snipping by dispatching Mondale to the area on July 1. The vice president would attempt to smooth the ruffled feathers of Israeli leaders and convince Jerusalem to attend the foreign minister's meeting. Mondale was a long–time friend and admirer of Israel and could expect a warm reception. Although Begin did not want to commit himself before seeing the Egyptian proposals, he finally consented to send Dayan to the July meeting in Britain.[186]

Mondale went to Alexandria on July 3 to receive the text of the Egyptian plan and obtain Sadat's commitment to join in the ministerial meeting. The U.S. vice president probably also sought assurances that Egypt's statement would contain no prior conditions that could torpedo the scheduled conference. Mondale received the Egyptian working paper and, through the good offices of the U.S. Ambassadors in Egypt and Israel, it arrived in Jerusalem on July 5.[187] The Israeli cabinet considered the plan unacceptable but voted on the 9th to send

Dayan to the ministerial talks anyway, undoubtedly in part because of American pressure. Some in Jerusalem, however, detected flexibility in the substance of Egypt's six-point plan.[188]

Ministerial delegations from the United States, Egypt, and Israel assembled at Leeds Castle outside London on July 18, 1978. Vance, the self-annointed host, opened the meeting by observing that the agenda consisted of two proposals -- the December 1977 Israeli autonomy plan and the new Egyptian one. Cairo's program, entitled "Proposal relative to Withdrawal from the West Bank and Gaza and Security Arrangements," contained six points. Its provisions included: A general statement that peace in the Middle East depended on a solution to the Palestinian question based on "the legitimate rights of the Palestinian people" and on the "legitimate security concerns of all the parties." The program proposed a transition period of five years at the end of which "the Palestinian people will be able to determine their own future." Talks would take place between Egypt, Jordan, Israel, and representatives of the Palestinian people with UN participation. The negotiations would work out the details of the transition regime, the "timetable for the Israeli withdrawal," mutual security arrangements during and following the transition period, and the implementation of relevant UN resolutions concerning the Palestinian refugees.

The plan stated that "Israel shall withdraw from the West Bank (including Jerusalem) and the Gaza Strip occupied since June 1967" as well as from the settlements in the occupied territories. "At the outset of the transitional period," Israeli military government in the territories would be abolished. Jordan would replace Israel in administering the West Bank, and Egypt would assume jurisdiction over the Gaza Strip. During this period, Amman and Cairo would cooperate with the freely elected representatives of the Palestinian people who would exercise direct authority over the administration of the West Bank and Gaza Strip in the future. Finally, the UN would supervise and facilitate Israel's departure and the restoration of Arab authority.[189]

Vance asserted that he would concentrate on the similarities between the two plans and avoid their obvious differences. He therefore listed points of agreement: A transitional period should last five years; the Israeli military government should be abolished; representatives elected by the inhabitants should administer the West Bank and

Gaza Strip; security arrangements would be necessary during and following the transition period; Jordan should participate in the negotiations and take some responsibility for administering the West Bank; and Egypt and Israel should establish a genuine peace including normalization of relations.[190]

The U.S. secretary of state then asked Dayan to clarify the Israeli stand. The Israeli official indicated that the Israeli plan did not represent a final, unalterable proposal. If Egypt desired to debate the merits of the autonomy plan and propose amendments, the Israeli delegation would do so.[191] Kamel countered that Jerusalem's self—rule program was too open—ended and reserved many matters for subsequent decision. He wanted the two sides to settle all of those matters at Leeds. The Egyptian foreign minister objected particularly to the Israeli insistence that a decision on sovereignty would have to wait until after the five year transition period. The United States had submitted clear and concise questions on the subject, but Israel had given imprecise and evasive replies.[192]

Al—Baz presented the Egyptian position. Dayan considered Mubarak's political adviser incisive, knowledgeable, and educated. But he was also curt, did not seem to like Israelis, and appeared unconvincing in his commitment to peace with Israel.[193] The Egyptians viewed the Palestinian issue as the central problem. They considered Israel's autonomy proposal inadequate and unacceptable to the Palestinians. Autonomy would not suffice for the Palestinian people, and any arrange—ment concerning the territories would require their agreement. The Palestinians wanted self—determination, and Egypt would not sign a treaty with Israel without solving the Palestinian problem. Moreover, the principles of an agreed solution would also have to apply to the Golan Heights.

Egypt's proposal, therefore, rested on two complementary principles: Israeli withdrawal from conquered territory and establishment of appropriate security arrangements to compen—sate Jerusalem. Thus, a peace agreement would accommodate Israeli defense needs by establishing demilitarized zones, limited force zones, UN peacekeeping forces, sophisticated early—warning stations, open shipping through the Gulf of Eilat, and finally full normalization of relations.[194]

Kamel began the afternoon session by expressing the hope that the two sides would resolve all outstanding disagreements over peace in the territories at the conference. Israel merely needed to pledge to withdraw.[195] Dayan responded by pointing to an Iraqi statement made that very week, promising to wage a fifth war against Israel no matter what happened in negotiations between Cairo and Jerusalem. The Israeli foreign minister thus rejected an Egyptian request that in his view ignored the political and military realities of the Middle East as well as the attitudes of surrounding Arab states.[196] Kamel retorted that Jerusalem should listen to the "voice of Cairo" and not the words of Baghdad.[197]

Dayan proceeded to probe Egyptian views on two crucial points. Israel's foreign minister wished to know whether Cairo regarded Jerusalem's peace proposal as a suitable basis for settlement, and he asked whether Egypt would discuss a territorial compromise in the West Bank along the lines of the 1974 Allon Plan.[198] Kamel responded that his instructions covered only the Palestinian problem and that he could therefore not respond properly to the first question. On the second point, Kamel stated that Egypt would countenance no division of the West Bank. Israel would have to withdraw from all the occupied territories, including East Jerusalem. Egypt would consider minor border adjustments but only on a reciprocal basis. Under no conditions would Egypt accept any enlargement of Israeli lands.[199]

The Egyptian plan called for resolving the Palestinian question in three stages. Israel would first accept the entire proposal at the Leeds Conference, and Cairo, Amman, and Jerusalem would negotiate the necessary arrangements for its implementation within a month. Then, again within a month, Israel would begin to withdraw and the transition period would start. The next stage would entail replacement of departing Israeli defense forces in the West Bank and Gaza Strip with UN troops and the simultaneous election of Palestinians to establish Arab institutions. The Palestinians covered by the agreement would include refugees who fled the area in 1948 and settled in Lebanon, Jordan, Syria, Kuwait, and Saudi Arabia, as well as those then residing in the disputed areas of the West Bank and Gaza Strip. Some of the refugees would receive adequate compensation for lost property -- subject to UN resolutions concerning refugee rights -- in the event that they chose not to return to their former homes.[200]

The Egyptian plan, according to Dayan, would fulfill Arafat's 1974 proposal. In a speech before the UN General Assembly that year, the PLO leader called for an Arab-Israeli state extending from the Mediteranean to the Jordan river in which Arabs would be in the majority. The Israeli foreign minister wondered whether Cairo really expected Jerusalem to assist in eliminating the only Jewish state that existed on the face of the globe.[201]

The first plenary session of the Leeds Conference concluded with an exchange between Kamel and Dayan over the stationing of UN troops in the territories following Israeli withdrawal. Dayan regarded the discussion as irrelevant, because Jerusalem would never rely on foreign troops to protect its citizens. Only the Israeli defense forces deployed along the Jordan River and at key strategic points in the West Bank and Gaza Strip could guarantee safety for the Jews.[202]

The American participants held consultations with Egyptian and Israeli representatives between sessions. Vance failed to moderate the stance of either side or to obtain specific Israeli concessions on territorial withdrawal in exchange for far-reaching security commitments. The American secretary of state hinted that Israel could even become a member of NATO if that would make Jerusalem feel more secure. Dayan appreciated the invitation but regarded it as an unsuitable substitute for Israeli military presence in the West Bank and Gaza Strip. The Israeli foreign minister nodded agreement to an American charge that no security arrangement would convince Jerusalem to pull back its military forces to the pre-1967 borders.[203]

An apparent deadlock in the discussions prompted Dayan to present a three-item statement of his personal assessment of the status of negotiations with Egypt. He wrote the following for Vance:

1. A proposal for a peace treaty which would be based upon the withdrawal of Israel to the pre-1967 demarcation lines (with minor modifications) and the establishment of Arab sovereignty over the areas will not be acceptable to Israel even if such a proposal is accompanied by a promise for security arrangements. Israel's opposition to any such arrangement stems from reason of principle (national) as well as from practical and security considerations.

2. Should a proposal for a peace treaty based upon a concrete territorial compromise be submitted, Israel in accordance with previous statements, would be ready to consider it.

3. If the Israel peace proposal (Self Rule) is accepted, Israel will be prepared, as provided for in two sections of the proposal, to discuss after five years the question of sovereignty (or permanent status) of the areas. Although these provisions do not call for a decision on the subject, it is the personal view of the Foreign Minister that an agreement on this question is possible.[204]

The meetings ended on July 9 amid uncertainty about whether the talks would continue at Leeds or elsewhere. Dayan accepted Vance's invitation for a further round of discussions.[205] But Kamel received no instructions from Sadat, who was attending a summit meeting of the Organization of African Unity in Khartoum.[206] But the heads of both delegations assured Vance that he could visit their respective capitals within several weeks.[207]

The conferees displayed at Leeds their usual unwillingness — or inability — to compromise or alter their positions substantially. In fairness, however, neither party desired to hold a conference. Carter arranged the meeting to prevent the process from quickly breaking down. Nevertheless, the conference achieved limited progress toward refining the basic views of the protagonists.

Jerusalem's foreign minister introduced a novel element into the proceedings — his assurance that Israel would discuss territorial compromise. It remained unclear, however, whether Cairo or Washington understood the significance of Dayan's step. In any event, the parties to the meeting at Leeds all apparently realized that only bold and imaginative American intervention could rescue the peace process.

NOTES

1. See, Washington Post, February 10, 1978. A December 1977 poll registered Begin's popularity at a rating of 78.3 percent.

2. New York Times, January 14, 1978.

3. Washington Post, January 5, 1978.

4. Ezer Weizman, The Battle for Peace (New York: Bantam Books, 1981), p. 143. See, also, Avner Yaniv and Yael Yishai, "Israeli Settlements in the West Bank: The Politics of Intransigence" in the Journal of Politics, Volume 43, Number 4, November 1981, p. 1122–1126.

5. Weizman, The Battle for Peace, p. 143.

6. Nadav Safran, Israel: The Embattled Ally (Cambridge: Harvard University Press, 1978), p. 473; also Eitan Haber, Zeev Schiff and Ehud Yaari, The Year of the Dove (New York: Bantam Books, 1979), p. 147.

7. Weizman, The Battle for Peace, p. 144.

8. Ibid., p. 143.

9. Ibid., p. 142–144.

10. See, Amos Perlmutter, "Ariel Sharon: Iron Man and Fragile Peace" in The New York Times Magazine, October 18, 1981, p. 106–112; also Weizman, The Battle for Peace, p. 140–142.

11. Weizman, The Battle for Peace, p. 142.

12. Ibid., p. 154.

13. Ibid. See, also, Haber, Schiff and Yaari, The Year of the Dove, p. 148–149.

14. New York Times, January 9, 1978.

15. Israel Atman, "Islamic Movements in Egypt" The Jerusalem Quarterly, Number 10, Winter 1979, p. 99.

16. Ibid., p. 97.

17. P. J. Vatikiotis, The History of Egypt, Second Edition (Baltimore: The Johns Hopkins University Press, 1980), p. 414.

18. Ibid. See, also, New York Times, February 15, 1978.

192

19. Vatikiotis, The History of Egypt, p. 415.

20. Ibid., p. 414.

21. Weizman, The Battle for Peace, p. 163–168.

22. Ibid., p. 176–184; also, Haber, Schiff and Yaari, The Year of the Dove, p. 155–164.

23. Ibid.

24. Haber, Schiff and Yaari, The Year of the Dove, p. 167–172.

25. Moshe Dayan, Breakthrough: A Personal Account of the Egypt–Israel Peace Negotiations (London: Weidenfeld and Nicholson, 1981), p. 111.

26. Ibid., p. 111–112.

27. Ibid., p. 112.

28. Ibid.

29. Ibid., p. 113.

30. Ibid., p. 114.

31. Tamar Yegnes, "Saudi Arabia and the Peace Process" in The Jerusalem Quarterly, Number 18, Winter 1981, p. 108.

32. Ibid., p. 114–115.

33. Foreign Broadcast Information Service (Hereinafter FBIS), Middle East and North Africa, January 11, 1978, D–1.

34. Ibid., D–11.

35. Ibid., January 16, 1978, D–15.

36. Ibid., January 17, 1978, D–5.

37. Ibid., January 23, 1978, D–19.

38. Ibid., January 26, 1978, D-4.

39. See Fouad Ajami, The Arab Predicament: Arab Political Thought and Practice Since 1967 (London: Cambridge University Press, 1981), p. 99; Jake Wien, Saudi-Egyptian Relations: The Political and Military Dimension of Saudi Financial Flows to Egypt (Santa Monica: The Rand Corporation) P-6327, p. 62.

40. Interview with William Quandt, Washington, D.C. September 23, 1981.

41. Interview with Zbigniew Brezinski, Issues and Answers, Transcript, December 11, 1977, p. 1.

42. See, Joseph Kraft, "Assad: Keeping His Cool" in the Washington Post, December 13, 1977; also, Washington Post, December 27, 1977; December 29, 1977; also Robert O. Freedman, Soviet Policy Toward the Middle East Since 1970, Revised Edition (New York: Praeger, 1978), p. 281, 242-260.

43. Washington Post, December 26, 1977; New York Times, December 27, 1977.

44. Time, January 9, 1978, p. 9.

45. William H. Sullivan, Mission to Iran (New York: W. W. Norton and Company, 1981), p. 131.

46. Ibid., p. 133.

47. Washington Post, December 30, 1977.

48. See Sadat statements at Ismailia and after in New York Times, December 27, 1977; December 28, 1977; December 29, 1977.

49. New York Times, December 29, 1977.

50. Yegnes, "Saudi Arabia and the Peace Process" in The Jerusalem Quarterly, Number 18, Winter 1981, p. 108-109.

51. Washington Post, January 4, 1978.

52. New York Times, January 5, 1978. Transcript.

53. Dayan, Breakthrough, p. 110.

54. Washington Post, February 8, 1978. See also Jimmy Carter, Keeping Faith: Memoirs of a President (New York: Bantam Books, 1982), p. 308 for discussion of National Press Club statement. While Carter endorsed Sadat's condemnation of Israeli statements and failure to withdraw from the West Bank, the U.S. president managed to wring concessions from Egypt's leader on continuing a dialogue with Israel.

55. Washington Post, February 9, 1978; February 11, 1978.

56. See, Adam Garfinkle, "Negotiating by Proxy: Jordanian Foreign Policy and U.S. Options in the Middle East" in Orbis, Volume 24, Number 4, Winter 1981, p. 865.

57. Ibid., p. 857–863.

58. Ibid., p. 864–865.

59. Ibid., p. 866.

60. Ibid., p. 866–867.

61. Dayan, Breakthrough, p. 115–118.

62. See Harvey Sicherman, Broker or Advocate? The U.S. Role in the Arab–Israeli Dispute, 1973–1978. Monograph 25 (Philadelphia: Foreign Policy Research Institute), p. 74–77; also, Washington Post, January 8, 1978; January 9, 1978; January 11, 1978; New York Times, January 9, 1978.

63. New York Times, January 10, 1978. Finance Minister Simcha Ehrlich predicted an inflation rate rise of 30 percent in 1978.

64. Washington Post, February 10, 1978.

65. Dayan, Breakthrough, p. 116.

66. Ibid., p. 119.

67. Ibid.

68. Ibid., p. 119–120.

69. Ibid., p. 33–37.

70. Ibid., p. 120.

71. New York Times, February 19, 1978.

72. Weizman, The Battle for Peace, p. 274–279.

73. New York Times, February 25, 1978.

74. For discussion, see, Andrew Pierre, "Beyond the 'Plane pledge': Arms and Politics in the Middle East" in International Security, Volume 3, Number 1, Summer 1978, p. 149–156.

75. Weizman, The Battle for Peace, p. 233–236.

76. New York Times, March 31, 1978.

77. Dayan, Breakthrough, p. 122–123; Haber, Schiff and Yaari, The Year of the Dove, p. 176–177.

78. Dayan, Breakthrough, p. 123–124; Haber, Schiff and Yaari, The Year of the Dove, p. 177.

79. Haber, Schiff and Yaari, The Year of the Dove, p. 177.

80. Dayan, Breakthrough, p. 123; Haber, Schiff and Yaari, The Year of the Dove, p. 178.

81. Haber, Schiff and Yaari, The Year of the Dove, p. 179.

82. Ibid., p. 178–179; Dayan, Breakthrough, p. 124.

83. Haber, Schiff and Yaari, The Year of the Dove, p. 125.

84. Ibid.

85. Ibid.

86. Ibid., p. 180–181; Dayan, Breakthrough, p. 125.

87. Haber, Schiff and Yaari, The Year of the Dove, p. 181.

88. Ibid.; Dayan, Breakthrough, p. 125.

89. Dayan, Breakthrough, p. 125–126.

90. Haber, Schiff and Yaari, The Year of the Dove, p. 183–184; Jimmy Carter, Keeping Faith, p. 312.

91. Ibid., p. 184.

92. Dayan, Breakthrough, p. 126–127.

93. Haber, Schiff and Yaari, The Year of the Dove, p. 186.

94. Ibid.

95. Dayan, Breakthrough, p. 127.

96. Ibid.

97. Ibid., p. 128.

98. Haber, Schiff and Yaari, The Year of the Dove, p. 186–187. See, also, Washington Post, March 26, 1978.

99. Dayan, Breakthrough, p. 125.

100. Ibid., p. 129; also, New York Times, March 24, 1978.

101. New York Times, March 12, 1978.

102. Dayan, Breakthrough, p. 129.

103. Haber, Schiff and Yaari, The Year of the Dove, p. 187.

104. Dayan, Breakthrough, p. 129.

105. Ibid., p. 130.

106. Ibid., p. 130–132.

107. Ibid., p. 131.

108. Ibid., p. 132.

109. Ibid.

110. Ibid., p. 132–133.

111. Ibid., p. 133–134.

112. Ibid.

113. Ibid.

114. Ibid., p. 136.

115. Ibid., p. 137.

116. Ibid.

117. Ibid.

118. New York Times, January 30, 1978.

119. Washington Post, April 29, 1978.

120. Ibid., April 13, 1978.

121. New York Times, March 8, 1978; February 26, 1978.

122. Ibid., March 28, 1978.

123. Washington Post, April 27, 1978; Newsweek, May 8, 1978, p. 50.

124. Time, March 6, 1978, p. 34.

125. Ibid.

198

126. FBIS, Middle East and North Africa, March 27, 1978, D1–2; also, New York Times, March 26, 1978.

127. New York Times, March 26, 1978.

128. Weizman, The Battle for Peace, p. 292–293.

129. Ibid., p. 293–294.

130. Ibid., p. 294.

131. Ibid., p. 295.

132. Ibid.

133. Ibid., p. 296.

134. Ibid.

135. Ibid.

136. Ibid., p. 296–297.

137. Ibid., p. 297.

138. Ibid.

139. Ibid.

140. Ibid., p. 297–298.

141. Ibid., p. 298.

142. Ibid.

143. Ibid.

144. Ibid., p. 298–299.

145. Ibid., p. 300.

146. Ibid., p. 300–301.

147. Ibid., p. 301–302.

148. Ibid., p. 302.

149. Ibid.

150. FBIS, Middle East and North Africa, March 31, 1978, D–2.

151. New York Times, May 15, 1978.

152. Washington Post, May 7, 1978.

153. Munir Nasser, Press, Politics and Power: Egypt's Heikal and Al-Ahram (Ames: The Iowa State University Press, 1979), p. 101–103.

154. New York Times, April 30, 1978.

155. Ibid.

156. Ibid., May 23, 1978; May 19, 1978.

157. Ibid., May 24, 1978; May 27, 1978; May 29, 1978; May 30, 1978; June 6, 1978; Washington Post, May 29, 1978.

158. New York Times, May 29, 1978.

159. R. Michael Burrell and Abbas R. Kelidar, Egypt: The Dilemmas of a Nation, 1970–1977 (Beverly Hills: Sage Publications, 1977), p. 17–18.

160. New York Times, June 21, 1978.

161. Jerusalem Post, International Edition, June 27, 1978.

162. Ibid., August 20, 1978.

163. Newsweek, May 8, 1978, p. 50.

164. Washington Post, June 16, 1978.

165. Jerusalem Post, International Edition, May 30, 1978.

166. Weizman, The Battle for Peace, p. 291–292.

167. Dayan, Breakthrough, p. 2.

168. New York Times, June 17, 1978.

169. Weizman, The Battle for Peace, p. 316.

170. Ibid., p. 316–318.

171. Ibid. The summer meeting in Austria with Peres was Sadat's second such discussion with Israel's Labor Party leader. The two had met in Austria during mid–February 1978. See, Washington Post, February 12, 1978.

172. Weizman, The Battle for Peace, p. 318–319.

173. Ibid., p. 319.

174. Ibid., p. 319–321.

175. Ibid., p. 321.

176. Ibid., p. 322.

177. Ibid., p. 323.

178. Ibid., p. 323, 326–329.

179. For discussion of Jihan Sadat's importance in Egypt during her husband's presidency see, Susan and Martin Tolchin, "The Feminist Revolution of Jihan Sadat" in The New York Times Magazine, March 16, 1980.

180. Interview with William Quandt, Washington, D.C. September 23, 1981. The discussions took place at Airlie House in nearby suburban Virginia.

181. Washington Post, June 23, 1978; New York Times, June 27, 1978.

182. FBIS, Middle East and North Africa, June 26, 1978, D–2.

183. Washington Post, June 23, 1978; New York Times, June 27, 1978.

184. New York Times, June 25, 1978; FBIS, Middle East and North Africa, June 27, 1978, D-2.

185. New York Times, June 28, 1978.

186. Weizman, The Battle for Peace, p. 336–338.

187. New York Times, July 6, 1978.

188. New York Times, July 13, 1978.

189. Dayan, Breakthrough, p. 141.

190. Ibid., p. 142.

191. Ibid.

192. Ibid.

193. Ibid., p. 141.

194. Ibid., p. 142–143.

195. Ibid., p. 143.

196. Ibid.

197. Ibid.

198. Ibid.

199. Ibid., p. 143–144.

200. Ibid., p. 144.

201. Ibid., p. 145.

202. Ibid.

203. Ibid.

204. _Ibid._, p. 146.

205. Haber, Schiff and Yaari, _The Year of the Dove_, p. 212.

206. _Ibid._

207. Dayan, _Breakthrough_, p. 146.

6
Meeting at Camp David

Prelude to Summitry: Domestic Context

Impasse at the Leeds conference coincided with renewed efforts by dissidents in Israel and Egypt to unseat Begin and Sadat. In Jerusalem, the clash between the Likud and Labor Parties in the Knesset intensified in part because of Shimon Peres's early July meeting with Sadat in Vienna. But, more important, the opposition wanted to exploit Begin's weakened physical condition and faltering leadership. Labor considered Likud's hardline policies a "recipe for isolation."[1] Begin had earlier derided Peres for his willingness to accept a division of the West Bank.[2] Some attributed the bitter invective hurled by the Israeli prime minister to the effects of medication he took daily to combat his various recurring ailments.[3] Others refused to accept this excuse, believing Begin's irascibility resulted from frustration with the decline of his authority.[4]

Defense Minister Weizman had challenged the beleaguered Israeli prime minister in the cabinet for neglecting opportunities to further peace with Egypt. On July 16, for example, Jerusalem deferred a decision on Sadat's request that Israel return El Arish and Mount Sinai to Egyptian control. A week later it rejected the proposal. What remained of the Democratic Movement for Change (DMC) in Begin's coalition also criticized the prime minister for resisting accommodation with Egypt.[5]

The DMC's looming collapse increased Begin's dependence in parliament on the smaller religious parties of the far right. Israel's prime minister rewarded Auguda Israel, whose four members joined the Likud coalition a year earlier, and other right wing parties by supporting some orthodox legislation they sought.[6]

Liberal Party leader Simcha Ehrlich, minister of finance, was also a target of severe criticism for his inability to stem the country's 40 percent inflation rate. Commerce and Industry Minister Yigal Hurvitz had threatened to resign over the government's failure to adopt reasonable budget cuts. He remained when Begin agreed to support parliamentary consideration of cutbacks. But a round of large government–approved public sector wage increases demonstrated Jerusalem's unwillingness to reverse the trend toward growth in the budget.[7] Despite the price spiral, Begin wanted to maintain government services. The cabinet was sensitive to charges of hostility to labor, particularly because Begin possessed many supporters among the Sephardic community of blue–collar workers. To curtail public services to those least able to shoulder the burden of rising inflation would strangle Begin's largest constituency.[8]

Thus, important segments of Israel's population — the peace movement, Weizman, and DMC — moved toward outright denunciation of Begin's leadership. Others, such as the lower class oriental laborers and the religious right, relished the prime minister's isolation from Israelis they regarded as nefarious and unpatriotic.

Meanwhile, in Cairo Anwar Sadat was struggling to maintain equilibrium in the face of protracted domestic turbulence. The drive in May to supress dissent broadened in the early summer of 1978.[9] The peace process was moving at a snail's pace, and the government's economic policy seemed to benefit only the managers and political confidants able to earn large commissions by locating opportunities for Western investment. The Arab Socialist Union (ASU) failed to spur broad grass roots political support for the regime despite efforts by Sadat to promote new programs and personnel.

Sadat possessed only two options: eliminate the opposition by restoring authoritarian rule and thus risk antagonizing Western aid donors as well as supporters of the peace process, or reorganize the political system in Egypt and rebuild the government party to make it more responsive to the special needs of its presidential leadership. The latter move could help dampen efforts by Egyptian elites to head off peace with Israel.

Thus the Egyptian president announced at a meeting of the ASU central committee in Cairo on July 22, 1978 his intention to form a new political party called the New Democratic Party (NDP). Sadat sought to establish a balance between the interests of the individual and those of society in setting the goals of his party and government. He maintained his support for social democratic principles and utterly excluded totalitarianism, opting instead to revitalize the multiparty system.[10]

The move undoubtedly came as a surprise and shock to a majority of Sadat's principal foreign and domestic advisers. Sadat had wanted to discuss establishment of the NDP at a July 26 NSC meeting but deferred the matter until August 1, largely as a result of disruptive Israeli behavior in the wake of the Leeds Conference.[11] An early NSC meeting would have occurred at a time when Mubarak was in Western Europe to explain the causes for Cairo's rapid estrangement with Jerusalem,[12] and Sadat would have had an easier time manipulating those present. As it turned out, he did not need to. At the August 1 meeting, Sadat emphasized the need to appoint new faces to every governorship in Egypt, revise the constitution, and establish a new committee to evaluate performance.[13]

Khalil had delivered a report on Egypt's domestic political needs to the ASU Central Committee on July 22 that assured him of a prominent position within Sadat's new order. He would replace Prime Minister Salim in October 1978 and assume a far greater role than his predecessor in government affairs. The appointment would reflect the president's desire to balance the military under Mubarak's increased control with strengthened technocratic leadership.

The competent but isolated Coptic Christian community was also a valuable resource in times of increased tension. Sadat gave Fikri Ubayd, a successful Coptic lawyer and businessman, titular responsibility for forming the NDP. Ubayd also had responsibility in parliament for foreign and domestic affairs while deputy head of the conservative Socialist Liberal Party.[14] His appointment to organize the NDP would add to Sadat's team a technocrat whose interests complimented Khalil's, who had the respect of the legislature and business communities, and who possessed direct ties to the Christian minorities.

Preparations

The United States seemed scarcely aware of the internal pressures besetting Sadat and Begin as it sought to rescue the increasingly troubled Egyptian–Israeli relationship in the days after the Leeds Conference. Vance, in fact, expressed optimism over the prospect for resuming bilateral negotiations, despite official Egyptian refusal to participate in new talks without meaningful changes in the Israeli posture.[15] On July 25, Dayan strayed from the official Israeli position advanced at Leeds, stating that if Egypt accepted five years of limited autonomy in the West Bank and Gaza Strip, then Israel would "find a solution" to the issue of sovereignty in the occupied territories. But the formula was imprecise, and the Egyptian foreign ministry condemned it. After a four hour meeting of the NSC on the 26th, Cairo announced that it had decided to expell Israel's military mission from Egypt.

Atherton went to both Jerusalem and Cairo on the 28th to seek approval for a new round of tripartite discussions at the U.S. monitoring station of Um Hashiba in the Sinai.[16] Sadat publicly turned down the offer on July 30, stating that Israel's refusal to commit itself in advance to total withdrawal from the occupied territories made further direct negotiations impossible. He also called on Washington to play a more central role in the peace process, conceding that only direct action by the United States could save the talks from collapse. Washington issued a mild rebuke to Cairo for spurning direct talks with Jerusalem.

Vance had expected to travel to the Middle East to host another round of foreign ministers' discussions. But with the Um Hashiba meetings cancelled, Vance left Washington on August 4 to attempt to save the peace process. The secretary first stopped in Jerusalem, where Begin and a large delegation of senior advisers and ministers greeted him effusively. Formal sessions between the American and Israeli delegations achieved no substantive progress. But in a private meeting Vance revealed to Begin the purpose of his visit to the Middle East.

President Carter wished to hold a summit meeting with Begin and Sadat together in Washington in early September. Should the Israeli prime minister accept the invitation, Vance would leave immediately for Cairo to seek Sadat's approval. Begin accepted the offer and agreed to delay the public announcement until Washington had received Sadat's assent to a summit meeting.[17]

Vance left for Egypt on August 7. William Quandt, the U.S. NSC aide charged with Middle East policy, returned to Israel on the 9th with news of Sadat's enthusiastic approval of the summit, scheduled to begin on September 5 without preconditions. Vance and Sadat had worked out the arrangements during private sessions in Alexandria.[18]

Each party would have a nine person delegation at the Camp David meeting and would be prepared to make final decisions. Many in Jerusalem believed that Sadat had agreed to attend the session only after receiving U.S. assurances that the Carter administration would favor Egyptian positions. Egypt's president, however, asserted that he had merely asked for an American commitment to become a full partner in the negotiations.[19]

Washington announced the meeting on August 8, asserting that it had arranged the extraordinary session "not because the chances for peace are right now so high, but because the stakes in peace are very high and because the risks, in fact, have risen."[20] Presumably the Carter administration feared that Egypt would not renew its UN peacekeeping mandate in the Sinai should Israel continue to resist compromise on withdrawal from the occupied territories and the Palestinian problem. In that event, either Washington would have to send American troops to the Middle East as a temporary measure to fill the void or allow tensions to rise in the area and risk the outbreak of conflict.[21]

Nevertheless, discussions at Camp David would have produced little had Sadat refused to compromise on Egyptian positions advanced at Leeds. Thus, Cairo went to Camp David without a prior Israeli commitment to withdraw totally from all occupied lands or grant the Palestinian people self-determination.[22] The Egyptian stance at Leeds reflected the positions of foreign office officials and other members of the country's elite who remained committed to the Palestinian cause. Sadat himself led Egypt's delegation to the Camp David meetings, while Mubarak remained in Cairo.[23] The seclusion of the American mountain retreat would allow Sadat, with U.S. assistance, to produce a viable compromise on matters involving deep principle for Israelis and Egyptians alike.

The absence of what Jerusalem regarded as pernicious Egyptian preconditions comforted Israeli officials. Nevertheless, senior advisers to the prime minister differed over the correct strategy to pursue at Camp David. Weizman feared that a failed conference would increase worldwide pressure on Israel to back down, while Egypt could always retreat to traditional Islamic positions and eventually return to the Arab fold.

Moreover, a serious and permanent rift between Israel and its diaspora, particularly with American Jews, might result from an unsuccessful Camp David meeting. For those reasons Weizman warned that Israel must avoid deadlock and oppose discussion of Jordanian demands.[24] Dayan, however, believed the future of the West Bank would be a main issue at Camp David and that Israel should alter its autonomy plan to offer Hussein a larger role.[25]

Begin viewed the conference from a distinctly more narrow perspective. The prime minister believed Sadat wanted the conference to produce agreements that would severely weaken Israeli positions. Begin desired to convince Washington that Israel advocated a just solution and had a positive attitude toward bilateral issues. He wanted to prevent a public breach between America and Israel at all costs.[26] Thus, he ordered work halted in mid–August on five new settlements secretly approved on June 28 by a special ministerial defense committee under the supervision of Agriculture Minister Sharon.[27] Jerusalem was determined, however, to resist more than minor adjustments to its self–rule plan in the West Bank and Gaza Strip and continued to believe that limits on Egypt's sovereignty in the Sinai might provide future security protection.

The Players

Egyptian and Israeli delegations arrived separately at Andrews Air Force Base just outside Washington on September 5, 1978 and were discretely flown sixty miles by helicopter to the 200–acre presidential retreat in the Catocin mountain range of northeastern Maryland. They would remain at Camp David for twelve days. The parties agreed to bar news media for the entire duration of the conference.

Anwar Sadat chose the members of his delegation carefully. Kamel, al–Baz, and Boutrus Ghali represented the foreign office. Dr. Nabil al–Arabi and Ahman Mahir, directors of legal and political affairs, respectively, in the foreign ministry provided legal and technical expertise. Ghorbal, Tuhamy, and Kamil completed Egypt's team.[28] Salim and Mubarak did not attend. The former had offered his resignation on August 21 in response to the formation of the NDP, and the latter ostensibly had to tend to the business of government at home in Cairo.

Mubarak had recently returned from Riyadh where he undoubtedly attempted to soothe Saudi Arabia's irritation about the Egyptian agreement to meet Israel at Camp David.[29] He opposed granting additional concessions to Israel and would likely have resisted any compromise on the West Bank. Sadat had to sever the Mubarak–Kamel link to avoid the kind of dead–lock that plagued negotiations at Ismailia, Jerusalem, and

Leeds. Al-Baz and Boutrus Ghali were both able and shrewd, and Sadat needed their counsel and expertise. Cut off from Mubarak, the two would provide less effective opposition to compromise in the week ahead. Sadat could handle Kamel more easily and personally.

Ghorbal became the direct link with U.S. policy makers conveying Egyptian views and helping ensure that the United States intervened when needed to encourage Israel to compromise. Finally, Tuhamy and Kamil performed crucial duties — as in Jerusalem in November 1977 — of arranging face-to-face meetings with key members of the Israeli team. Sadat remained in total control of his delegation throughout the Camp David spectacular.

Menachem Begin similarly tailored the Israeli delegation to fit his own personal and political needs. Dayan and Weizman were Begin's senior advisers at Camp David. Supreme Court Justice-designate and former Attorney General Barak handled legal matters with the assistance of Rosenne. General Avraham Tamir, chief of planning of the Israeli defense forces, contributed considerable military expertise. Israel's Ambassador to the United States Simcha Dinitz, soon to retire, would be a link to the past in seeking to resurrect special ties between Jerusalem and Washington. Begin and Dayan each brought personal aides.[30]

Deputy Prime Minister Yadin did not attend the summit. Associated with the leftist "peace now" movement, Yadin's presence on the delegation would have caused indignation among the leaders of the far-right National Religious Party who might have demanded equal representation. The deputy prime minister also possessed virtually no political power, as the Democratic Movement for Change had recently splintered.[31]

Thus Begin led a seasoned, technically competent, and apparently united group. Weizman had suffered severe criticism in Israel for his sensitivity to and association with Sadat and was therefore suspect to some. Dayan had recently begun to move toward compromise on Begin's more extreme positions on the West Bank. Barak and Tamir were also determined to achieve a reasonable peace arrangement with Egypt and demonstrated complete flexibility in their approach.

Carter's team at Camp David contained many of the individuals most closely associated with the U.S. mediation effort. Vance, Atherton, and Saunders represented the State Department. Brezinski and Quandt were there from the NSC. Defense Secretary Harold Brown came and went. Carter brought three trusted White House aides — Press Secretary Jody Powell, White House Chief of Staff Hamilton Jordan, and Appointments Secretary Phil Wise — and also invited the U.S. Ambassadors to Israel and Egypt — Samuel Lewis and Herman Eilts respectively — to attend the summit.[32]

The president was determined to achieve a breakthrough. His extraordinary grasp of technical matters served him well during talks with Sadat and Begin, both crafty negotiators. Vance, Atherton, and Saunders all possessed intimate knowledge of the peace process. Brezinski overshadowed Quandt, his more knowledgeable Middle East adviser on the NSC. But the Israelis did not trust Brezinski. Most of the guests at Camp David knew little about Brown but considered him valuable to Carter on military matters. Lewis and Eilts were in the best position to decipher the responses of Israel and Egypt to U.S. proposals and interpret their moods during periods of tension. The White House guard — Jordan, Powell and Wise — knew Carter better than almost anyone and could provide him with an assessment of America's political disposition during the summit and the country's likely reaction afterward.

These three delegations gathered at Camp David on September 5 for twelve days of difficult and risk-filled negotiations.

A Clash of Personalities

Anwar Sadat and Menachem Begin met several times during the initial working sessions of the Camp David talks. The two leaders would not, however, come into direct contact again until shortly before they signed the Camp David agreements in the White House ten days later. Carter's own observations and personality profiles of Sadat and Begin prepared for the meeting convinced the American president that Sadat and Begin would likely clash if they met too often.

Anwar Sadat spent his formative years along the banks of the Nile. He had pleasant memories and nostalgia for the simple rural life of his childhood. He revered his grandmother, whose wisdom he admired and whom he described as kind and gentle. He had almost religious respect for his father, who had risen to become an effendi — in a society controlled by the British. At seven, the future president moved to the city with his father and began his education.[33]

The values of the village remained with Sadat throughout his years in Cairo, where he attended secondary school, distinguished himself as a member of the class of 1938 in Egypt's Royal Military Academy, and became a firebrand nationalist officer who landed in a British prison for anticolonialist activity. A devout Muslim, Sadat flirted with the notion of joining the virulently anti-British Muslim Brotherhood. But the attraction of Nasser's ideals and of the emerging Free Officer Corps pulled him away from religious extremism. The early years of Nasserism exposed Sadat to the chicanery and insecurity of political struggle.[34]

As a mature leader and later as president, Sadat became more aloof and reflective, traits that led some to describe him as a visionary. In fact, Anwar Sadat regarded himself as a pragmatist who despite his great self-confidence shouldered the burdens of office with trepidation.[35] He often observed that compromise rather than absolutism and rejectionism could best assure success.[36] Sadat possessed an unusual degree of flair for the dramatic and a certain eastern fatalism. His humble origins often clashed with his urbanity. Anwar Sadat was the heir of the Egyptian pharaohs and a symbol to his people of that proud and everlasting heritage.[37]

In stark contrast, the scourge of anti-Semitism that swept Europe during and after World War I molded the character of Menachem Begin. While a small boy, Begin witnessed the daily suffering of Polish Jews from his native Brest-Litovsk wrongly suspected of harboring German sympathies by partisans of the Russian Tsar. The Russians accused his own father of complicity with Berlin and exiled him from Brest-Litovsk. Dov Begin's family joined him in time near Warsaw after abandoning their home before the conquering German armies.[38] Menachem Begin's earliest memories thus included experience as a modern-day "wandering Jew."

A half-dozen years of moving from place to place within Poland eventually led them back to Brest-Litovsk. There the family lived under a succession of German, Polish, and Bolshevik rulers, as the territory became pawn in the European power struggles of the interwar period. The younger Begin excelled at oratory and at the age of ten received public notice of his talent. Menachem Begin's home environment was intensely religious and scholarly in the tradition of east and central Europe. The elder Begin, a respected timber merchant, had been a town leader prior to the war and resumed his position in the community afterward. At fourteen, Menachem

Begin transferred to a Polish governmental school, where he studied Latin and the classics. Polish nationalism permeated the _gymnasium_. The youngster combined this example of national spirit with his father's rabid Zionism and began to long to participate in the settlement of Palestine by Jews.[39]

At eighteen he had already become active in the youth organization of a Zionist movement formed in Russia. He pursued those activities while attending law school at the University of Warsaw. He served a prison term in the Soviet Union for his political deeds. He then spent a brief period in the Polish Army before assuming command of a guerrilla effort to dislodge the British from Palestine and establish an independent state of Israel there. Begin's parents and brother died at the hands of the Nazis during Hitler's 1941 drive to Moscow.[40] After the establishment of Israel, the guerrilla leader became head of an opposition party for nearly thirty years until his accession to the prime ministership in May 1977.

Despite the differences between the upbringings of Sadat and Begin, their backgrounds did contain similarities. Both men had strived for power for many years. Both suffered personal attacks and charges of incompetence during their long climb to the top. The two men followed a discredited leadership to power. Sadat and Begin derived inner strength from fervent religious beliefs. Neither leader sought nor welcomed advice, and both treated advisers with a certain disdain. Both had wide experience in foreign affairs.

However, their differences were fundamental. The Egyptian president regarded concessions in politics as normal and essential. Israel's prime minister considered compromise an option only for marginal questions. He would not negotiate over matters of principles. Sadat had been taught to view resignation from office -- even on principle -- as an abdication of responsibility. The Egyptian leader preferred to view problems in terms of their wider implications while the Israeli leader wished to master every technical detail and thus avoid an oversight that could later lead to tragedy. The distrust of people and their motives that characterize urban life had left its mark on Begin, as did his encounter with persecution as a Jew without protection. The trust and simplicity inherent in village life dominated Sadat's images and assumptions.

Begin and Sadat were both strong and dominant individuals committed to achieving peace. But the bargaining at Camp David would entail long hours of deliberation during which Begin's quibbling with the most trivial detail would surely clash with Sadat's desire to draw the broad outlines of an agreement. If Carter allowed such a confrontation to occur, breakdown would most likely follow.

The U.S. Role

American policy makers approached the negotiations at Camp David with caution. Vance, Atherton, Saunders, and Quandt had already noted the personal and substantive differences between Sadat and Begin during presummit discussions in Israel and Egypt. They wanted Carter to meet with each separately once the two sides had presented their positions. The U.S. president would act as mediator.

But the opening discussions of the conference were devoted to a review of both Egyptian and Israeli positions on the major unresolved issues. Carter, Sadat, and Begin met three times during September 6–7 but emerged from the meetings further apart than before. Sadat opened with an eleven-page document that expressed extremist views on Israeli withdrawal from the occupied territories, transfer of authority in the West Bank and Gaza Strip to Palestinian rule, and redivision of Jerusalem.[41] Begin responded the following morning with a pointed rejection of Egypt's proposal and took a hard line on the issue of dismantling settlements in the Sinai.[42] The group's third and final tripartite meeting in the afternoon of September 7 achieved no progress.

The stridency and lack of movement that marked the joint meetings convinced the Americans to embrace the suggestion of an Israeli participant that no further direct meetings take place between Begin and Sadat.[43] Egyptian and Israeli aides conducted the joint negotiations instead, and Carter would meet with Sadat and Begin individually. The United States also decided that it could only break the deadlock by offering its own proposal.[44]

The American delegation prepared a draft proposal and presented it first to the Israeli team on the afternoon of September 10. It focused on the issues concerning the future of the West Bank and Gaza Strip. According to the plan, talks to determine final status of the territories, including borders and Palestinian participation, would commence during a three-year transition at the end of which a plebiscite would be held.

A Palestinian self-governing authority would replace Israeli military administration of the West Bank and Gaza Strip during the transition. Jordan would play a special role in the West Bank, and Israel would not be allowed to add settlements or expand existing ones in the area. The preamble stressed that "the acquisition of territories by force cannot be accepted."[45]

The United States formulated its plan following several days of discussion with members of Israel's delegation to better understand their views on withdrawal from the West Bank and resettlement of refugees. Dayan, for example, was asked about the practical problems and implications of resettling Palestinians in the West Bank.[46] Weizman was queried as to how Israel planned to redeploy its forces in the West Bank and Gaza Strip after abolishing the military government there.[47] The Americans also asked Barak and Rosenne to explain what Israel would consider the source of authority in the territories under an agreement and to help devise language that would commit Israel to withdraw but would not require total removal of forces.[48]

Although Carter wanted an immediate Israeli response to the American plan, Begin insisted that his delegation needed time to give the elaborate proposal careful consideration before replying. The Israeli party considered the plan a first draft. Thus it concentrated on devising a new formula that would bridge the gap between incompatible Egyptian and Israeli views.[49] The delay in receiving the Israeli response forced cancellation of a planned discussion between Carter and Sadat.

Earlier during the conference the American delegation had criticized Israeli positions on four issues: settlements, sovereignty in the West Bank and Gaza Strip, the source of authority in the territories after Israeli withdrawal, and the implementation of UN Resolution 242 calling for withdrawal from territories conquered in 1967.[50] Carter now began to press his views on the Israelis as he debated the U.S. proposal with Begin late into the evening of September 10. The U.S. president wished to discuss the national rights of Palestinians, including the freedom of self-determination. He further advised Begin that Israel would have to stop creating new settlements in the West Bank and remove those in the Sinai.

The U.S. leader stressed most firmly, however, that Israel would have to accept the clause in the U.S. proposal's preamble condemning "acquisition of territory by force." Carter achieved agreement only over his suggestion that Israeli military units should remain somewhere in the West Bank through and beyond a five-year transition period.[51]

Begin ruled out any mention of legitimate rights of Palestinians for fear that it would amount to the first step toward statehood. Similarly, Israel's prime minister refused to limit Israeli settlements activities or to eliminate enclaves already in place. The Israeli team also refused to accept the clause condemning the acquisition of territory by force, asserting that it might be subsequently used as an excuse to dislodge the Israelis from the Golan Heights. Retention of the air fields in the Sinai remained a serious objective of the Israeli delegation, although some members expressed interest in a suggestion that Washington take control of the facilities for training purposes while Israel constructed alternative bases in the Negev.[52]

After receiving a written Israeli response to his plan during the morning of September 11, Carter spoke to Sadat. The U.S. president, as expected, received an immediate negative reply from the Egyptian leader on each Israeli comment. Sadat was particularly angry over Begin's insistence on retaining the Sinai settlements and airfields and threatened to leave the conference. The Egyptian president agreed to separate discussion of the West Bank from talks on the Sinai. But Sadat added a new element to Egyptian demands by calling for the deployment of Egyptian Army units in the Gaza Strip and West Bank pending final disposition of the territories.[53]

Carter then spent the afternoon meeting privately with various members of the Israeli delegation hoping to stimulate greater willingness to compromise. Carter reminded Weizman and Tamir that the Egyptian president would not -- could not -- permit any Israeli presence in the Sinai following its return to Egyptian control.[54] The American president made similar comments to Dayan and Barak.[55] The Israeli foreign minister flatly rejected Sadat's proposal to place Egyptian military units in the West Bank and Gaza Strip.[56] Carter attempted to resolve the dispute over the airfields in the Sinai by proposing that Israel maintain control of one base for three years and that the second serve as a trade and tourist link between Egypt and Jordan.[57]

Carter spent the entire day of September 12 moving between delegations in an effort to fashion an acceptable solution for the Sinai.[58] He was undoubtedly aware of Dayan's belief that the conference would soon collapse and of the Israeli foreign minister's plan to return to Israel as a result.[59] Carter therefore accepted Begin's request for a private meeting that evening in order to lighten the somber mood permeating the Israeli delegation.[60]

The two leaders met at 8 p.m. in Carter's cabin and began the discussion with the most divisive issue separating the two sides -- territorial compromise. The president noted that the majority of respondents in recent Israeli polls supported territorial compromise. Begin questioned the validity of public opinion surveys and vowed not to alter his opposition. The prime minister then threatened to publicize the differences between Egyptian and Israeli views unless American participation in the conference became more evenhanded. Carter responded that he did not wish to favor either side and offered to delete from the preamble language prohibiting under all circumstances the retention of areas by force. The president also reiterated support in principle for continued Israeli military presence in the West Bank. In return, Begin agreed that after the five-year period the parties would "decide" rather than merely "consider" the future of the West Bank.[61]

Carter returned to his proposal to separate the negotiations on the West Bank and Gaza Strip issues from those relating to the Sinai. Begin approved the idea, as Sadat had earlier. Begin and Sadat agreed to name a single representative from each delegation to meet with Carter and establish the basis for negotiating two separate agreements that would nevertheless be linked in some fashion. Al-Baz represented Egypt and Barak stood for Israel in the meetings that began the next day.[62]

Carter had worked hard beforehand to construct a draft Sinai agreement that envisaged Israeli withdrawal and restoration of Egyptian control in stages. He produced a remarkable document delineating demilitarized zones and assigning specific timing -- within hours -- to each phase. Except for minor modifications the plan received Sadat's enthusiastic approval.[63]

The Carter-al-Baz-Barak discussions therefore sought to address the more fundamental unresolved issues -- the Sinai settlements, the future role of Palestinians under Begin's autonomy plan or an alternative, the relevance of UN Resolution 242 to the West Bank, Jordan's relationship to the area, and the status of Jerusalem.[64] During a meeting on the evening of the 13th the Egyptian and Israeli representatives made a list of the matters the two sides had resolved and those they had not. They included all points even those involving seemingly unalterable principles, such as Jerusalem.[65]

Late that night, Carter achieved agreement on an amended draft of the American proposal submitted three days earlier. The new version contained concessions made by both sides during the twenty-four hours of laborious negotiations with the American president. Toward the end of the night of talks, Carter attempted once again to achieve agreement on the Sinai settlements. Begin again rebuffed Carter's effort.[66]

Despite the day's achievements, Carter worried through the night about the lack of real progress toward narrowing the differences in perception or policy between Egyptians and Israelis. The Egyptians had informed him that Sadat intended to leave the conference within a day or two; Dayan had delayed his departure only temporarily. The U.S. president therefore rose at dusk on September 14 and summoned Brezinski and others to review options that might revive the efforts to resolve the remaining issues.[67]

Carter called Dayan and Barak to his cabin in mid-morning and the group, later joined by Weizman, discussed the impasse over the Sinai settlements. Carter expressed his belief that the meeting would end without further progress if that issue remained unresolved.[68] During a morning stroll Carter persuaded Sadat to remain at Camp David for a few more days as a personal favor. The Egyptian agreed but repeated, as he did that afternoon during soliloquies before Dayan and Weizman, that he would not sign any agreement that did not guarantee total Israeli evacuation of the Sinai settlements.[69]

Meanwhile, the Israelis had not yet expressed their views on the redrafted American plan, and Vance went to Begin's cabin to receive his formal response. The prime minister expressed his disappointment and feeling of betrayal over language describing the eventual Palestinian role in the West Bank and Gaza Strip. To Begin, the new formulations favored the eventual establishment of a Palestinian state. The United States had earlier pledged to oppose that very development. The Israeli prime minister also complained that the new wording retreated from earlier positions approved by both Americans and Israelis at Camp David and elsewhere. Vance agitatedly conceded that the Egyptians had rejected some of the points agreed to by Carter and Begin.[70]

Barak outlined additional areas of the U.S. plan the Israeli delegation considered unacceptable, including proposals to hold a referendum in the West Bank and Gaza Strip and to create a Palestinian government there.[71] Carter, eager for a briefing on Israeli attitudes toward the American proposal, called Vance out of the meeting. Before going, Vance asked the Israelis to review their position further, and Begin agreed to instruct members of his delegation to search for new alternatives. Fears that the conference might have to end without an agreement increased.[72]

Harold Brown arrived at Camp David on September 15 to help bolster America's sagging fortunes and focus on the practicalities of Israeli military withdrawal from the Sinai. Brown met with Weizman to discuss the possibility of replacing the Sinai airfields with ones the United States would build for Israel in the Negev.[73]

During a meeting in Carter's cabin the Americans informed Dayan that they had begun preparations to conclude the conference on the 17th and, if no agreement was achieved by then, to report the reasons for the failure to Congress and the media the following day. In this manner, the Americans warned Dayan that Israel would be blamed in the event of a total impasse.[74]

Meanwhile, Sadat advised Vance that Egyptian concessions would have to be renegotiated in the future if the meeting collapsed. In a subsequent conversation with Egypt's president, Carter acknowledged that each party's position would become moot if the conference failed to resolve disputed matters.[75]

In addition to gaining Sadat's agreement to extend his stay at Camp David, Carter extracted a key concession from the Egyptian president: Cairo would agree to drop the provision condemning the acquisition of territory by force and instead rest its position on UN Resolution 242 and the Aswan formula of January 1978.[76] Armed with that significant compromise, Carter now sought an Israeli concession on the Sinai settlements. The Israeli prime minister seemingly already had decided to back down as he quickly agreed to submit the matter to the Knesset and abide by its judgment although he opposed giving up the settlements.[77] He promised that he would not invoke party discipline during the Knesset debate. He also agreed to give up the Sinai airfields and to include mention of "legitimate rights of the Palestinian people" in the framework agreement. Begin stressed, however, the Israeli consent to the language did not in any way imply acceptance of Palestinian statehood.[78]

The sudden breakthrough nearly collapsed within hours when the Israelis discovered that Carter had promised Sadat a letter declaring U.S. recognition of East Jerusalem as occupied territory. The entire Israeli delegation rejected the implication of the American position and threatened to return home immediately. Carter rushed to save the situation and, together with legal representatives of all three delegations, arranged a settlement. Begin and Sadat would prepare public statements for Carter detailing their differing positions on Jerusalem. The American leader would then respond to each side, mentioning America's traditional posture as outlined in the United Nations by successive U.S. representatives.[79]

The glare of publicity awaited the three leaders as they arrived at the White House by helicopter and participated in an official ceremony to sign the Camp David Accords. Months of frustrating, erratic, and sometimes conterproductive behavior on the part of all parties would follow, as they struggled to conclude a peace treaty between Israel and Egypt. But on the evening of September 17, in the glow of success, the difficulties ahead were far from anyone's mind.

The Issues

The Camp David Accords demanded enormous skill on the part of all those involved in the negotiations. The talks would have achieved nothing had the participants not demonstrated the will and ability to move away from extreme opening positions and seek compromise on the issues that sharply divided them.

Sadat began the conference on September 6 by presenting the text of a proposal entitled "Framework for the Comprehensive Peace Settlement of the Middle East Problem." It contained an eight-clause preamble and two major articles. The plan's major provisions included:

o withdrawal of Israel to international boundaries and armistice lines -- the pre-1967 borders -- in the Sinai, the Golan Heights, the West Bank, and Jerusalem with only minor modifications;

o removal of Israeli settlements from the occupied territories;

o supervision of the administration of the West Bank by Jordan and of the Gaza Strip by Egypt "with the collaboration of the elected representatives of the Palestinian people..." at the end of a period not to exceed five years;

o establishment of a national entity for the Palestinian people -- linked to Jordan if the inhabitants so choose — after they have exercised their right of self-determination six months prior to the end of the interim period;

o recognition of the right of Palestinian refugees to return or to receive compensation in accordance with UN resolutions;

o formation of a committee composed of equal numbers of Palestinians and Israelis in Jerusalem to administer the city;

o implementation of these points within a framework of peace recognizing the principles of "non-acquisition of territory by war;

o finally, payment by Israel of full compensation for all damages caused by the operations of its armed forces and the exploitation of natural resources in the occupied territories.[80]

Begin found Egypt's proposal repugnant, observing that it would lead to a Palestinian state.[81] The Egyptian president acknowledged that his plan envisaged the establishment of a national entity for the Palestinians but suggested that the entity would be inextricably linked to Jordan.[82] The Israeli prime minister ignored the distinction and noted that under Egypt's proposal the Jewish state would revert to its 1949 borders including redivision of Jerusalem.[83] The two leaders exchanged charges and countercharges, as each considered his country as the aggrieved party in previous conflicts and therefore as the one that deserved compensation. The meeting ended on that bitter note. It was clear that the conference would result in an impasse unless the two sides agreed to compromise on fundamental issues such as the future role of Palestinians in the West Bank and elimination of Israeli settlements and airfields in the Sinai.

Most Israelis and Americans wondered why Sadat had put forth a document so obviously unacceptable and whether he was prepared to modify it in return for suitable compromises from Jerusalem. The tone and wording of the plan did not seem consistent with Sadat's previous public and private declarations. It surprised even Carter.[84]

The September 6 Egyptian proposal appeared almost immediately in the Cairo papers, suggesting that Sadat wished to elicit a favorable response in the Arab press.[85] The document resembled closely the one presented at Leeds by the foreign office officials. Both proposals called for Israeli withdrawal from the West Bank and Gaza Strip — including Jerusalem — the end of Israel's military government in the territories, supervision of the liberated areas by Egyptian and Jordanian authorities, and establishment of a Palestinian entity selected by the inhabitants of the area at end of a five-year transition period.

The Camp David version, however, exceeded the Leeds proposal by focusing on all occupied territories, not just the West Bank and Gaza Strip. The September 6 document also envisaged no serious role for the United Nations. It placed special emphasis on the settlements, particularly those in the Sinai, and in emotional terms demanded that Israel pay reparations for its past military transgressions. Sadat's Camp David plan would have granted Palestinian refugees the right to return to their former homes or receive adequate monetary compensation, a condition not included in the Leeds plan but discussed during debate there.

To attribute Egypt's initial position at Camp David only to Sadat's political need to placate the foreign office officials by remaining consistent with positions offered at Leeds would be simplistic and misleading. Sadat had his own carefully prepared agenda that coincided with his need to protect himself against harsh criticism at home during initial stages of the conference. Sadat wanted above all to arrange for the unconditional return of the Sinai, including the Rafah settlements and adjacent airport facilities. Neither threats nor personal pleading with Weizman in previous negotiations had achieved this objective. Thus, Sadat may have calculated that an extreme opening position would provide him with bargaining chips.

The tactic could only work, of course, if Sadat intended to compromise. The demand that Israel pay damages for the destruction of previous wars was preposterous and easy to withdraw if Begin appeared ready for serious negotiations. Although most other provisions of Sadat's plan had some validity, they too contained unacceptable aspects probably intended as bargaining tools in the effort to regain the Sinai settlements and airfields. Egypt's claim to a role in the administration of the Gaza Strip, however, was nearly sacrosanct. For this issue, like the Sinai settlements, involved a question of Egyptian sovereignty — Egypt had lost the area in the 1967 war. To abandon any claim to at least a role in the area, therefore, might severely undermine Sadat's authority in Cairo.

The Israelis feared that Sadat may have composed such a harsh program to ensure the collapse of negotiations and allow him to cast Jerusalem as the culprit.[86] Begin ordered his aides to prepare a set of meticulously reasoned, positive counterproposals, although Dayan convinced him to withhold them until the delegation had had a chance to assess the situation more carefully. Otherwise, both Egyptians and Americans might misinterpret the Israeli response as a form of ultimatum.[87]

Carter regarded the Egyptian statement as needlessly provocative but sympathized with some of Sadat's arguments.[88] The American delegation, therefore, searched for compromise that would modify the Israeli position on several matters. Vance and Brezinski, unfortunately, failed to grasp Sadat's priorities and during early bilateral discussions with Begin accorded equal treatment to achieving a freeze of Israeli settlement activity on the West Bank and to eliminating the Sinai settlements. The Israeli prime minister avoided the issue, pointing out the historical differences behind the settlements in the two areas.[89] Begin then chided Carter for failing to achieve an agreement with Egypt that would bring the Sinai settlements under the control of a third-party, such as the United Nations.[90] But Sadat, during the final meetings between heads-of-governments on the 7th, emphasized that the removal of Israeli settlements and airbases from the Sinai was a matter of deep principle upon which he could not compromise. Any agreement that did not provide for their evacuation would threaten his leadership and place Egypt "under the influence of the extremists."[91]

Begin's demur was attenuated somewhat by Carter's appraisal that if the Sinai settlements became the sole obstacle to an accord at Camp David the final decision on their fate -- and therefore on the fate of the accord itself -- could be placed in the hands of the Knesset.[92] The Israeli prime minister believed even then that a majority of the Israeli legislature would oppose renouncing control of the Sinai settlements.[93] The indication that Carter was actively probing for the outlines of a solution in the first days of the conference encouraged Sadat, even though the American leader had misread the significance to Egypt of the Sinai settlements issue.

A private meeting among Sadat, Weizman, and Tamir on the 8th did little to dispel the Israeli belief that the Egyptian president's tough performance of the previous day presaged a difficult and perhaps fruitless conference. Sadat rejected a proposal by Weizman to link the Rafah Salient to the Gaza Strip, thereby allowing the IDF to protect the settlements on Egyptian soil following Israeli withdrawal. The Egyptian leader asked.

> How can I show my face before the other Arab states
> if that is the price I pay for peace? I refuse to
> have settlements with Israeli protection! I will not
> be able to receive my peoples' consent, and I cannot
> consent, either, because whoever succeeds me will
> blame me for my consent. This will cause problems
> between us in the future.[94]

Sadat also advised Weizman that Israel would have to evacuate Etzion and Etam airfields within two years. The Egyptian president was committed to achieving a step-by-step Israeli withdrawal from the Sinai Peninsula, with the first phase encompassing the territory within the El-Arish–Ras Mohammed line. In return for regaining the entire Sinai, Egypt would grant Israel full recognition, free passage for its ships through the Tiran waterway, and other such incentives. How far Sadat would, however, allow diplomatic and commercial relations between Egypt and Israel to develop would depend on Begin's willingness to make the concessions necessary for a broader peace.

He believed that neither Israeli nor Jordanian claims to sovereignty over the West Bank were persuasive. He therefore suggested that the area ultimately belonged only to its population, although Israeli military forces should be allowed to remain at least through the interim period. After the transition the parties would renegotiate military arrangements there. Sadat expressed confidence that King Hussein would finally join the peace process but offered to take Jordan's place in the West Bank and Gaza Strip and, if necessary, to station Egyptian forces there.[95]

The Egyptian president's businesslike manner during the brief weekend meeting surprised Weizman. The Egyptian president was unsparing in his criticism of what he considered Begin's inflexibility. But to Weizman Sadat appeared determined to secure agreement. Israel would only have to satisfy minimum conditions, in particular eliminate the settlements and airfields from the Sinai.[96]

Nevertheless, the American proposal submitted on September 10 centered on the West Bank and Gaza Strip. It emphasized the Palestinian problem because Washington viewed the issue as the key to an accord. Egyptian foreign office representatives repeatedly stressed in private and public meetings prior to Camp David that a framework agreement must cover Palestinian self-determination. In his opening statement and during the three unsuccessful sessions with Begin, Sadat repeatedly called for the establishment of a Palestinian entity linked to Amman. Al-Baz and Kamel never failed to mention the importance of the Palestinian issue when discussing Egyptian positions during ministerial conversations with American delegates at Camp David. Perhaps most crucial, the United States wished to fashion an agreement that would attract moderate Arab states such as Saudi Arabia and Jordan.

The Americans did not know, however, that Sadat wanted above all to restore Egyptian honor and sovereignty over the Sinai. To do so he would alternately have to placate and undercut domestic opponents who preferred to sacrifice Western economic ties and the prospect of peace to strengthen relations with the Muslim world.

The U.S. document unnecessarily alarmed and angered the Israelis. The Israeli negotiators had problems with the plan's treatment of four issues: Settlements, sovereignty in the West Bank and Gaza Strip, source of authority in the territories after the transition period, and withdrawal from lands acquired in 1967 covered by UN Resolution 242. The plan damaged American credibility with Israel as an unbiased mediator. Some in the Israeli delegation -- particularly Dayan -- regarded the United States as a frivolous power that possessed only a superficial grasp of Middle East <u>Realpolitik</u>.[97]

The most controversial clauses in Carter's September 10 proposal dealt with issues concerning the West Bank and Gaza Strip that most divided Egypt and Israel. The American formulations seemed to tilt heavily toward Egyptian positions. For example, the Begin autonomy plan called for the election of an eleven-member Palestinian administrative council to serve for four years. At the conclusion of the fifth year, the parties would negotiate procedures for settling sovereign claims to the territories. The American plan called for negotiations over the final status of the West Bank and Gaza Strip to begin within three years. Israel wanted an elected Palestinian administrative council to oversee the area's affairs. The Americans would allow the local residents to vote

on what sort of self-administration they desired. Under the
U.S. program, the self-governing authority would operate within
the bounds of some still undetermined relationship with Arab
neighbors, instead of drawing powers from the existing Israeli
military administration. The Israeli delegation reserved
special opprobrium for Carter's suggestion that the inhabitants
of the area should approve the final disposition of the
territories through a plebiscite at the end of the five year
transition.[98]

The Israeli team would not accept any formula that might
be interpreted as granting Palestinian self-determination or
statehood. Instead, the Israelis believed the future of
Palestinian Arabs residing in the West Bank and Gaza Strip
should be resolved in talks among representatives of Israel,
Egypt, Jordan and the Palestinians. The Israeli delegation
reconfirmed its determination not to withdraw militarily from
the West Bank or Gaza Strip by adamantly opposing the wording
in the preamble that declared the acquisition of territory
through war inadmissable.

Israel also insisted that it would retreat to the
international boundary in the Sinai but would preserve Israeli
control of the settlements and airfields located in the
northeastern and southeastern portions of the peninsula.
Differences also remained with the United States on the
settlements in the West Bank, Gaza Strip, and East Jerusalem.
But Carter's document did not emphasize these matters, and
Begin chose to disregard them.

Carter's failure to alter Israel's opinion of the American
proposal — and Egypt's own tepid support for it — spurred him
to redirect his mediation effort. The minutiae of America's
ideas toward the Palestinian and West Bank issues did not worry
Sadat a great deal, but refusal to budge from the Sinai
settlements and airfields infuriated the Egyptian president.
In a crucial move, Carter gained the approval of the Israelis
and Egyptians to separate the issues involving the Sinai from
those concerning the West Bank and Gaza Strip.

The U.S. president then succeeded in limiting the
participation of Egyptian and Israeli negotiators to single
jurists in order to simplify matters and gain adroit and
flexible collaborators. Carter undoubtedly expected that Barak
and al-Baz would become his partners in the negotiation. The
president respected and admired Israel's former attorney
general. Although often difficult, al-Baz was a master of
detail and was believed to enjoy the confidence of Sadat.

Al-Baz had advocated uncompromising solutions toward West Bank–Gaza Strip and Palestinian issues and generally identified with traditional pan–Arab causes. But Carter's request for a negotiating partner with judicial talent from each camp limited Sadat's choices. Neither the more sympathetic and controllable Tuhamy nor Ghali possessed legal qualifications. The only other lawyers in the delegation were junior officers attached to the foreign ministry. To bypass al–Baz at this juncture would have caused puzzlement among other members of the delegation and political problems at home, particularly if the conference produced an unsatisfactory result. Thus, contrary to the perception at the time, Sadat did not trust al–Baz.

Carter quickly became disenchanted and angry with al–Baz, who repeatedly tried to resurrect the language condemning the acquisition of territory by force. The Egyptian delegate added to his unpopularity by insisting on a provision that called for hoisting an Arab flag at the Temple Mount in Jerusalem. Carter accused al–Baz of "...sabotaging the peace process and obstructing the negotiations."[99] At this point the entire Israeli delegation started to wonder whether the conference had not reached a dead end. Begin, in fact, began to prepare his version of a final communique announcing the failure of the Camp David meeting.[100]

The rapid deterioration of peace prospects and the grim implications of failure triggered one last attempt to devise an original solution that might break the deadlock. In the meeting with Dayan, Weizman, and Barak, followed by a discussion with Sadat alone on the 14th, Carter reasoned for more time and renewed faith. The U.S. president presented an especially convincing case to the Israeli delegation that if Jerusalem wanted to achieve an agreement it would have to withdraw from its settlements and airfields in the Sinai.

Dayan's suggestion that a solution to the Sinai settlements problem might lie in placing the issue before the Israeli cabinet and Knesset came on the heels of a successful attempt within the Israeli delegation to bring Begin closer to compromise. General Tamir contacted Ariel Sharon in Jerusalem and persuaded the agriculture minister to call Begin and recommend that Israel agree to evacuate the Sinai settlements. The idea worked and after his talk with Sharon, Begin told his colleagues that "Arik" Sharon — who had supervised the erection of the Rafah settlements — saw no "military objection" to their removal.[101]

For his part, Sadat also made an effort to stimulate greater Israeli flexibility. He invited Dayan to meet him for tea that afternoon. During the meeting in the Egyptian president's cabin, Sadat explained in clear and concise terms why Israel must cede control over its settlements and airfields in the Sinai. Sadat angrily observed that his options were narrowing rapidly as a result of Kamel's anxiety and al-Baz's venomous attitude.[102] He warned that

> My people will not agree to any foreign regime on our soil, neither to American forces in the Sinai airfields, nor to your settlements, not even one, not even for a brief period. If you want peace with us, the table must be clear.[103]

Dayan reported to Begin, as Weizman already had, that if Israel refused to withdraw totally from the Sinai, the Camp David Conference would end in failure.[104]

Jimmy Carter's decision on September 15 to announce that the conference would end two days later reflected his belated recognition that final agreement depended on a tradeoff between the parties' minimal conditions and that goodwill would run out if such an exchange did not occur soon. But the American president's open threat to blame Israel if the conference failed risked provoking Israeli wrath, thus ending any chance for success at Camp David. Begin was already under intense pressure from within his delegation to relinquish the Sinai settlements and airfields, an issue involving deep principles for the prime minister. Begin had exploded the evening before during talks with Vance against what he considered Egyptian perfidy on the future of the Palestinians in the West Bank.

This episode convinced Carter to seek clarifications directly from Sadat, as discussions with al-Baz had led nowhere. Sadat feared that concessions already granted to Jerusalem, although limited, could become open-ended if the conference failed. His nervousness reflected his tenuous political position. Already Kamel had offered his resignation over Sadat's apparent willingness to exchange ambassadors with Israel prior to achieving a final solution of the Palestinian problem. The Egyptian president accepted the resignation effective upon their return to Cairo.[105] But a total or even partial failure at Camp David could end Sadat's presidency.

Carter agreed that commitments made at Camp David would not take force unless the parties achieved an accord there.

Carter's gesture probably had as much to do with his desire to extract an important concession from Sadat as with sensitivity to the Egyptian leader's domestic vulnerability. Thus, Carter was able to convince Sadat to abandon the principle condemning the acquisition of territory by force in exchange for the elimination of Israel's settlements and airfields in the Sinai.

However, it was Menachem Begin's unexpected approval of a clause recognizing the "legitimate rights of the Palestinians" on the 15th that enabled the parties to sign a framework agreement with greater confidence. The Israeli prime minister allowed a deviation from his rigid approach to the Palestine issue in order to secure peace. He had earlier convinced others that to attribute any form of "legitimacy" to matters regarding the Palestinians would inevitably produce statehood. In a transparent move calculated to reassure the faithful at home, he lamely questioned whether a right indeed could be "illegitimate."[106] In any case, Begin provided Sadat with a crucial concession that strengthened an achievement that appeared questionable to those in Cairo expecting grandiose results.

The Results

The Camp David Accords, initialed and released at White House ceremonies during the evening of September 17, 1978, were remarkable documents. The first accord, entitled "The Framework for Peace in the Middle East," contained a preamble and three major sections setting guidelines for a settlement on the West Bank and Gaza Strip involving Egypt, Israel, Jordan, and representatives of the Palestinian people. The second accord, called "Framework for the Conclusion of a Peace Treaty Between Israel and Egypt," described detailed procedures for a step-by-step transfer of the Sinai Peninsula from Israel to Egypt within specified time periods.[107]

The preamble to "The Framework for Peace in the Middle East" confirmed that the basis for any future dealings between Israel and its neighbors would remain UN Resolutions 242 and 338, as the Israeli delegation insisted it should. It called on the parties to seek peace founded on "respect for sovereignty, territorial integrity, and political independence of every state in the area [including Israel] and their right to live in peace within secure and recognized boundaries free from threats or acts of force."[108] It stated that Israeli insecurity should be relieved by adopting special measures, such as "demilitarized zones, limited armaments areas, early warning stations, the presence of international forces, liaison, agreed measures for monitoring and other arrangements."[109] And it noted that the framework could serve as basis for peace between Egypt and Israel and each of the latter's neighbors prepared to negotiate an end to hostilities. The preamble did not condemn the acquisition of territory through war.

The "Framework for Peace in the Middle East" addressed the issues surrounding the West Bank and Gaza Strip. Egypt, Israel, Jordan, and representatives of the Palestinian people would participate in three-stage negotiations to determine the area's future. First, Cairo and Jerusalem would negotiate and then supervise transitional arrangements for a maximum of five years. The current Israeli military and civilian administration would withdraw when the inhabitants of the areas had elected a self-governing authority in free elections. Jordan would assist in the details of the change but Egypt and Israel would possess the right to review any adjustments.

Second, Egypt, Israel, and Jordan would determine the powers and responsibilities of an elected self-governing authority in the West Bank and Gaza Strip. Israel would redeploy its withdrawn IDF forces into specified locations. Local constabulary forces consisting of Israeli and Jordanian forces would patrol and thereby ensure proper border control.

Third, after the establishment of the self-governing authority a transition period of five years would begin. No later than the third year, negotiations to determine the final status of the territories would begin. The discussions would include Egypt, Israel, Jordan and elected representatives of inhabitants of the West Bank and Gaza Strip. The talks would be based on the provisions of UN Resolution 242 and involve discussion of boundaries and future security arrangements. And the solution would "...recognize the legitimate rights of the Palestinian people and their just requirements. In this way, the Palestinians will participate in the determination of their own future..."[110]

Finally, Egyptian, Israeli, Jordanian, and representatives of the self-governing authority would form a committee to monitor and restrict the resettlement of refugees into the West Bank and Gaza Strip.

A smaller section of the Framework established principles for resolving peacefully disputes arising from the settlement and fixed a goal of three months to negotiate a final peace treaty between Israel and Egypt. The concluding portion of the first accord asserted the parties' intention to enter into full recognition, abolish economic boycotts, and guarantee that each country's citizens enjoyed equal protection of the law in the other's jurisdiction. The United States was invited to participate in treaty talks, and the United Nations would be asked to endorse the resulting treaty and ensure full compliance.[111]

The terms of The Egyptian–Israeli bilateral agreement on the Sinai would be implemented within a two- to three-year period. Israel would withdraw its armed forces, including those based at the airfields, to the internationally recognized border between Egypt and mandated Palestine. Jerusalem would possess the right of free passage through the Straits of Tiran and the Gulf of Aqaba. Specified limitations on the stationing of Egyptian, Israeli, and UN forces in the Sinai during and after the implementation of the agreement concluded the substantive portion of the document.

Following the signature of a peace treaty and upon completion of the interim withdrawal, the two countries would establish diplomatic, economic, and cultural relations, terminate commercial boycotts, and apply legal due process to each other's citizens. The interim withdrawal itself would occur between three and nine months after the signature of the peace treaty. All Israeli forces would retreat east of a line extending from a point east of El Arish to Ras Mohammad, to an exact location to be determined by mutual consent.[112]

Letters exchanged between Carter and Begin on the one hand and Carter and Sadat on the other concerning Knesset consideration of the Sinai settlements issue and the two countries' sharply divergent perceptions of Jerusalem's status added a note of caution to the proceedings at the White House. The Camp David Accords shattered the psychology of mistrust that pervaded previous relations between Egypt and Israel and set a pattern that with skill and luck could be imitated with other Arab countries.

U.S.–Israeli discord over settlements in the West Bank and Gaza Strip marred the generally festive mood that enveloped the White House signing ceremony. A sharp exchange among Carter, Begin, and aides preceded the signing. An Israeli agreement to refrain from building new settlements anywhere in the administered territories during the period of negotiations relieved the dispute temporarily.[113] The issue would soon cause a rift between the United States and Israel, which interpreted the pre-signing agreement differently. Begin claimed the prohibition covered only the three months of negotiations over the Egyptian–Israeli treaty. Carter asserted the freeze applied to the entire five-year transition period.[114]

Camp David was a milestone toward achieving peace in the Middle East. The parties reached agreement because Anwar Sadat and Menachem Begin chose to place pragmatism ahead of principle and statesmanship over self-interest.

NOTES

1. New York Times, July 20, 1978.

2. Washington Post, July 20, 1978.

3. Washington Post, July 22, 1978. For discussion of illness, see, also, Ezer Weizman, The Battle for Peace (New York: Bantam Books, 1981), p. 307, 333. Also, Uzi Benziman, Prime Minister Under Siege (Jerusalem: Adam Publisher, 1981) Translated from the Hebrew by Mordecai Schreiber, p. 155–156. Benziman attributes Begin's mood swings — first supporting Dayan positions toward autonomy questions at the end of five years than opposing them — to the prime minister's declining health.

4. New York Times, July 22, 1978; July 25, 1978; Washington Post, July 22, 1978.

5. New York Times, July 23, 1978.

6. New York Times, July 21, 1978.

7. Washington Post, August 1, 1978.

8. Ibid.

9. New York Times, July 13, 1978; August 1, 1978; Washington Post, July 20, 1978; August 23, 1978.

10. Foreign Broadcast Information Service (Hereinafter FBIS) Middle East and North Africa, July 24 1978, D1–23.

11. _Ibid._, August 1, 1978, D–5.

12. _Ibid._, July 26, 1978, D–1.

13. _Ibid._, August 2, 1978, D–3.

14. See, Assem Abdul Moshen, "Democracy Revisited" in the _Middle East_, October 1978, p. 39.

15. _New York Times_, July 20, 1978.

16. Moshe Dayan, _Breakthrough: A Personal Account of the Egypt–Israel Peace Negotiations_ (London: Wiedenfeld and Nicholson, 1981), p. 149; _New York Times_, July 29, 1978.

17. Dayan, _Breakthrough_, p. 150.

18. _Ibid._, p. 152.

19. _Ibid._, p. 153; _New York Times_, August 9, 1978.

20. _New York Times_, August 9, 1978.

21. _Ibid._, _Washington Post_, August 9, 1978.

22. Dayan, _Breakthrough_, p. 153.

23. Interview with William Quandt, Washington, D.C. September 23, 1981. Elsewhere Sadat was quoted as suggesting that Mubarak was needed at home to maintain a smoothly running government. The Egyptian vice president was also involved in assuring his reelection to the People's Assembly.

24. Weizman, _The Battle for Peace_, p. 341.

25. _Ibid._

26. Eitan Haber, Zeev Schiff and Ehud Yaari, _The Year of the Dove_ (New York: Bantam Books, 1979), p. 216–217.

27. _Washington Post_, August 15, 1978.

28. Jimmy Carter, Keeping Faith: Memoirs of a President (New York: Bantam Books, 1982), p. 326.

29. New York Times, August 22, 1978.

30. Uzi Benziman, Prime Minister Under Siege (Jerusalem: Adam Publishers, 1981) Translated from the Hebrew by Mordecai Schreiber, p. 163.

31. Jerusalem Post, International Edition, August 29, 1978.

32. Carter, Keeping Faith, p. 326.

33. Anwar Sadat, In Search of Identity (New York: Harper and Row, 1977), p. 2–6.

34. Ibid., p. 8–40, 94–103.

35. Time, October 19, 1981, p. 32–33.

36. Ibid.

37. Ibid.

38. Eitan Haber, Menachem Begin: The Legend and the Man (New York: Delacorte Press, 1978), p. 14–18.

39. Ibid., p. 17–22.

40. Ibid., p. 23, 46–60, 83–249.

41. Dayan, Breakthrough, p. 160–162.

42. Ibid., p. 162.

43. Weizman, The Battle for Peace, p. 357.

44. Carter, Keeping Faith, p. 370; Dayan, Breakthrough, p. 163.

45. Carter, Keeping Faith, p. 27–271; Weizman, The Battle for Peace, p. 363–364.

46. Dayan, Breakthrough, p. 164.

47. Ibid., p. 164–165.

48. Ibid., p. 165.

49. Ibid., p. 167.

50. Ibid., p. 165.

51. Carter, Keeping Faith, p. 372–374; Haber, Schiff and Yaari, The Year of the Dove, p. 250–251.

52. Carter, Keeping Faith, p. 374–376; Haber, Schiff and Yaari, The Year of the Dove, p. 251–252.

53. Carter, Keeping Faith, p. 379–380; Haber, Schiff and Yaari, The Year of the Dove, p. 253.

54. Carter, Keeping Faith, p. 381; Weizman, The Battle for Peace, p. 367–368.

55. Carter, Keeping Faith, p. 382; Haber, Schiff and Yaari, The Year of the Dove, p. 354.

56. Ibid.

57. Haber, Schiff and Yaari, The Year of the Dove, p. 254.

58. Ibid., p. 253.

59. Weizman, The Battle for Peace, p. 368.

60. Carter, Keeping Faith, p. 385; Haber, Schiff and Yaari, The Year of the Dove, p. 260.

61. Carter, Keeping Faith, p. 385–387; Haber, Schiff and Yaari, The Year of the Dove, p. 260, 257.

62. Carter, Keeping Faith, p. 387; Haber, Schiff and Yaari, The Year of the Dove, p. 257–258.

63. Weizman, The Battle for Peace, p. 368.

64. Carter, Keeping Faith, p. 387–388; Weizman, The Battle for Peace, p. 368–369.

65. Haber, Schiff and Yaari, The Year of the Dove, p 260.

66. Dayan, Breakthrough, p. 173; Haber, Schiff and Yaari, The Year of the Dove, p. 260–261.

67. Carter, Keeping Faith, p. 389; Haber, Schiff and Yaari, The Year of the Dove, p. 262–263.

68. Carter, Keeping Faith, p. 390; Weizman, The Battle for Peace, p. 371.

69. Carter, Keeping Faith, p. 389–393; Haber, Schiff and Yaari, The Year of the Dove, p. 264; Dayan, Breakthrough, p. 172; Weizman, The Battle for Peace, p. 360.

70. Dayan, Breakthrough, p. 173–174.

71. Ibid., p. 174.

72. Ibid., p. 174–175.

73. Weizman, The Battle for Peace, p. 371.

74. Haber, Schiff and Yaari, The Year of the Dove, p. 268.

75. Carter, Keeping Faith, p. 393; Haber, Schiff and Yaari, The Year of the Dove, p. 268–269.

76. Weizman, The Battle for Peace, p. 372.

77. Carter, Keeping Faith, p. 396; Weizman, The Battle for Peace, p. 372; Dayan, Breakthrough, p. 176–177; Haber, Schiff and Yaari, The Year of the Dove, p. 270.

78. Carter, Keeping Faith, p. 398–400; Dayan, Breakthrough, p. 177–179.

79. Carter, Keeping Faith, p. 398–400; Dayan, Breakthrough, p. 351–352.

80. Dayan, Breakthrough, p. 161–162; Weizman, The Battle for Peace, p. 351–352; Carter, Keeping Faith, p. 340.

81. Dayan, Breakthrough, p. 162.

82. Ibid., p. 163.

83. Haber, Schiff and Yaari, The Year of the Dove, p. 238.

84. Carter, Keeping Faith, p. 342–345; Haber, Schiff and Yaari, The Year of the Dove, p. 232, 236; Weizman, The Battle for Peace, p. 353.

85. Dayan, Breakthrough, p. 163.

86. Haber, Schiff and Yaari, The Year of the Dove, p. 233; Dayan, Breakthrough, p. 162; Weizman, The Battle for Peace, p. 353.

87. Dayan, Breakthrough, p. 162; Haber, Schiff and Yaari, The Year of the Dove, p. 233.

88. Carter, Keeping Faith, p. 345; Weizman, The Battle for Peace, p. 355–356.

89. Haber, Schiff and Yaari, The Year of the Dove, p. 241.

90. Ibid.

91. Ibid., p. 240.

92. Carter, Keeping Faith, p. 359; Dayan, Breakthrough, p. 164; Haber, Schiff and Yaari, The Year of the Dove, p. 241.

93. Carter, Keeping Faith, p. 347; Haber, Schiff and Yaari, The Year of the Dove, p. 241.

94. Weizman, The Battle for Peace, p. 360.

95. Ibid., p. 361–362.

96. Ibid., p. 362.

97. Dayan, Breakthrough, p. 166–167.

98. See, Carter, Keeping Faith, p. 370–379; Weizman, The Battle for Peace, p. 364.

99. Haber, Schiff and Yaari, The Year of the Dove, p. 259–260.

100. Weizman, The Battle for Peace, p. 369.

101. Ibid., p. 370; Benziman, Prime Minister Under Siege, Translated from the Hebrew by Mordecai Schreiber, p. 195.

102. Dayan, Breakthrough, p. 172.

103. Ibid.

104. Ibid.

105. Haber, Schiff and Yaari, The Year of the Dove, p. 267.

106. Weizman, The Battle for Peace, p. 373.

107. See, United States Department of State, The Camp David Summit — September 1978. (Washington: Department of State) Publication 9054, p. 6–15.

108. Ibid., p. 7.

109. Ibid.

110. Ibid., p. 7–8

111. Ibid., p. 8–9.

112. Ibid., p. 10.

113. Dayan, Breakthrough, p. 181–185.

114. Ibid., p. 186.

7
"Peace is at Hand"—Almost

Both Sadat and Begin waged intense struggles to obtain popular acceptance and parliamentary approval of the Camp David Accords.   When Sadat returned to Cairo, huge crowds filled the streets, proclaiming their leader a "hero of peace."[1]   The public display, however, concealed deep divisions over the substance of Sadat's achievement.

Leftists, Nasserists, former members of the Free Officer Corps, fanatical members of the religious right, and the Moslem Brotherhood opposed the Camp David agreement utterly.   But the government had anticipated their disorganized efforts.[2]   Sadat had not expected members of Parliament and of his own cabinet to give him as much trouble as they did.

Sadat's speech to the People's Assembly presenting and defending the terms of the accords met with heckling and grumbling from representatives of both urban and rural constituencies who feared isolation from the Arab world.[3]   Members of professional syndicates, for example, believed their professions vulnerable to boycott by the rest of the Arab world.   Camp David might undermine the exalted status among villagers of rural notables who became identified with the accords.   Urban leaders allied with the military were also confused by the sudden rapprochement with Israel.   Some officers were jealous of Israeli technical superiority and wondered if peace would reverse the deterioration of the armed forces.[4]   Many worried that peace might jeopardize the security, good pay, and perquisites the military enjoyed as long as war with Israel remained possible.[5]   The urban poor had the most to gain from the influx of Western investment expected to follow peace.   The Muslim Brotherhood and others of the right tried hard to belie the belief among Old City dwellers that Camp David would improve their lot.[6]

Sadat sought to counter this somber mood by kindling optimism about the benefits of peace among the urban poor and at the same time dispelling the fears of rural Egyptians that peace would disrupt their pious existence. Thus in the weeks immediately following Camp David, Sadat launched a policy designed to cleanse the bureaucracy and streamline decision making.[7] Corruption had spread among the nouveau riche who had profited handsomely from the economic opening to the West and had worsened within the already venal bureaucracy. A public government campaign to eradicate corruption could polish the image of the Sadat regime among the Egyptian masses and create hope that real economic benefits would result from peace. Sadat convinced Mustapha Khalil to lend his considerable prestige and talent to the effort by becoming prime minister.[8]

Few had expected the appointment of Khalil, although the ASU leader had often performed foreign and domestic tasks for Sadat on an ad hoc basis. For example, he had figured prominently on the delegation that had accompanied Sadat to Jerusalem and had prepared the agenda that would form the basis for the National Democratic Party platform. But Khalil possessed a far broader and more compelling appeal than provided by his previous employment.

Sadat had excluded Hosni Mubarak from the Camp David conference and associated developments. But the Egyptian vice president had hardly lost his power and influence. His perspicacious political adviser, Usama al-Baz, provided a full account of events at Camp David. Mubarak could be expected to exploit any misstep by Sadat that might permit a retrenchment from the more controversial Egyptian concessions at Camp David, in particular on issues involving the future of the West Bank and Palestinian rights.

Khalil could act as a counterpoise to Mubarak. The new prime minister enjoyed immense popularity and wielded significant influence within the techno-managerial elite.[9] Consequently, he could help frustrate moves stimulated by Mubarak within the military to undermine the peace process. And probably more than any other, the scrupulously honest Khalil possessed the skill to maintain some control over Egypt's bloated and inefficient bureaucracy.[10]

To strengthen and liberalize the economy, Cairo needed a greater inflow of Western aid and loans. But an unstable peace with Israel could significantly reduce the prospects for a substantial increase in U.S., West European, or multilateral investment in Egypt. Thus Khalil and his associates had sufficient incentive during early October to argue vigorously for the implementation of peace with Israel, asserting that only peace could ensure a measure of improvement in the future for the impoverished and disaffected in Egyptian society.

Sadat's survival in power depended on a careful balancing of interests that precluded any of several rival power centers from gaining too much strength. Sadat could not allow a military—industrial alliance or one between party and bureaucracy from forming.[11] Khalil and Gamassy were close friends and often viewed matters from the same perspective.[12] The appointment of the former to the prime ministership therefore dictated the replacement of Gamassy -- whose visibility with the foreign press had already strained relations with Sadat -- as minister of war.[13]

Mubarak undoubtedly viewed the removal of Gamassy as a major victory. The appointment of Ali, a Mubarak client, to replace the minister of war appeared to confirm the vice president's success. But with his new position Ali attained equal status relative to Mubarak, altering their relationship and weakening the vice president's authority.[14] By elevating Ali -- a competent and popular officer -- and placing him in charge of peace negotiations, Sadat bolstered morale and support for the peace process within the military. Mubarak's position suffered as a result.

Sadat moved swiftly in the first week of October 1978 to alter the composition of his government and senior military staff. He announced the appointment of Khalil as prime minister on October 2 and delivered his speech to the parliament defending the Camp David agreements the following day. Khalil began to form his cabinet on the 4th. On the same day Sadat offered Gamassy the post of special presidential advisor and appointed a new Army Chief of Staff -- Major General Ahmad Badawi, the head of military training. Badawi was a hero of the 1973 war and, most important, well regarded by his peers and subordinates.

The Egyptian president swore in the restructured cabinet on October 5. It did not include a foreign minister; Khalil himself later added that position to his already long list of responsibilities. The new cabinet formally approved the Camp David Accords on the 10th, and the parliament followed suit on the 14th.

Menachem Begin encountered a less enthusiastic reception in Jerusalem than the public welcome accorded Sadat in Cairo. In private, informal consultations with selected cabinet members prior to official presentation of the accords, Begin faced sharp questioning. Most criticized the prime minister for accepting language that granted the Palestinians a role in determining the future of the West Bank. They regarded the agreement as the first step toward Palestinian statehood.[15]

Elikaim Rubinstein, an aide of Dayan who had attended the Camp David conference, participated in the meetings. The foreign ministry adviser expressed his opposition to the Israeli commitment to remove its settlements from the Sinai, asserting that Israel may have made an unnecessary concession. For he believed Sadat would not have renounced other Egyptian gains if the Sinai settlements remained. Rubinstein also decried what he described as unceasing U.S. pressure on Israel to satisfy Egyptian demands. He was suspicious of Washington's intentions and feared that it might attempt to use the Sinai accord as a precedent for efforts to reach a solution for the West Bank. Rubinstein's arguments made sense to many at the meeting.[16]

Begin convened a formal cabinet meeting to review the Camp David agreements the next day, September 24. After eight hours of acrimonious debate, the cabinet approved the accords by a vote of eleven to two. One minister abstained and four did not participate. The prime minister argued during the session that the accords would benefit Israel in six ways: They would establish a secure peace with Egypt; allow Israel to maintain a military presence in the West Bank after a five-year autonomy period; lead to full peace before Israeli withdrawal from the Sinai and regardless of the amount of progress made or the result of negotiations on Palestinian self-rule and the future of the West Bank and Gaza Strip; impose no preconditions on the talks over Palestinian autonomy; enhance the prospects of obtaining a self-rule plan that resembled closely Begin's own proposal; and permit Israel's settlement program in "Judea and Samaria" to proceed after a temporary halt of three months. Begin told the cabinet that he believed Sadat had made far greater concessions for peace but urged them not to express this view in public for fear of embarrassing the Egyptian president.[17]

During the tense debate in the Knesset over the accords a member of Begin's Herut Party who attempted to sponsor a motion demanding the prime minister's resignation was thrown out of the party. Other members of the extreme right punctuated the discussions with catcalls. Opposition leader Shimon Peres's comments contained a mixture of praise and sharp criticism. He too feared that Palestinian self-government would lead to a Palestinian state. He believed Israel could have avoided yielding the Sinai airfields and settlements. Nevertheless, he conceded that the agreements' drawbacks could not outweigh the single advantage of true peace with Egypt. Finally, Peres echoed the sentiment of a widow who had lost two sons in battle. At a Labor Party caucus preceding the debate she asked: "Can we allow this moment to slip away?"[18]

Moshe Dayan attempted to relieve anxiety that the accords would facilitate the birth of a Palestinian state. He noted that the accords clearly limited the role of representatives of Palestinians in the occupied territories to matters of strictly local concern. Negotiations to draw Israel's permanent eastern border or to establish the terms of peace in the area would only be conducted with Jordan, not the Palestinians, consistent with UN Resolution 242.[19]

On September 27, 1978, after seventeen hours of debate during two sessions of parliament, the Knesset approved the Camp David accords by a vote of 84 to 19 with 17 abstentions.[20] Begin won approval of the accords from his cabinet and the Knesset at considerable political cost within his party and nation. The prime minister customarily presented all major policy decisions -- the Camp David accords certainly fit into that category -- to his party before submitting them to the Knesset for debate and approval. But the rough treatment Begin encountered during the September 23 meeting at his residence and reports of similar behavior by hardline members of Herut when Dayan and Weizman met with a ministerial review committee on the 20th[21] apparently convinced Begin to alter the normal process. In order to prevent the right wing from organizing well-orchestrated attacks in the Herut Party or in the important parliamentary Foreign Affairs and Security Committee, he bypassed his party's political caucus, accelerated cabinet consideration of the agreements, and requested that the Knesset schedule an early debate and vote on the accords.

The prime minister correctly judged that his domination of the Herut Party's machinery assured that it would sponsor the accords even without formally approving them. The Liberal Party advocated a moderate position on territorial issues and thus would endorse the Camp David agreements. The remaining members of the Likud found the accords objectionable, but these extremist factions on the right — such as La'am — were small and politically weak.[22]

Unlike the different factions in the Labor Party, the members of the Likud coalition had not yet formed strong ties to well-positioned, articulate interests in Israeli society.

If a faction of the Labor Party wanted to assert its strong beliefs within the party on a particular issue it could mobilize independent structures outside of government to help bolster its cause. No such capability existed for the members of the Likud. Thus, Begin used his near total control of the Herut party apparatus, his national stature, the relative moderation of Likud's liberal party faction, and the lack of any real alternative leadership in the coalition to achieve quick approval of the accords.[23]

But Begin's opponents within the coalition were angered by his willingness to make concessions at Camp David that violated cherished right-wing causes and by his apparent drift toward the center. They questioned the prime minister's ability to speak on behalf of the coalition, which in their view did not accept his revisionist philosophy.[24] These critics blamed Dayan and Weizman for leading Begin astray.[25] The right-wing ideologues — both in Herut and the NRP — enjoyed considerable support among important constituencies, including the Sephardic community. Gush Emunim continued its campaign to construct additional settlements near the West Bank town of Nablus.[26]

Thus Begin faced an unhappy and, in the case of such groups as Gush Emunim, potentially disruptive right wing. He could not fully desert the rightists, or he would free the ultranationalists to trample on the Camp David accords with impunity. The Israeli prime minister consequently acknowledged the necessity to allow his more conservative ministerial colleagues to play a greater role in the formulation of policy toward the peace negotiations. He also decided to assert tighter control over Dayan and Weizman during the forthcoming talks with U.S. and Egyptian representatives scheduled for mid-October in Washington.

Saunders and the Jordanians

Meanwhile, U.S. policy makers sought to attract the support of moderate Arab states for the Camp David agreements and enlist their participation in future attempts to achieve a comprehensive agreement. Secretary of State Vance went to Amman, Riyadh, and Damascus during September 20 to 24 but failed to persuade a single leader to join the peace process.

In the eyes of Syrian President Hafez Assad, the accords did nothing to fulfill Palestinian rights. Damascus, in fact, became a leader of the so-called "rejectionist front" comprised of Syria, Algeria, South Yemen, Libya, and the PLO. The rejectionists would soon suspend diplomatic and economic ties with Egypt over the accords.

The Saudi monarchy issued a statement just prior to Vance's visit that noted: "What has been reached at the Camp David conference cannot be considered a final accepted version of a formula for peace."[27] The Riyadh declaration further stated that the Camp David accords had failed to produce a formula for Israeli withdrawal "from all occupied Arab territories, the chief among them Jerusalem."[28] Finally, the statement decried the failure of the accords to ensure a PLO role in future negotiations.[29]

Saudi Arabia was upset about the Camp David conference and resulting agreements, as they exposed Riyadh to twin perils -- rapprochement between radical Syria and Iraq and a Khomeini-style revolution, both of which posed a threat to the Saudi regime. Riyadh had earlier expressed interest in organizing a conference to reconcile the Arab states, thwart any designs to destabilize the Persian Gulf, and seek to narrow differences over the Palestinian issue.[30] Camp David now doomed that effort.

U.S. officials suffered their greatest disappointment in Amman. King Hussein's belligerent attitude toward the accords jolted Vance. The king's somewhat vague views on peace with Israel in the months preceding Camp David had encouraged Washington. He had not endorsed Israeli proposals for the West Bank but neither had he rejected totally all notion of negotiating peace.

The United States believed that Hussein's dependence on Saudi financial subsidies and his warming relations with Syria restrained him. The Jordanian leader undoubtedly welcomed Egyptian and American pressure on Israel and decided to allow their combined efforts to weaken Jerusalem's fundamental positions before joining the process. He expected Sadat and Carter to extract concessions from Israel that would benefit Jordan without his own direct involvement. This approach permitted Hussein both to remain a member in good standing of the Arab world and to preserve an image of moderation in Washington.[31]

But the Camp David accords contained far less of interest to Hussein than presummit activities had suggested it might. Egyptian and American officials failed to budge Israel on many crucial matters. Jerusalem had not categorically agreed to transfer the West Bank to Arab sovereignty after a five year transition period and had not recognized the principle of Palestinian self-determination. The Camp David agreements did not require the removal of Israeli settlements in areas west of the Jordan River. The accords had addressed the final status of Jerusalem simply as an issue to be discussed bilaterally between Israel and Jordan, but made no mention of restoring its eastern portion to Arab control. In Hussein's eyes, the accords relegated Jordan to the role of a policeman in the West Bank and -- even worse -- seemed to ensure the birth of a Palestinian state there. He could not accept either.

Hussein had wrongly assumed that Sadat and Carter could modify and moderate Israeli demands concerning the West Bank and Gaza Strip. The final agreement reached at Camp David was so vague as to allow Egypt and Israel to interpret it in whatever way they chose and thus accomplished little of substance for Jordan.

As a result, Hussein turned to America to achieve his goals. He wanted to build on the limited Israeli concessions at Camp David by negotiating a firm linkage between the two Camp David documents -- making any peace treaty with Israel dependent on a satisfactory solution to the Palestinian problem -- thus satisfying Palestinian demands without simultaneously creating a Palestinian state. [32] The Carter administration already believed that it would have to attract Jordanian participation in the next round of discussions if it wished to transform the Camp David accords into a more comprehensive and stable peace agreement. American decision makers thought they could convince Jordan to join the peace process without undermining the accomplishments gained at Camp David.

But Vance left empty handed. Hussein had merely promised to send Washington a list of questions, which he wanted the United States to answer in writing, about the future of the West Bank and Gaza Strip during and after the transition period. [33] In the meantime, the king embraced hardline positions toward Camp David formulated by Arafat, Qhaddafi, and Assad and accepted an invitation to attend an anti-Sadat Arab conference in Baghdad during November. [34]

Hussein's detailed, 14-point questionnaire arrived in Washington on September 29, and U.S. Assistant Secretary of State Harold Saunders carried Washington's official responses to Amman on October 16. After several days of meetings in the Jordanian capital and a brief stopover in Jerusalem on the 20th, Saunders returned to Washington. [35] The questions covered a variety of subjects but concentrated on: the extent of the

U.S. commitment to negotiations over the West Bank; the present and future status of Arab Jerusalem; the supervision of self-rule during the transition period; the deployment of Israeli forces during the transition; the future of Israeli settlements in the West Bank; the rights of Palestinian refugees; the future of occupied territories not mentioned in the Framework Agreement; the American role in improving the security of Arab states; and clarifications of UN Resolution 242.

Clearly, Hussein would participate in the peace process only if the U.S. interpretation of the accords envisaged a significant Jordanian presence in East Jerusalem and the West Bank and safeguarded the king's own interests. For any agreement to enjoy Jordanian support it would have to require the removal of Israeli settlements in the West Bank and Gaza Strip, bar equal rights for Israelis to reside and purchase land there, and curtail severely Israel's military presence there both before and after the five-year period.[36] Implicit in Hussein's questions was a reminder that America possessed long-term interests in the Arab world that it could protect only by fulfilling its long-standing commitment to restore Arab sovereignty over captured lands.

Carter's responses were briefer than Jordan anticipated but nevertheless momentous in their implications for peace. Concerning the Israeli settlements Carter asserted "Whatever number that might remain beyond the transitional period...would presumably be agreed to in the negotiations concerning the final status of the West Bank and Gaza."[37] He indicated that the Palestinians would be able to fulfill their "legitimate aspirations", instead of their "legitimate rights" as called for in the text of the Camp David accords.[38] He reiterated the U.S. position that negotiations should allow the stationing "of limited numbers of Israeli security personnel in specifically designated areas if agreed to by the parties."[39] Finally, with respect to East Jerusalem he stated that "the U.S. will support proposals that would permit the city's Arab inhabitants...who are not Israeli citizens to vote in future elections in the West Bank as well as sharing...in work of the self-governing authority itself."[40]

Saunders spent his final day in Amman clarifying the U.S. answers for Hussein. Late in the afternoon on October 19th, the American assistant secretary of state met with seven Palestinians and during their conversations described the withdrawal of Israeli settlements from the Sinai as a model for the West Bank and Gaza Strip. "The Egyptian experience with

Sinai," he said, "could explain what would happen in the West Bank and Gaza Strip if the Palestinians join in the negotiating process."[41] Saunders assured Hussein and the Palestinians that America would remain a "full partner" in the peace process and use its influence to obtain a West Bank settlement. Carter, he asserted, would continue to "...take an active personal part in the negotiations."[42]

Saunders, as expected, encountered harsh criticism in Israel of America's interpretation of the Camp David accords. Dayan had been shown the Jordanian questions in New York on October 6. In his view they possessed an obviously "propagandistic character" and did not merit a reply.[43] Nevertheless, Saunders and Atherton informed Dayan on the 15th that Washington would deliver American responses to Amman the following day.[44] An acrimonious discussion ensued. Washington did not give Dayan the text of Carter's replies to Hussein until the 18th. The Israeli foreign minister, who was participating in talks in Washington, informed Jerusalem the same day by cable.[45] In response to the Saunders mission, Begin announced his government's intention to expand settlements in Judea and Samaria.[46]

The deterioration of relations between Washington and Jerusalem no doubt delighted Hussein. The Jordanian monarch had convinced the United States to endorse in writing a form of linkage between the two Camp David accords. Washington also promised to take Jordanian interests and goals into account in its policies toward Israeli settlements in the West Bank, the rights of the Palestinians, the status of East Jerusalem, and the presence of Israeli forces in the territories. These agreements between Jordan and the United States formed the foundation of Hussein's peace strategy, which he had sought unsuccessfully to impose on the Camp David conference, of greatly and permanently reducing Israeli strength and influence in West Bank affairs. This time, however, the king would rely exclusively on Carter without the aid of Sadat -- to elicit from Israel the necessary compromises.

Hussein's effort to sway the peace process and America's tacit cooperation with the attempt reduced Sadat's ability to achieve his objective of accelerating the negotiations with Israel. For example, Jordan's diplomatic activities hindered discussions between Egyptian and Israeli representatives over the extent and timing of linkage between the two Camp David accords.

The Washington Meetings

Talks between Egypt and Israel to complete negotiations begun at Camp David opened at Blair House in Washington on October 12. Recently appointed Defense Minister Kamal Hassan Ali led the Egyptian delegation, which included Boutrus Ghali, Usama al-Baz, Ambassador to Switzerland Abdullah al-Aryan, Ambassador to the United States Ashraf Ghorbal, General Majdub, Sharab, and Commodore Hamdi. Dayan, Weizman, Rosenne, Tamir, General Ephriam Poran -- Begin's military assistant -- and Dinitz represented Israel. Vance led the American delegation.[47]

Discussions between Carter and Dayan on October 10 followed by conversations between Dayan and Ghali on the 11th preceded the formal meetings. Neither encounter, however, eliminated the tension surrounding the talks. Carter told Dayan that Sadat wanted to link resolution of the Palestinian question with the implementation of the bilateral treaty between Egypt and Israel, which the two sides would negotiate at Blair House.[48] Dayan rejected any linkage between Palestinian issues and the talks at Blair House, reminding Carter that the meetings in Washington were intended to conclude a peace treaty between Egypt and Israel as specified in the Camp David accords, not a solution to the Palestinian problem.

The Israeli foreign minister also argued that a successful peace agreement between Cairo and Jerusalem could itself induce Palestinian participation in the peace process. Palestinians in the West Bank and Gaza Strip, he said, would regard continued meddling by the United States, Egypt, and Israel in their affairs as patronizing and might stiffen their rejection of the Camp David accords as a result.[49]

Ghali, in conversations with Dayan the following evening, pointed to Cairo's growing isolation from its Arab neighbors and asserted that Israeli gestures toward resolving the Palestinian problem could reduce Arab hostility. Ghali suggested three steps that could build confidence in the Arab world: The redeployment of Israeli forces in the West Bank and Gaza Strip away from Arab population centers; the abolition of military government in the territories; and the release of Arab prisoners suspected or convicted of terrorism.[50] The Israeli foreign minister responded by merely expressing regret over Sadat's difficulties and repeated his refusal to consider any linkage between the Palestinian problem and the Egyptian–Israeli peace treaty.[51]

Vance established a format for the negotiations at the initial session of the Blair House talks on October 12. U.S. delegates would hold separate but simultaneous talks with the Egyptian and Israeli delegations; those sessions would be followed by joint meetings of the three parties. The U.S. delegation presented a draft peace treaty to Egypt and Israel individually. Both approved the general outlines of the draft although each sought modifications.[52]

The Israelis were principally concerned about when official diplomatic relations with Egypt would begin — Jerusalem wished them to coincide with Israeli withdrawal to the El–Arish–Ras Mohammad line in the Sinai — the responsibilities a UN force in the Sinai would have, and a suggestion that the International Court of Justice would arbitrate disputes arising from differing interpretations of the agreement. The Egyptians objected primarily to the lack of a firm link between the treaty and the Palestinian Issue.[53]

Disagreement over other issues would emerge during subsequent meetings. One major obstacle arose over the status the Egyptian–Israeli treaty would have in relation to existing bilateral agreements between Cairo and other Arab states. Jerusalem feared that in the event of hostilities with the Arabs, Egypt might choose to honor previous commitments to join its Arab allies rather than observe its peace treaty with Israel. The Israelis wanted to insert a clause in the treaty with Egypt specifying that the Egyptian–Israeli peace agreement would have "priority of obligations."[54] Difficulties also arose over the designation of a line east of the Naot–Sinai settlement for the first phase of Israel's withdrawal from the Sinai, the definition of the Israeli right to use the Gulf of Eilat unmolested, and the supply of oil to Israel in the event that the burgeoning crisis in Iran shut off what was Jerusalem's main source.[55] When and how the two sides could submit the treaty to review, who would determine breaches of its conditions, and how much financial assistance the United States would offer Israel as compensation for removing its airfields from the Sinai and reestablishing them in the Negev Desert completed the list of unresolved issues.[56]

On the 17th, Carter invited the Israeli and Egyptian delegations separately for discussions at the White House and met with them together at Blair House two days later. In each of the October 17 sessions, the president merely took note of the most difficult questions and requested that each side show greater flexibility.[57] But at the combined meeting Carter addressed the most intractable issues. He warned those assembled that he would seek to impose his own solution on the two countries if they did not begin to make progress.[58]

Linkage of the Palestinian issue to the peace treaty remained the most divisive issue, and Carter attempted to break the impasse by suggesting compromise positions. For example, although the president regarded linkage as essential, he considered a political rather than legal link as perfectly acceptable. He recognized the validity of Dayan's view that it would be ridiculous for "...the maintenance of the Israel–Egypt treaty to be dependent upon the Palestinians or Jordan."[59] Carter proposed the following tradeoffs: Israel would agree to a provision in the preamble establishing linkage between the two issues and would commit itself to end military government in the territories in an exchange of letters between Begin and Sadat; Egypt would agree to exchange ambassadors immediately upon completion of the first phase of Israeli withdrawal from the Sinai; the United States would itself put together a multilateral force with Canadian or Australian troops should the UN Security Council fail to agree on the composition of a peace keeping force for the Sinai.[60]

The Israeli cabinet decided to recall Dayan and Weizman for consultations on October 22.[61] The U.S. president therefore began to race the clock at mid–day on the 20th in an effort to achieve a mutually agreed draft treaty before the Israeli ministers left Washington. Carter held separate meetings with the two delegations at the White House in the afternoon and again during the evening and concluded with a morning meeting on the 21st.

The parties agreed to allow Israeli ships through the Suez Canal upon ratification of the peace agreement and to establish diplomatic relations at the ambassadorial level a month after the treaty was signed. But Egypt rejected the clause giving its treaty with Israel priority over all other obligations, and the two sides failed to find a mutually acceptable formula for linking the treaty to resolution of the Palestinian problem. After a great deal of hard bargaining the negotiators agreed to language that encompassed the position of each country on disputed matters in the late afternoon of the 21st.[62] Dayan and Weizman left for Jerusalem carrying a draft treaty with Egypt.

Bases and Energy

Two issues -- Israel's energy supply and the cost of replacing its bases in the Sinai -- would prove among the most difficult to resolve at Blair House. Jerusalem and Washington appointed a joint committee of technical experts to determine the best way of ensuring adequate supplies of fuel to Israel after it relinquished oil installations in the western Sinai. A team of Israeli energy specialists flew to the United States and participated in intensive discussions for several weeks.[63] U.S. negotiators refused to pressure Egypt to fill Israel's oil needs at fixed prices.[64] Cairo maintained that following the normalization of relations Jerusalem could purchase supplies on the same basis as any other country. The issue thus remained unresolved when the Blair House meetings ended in mid-November.[65]

The promised expansion of U.S. and Israeli military-economic relations implicit in the accords had begun to play a central role in the discussions. Ezer Weizman reminded Carter during the October 10 meetings before the Blair Conference that an Israeli decision to evacuate the Western Sinai early depended on the American willingness to finance new airfields in the Negev. The Israelis set cost of replacing the airbases at $2.5 billion. Carter questioned whether a U.S. commitment existed to finance the replacement of both new facilities, but Vance confirmed that the United States had made such a promise during the Camp David meetings.[66]

Dayan raised the matter again on October 17 during a White House session with Carter. The Israeli foreign minister advised Carter that Israel would soon face enormous expenditures for the transfer of men, materiel, and facilities from the Sinai to Israeli territory. Egypt, he pointed out, would receive "an ordered and well organized Sinai" with infrastructure and installations constructed by Israeli forces over a decade.[67] Carter indicated he would send Pentagon personnel to inspect the area. But he believed peace would reduce the huge sums America provided Jerusalem. U.S. Secretary of Defense Harold Brown similarly informed Weizman on the 20th that the amount Israel had requested appeared excessive. He also hinted that Jerusalem should not seek American financial help as a prerequisite to making peace.[68]

Begin, en route to Canada for an official visit, stopped in New York on November 1 to meet with Vance. He urged the U.S. secretary of state to support the economic assistance requested by Israel and indicated that it could take the form of a 25-year loan at a rate of interest of two to four percent.[69] In the face of public outcry over such a huge request, Begin modified his position on November 4. The $700 million needed to build the air bases could, he conceded, take the form of grant aid, and Washington could provide the rest under the same, less favorable credit provisions as previous loans.[70] But in later meetings with American policy makers in Washington and New York, Dayan and Begin failed to extract a firm U.S. commitment to provide the money, either as grants or loans. Moreover, Israeli and American finance ministers were barred from holding any meetings, undoubtedly a sign of U.S. displeasure with Jerusalem's unyielding attitude on a number of more central matters pertaining to autonomy and settlements.

The Settlement Controversy

Carter's refusal to accept Begin's interpretation of the freeze on Israeli settlements in the Sinai and the West Bank agreed to at Camp David introduced enormous strain in their bilateral relationship. The U.S. president raised the issue during his October 10 discussions with Dayan. The Israeli foreign minister reiterated Begin's position that the freeze applied only to the three-month period established for negotiations to conclude the Israeli-Egyptian treaty and not the entire five-year transition period.[71] Carter did not press the matter further during the October 12-21 period because even under the Israeli interpretation, settlement activity had ceased.

Following Dayan's return to Israel on October 22, however, he broached the subject of settlements with Begin. The discussion came on the heels of Saunders' mission to Jordan and his public statements that the Israeli settlements were temporary. Dayan counseled Begin to notify America that the freeze on settlements would expire on a specific date and that Israel intended to strengthen existing enclaves. Jerusalem would not, however, extend settlement activity to private Arab property and would not expropriate land.[72]

Begin announced on October 26 that Israel would begin expanding the West Bank settlements as soon as the freeze ended. The Carter administration's response was swift and bitter. Atherton and Vance separately conveyed Carter's anger over what he considered a violation of an agreement made at

Camp David.[73] In a meeting with Atherton, Dayan reasserted the Israeli view that it had not agreed to halt its settlement activity beyond three months and repeated the argument advanced at Camp David that the settlements would only remain viable if their population increased at a rate sufficient to require educational, health, security, and commercial services.[74] Dayan also sought to deflect the stinging criticism by noting that unilateral American statements that Israel must dismantle its settlements harmed efforts to achieve a satisfactory peace, particularly when Americans issued the announcements in the midst of negotiations between Cairo and Jerusalem.[75]

Boutrus Ghali reproached Israel during a meeting with Dayan on the 29th for creating "accidents."[76] The Israeli foreign minister replied that Israel had never agreed to refrain from expanding existing settlements either during or after the three-month freeze. He also warned that Egypt should not view Israeli willingness to withdraw from the Sinai as a precedent that would apply to the settlements in the West Bank and Gaza Strip. Israeli villages in those territories would remain even after completion of the autonomy negotiations.[77]

Autonomy: Coalition Politics in Israel

Begin recalled Dayan and Weizman from Washington in late October in response to vocal demands of some cabinet members to learn more about progress in the Blair House talks. The skeptics distrusted the negotiators. Begin himself had argued with Dayan on the telephone in the first days of the conference over the foreign minister's request that Barak join the Israeli delegation and over the degree of independence the negotiators should have.[78]

Dayan successfully convinced Begin to name Barak to the delegation.[79] It was a controversial decision. The former attorney general's new position as supreme court justice gave rise to private concern that the appointment violated the separation between judicial and political matters. Barak's participation in the negotiations was also sensitive because Rosenne opposed it. Rosenne regarded Barak as too accommodative toward U.S. and Egyptian views.[80]

For those very same reasons, the appointment of Barak was attractive to Dayan. The Israeli foreign minister desired to strengthen the hand of those on the delegation who supported a flexible Israeli negotiating posture. He also wanted to add a relatively independent voice that could stand up to Begin and recalcitrant ministers.[81] Dayan continued to resist efforts to impose tight restrictions on his authority. For example, he refused orders to submit all U.S. and Egyptian proposals to cabinet review. Time constraints and rapidly changing circumstances, he claimed, made such a procedure impractical.[82] The foreign minister knew that other members of the delegation would add their personal reports to his own and keep Begin well informed of developments at the Blair House meetings.[83]

Dayan and Weizman knew that the effort to gain cabinet approval of the draft treaty negotiated in Washington would involve a bitter struggle and would therefore require a carefully devised strategy. Above all they needed to convince Begin personally to direct the effort. For only the prime minister could neutralize key ministers expected to mount staunch opposition to the draft treaty.[84]

Foremost among the dissidents was Education Minister Zevulun Hammer. Hammer had emerged as a strong leader of the NRP. The dominant figure among the party's aggressive younger members, he was a strong contender to head the party. He was a visceral proponent of expanding the settlements in "Judea and Samaria" and sympathized with the activities and zeal of extremist groups such as Gush Emunim. Hammer even threatened to resign on October 26 over what he considered the government's indifference to the plight of prospective settlers as well as his fear that the withdrawal from the Sinai might become a precedent for the West Bank.[85] Dayan quickly offered Hammer an olive branch by promising to support an immediate program to increase and expand existing settlements. The education minister accepted the offer and remained in the cabinet.[86]

The Israeli foreign minister thus helped resolve a troublesome political problem for the prime minister and satisfied many members of the angry, vocal, ultra-nationalist wing of the Likud coalition. Dayan's actions also cleared the way for the strongest possible commitment by Begin to achieve cabinet approval of the draft treaty. An earlier, informal poll of the cabinet had revealed narrow support for the treaty — 9 to 7 in favor with one abstention.[87] The combination of Begin's decision to impose party discipline and his fiery advocacy of the accord, however, altered the vote near the end of October to 14 to 2 in favor.[88] The cabinet did attach reservations to the draft and forbade Dayan to accept any new formulation submitted in Washington without approval from Jerusalem.[89]

Most ministers remained uncertain about the terms of the draft treaty. They feared that it created a specific link between Israel's withdrawal from the Sinai and the future of the West Bank and Gaza Strip. It did not establish itself as the agreement superceding all other Egyptian obligations in case of hostilities between Israel and other Arab states and did not set a clear schedule for the beginning of full bilateral diplomatic relations. It remained vague concerning the promises of U.S. economic assistance. And it encouraged premature expectations that negotiations on the West Bank would begin within one month of the signature of the peace treaty.[90] The cabinet ignored Dayan's claim that the draft treaty favored Israel far more than previous versions circulated by the Egyptians. The Israeli foreign minister pointed out that early drafts contained language granting the Egyptian air force free movement in the Sinai and its Navy unrestricted use of the Gulf of Aqaba, limited the life of the agreement to five years, and contained a strong connection between the treaty and the West Bank and Gaza Strip. According to Dayan, the Israeli negotiating team had expected Cairo to reject the draft under consideration.[91]

External Influences on Egyptian Positions

The issue of linkage plagued the negotiations up until the final agreement was signed in March 1979. Growing unease among the members of Cairo's governing elite over the country's rapidly eroding position in the Arab world increased Egypt's sensitivity on this point. Sadat was receiving very little good news. Ali, chief of the Egyptian delegation to the Blair House talks, met with Arab ambassadors to the United States on the 22nd. They warned him that Cairo must not expand economic and cultural ties with Israel after ratification of the treaty.[92] Khalil also reported that Egypt was fast losing its authority and respect among Arab nations. Al-Baz left the Blair House talks on the 19th to brief Mubarak — then in the midst of a diplomatic tour of Western Europe and Iran — in London. Already skeptical of the value of the peace process, the vice president had encountered little enthusiasm from other Arabs and only uncertain support from his hosts during his travels. He too delivered discouraging news to Sadat.

Linkage between the treaty and the future of the West Bank and Gaza remained weak and ill-defined in the draft submitted to Sadat. For example, the preamble — written by the Israelis and approved by Ali -- vaguely noted that peace would be maintained in the West Bank through arrangements with both the Palestinians and Jordanians. And although an annex raised the possibility of beginning the autonomy talks one month after the ratification of the Egyptian-Israeli treaty, no deadline for resolving the issues surrounding the future of the West Bank and Gaza Strip figured in the text placed before Sadat.[93]

Sadat remained convinced that restoring Egyptian sovereignty over the Sinai must take precedence over all other issues and that it would ensure his political survival. But Khalil and most of Sadat's advisers told the president that efforts to form an effective new political party, to retain full control over a restive parliament, and to solidify economic gains would founder if Egypt did not maintain at least the appearance of a community of interests with moderate Arab states.

Thus, more than a week prior to the Baghdad Conference that would denounce Egypt and before Begin's announcement that Israel would expand its settlements on the West Bank, Sadat instructed Ali in Washington to strengthen the linkage between the treaty and the autonomy talks.[94] Ali convened a meeting of his delegation on October 24 to devise a strategy to accomplish Sadat's order.[95]

On the 25th, special presidential emissary Sayed Marei returned to in Cairo from Riyadh without a clear promise of Saudi support for Sadat's peace moves,[96] adding to the Egyptian leadership's feeling of insecurity. The Saudi refusal to back Egypt dashed any hope that Riyadh and Amman would assume a moderate posture toward Egypt at the upcoming Baghdad summit. Equally significant, the Saudi government's negative response cast a pall over discussions concerning bilateral military and economic assistance, including Riyadh's promise to finance the purchase of high-performance fighter planes for Cairo from the United States.[97] Retraction of that commitment would jeapordize Sadat's relations with the military-security establishment in Egypt.

The Carter administration suspected just how precarious Sadat's position had become; Jerusalem did not. Dayan and Weizman suffered severe criticism at home for the modest compromises they had agreed to in the draft treaty and obtained cabinet approval only after backing a hardline policy toward the settlements in the West Bank. Carter now redoubled his efforts to reach a solution and persuaded Sadat to leave Egypt's negotiating team at the Blair House Conference intact.[98] Domestic political problems and a desire to express dissatisfaction with Israel's settlements policy had led Sadat to consider recalling senior members of the delegation.

Egyptian–Israeli talks resumed in Washington in late October. But neither Cairo nor Jerusalem had given their respective delegations sufficient leeway to conclude a peace treaty. Dayan informed Ali and Ghali on the 29th that Jerusalem could not agree to a special Egyptian role in the Gaza Strip.[99] Moreover, during a November 1 stopover in New York before traveling to Canada, Begin sought in talks with Vance to eliminate from the draft treaty even the limited mention of linkage agreed to by Israel on October 21 in Washington but amended by the Cabinet five days later.[100]

Egyptian representatives naturally turned down Begin's request. After Dayan returned to Blair House from Jerusalem, the Israeli cabinet became more anxious over the treaty terms they had reluctantly approved. Begin agreed to submit each clause to full cabinet review and appoint a ministerial committee to study revisions.[101]

Meanwhile, the Baghdad summit began, and the participants — including Saudi Arabia and Jordan — mounted a fierce verbal attack on the Camp David Accords. Midway through the conference, a delegation led by Lebanese Prime Minister Salim Hoss was dispatched to Cairo with instructions to offer Sadat $5 billion over ten years if he disavowed the Camp David agreements.[102] Sadat refused even to receive the mission, asserting that his nation's future was not for sale.[103]

The meeting in Iraq concluded on November 5 with a decision to grant Syria, Jordan, and the PLO a war–chest of $3.5 billion annually to combat the accords and Israel. The conference also decided that if Egypt concluded a peace treaty with Israel, the Arabs would suspend Egypt from the Arab League, remove the organization's headquarters from Cairo, and boycott all Egyptian firms that dealt with Israel.[104]

Khalil convened a cabinet meeting on November 7 to listen to a review of the Blair House conference by Boutrus Ghali. The four–hour discussion concluded with a reiteration of the need to defend the rights of the Palestinian people by creating a link between the Egyptian–Israeli treaty and the autonomy negotiations.[105] On the same day, Sadat told Washington Post columnist Joseph Kraft in Cairo that Egypt desired a precise timetable for resolving the Gaza Strip and West Bank issues.[106] The Egyptian president announced on November 8 just before Ghali and al–Baz returned to Washington that he could not accept a treaty that did not provide explicitly for the start of negotiations on the Palestinian problem within a month of ratifying the Egyptian–Israeli agreement.[107]

Boutrus Ghali arrived in Washington on November 9 and, accompanied by Ghorbal, immediately contacted Dayan. Weizman and Dayan's top aide, Eliakim Rubinstein joined them. After three hours of intensive discussions the Egyptian officials informed their Israeli counterparts that Sadat would insist on five demands: a joint letter with Begin containing a specific timetable for the implementation of Palestinian autonomy; a commitment in the treaty to begin negotiations on autonomy within a month of ratifying the accord; elections for a Palestinian council four months after the beginning of negotiations; transfer of authority in the West Bank and Gaza Strip from the Israeli military government to the Palestinian council one month after the vote; and then redeployment of Israeli forces to new security locations in the territories.

In the meantime, Cairo wanted the Israelis to make gestures of goodwill that would help it build confidence in the peace process among the Palestinians. Israel could, for example, remove headquarters of its military government from Arab towns, free Arab prisoners, allow political activity in the territories, permit Arabs who fled the West Bank during the 1967 war to return, and agree to a permanent Egyptian mission in the Gaza Strip.[108]

Dayan and Weizman responded in muted tones that the Blair House talks were supposed to finalize the terms of a peace treaty between Israel and Egypt, not the details of Palestinian autonomy. Nevertheless, Dayan asserted unofficially that Begin would agree to begin autonomy negotiations one-month after ratification of the treaty. Israel could not, he continued, commit itself to holding elections for a Palestinian council four months later. Egypt proposed the move because it might help create a strong link between the treaty and Palestinian autonomy. Israel rejected the proposal for the very same reason. Jerusalem insisted that the exchange of ambassadors and opening of cultural and economic ties should begin before the implementation of autonomy.

The Israelis promised to recommend that IDF headquarters be removed from the Gaza Strip and Nablus, although they stressed that such a move would not diminish the authority of the Israeli military government there. A decision to permit a permanent Egyptian mission in the Gaza Strip, they said, would have to wait for the establishment of diplomatic relations between Jerusalem and Cairo and would depend on Egyptian willingness to allow a similar Israeli presence in Alexandria. The Israelis also asserted that procedures for the return of refugees to the West Bank and Gaza Strip, including security checks, would have to be devised in separate talks.[109] In effect, Israel rejected the imposition of preconditions on the Arab–Israeli peace treaty.

Separate U.S.–Egyptian and U.S.–Israeli meetings on the 10th and 11th produced little change in the positions of the two sides on autonomy and its relationship to the treaty. Ghali reviewed Egypt's stance with Atherton,[110] and the U.S. team altered the Egyptian proposals slightly –– making the timetable on autonomy a goal instead of a fixed schedule –– before formally resubmitting them to the Israeli delegation.[111] During a discussion between Vance and Dayan at the State Department, the U.S. secretary of state suggested that the two sides adopt nine months rather than six as a goal to complete talks on the West Bank and Gaza Strip.[112] Dayan countered that Israel might agree to a one year objective but cautioned that the decision rested with Begin.[113] Vance said he would go along with Dayan's proposal if Egypt accepted it. According to Atherton, Vance was reticent to back Dayan's suggestion because Sadat had warned he would normalize relations with Israel –– set for nine months after ratification of the treaty –– only after completion of the autonomy talks. Dayan desired a one-year period because he wanted diplomatic relations established three months prior to the end of autonomy talks.[114]

There remained one final opportunity to reach an accommodation on this point before the end of the Blair House talks. Begin flew from Toronto to New York on November 12 to meet with Vance, Atherton, and Saunders. The Israeli prime minister rejected Dayan's one-year target.[115] First, Begin was unhappy over the appearance of collusion between Dayan and Vance on the matter. Second, he was apprehensive about committing Israel to a specific goal without assurances that failure to meet the objective would not jeapordize the entire Egyptian–Israeli treaty. Finally –– and most important –– the Israeli cabinet would probably reject out of hand any joint letter setting deadlines for achieving a settlement in the West Bank and Gaza Strip.[116]

The Sinai

There was little disagreement among the parties over the provisions for Israeli withdrawal from the Sinai at the Blair House Conference. The Israeli government agreed to complete its departure within three years after ratification of the treaty.[117] Israel would complete phase one of a two-step arrangement within nine months of ratification. This phase would include withdrawal behind a line running east of El Arish to Ras Muhammed.[118] The Egyptian delegation at Blair House indicated as early as October 17 that they favored stepping up the transfer of El-Arish and recommended moving up the date by three months.[119] Carter apparently opposed the change, but Dayan and Weizman viewed the matter within an entirely different context.[120]

The two Israeli officials wished Cairo to establish diplomatic relations with Jerusalem at the earliest possible date. In a sense, the entire bargain would mean nothing if Israel failed to achieve recognition of its right to exist and secure some promise of a safe future. Thus, Dayan recommended to Begin upon his return to Jerusalem on October 22 that Israel agree to advance the date for evacuation of the western Sinai. Such a move, he argued, could accelerate the process of normalization and permit a longer period for total withdrawal from the Sinai, thereby testing Egyptian behavior. Moreover, he pointed out that the majority of Israeli airfields and settlements were located in the eastern Sinai.[121]

The Israeli cabinet informed its Blair House delegation on November 2, however, that Israel would not agree to withdraw to the El-Arish line within six months of ratifying the treaty. Jerusalem would adhere to the timetable agreed upon at Camp David — evacuation after nine months.[122] Weizman returned to Israel to seek a reversal in the government's position. He failed.[123]

The Egyptian reaction was quick and sharp, although Cairo had downplayed the matter a few weeks earlier. Its increased concern presumably reflected national anxiety following the Baghdad summit. Ghali and Ghorbal even charged that the Israeli refusal amounted to a violation of the prospective peace agreement.[124] On November 11 the U.S. government conveyed to the Israeli delegation its disappointment about the Israeli cabinet's decision.[125] The parties did not resolve the impasse fully for several months.

Deadlock

Negotiations slowed after the Blair House Conference. In Egypt, the peace process faced serious troubles. Sadat had devised a meticulous plan to achieve a settlement with Israel by the anniversary of his spectacular trip to Jerusalem. The strength of opposition both among Egypt's elites and in leading Arab states, however, surprised and inhibited Sadat. He had expected radical Arab states to mount fierce opposition to the Camp David accords, but the strong anti–Egypt stand taken by moderate Saudi Arabia and Jordan at Baghdad startled the Egyptian president.[126]

Sadat refused to allow his foes to cow or discourage him. He was not willing to adopt a hardline policy toward Israel that held little promise for producing a solution. He therefore set in motion a kaleidoscope of activity intended to confound and defeat foreign and domestic opponents, influence Jerusalem, and impress Washington. He proposed that autonomy be implemented in the Gaza Strip first, with Egypt playing an important role there. He hoped such an early implementation of autonomy might demonstrate the sincerity of Israeli and Egyptian intentions toward the Palestinians and help reduce fear in Israel that to relinquish the West Bank would pose a deadly threat to the country's existence. Sadat also put forth new linkage proposals that Jerusalem might find acceptable.

Sadat dispatched Mubarak to Washington on November 15 with a proposal to hold elections in the Gaza Strip and the West Bank at different times following ratification of the treaty between Egypt and Israel.[127] The implementation of autonomy in the West Bank would begin within a year of ratification. In the Gaza Strip, however, it would start within six months.[128] By sending Mubarak to deliver the new proposal, Sadat co–opted the vice president into supporting the policy. The president then named Mubarak head of a special leadership group charged with oversight of Egypt's strategy in the peace process.[129]

America and Israel carefully examined Egypt's new linkage proposal presented by Mubarak. Washington had serious reservation about the plan's substance, and Jerusalem rejected it outright.[130] The Egyptian president recalled his negotiators from Washington. Cairo explained publicly that since the Israeli delegation had already returned to Jerusalem there was little reason for the Egyptians to remain at Blair House without bargaining partners.[131] But the move also strengthened Sadat's position by ensuring that his decisions would not be criticized by Egyptian officials based in Washington. And certain members of the delegation could help promote support for the policies that would inevitably result from Mubarak's review of the peace process. Several days after the recall of the Egyptian delegation Sadat issued an optimistic statement regarding future negotiations despite Israel's rejection of his linkage proposal.[132]

Sadat now had to convince his domestic audience that a month of discussions with Israel in Washington had been worthwhile and warranted serious efforts to break the impasse. The pro—regime daily newspaper Al—Ahram disclosed the text of the draft treaty without annexes in its November 23 editions.[133] It almost certainly would not have done so without the approval and connivance of Sadat. The Egyptian president probably believed that to reveal the details of Israel's return of the Sinai to Egyptian control would enhance the public appeal of the peace process.

Mubarak and his committee presented their report to Sadat on the 26th. Sadat approved a working paper that recommended strategies and positions for future talks with Israel.[134] He asked Khalil, who would henceforth become Sadat's point man in the peace process, to deliver the document to Carter.[135] The Egyptian prime minister arrived in Washington on December 1 accompanied by al—Baz —— who went along to represent Mubarak and, as one of the foreign office's most experienced negotiators, to assist Khalil in his first official diplomatic mission.[136] The White House discussions centered on a three-point Egyptian solution to the impasse over linkage. Cairo suggested that councils to administer the West Bank and Gaza Strip be set up within a month of ratification of the treaty; that elections be held in the territories before the end of 1979; and that Israeli authority then be transferred to local groups and IDF forces be withdrawn to secure locations in the area.[137]

Sadat's new plan contained elements that would satisfy the supporters of linkage as well as concessions that would meet some Israeli objections. And it differed enough from previous Egyptian stances to attract American approval. Crucially, the offer enjoyed considerable support from Khalil and the Egyptian techno—managerial class and as a result helped further isolate Mubarak's pan—Arabists.

When Begin returned to Israel from the United States and Canada in mid—November, he encountered official disquiet. Many in the cabinet remained unconvinced of their negotiators' commitment to preserving Israel's security perimeter as outlined in the Camp David Accords. Dayan and Weizman launched a media blitz in mid-November to attract support for a specific timetable for concluding an agreement on the West Bank and Gaza Strip, confirming the doubts of their opponents.[138] These suspicions came to the prime minister's attention during his stay in Canada. Begin was informed that during one cabinet meeting held in his absence Education Minister Zevulun Hammer had asked: "What did they (Dayan and Weizman) sell us this morning?"[139] Thus, the prime minister's refusal to accept a timetable for the autonomy talks resulted in part from a need to placate rebellious members of his cabinet.

Israel's foreign and defense ministers argued that delay would not help Israel gain more favorable peace terms. The deterioration of Egypt's position in the Arab world and mounting domestic and pan-Arab pressure on Sadat to return to the fold, they pointed out, would only make talks more difficult in the future.[140] Sadat unwittingly bolstered Dayan and Weizman's argument toward the end of November by sending Begin a ten-page statement complaining about the lack of progress in the negotiations. He reiterated the Egyptian demand that the implementation of a peace treaty must be linked to a commitment to achieve a satisfactory settlement in the West Bank and Gaza Strip. Sadat also rejected the Israeli demand that the treaty contain a clause establishing the treaty's precedence over all other Egyptian obligations.[141]

The Israeli prime minister was, if anything, a consummate and skilled negotiator. He knew when and how to bluff. Begin must have realized that Sadat had just raised the ante. He knew the cost of withdrawing from the negotiations was too high. He chose instead to adopt a strategy devised by Dayan. Israel would sign a peace treaty with Egypt based on the terms agreed to before November 11. Thus, it would include no firm timetable for concluding autonomy negotiations, and Dayan would call Vance and withdraw the offer to settle West Bank and Gaza Strip issues one year from treaty ratification.[142] But suspicion among cabinet members remained a formidable obstacle. Dayan helped convince Begin to adopt the plan and to make a major effort to persuade the ministers to support it by producing a set of legal opinions, co-signed by Barak, Rosenne, and new Attorney General Yitzhak Zamir, that argued Israel would retain complete freedom of action despite the linkage contained in the treaty.[143] Carter contributed with yet another personal plea to Begin for flexibility toward Egypt.[144]

The Israeli prime minister finally approved the strategy on November 21 and in a spirited defense informed the full cabinet that he favored the draft treaty presented in October. He told the ministers that he would agree to sign a joint letter with Sadat promising to seek a settlement for the West Bank and Gaza Strip "at an early date" but that he would reject any formula establishing a fixed timetable.[145]

Meanwhile, Dayan attempted to regain the confidence of his ministerial colleagues by issuing a tough statement about the draft treaty on the 22nd, asserting that Egypt would have to "take it or leave it."[146] Few ministers accepted Dayan's apparent turnabout, and the cabinet reiterated its determination to place sharp limits on the foreign minister's latitude in negotiations with Egypt.[147]

Israel responded to Al-Ahram's publication of the draft treaty by releasing its version of the text with annexes on the 25th.[148] Washington followed suit.[149] The Israeli cabinet then announced formally its position on peace with Egypt after a special session held on November 30. The statement read:

> The Government of Israel is prepared to sign the peace treaty with Egypt which was brought before them for consideration by the negotiating delegation, if the Egyptian delegation is willing to do so.
>
> The latest Egyptian proposals (November 11) are a deviation from the Camp David Accords and are not acceptable to Israel.
>
> When the peace treaty between Egypt and Israel is signed and ratified, Israel will be ready to start negotiations towards an agreement on the introduction of administrative autonomy in Judea, Samaria and Gaza, in accordance with what was stated in the Camp David Accords.[150]

Carter observed events since the Blair House talks with a mixture of irritation and impotence. The period envisaged in the Camp David Accords to negotiate an Egyptian–Israeli Peace Treaty would expire on December 17. The freeze on Israeli settlement activity would also end on that day, according to the Israeli interpretation of the promise made at the September summit.

Egypt and Arab moderates such as Jordan and Saudi Arabia were certain to view any expansion of the settlements in the occupied territories as an affront and a violation of the Camp David Accords. Such a move might even cause Cairo to withdraw from the recessed negotiations altogether. Washington opposed any resumption of settlement activity, which it viewed as an obstacle to peace and a violation of international law. If Israel ended the freeze, the Arab world would insist that American policy makers back their tough rhetoric with strong measures against Israel. America would then face a difficult decision, particularly because the Shah of Iran was rapidly losing authority, which threatened U.S. oil supplies from Iran and increased U.S. dependence on oil supplies from Saudi Arabia. Jordan continued to follow Riyahd's lead and refused to join the peace process without firm assurances of rapid Israeli withdrawal from the West Bank.

Carter dispatched Vance to the Middle East in an attempt to break the impasse.[151] The Egyptian proposals presented by Khalil and the Israeli cabinet announcement of November 30 narrowed differences somewhat but core disagreements remained over linkage and over the status of the Egyptian–Israeli treaty relative to other Egyptian commitments. But neither side appeared anxious over the possibility that they might not achieve agreement before December 17.

Vance arrived in Egypt on December 10 and proceeded to Israel two days later. The meetings in Cairo resulted in some shifts in the Egyptian position. Cairo sought alterations related to security arrangements in the Sinai following Israeli withdrawal and to the stationing of UN troops on the border between opposing forces. Egypt wished the treaty to permit either side to request a review of the Sinai agreement five years after ratification, although changes would require the consent of both partners. Cairo also desired to establish a time limit for the UN peace–keeping presence in the Sinai. Sadat may have wanted to change the status of the UN force in order to confirm further Egyptian sovereignty over the Sinai.[152]

The most troublesome change requested by Egypt concerned the exchange of ambassadors. The two sides had earlier agreed to establish full diplomatic ties one month after completion of the first phase of Israeli withdrawal from the Sinai. Under Sadat's latest proposal, only consuls and charges d'affaires would be appointed after the redeployment of Israeli troops to the El-Arish–Ras Muhammed line. The exchange of ambassadors would occur only after the introduction of Palestinian autonomy at least in the Gaza Strip. Difficulties over the relative priority of Egypt's conflicting obligations and over the timetable for a settlement in the West Bank and Gaza Strip remained a top concern of Egyptian officials. The Egyptians recommended a solution to the former whereby the treaty would contain language merely declaring mutual respect for treaty obligations. On the latter, Egypt did not budge from its insistence on specific dates.[153]

Vance carried the Egyptian ideas to Jerusalem and on December 13 met twice with Israeli government leaders and members of a ministerial defense committee. The U.S. secretary of state told the Israelis that he had convinced Sadat not to reopen the entire treaty for renegotiation but to accept explanatory letters and documents instead.[154] The Israeli prime minister, recently returned from Oslo where he had shared the Nobel Peace Prize with Sadat, responded by making harsh comments about the American role in the negotiations. Begin reminded Vance that after considerable internal dispute the Israeli government had agreed to relinquish the entire Sinai, including the settlements.[155] Dayan interjected that Israel would never abandon Judea, Samaria, and the Gaza Strip, that the status of those areas would affect the very survival of Israel and Israeli citizens.[156] Vance reminded his hosts of Sadat's delicate position both at home and abroad and asked them to show greater generosity and historical vision.[157]

Most cabinet members regarded Vance's performance as totally insensitive to Israeli security requirements. Many in the government believed America had lost all credibility as a mediator. They considered the United States an apologist for Egypt and complained that Washington placed undue emphasis on Sadat's internal and external troubles.[158] A majority of the ministers went so far as to advocate recanting on Israel's November 30 decision to approve the draft treaty prepared in October.[159]

Begin and Dayan, however, united the cabinet behind a policy that firmly rejected new Egyptian demands without retreating from existing positions or precluding flexibility in the future. The ministers approved a statement on December 15 that blamed Egypt for the impasse and described Cairo's new demands transmitted by Vance as deviations from the Camp David Accords.[160] Finally, the cabinet left open the possibility that it might consider approving a joint letter with Egypt concerning autonomy negotiations.[161]

Brussels — December 1978

U.S.-Israeli relations plummeted following Jerusalem's rebuke to the Vance mission for attempting to reconcile the differences between Israel and Egypt. The Carter administration publicly accused the Israeli government of obstructing peace, and American Jewish leaders leaped to Jerusalem's defense.[162]

Meanwhile, efforts to arrange face-to-face meetings between high-level Israeli officials and Egyptian Prime Minister Mustafa Khalil resumed. The process began in early December during Khalil's visit to Washington. Khalil intended to return to Egypt through Western Europe and may have requested that U.S. officials assist in arranging a meeting there with Weizman, Dayan, or both.[163] Vance's failure to move the parties perceptively toward signing a treaty encouraged the secretary to urge a meeting between Dayan and Khalil. Sadat and Begin accepted the suggestion, and Khalil, Dayan, and Vance met in Brussels on December 23. The purpose of the conference was to seek ways to restart the peace negotiations.[164]

Vance's arrival in Brussels was delayed. Dayan proceeded to the Hilton ahead of schedule and was invited by Khalil to an informal, private dinner on the 22nd at the nearby Hyatt House. Khalil's brother -- the Egyptian Ambassador to Belgium -- and Usama al-Baz accompanied the Egyptian prime minister. Dayan brought Rosenne and Israeli Ambassador to Belgium Yitzhak Minesir. Dinner conversation was amiable. Vance, Saunders, and Quandt joined the group near midnight.[165]

A brief business meeting ensued. Dayan advised the Egyptians and Americans that Jerusalem's position had not changed since Vance's trip to the Middle East. Khalil stressed the deterioration of Egypt's relations with other Arab states. He asserted that although he did not expect most Arab nations to endorse the treaty, many could become reconciled to it if its provisions went at least part way toward satisfying the demands of the Arab world's leading moderate states.[166]

Dayan asked whether accommodating Arab views meant Israel would have to withdraw from the West Bank, East Jerusalem, and the Golan Heights and endorse Palestinian self-determination. Khalil responded that it did. The Americans were not surprised that the Egyptians had revived old positions unacceptable to Israel. Vance had reportedly learned in Cairo that Sadat had to restrain Khalil and al-Baz, who wanted to renegotiate the entire treaty. The late—evening meeting, however, ended on a positive note: The Egyptian prime minister assured his negotiating partners that he desired to create an atmosphere of trust and concentrate on general formulas for achieving peace. But he wanted to avoid the isolation of Egypt from the Arab world.[167]

The same group met again for breakfast on the morning of the 23rd. Vance, Dayan, and Khalil shortly broke away and held a private, unrecorded discussion. The Egyptian prime minister placed the clause concerning the relative priority of Egypt's various obligations within the context of radicalism and fundamentalism that had begun to sweep the Islamic world. The United States and Israel should, he asserted, value its Egyptian ally and encourage the growth of Cairo's influence among moderate Arab neighbors. Egypt could only achieve that goal if Cairo commanded respect in the region. Placing treaty restrictions on Cairo's relations with other Arab states would doom the effort. He reminded his interlocutors that Pakistanis and Koreans had already replaced Egyptian technicians in the Gulf States as a result of Sadat's visit to Jerusalem.[168]

Dayan listed the dangers to Israel posed by Cairo's alliances with its Arab neighbors. Syria, for example, could attack Israeli forces on the Golan Heights and characterize the move as defensive or as a justifiable attempt to regain its land. The Israeli foreign minister asked Khalil what Egypt would do under that set of circumstances. The Egyptian prime minister's answer surprised Dayan. He asserted that Cairo would support Syria's position but refuse to enter the conflict. Without Egyptian participation, he pointed out, the Arabs possessed only a limited ability to wage war against Israel.[169]

Dayan then questioned the Egyptian representative on other possible scenarios. He wanted to know what Egypt would do if Israeli forces crossed into Lebanon to counter PLO terrorism launched from bases there and the Arabs used the Israeli military response as a pretext to launch a military campaign against Israel. Would, he asked, the Egyptian—Israeli peace treaty remain in force? Khalil repeated his previous answer: Egypt would join in the condemnation of Israel but would not go to war. It would support Arab unity politically and diplomatically, but not militarily.[170]

The discussion moved on to other subjects. Differences over the West Bank, East Jerusalem, and the Palestinian problem remained profound. Khalil warned, for example, that if Israel expanded its settlements in the West Bank, Egypt would refuse to send an ambassador to Jerusalem. Dayan replied that to make exchange of ambassadors dependent on settlement restrictions would doom the treaty. Vance refrained from comment throughout most of the discussion.[171]

Both Egyptian and Israeli representatives at the Brussels meeting were constrained by the narrow limits placed on their freedom to make independent decisions. Khalil had fewer personal restraints than Dayan. But public attitudes in Cairo toward ties with Israel were hardening. The press damned the lack of progress toward peace. Members of the Egyptian parliament openly criticized Begin and attacked Israeli military actions in southern Lebanon. Even Jihan Sadat, the president's wife, had cancelled plans to attend an international medical conference in Cairo when she learned Israeli delegates would be among the guests.[172]

Despite the growing ferment, however, Khalil retained wide public acceptance. He had begun to crack down on urban corruption. He wielded considerable power within the New Democratic Party structure[173] and was both prime minister and foreign minister. He retained primary responsibility for the daily conduct of talks. The constant presence of al-Baz at Khalil's side at bilateral meetings with the Israelis indicated that Mubarak still possessed some influence on the peace process. Moreover, Khalil remained on good terms with Mubarak and other Egyptian pan-Arabists as he shared and voiced many of the same concerns.

Dayan, however, did not enjoy the full confidence of Israel's suspicious cabinet, which was determined to limit his freedom to maneuver. And the foreign minister's relationship with Begin had begun to deteriorate. Nevertheless, the Liberals and Yadin backed Dayan's position on peace with Egypt, and the foreign minister retained the confidence of U.S. and Egyptian diplomats, replacing Weizman — an early favorite — who had fallen into obscurity.

The Atherton Shuttle — January 1979

Egyptian-Israeli peace negotiations disappeared from public attention during the first weeks of 1979 as the Carter administration struggled vainly to prevent Shah Mohammed Reza Pahlevi's fall from power in Iran.[174] But during this partial eclipse, Israel moved a step closer to compromise with Egypt.

Dayan recognized the value of meeting personally with Khalil and sought to give the dialogue greater substance. He was convinced the Egyptian prime minister desired peace with Israel. The Israeli foreign minister, therefore, drafted and received government approval on December 31 for a slightly modified position.

Jerusalem had previously asserted that it would no longer negotiate but merely wait for Egypt to sign the treaty submitted before November 11. Now, however, Israel would agree to resume the talks on Palestinian autonomy and security arrangements in the Sinai, although it would continue to reject any firm timetable for either.[175] The language of Dayan's proposal was sufficiently imprecise to ensure the support of even the most right-wing ministers. Dayan also took two initiatives, intended to swing recalcitrant cabinet members. First, he sent a letter to Vance bitterly complaining about the secretary of state's performance during his mid-December visit to the area. Second, he told Education Minister Hammer that he would again endorse a recommendation to strengthen Israeli settlements in the West Bank.[176] Hammer's supporters, particularly among the radical Gush Emunim, threatened to establish new encampments in the Jordan Valley even if the government forbade them to do so and warned that they would use force if necessary.[177] Dayan's offer, if accepted, would permit Hammer to placate his restive constituency.

The hiatus in talks enabled those in both Cairo and Jerusalem who opposed the direction the process had taken to assert themselves. On January 6 Ghali revived the claim that the Camp David Accords did not prohibit the creation of a Palestinian state.[178] In Jerusalem, wavering cabinet members worried about the probable loss of their major oil supply in the wake of Iran's revolution and wondered whether it would not be wiser to back out of the peace process as a result.[179] Serious concern about what sorts of limits the autonomy talks would impose on Israel led some to consider delaying the Israeli evacuation from the Sinai until those negotiations had started. Others, such as Dayan and Weizman, feared the process was losing momentum and that a permanent break in the negotiations might result.[180] Under those circumstances, Washington sent Atherton to the Middle East. Should the mission prove unsuccessful, Vance, Khalil, and Dayan would meet again to discuss intractable issues.[181]

Atherton and State Department Legal Adviser Herbert Hansell stayed in Jerusalem from January 17 to 25 to devise acceptable language for several clauses. The articles in dispute dealt with the priority of obligations and the right of each party to review security arrangements in the Sinai after Israeli withdrawal.[182] An Israeli negotiating team, led by Ben-Elissar and consisting of Rosenne, Zamir, and Ruth Lapidot — a law professor at Hebrew University — conducted marathon sessions with the Americans until they agreed on a draft.[183] A letter clarifying specific clauses or offering additional interpretations would also be attached to the new version of the treaty.

The letter would be addressed to Begin from Vance. It would stipulate that Egypt and Israel would seek to resolve the Arab-Israeli conflict through peaceful means and that neither had the right to use or threaten the use of military action against the other to accomplish its goals. Thus, Egypt would have neither the obligation nor the right to assist the Arab allies in a war against Israel. Israeli presence in the West Bank, Gaza Strip, or the Golan Heights would henceforth not justify armed action against Jerusalem. Israeli military action launched in self-defense — in response to terrorism, for example — would not be grounds for military action against Israel. Finally, the letter would state that both sides would have the right to review security arrangements in the Sinai after Israeli withdrawal. Any changes would require mutual agreement.[184]

The Atherton mission accepted one other important compromise before leaving for Cairo on January 25. Begin objected to calling the Israeli presence in the territories as "occupation." U.S. representatives regarded it as an occupation and refused to call it anything else. But wishing to preserve the spirit of compromise, Atherton accepted a formula that stated "Israel's presence in the territories is not aggression."[185] This phrase caused America's eleven-day peace effort to collapse. Egyptian officials were furious. They charged that Washington had granted legitimacy to the Israeli occupation.[186] Cairo did not even consider the draft treaty and accompanying interpretative notes and letter as a result, and Atherton returned to Jerusalem without a useful response. Nevertheless, each side expressed its hope for an early return to the bargaining table.[187]

Camp David II — February 1979

The failure of the Atherton mission coincided with troubling domestic and regional events. Doubts about the peace process were growing among the Egyptian military, and attacks against the regime inspired by the left were increasing. Defense Minister Ali attempted to dispel criticism of the treaty within the army by noting that any agreement signed with Israel would not prevent Egypt from protecting itself against its enemies. In an address to officers in Luxor and Aswan in early January, Ali emphasized the necessity to maintain strong deterrent forces. He was cognizant of charges that a peace treaty with Israel would lead to reductions in Egyptian strength and assured his audience that he would not allow that to happen.[188]

Sadat in the same month ordered the construction of five new cities within twenty-five miles of Cairo to house the poor who overcrowded the capital. The government feared that discontent with a failure of the peace process to produce benefits for old city dwellers and agitation by fundamentalist opponents of peace with Egypt might fuel urban disruptions. Sadat chose, however, to avoid a confrontation with his real enemies by ordering roundups among the less numerous and relatively impotent leftists.[189] The Sadat regime thus indirectly warned those in alliance with Muslim fanatics that he would not tolerate open dissent.

Egypt's campaign to persuade the Arabs of its fidelity to the Palestinian cause by insisting on a linkage between the Arab-Israeli treaty and resolution of the Palestinian problem did not win over the Islamic states. In fact, rather than consider joining the Egyptian-israeli peace process, Jordan's King Hussein was calling for a broader framework sponsored by the United Nations.[190] Syrian and PLO officials felt confident that Cairo would soon return to the fold when it recognized Israel's intention permanently to avoid relinquishing captured territory.[191] The Saudis remained quietly critical of Egyptian policy and doubted it would achieve comprehensive peace in the region.[192]

Thus, Egypt's isolation from the Arab world, growing doubts about the peace process within the army, and urban discontent exploited by right-wing fanatics became formidable obstacles to Sadat's desire to conclude swiftly a treaty with Israel. The disappointing Western commercial response to Sadat's generous peace moves only reinforced the lack of enthusiasm among leading Egyptians. The few investment projects undertaken suffered from serious graft and corruption, and profiteering by middlemen nearly wiped out any advantages to the poor. Under the circumstances, Egypt's elites advocated caution in moving toward accommodation with Jerusalem.[193]

The Israeli government faced similar domestic opposition to its peace proposals. Many Israelis feared that a Palestinian state would emerge from any agreement to link the Egyptian-Israeli treaty and the autonomy talks.[194] Begin's autonomy plan was a thinly veiled attempt to preserve Israeli control of the West Bank and Gaza Strip. Egypt's proposals, according to many Israelis, threatened to eliminate any Jewish presence in the area. The peace now movement, which had seemed to represent the national mood in mid-1978, had withered by early 1979.[195] Moves by the government to establish new settlements in the Jordan Valley during mid-January received enthusiastic support.[196] Although Begin's popularity remained high, the strength of the Likud party was ebbing among Sephardic Jews anxious about rapidly rising inflation and uncertain security prospects.[197]

The shah of Iran's flight from Teheran in mid-January 1979 complicated matters for Begin and Sadat as well as Jimmy Carter. Israel faced the difficult task of replacing its loss of Iranian oil.[198] Jerusalem would have to rely on Egypt to sell Israel energy from its oil fields in the Sinai, or America and its allies would have to supply Israel from their stocks. Sadat unwisely received the shah when the latter left Teheran and briefly considered offering the monarch permanent refuge in Egypt. By thus identifying himself with the fallen regime in Iran, Sadat further soiled his image in an Arab world under pressure from Moslem fundamentalists. He also provided the radical fringes in Egypt with yet another target.[199] And Carter knew that on the heels of the Iranian revolution America's position in the Middle East would erode further if Washington failed to deliver a peace treaty tied to a settlement in the West Bank and Gaza Strip.

In order to arrest the erosion of support for the peace talks in Cairo and Jerusalem and relieve the pressures created by the Iranian revolution, Washington sought to accelerate the negotiations. In mid-February, Begin and Sadat accepted an American suggestion to hold a new round of ministerial-level meetings at Camp David beginning on the 21st.[200]

Dayan headed the Israeli delegation to the talks. But the cabinet again gave him no freedom to suggest new solutions.

Dayan could express his own personal opinion, but final authority rested with the government in Jerusalem.[201] A public statement made by the foreign minister prior to his Washington visit contributed to the cabinet's decision to limit Dayan's authority. He stated: "The PLO is not a state, but we cannot overlook their status and value in the conflict, in order to reach a solution..."[202]

Zamir, Rosenne, Yehuda Blum, Ben-Elissar, and Poran accompanied the Israeli foreign minister. Khalil, Boutrus Ghali, and al-Baz represented Egypt. Vance, Saunders, and Atherton attended for the United States.[203]

The conference lasted four days and ended on February 24 without moving the parties visibly closer to resolving their impasse. Atherton presided at the first meeting as Vance was absent. He sought to convince the delegates that the opportunities for peace were dwindling, especially in light of Khomeini's accession to power in Iran. A peace treaty between Israel and Egypt would, he said, provide an important foundation for stability in the Middle East.[204]

Vance met separately with Khalil and Dayan on the morning of the 21st -- the conference's first formal session -- and established procedures for the talks. Vance confided to Dayan that Washington believed the treaty could stand on its own. He cautioned, however, that it would be dangerous and irresponsible to disregard existing ties between Egypt and other Arabs, or reject any political link between the treaty and autonomy, or deny the pact represented only a first step toward a comprehensive peace.[205]

Khalil opened an afternoon meeting of all three delegations by delivering a long discourse on the effect of Khomeini's revolution on regional stability. The Egyptian prime minister concluded that to sign a peace treaty with Israel in the face of the Islamic fanaticism sweeping the Arab world entailed great risks for Cairo. Even the Sudan and Oman, Egypt's two closest Arab friends, might sever relations with Egypt, according to Khalil. And a treaty between Egypt and Israel that caused such a rupture would shock the Egyptian public. He had come to Camp David, Khalil continued, to conclude an agreement with Israel, but he could not accept a separate peace. The treaty would have to be linked with an Israeli promise to grant the Palestinian people self-determination.[206]

Dayan asked what points needed to be resolved at Camp David to achieve a settlement. Khalil questioned the extent of

Dayan's authority to make decisions. The Israeli foreign minister reminded his interlecutors that the restrictions placed on him by Jerusalem were well-known to all before the conference began and pointed out that he could make recommendations to his government. If that arrangement did not suffice, he said, the meetings could end. The Israeli foreign minister then expressed his nation's very real commitment to peace and outlined sacrifices entailed by Israel's agreement to withdraw totally from the Sinai. Dayan defended the Israeli military presence in the occupied territories as necessary to root out terrorism.[207]

The two sides exchanged harsh words over more substantive issues, including the Egyptian suggestion that autonomy begin in the Gaza Strip first if West Bank Palestinians refused to participate in scheduled elections. Dayan informed the Egyptians that he was prepared to recommend the Gaza-first option to the cabinet if Egypt would agree not to stand in for Jordan in the negotiations over the West Bank. The Egyptian prime minister refused the condition. Khalil then asserted that Cairo should possess the right to send Egyptian police into the Gaza Strip during any disturbance. Dayan immediately ruled out any such right, remarking that the Camp David accords contained nothing to that effect. The Israeli foreign minister asked whether Egypt would supply oil to Jerusalem. Khalil responded that Cairo would discuss the matter only after signature of the peace treaty, not as a precondition to ratification nor as part of the agreement.[208]

As the talks progressed the gap between the Egyptians and Israelis appeared to widen, threatening a breakdown in negotiations. Khalil, for example, moved away from an agreement to exchange ambassadors after the Israeli evacuation of El-Arish -- terms earlier agreed to at Blair House and included in an appendix to the draft treaty under consideration. He preferred to delay formal relations at the ambassadorial level even if Israel advanced the timetable of the first phase of its withdrawal from the Sinai or consented to link the exchange to autonomy. Khalil wanted diplomatic relations to begin at a lower level first. He informed Dayan that the earlier agreement counted merely as a proposal subject to new interpretations. Vance seemed to agree. Dayan retorted that arguments of that type could only produce stalemate. Israel might, for example, delay its withdrawal from Egyptian oil fields located in the Sinai, Dayan warned.[209]

Faced with continued stalemate, President Carter held a one-hour meeting in the White House with the Israeli and Egyptian foreign ministers on Sunday, February 24. Carter informed Dayan and Khalil that he expected to reexamine U.S. policy toward the Middle East within ten days. He hoped that all outstanding problems between Egypt and Israel could be settled by that time. The president's demeanor conveyed a sense of urgency.[210]

Khalil approved of Carter's desire to complete the treaty within a limited time frame. He indicated that Riyadh was calling for a second Arab summit conference that could only increase Egypt's isolation and pressures on Cairo to abandon the peace process. Dayan characterized the past several days' peace efforts as disappointing and regressive, complaining that Egypt's turnabout on the exchange of ambassadors revealed a desire to obtain total Israeli withdrawal from the Sinai in return for only partial normalization. Carter interjected that by reneging on its promise to advance the date it would evacuate El-Arish, Israel had prompted Egypt's retreat on diplomatic relations. The president promised, however, to settle the matter personally if Jerusalem and Cairo resolved all other subjects.[211]

The clause concerning the priority of obligations received the most attention during the White House conference. Carter did not comprehend why Israel attached such great importance to the issue. Dayan explained that Syria or other Arab states might involve Egypt in a war against Israel by calling on Cairo to fulfill bilateral agreements. Carter dismissed speculation that Cairo would do any such thing. The Egyptian prime minister, either unwilling to renounce the possibility that Egypt might one day side with an Arab state against Israel or forced by events in Iran and at home to adopt a more hardline position, remained silent. Dayan expressed dismay about what he considered the similarity between U.S. and Egyptian positions. As evidence he cited the Egyptian proposal that Vance delivered to Jerusalem several months earlier. It was, he said, nearly word-for-word the same as the American plan presented to the Israeli delegation at Camp David on the 22nd of February.[212]

Carter closed the meeting by announcing that he would invite Begin to attend a tripartite summit in Washington on March 1. Khalil would represent Egypt; Sadat declined an invitation citing the Egyptian prime minister's full authority to make final decisions.[213] The Egyptian president evidently did not wish to engage his prestige in yet another high-profile negotiation at this delicate point in regional and personal politics.

Begin Visits Washington — March 1979

The debate over whether Begin should participate in a meeting in Washington with Khalil and Carter began even before the adjournment of Camp David II. Vance apparently broached the subject with Dayan on February 23.[214] Dayan favored the idea.[215] But Ben-Elissar believed Washington wanted to lure Begin onto a world stage, forcing him to make undesirable concessions or appear intransigent. The prime minister's aide evidently believed an alliance between Washington and Cairo had been formed to pressure Israel.[216] The Americans countered Ben-Elissar's lack of enthusiasm by conveying their belief that U.S.-Israeli relations would suffer severe strains if Begin did not attend.[217]

The Israeli cabinet met in Jerusalem on the 25th to discuss the matter. Vance had personally telephoned Begin to request his participation. The Carter administration enlisted the aid of Dayan and others in Israel's Camp David delegation to advocate Israeli attendance.[218] The cabinet advised Begin to delay until Dayan returned to Jerusalem and reported the results of Camp David II. It also asked that the discussions concerning a possible summit remain private.[219] Carter, however, publicized his request for tripartite talks.[220] Jerusalem once again felt cornered.[221]

Ignoring a substantial portion of Israel's Camp David delegation, Begin rejected the invitation. He apparently believed that to go to Washington would worsen the deadlock in the negotiations rather than lead to settlement. Begin believed Carter would subject him to intense pressure, while Sadat remained comfortably out of range in Cairo. Should Begin resist Egyptian demands and U.S. government intervention, Carter was certain, in Jerusalem's view, to attack Israeli intransigence before the American Congress and public. Begin believed that by staying in Jerusalem he would actually enhance rather than reduce the prospects for peace.[222]

Soon after Jerusalem rejected Carter's invitation, the U.S. president telephoned Begin and asked for a bilateral meeting. The Israeli prime minister accepted the request and agreed to visit Washington on March 1.[223] Carter then announced publicly that he would hold parallel talks with Sadat or Khalil at a later date.[224]   Prior to leaving for Washington, Begin pledged before his cabinet that:

> ...It won't be a unilateral withdrawal, and if there
> is no real treaty, we will remain in the Sinai and we
> will keep the settlements.   This hand will not sign
> any treaty which is not an honest one.[225]

Some in Israel, however, predicted that Begin would soften his stand once in the United States.[226]

Begin and Carter held four meetings at the White House in as many days.   The two leaders narrowed differences on crucial matters that stood in the way of the peace treaty.   They devised a formula that satisfied Israel's desire to ensure Egypt would not join other Arabs in a war against Israel and Cairo's wish to preserve its relationships with other Arab states.   Thus, they agreed to add the following to Article 6:

> The instructions of section six will not be
> interpreted in contradiction of the instructions on
> the framework for peace in the Middle East agreed on
> at Camp David.   The controversy on the status of the
> treaty in relation to international commitments which
> the two countries may have will be resolved by a
> comment...in the treaty which...state: it is agreed
> by the parties that there is no assertion that this
> treaty is preferable to other treaties or
> agreements...[227]

The two leaders also drafted a joint letter concerning Palestinian autonomy that revived an earlier concept.   Instead of a specific target date, the letter asserted autonomy negotiations would begin one month after ratification of the treaty and that the parties would seek to conclude the talks within a "goal" of one year.   Elections to the self-governing Palestinian authority would be held promptly after the conclusion of the talks.[228]

Begin consulted his cabinet in Jerusalem twice on March 4 and 5.   Minutes of the four Begin-Carter sessions were read to the assembled ministers, who reviewed all changes in the treaty with care.   Some detected little real change from previous submissions.   Others criticized the prime minister for reversing his opposition to amending the provisions of the draft treaty accepted by both sides in November. The ministers desired to know Sadat's opinion of the American formula, the date diplomatic representatives would be exchanged, the status the Gaza Strip would have in autonomy negotiations, whether Egypt would supply oil to Israel, and how committed Washington was to meeting future Israeli defense needs.[229]

Begin cabled his responses to the questions. For the most part he remained vague but did inform the cabinet that Washington had agreed to provide $3.5 billion for the relocation of the Sinai airfields and had promised to seek preferential treatment for Israel in the purchase of Egyptian oil. The prime minister also reported that the United States had offered to sign a defense treaty with Israel. The ministers initially defeated a resolution to adopt the compromises devised in Washington as a basis for negotiations and insisted on clarifications. Ariel Sharon then advanced a proposal that appeared to have majority support. It would approve the prime minister's recommendations on all matters except those relating to Palestinian autonomy, which would await fuller discussion upon Begin's return to Israel. After some debate Sharon's motion was dropped, and the cabinet finally approved a statement offered by Deputy Prime Minister Yadin that unequivocably endorsed the changes to the draft treaty. Nine ministers voted in favor of the resolution, three against, and four abstained.[230]

The battle for peace was still only half won. Before Begin left the United States Carter announced that he would visit Cairo and Jerusalem beginning on March 7 to conclude the negotiations, a task that would prove very difficult.

Breaking the Deadlock

Carter's mission to secure final agreement on an Egyptian–Israeli peace treaty lasted seven days. The Carter team flew first to Cairo, arriving at Sadat's luxurious Tahara Palace on March 8 and the two held talks there and in Alexandria through March 10.[231] The Americans carried with them the notes and letters agreed to in Washington with Begin. Carter then went to Israel and returned to Cairo on the 13th. During the shuttle, the final major compromises were achieved.

o The Priority of Obligations. The most critical U.S.–Israeli understanding concerned the priority of obligations. The Egyptians, determined to prevent any implication that the treaty amounted to cancellation of their existing agreements with other Arab states, subjected the language devised by Begin and Carter to careful scrutiny. After some haggling over the changes, the Israeli cabinet offered a compromise position during Carter's talks in Israel from March 10 to 12,[232] which Sadat approved on the 13th.[233] The appropriate section of Article 6 thus read:

> It is agreed by the Parties that there is no assertion that this Treaty prevails over other Treaties or agreements or that other Treaties or agreements prevail over this Treaty. The foregoing is not to be construed as contravening the provisions of Article VI(5) of the Treaty which reads as follows:
>
>> 'Subject to Article 103 of the United Nations Charter, in the event of a conflict between the obligations of the Parties under the present Treaty and any of their other obligations, the obligations under this Treaty will be binding and implemented.'[234]

Israel worried less during Carter's visit about the specific Egyptian alterations than about the American willingness to allow the Sadat government to change a text agreed upon only days earlier in White House discussions. Begin complained that he had wasted his time hurrying to Washington when it appeared that Sadat could merely sweep aside agreements arduously negotiated in the United States.[235] Despite its indignation, however, Jerusalem had succeeded in alleviating one of its primary concerns.

o <u>Exchange of Ambassadors.</u> At Camp David II Khalil had opposed establishing diplomatic relations rapidly at the ambassadorial level. And Carter had promised to intercede on Israel's behalf if the Israelis agreed to advance the date of their evacuation from El-Arish. Although the Israeli cabinet had rebuffed an attempt by Weizman during the Blair House talks to secure its approval for such a compromise, the ministers reversed themselves on March 12.[236]

o <u>Autonomy in the West Bank and Gaza Strip.</u> The agreement negotiated by Carter and Begin called for autonomy discussions to begin within a month of treaty ratification and set a goal of one year in which to conclude the talks. It did not, however, establish a difference between autonomy in the West Bank and the Gaza Strip. The issue meant a great deal to Sadat, as it involved an area -- the Gaza Strip -- over which Egypt had possessed sovereignty. The Israeli withdrawal from the Sinai and the restoration of Egyptian sovereignty there would provide Cairo with obvious practical benefits and, just as significant, fill a psychological need to regain lost territory and pride. But Israeli evacuation would occur slowly over a three-year period. Restitution of Egyptian sovereignty over the Gaza Strip, or at least recognition of a special Egyptian role there, could happen more quickly and help muffle the outcry certain to emanate from the Arab world after Sadat signed the treaty with Israel. Sadat's proposal for the Gaza Strip also enjoyed the support of other Egyptian officials and would help relieve some of the domestic pressure on the president.

Egypt's plan for the Gaza Strip was folded into its draft of a joint letter on autonomy. Cairo requested the right to station liaison officers in the Gaza Strip and suggested that autonomy be implemented there first.[237] Carter urged Israel on March 12 to permit Egypt to send liaison officers to the Gaza Strip and to grant Egyptians the same rights as Americans to enter freely into the territory.[238]

The cabinet in Jerusalem, however, ruled out the Gaza-first option. Carter, disappointed, pressed hard in a March 12 meeting for Israel to allow Egypt to open a liaison office in the Gaza Strip. According to the U.S. president:

> There will be tragic consequences to your refusal to open a liaison office in Gaza. Your responding to this demand is a supreme national interest of the United States. I have personally promised President Sadat to secure your agreement to this request and my personal credibility is put to the test. Your approach to this question is the yardstick of testing whether your attitude toward the negotiations as a whole is sincere. I could bring Sadat to Jerusalem to sign the peace treaty, and only petty problems are preventing it.[239]

Carter further noted that Begin's refusal to budge on this issue revealed a lack of seriousness about autonomy and raised questions about Israeli intentions in general.[240] The Israeli prime minister failed to see the connection.[241] Dayan ended the exchange by pointing out that the Egyptian proposal would create an entirely different situation than that envisioned in the Camp David accords. He concluded therefore that to grant Egypt special rights in the Gaza Strip would require renegotiation of the Camp David agreement.[242] No one at the meetings in Jerusalem favored that option, and the matter was dropped.[243]

o <u>Oil Supplies to Israel.</u> The last and most divisive issue was how to compensate Israel for relinquishing oil fields in the Sinai at a time when it had lost its principal foreign source — Iran. Carter proposed a ten-year agreement whereby the United States would purchase oil from Egypt at market prices and resell the fuel to Jerusalem as part of its obligation to ensure Israeli petroleum needs.[244]

Israeli cabinet members quickly rejected the American suggestion. For by obtaining the oil from a U.S. company, Jerusalem would allow Egypt to maintain at least the appearance of adhering to the Arab boycott against Israel. The Israeli cabinet considered the issue as a test of Cairo's willingness to accept full normalization of relations. A peace treaty should, Jerusalem believed, grant Israel the opportunity to buy reserves directly from Cairo and transport the petroleum on Israeli vessels through the Gulf of Suez.[245]

In response to a question from Carter, Begin explained that Israel felt entitled to preferential treatment by Egypt because Jerusalem had discovered and developed the oil fields in the first place.[246] But in later conversations with Vance, Dayan acknowledged that Israel could not expect the Egyptians to offer it a long term oil-supply contract. He therefore suggested a compromise solution: A U.S. oil company would commit itself to supply Israel for twenty years instead of ten and the treaty would state that Israel possessed the right to buy oil directly from Egypt. Thus, Israel's oil supply would be guaranteed, and Egypt would no longer be part of the Arab boycott.[247] The American delegation wrote language to accommodate Dayan's proposal. The relevant provision read:

> The Treaty of Peace and Annex III thereto provide for establishing normal economic relations between the Parties. In accordance therewith, it is agreed that such relations will include normal commercial sale of oil by Egypt to Israel, and that Israel shall be fully entitled to make bids for Egyptian—origin oil not needed for Egyptian domestic oil consumption, and Egypt and its oil concessionaires will entertain bids

made by Israel on the same basis and terms as apply to other bidders for such oil.[248]

The United States offered a 15-year guarantee to supply petroleum to Israel if Jerusalem was unable to obtain comparable oil from other foreign sources.[249] Sadat subsequently agreed to the arrangement, although the generous bargain was not finalized until a meeting in Washington between Egyptian and Israeli heads of government on March 23, just prior to the signature of the treaty. Israel agreed to advance the date it would evacuate the Sinai oil fields, and Egypt consented to sell Jerusalem petroleum from those fields at market prices. Israel would also be entitled to ship the oil directly to Israeli ports through the Gulf of Suez.[250]

The Domestic Fight for Peace

The popular mood in Israel at the time of Carter's March 1979 trip to the Middle East had moved sharply to the right, and the shift was reflected in the cabinet and Knesset. Nevertheless, a rapid acceleration in the rate of inflation — which had risen to a peacetime high of over 50 percent — and soaring military expenditures reduced both public and official opposition to compromise with Egypt.[251] In February, government budget cutters had prevailed on the cabinet to approve spending reductions of three percent and raise taxes as a method of reducing inflation.[252]

The pact with Egypt weighed heavily in the struggle to improve the Israeli economy. Military expenditures alone in the coming decade were projected to reach $12 billion.[253] Over thirty per cent of the Israeli budget and one fifth of its annual gross national product was allocated to defense or defense-related matters.[254] Israelis estimated that their long-term military expenditures would fall by as much as 25 percent as a result of a peace with Egypt.[255]

In the short term, however, military needs would increase.[256] The defense committee of the cabinet recommended on February 9 a plan intended to assure Israeli society sufficient military protection after the expected implementation of autonomy. The principal features of the proposal were: maintenance of IDF forces as the source of authority in the West Bank and Gaza Strip; continuation of army training activities there while IDF units relocated to secure areas;

perpetuation of Israel's internal security responsibilities
there despite the existence of local police forces under the
self-governing authority; and preservation of Israeli
sovereignty over state-owned lands there, including an
expansion of settlements.[257]

Despite its many doubts about the peace process, the
Israeli cabinet gave Begin ample freedom to negotiate
compromises during his visit to Washington, provided all
arrangements pertaining to autonomy were subjected to full
ministerial debate. Sharon's support in that regard assured
the Israeli prime minister of majority support in the cabinet.
Ministerial endorsement of peace terms could not guarantee
Knesset approval, but a narrow endorsement or rejection by the
ministers would assure defeat. Begin's coalition majority in
the parliament remained unreliable. The far right within Likud
was opposed to the peace process viscerally, regardless of its
potential benefits.

Thus, when Carter arrived in Israel on March 10 carrying
alterations to proposals previously approved by Begin, the
Israeli cabinet was outraged. Begin felt whipsawed by Carter
and Sadat. The two leaders had in Begin's view left him
betrayed and vulnerable, and he lashed out against both. But
the Israeli prime minister knew Carter could ill-afford to
return to Washington without a settlement and took advantage of
that fact.[258] Begin reminded the American president that any
text approved in bilateral discussions would require final
Knesset ratification, implying that any agreement that did not
satisfy him and the cabinet had no chance of approval.[259] He
wished thereby to warn the United States that Israel would not
accept just any accord and to reassure vascillating ministers
of his commitment to protect Israeli security.

Yet Begin probably believed Israel could no longer turn
away from peace with Egypt. Under the circumstances, with both
sides under intense pressure to achieve an acceptable final
agreement in little time, the rhetoric became bitter. Thus,
Begin asked Carter:

> How can you ask us to agree to new formulations,
> after we have agreed in Washington on the solutions
> for all the problems? Why is something which we
> considered a stroke of genius a week ago is no longer
> so? What you are suggesting now is a change in the
> fundamental elements of the treaty...I will not
> recommend to my colleagues to sign this agreement.

When I left the United States, we agreed on a certain text. Now you come back from Egypt without securing Sadat's consent, and you're asking me to change my positions. We are free people and we're allowed to accept or reject proposals made to us. We reject the Egyptian proposal.[260]

Carter's request for counterproposals met with evasion and obstreperousness. Begin proposed a delay of several days while his government examined alternatives, and Sharon reminded the American president that Israel could not tolerate any conditions leading to a Palestinian state.[261] In private, however, Begin talked his cabinet colleagues into supporting most of the Egyptian changes and altering the others. But he continued to berate the United States and Egypt for their apparent collusion.[262]

Begin chose to take a stand on matters of principle that would trouble even the strongest supporters of compromise within the Israeli cabinet -- the Egyptian desire to open a liaison office in the Gaza Strip and its wish to avoid selling oil directly to Israel. These matters, he believed, involved issues of equity American officials would have difficulty opposing.[263] At one particularly tense point during the dialogue Begin warned: "We will not sign this document." Carter responded icily "You will have to sign it."[264] Tempers cooled, and Carter apologized for his remark.[265] The two sides then began to make progress toward a compromise. They eventually dropped Egypt's proposal for the Gaza Strip and negotiated a compromise on the oil supply question. The Israeli cabinet approved the treaty, including some Egyptian changes and the energy compromise, by a 15 to 1 margin, with one abstention.[266]

Sadat and His Opposition

Sadat approved the peace terms at Cairo's International Airport on the afternoon of March 13.[267] The U.S. embassy in Cairo had kept him informed of developments in the U.S.-Israeli negotiations, thus helping pave the way to quick Egyptian approval. But Sadat's apparent delight masked deep anxiety.

He needed to obtain from the United States vast amounts of weapons and economic assistance crucial to his political survival. Negotiations to acquire U.S. fighter planes had nearly broke off in late February, as the Egyptians requested too much sophisticated gadgetry the United States would not provide.[268] Loss of American arms could turn Egypt's already restive military against Sadat and foster support for an alternative. Despite Sadat's attempts at reform, continuing government waste and inefficiency, severe unemployment, widespread poverty, and rampant corruption presented an equal threat to the president's power. American economic assistance — in particular food and development aid — was essential to alleviating discontent.

For the time being at least Sadat was also estranged from the Palestinians. The mayor of Gaza and some other local Palestinians privately expressed their gratitude for the Egyptian president's efforts on their behalf.[269] But the fact remained that he had failed and other, equally numerous Palestinians accused him of selling out. Sadat might still achieve an acceptable solution to the Palestinian problem during the autonomy talks, but little ground for optimism seemed to exist. Sadat also knew the rest of the Arab world would subject him to bitter attack, with potentially severe domestic impact. The Egyptian press and New Democratic Party organs would help reduce the consequences of Arab outrage. But the isolation from the Arab world Sadat expected would be impossible to counter totally.

Despite these difficulties, Egypt would reap some foreign policy benefits from the peace treaty with Israel. The West Europeans were becoming more openly involved in the search for a Middle East peace — a natural result of increased dependence on Arab oil. Sadat could seek to persuade them to help reverse his worsening economic and military conditions, thus diversifying his sources of support. Meanwhile, the fall of the Shah of Iran might encourage the United States to turn to the Egyptian military to help protect U.S. and Western interests in the area. Such a development would enhance Sadat's reputation within the military and help ensure a steady flow of Western aid.

Sadat sought to reduce distaste for the treaty among members of his regime by keeping them busy. He sent Mubarak to brief friendly African states and West European nations. He directed Khalil to resume direction of the nation's economic and development programs and to prepare plans for massive recovery financed with U.S. assistance. He placed Ghali and al-Baz in charge of the autonomy talks, a task certain to present enormous difficulties. Finally, he ordered Ali to head negotiations to acquire American weapons and devise a plan to ensure their efficient integration into the Egyptian armed forces.

The Egyptian president had concluded a treaty with Israel; he now faced the daunting task of managing the peace. Egypt's ruling elites were at best ambivalent toward the new world created by the treaty. For every diplomatic and economic benefit there appeared to be a disadvantage. In particular, the Egyptians were deeply troubled by their isolation from the rest of the Arab world. But for the time being at least war with Israel seemed the least promising of all available options.

The members of the Egyptian elite, whatever their attitudes toward the peace process, were nationalists. Sadat had promised peaceful relations with Israel would lead to a better life for Egyptians. With Western assistance, he hoped Cairo would again become a flourishing center for culture and trade. At the same time, however, increased Western money and influence could only upset those who hoped for a return to religious piety and traditional ways. Sadat was regarded as a religious man sometimes given to excess. He would have to demonstrate his orthodoxy and reduce opportunities for the Muslim Brotherhood and its radical allies to exploit discontent among the urban and rural poor. The challenges facing Sadat would prove as difficult to master as peace was to achieve.

The Egyptian-Israeli Peace Treaty

The Egyptian-Israeli Peace Treaty was signed on March 26, 1979, on the White House lawn by Anwar Sadat and Menachem Begin, with Jimmy Carter as witness.[270] The treaty contained a preamble, nine main articles, three annexes, an agreed record of the negotiations, several letters of understanding — some from President Carter to Sadat and Begin and others from each of the principals to the American president.[271]

The preamble stressed the continuity of the peace treaty with the framework agreement signed at Camp David and with UN Resolutions 242 and 338. It also stated that the treaty would constitute an "important step in the search for comprehensive peace...an attainment of...settlement of the Arab-Israeli conflict in all its aspects..." Finally, it invited other Arab parties to the dispute to join in the peace process.[272]

The nine articles in the main portion of the document dealt with the general principles governing the termination of war and establishment of peace; withdrawal by Israel from the Sinai to an internatonal boundary; normalization of relations between Egypt and Israel under the provision of the UN Charter; security arrangements, including limited force zones patrolled by UN observers; transit rights in international waterways such as the Suez Canal, Strait of Tiran, and Gulf of Aqaba; priority of obligations; and procedures to settle disputes arising from the treaty peacefully.[273]

The annexes contained the details of the phased withdrawal of Israeli forces from the Sinai, established the timing for the exchange of ambassadors, and defined the nature of relations in the fields of economics, trade, culture, travel, transportation, and telecommunications.[274] The agreed record covered issues that had remained in dispute for many months of hard bargaining, such as treaty review procedures, priority of obligations provisions, the composition of observer forces, and the Israeli right to purchase Egyptian oil from the Sinai fields. The letters dealt with sensitive bilateral issues, including the implementation of autonomy and U.S. responsibilities in the event of treaty violations.[275]

The peace treaty was a reasoned effort to balance return of the Sinai with a complex web of measures that would adequately protect Israeli security. But both parties were determined that the pact would be more than simply an agreement on territorial rights. They considered it a solemn undertaking, the first step toward healing the wounds of over thirty years of war and hatred.

Cairo requested and received an agreement that initiated a process that in time could lead to settlement of the Palestinian problem, the key to a comprehensive peace and to the restoration of an Egyptian role in the Arab world. Israel had dreamt for thirty years of gaining acceptance among Middle Eastern nations. The Treaty achieved recognition and relationships with at least Egypt -- the most populous and powerful Arab state. The trade and cultural exchanges initiated by the pact could help change the views of nations accustomed only to mutual hatred. Finally, the Egyptian-Israeli Peace Treaty placed America squarely at the center of the Arab-Israeli conflict.

The American Guarantee

Israel's overriding desire to protect its security led Jerusalem's leadership to seek ironclad guarantees. The Begin government sought to extract the clearest expression of American intentions should the treaty collapse, whether through neglect of its provisions or malevolence. Thus, within hours of the White House ceremony marking signature of the peace treaty between Egypt and Israel, Vance and Dayan initialed for their respective governments a memorandum of agreement listing the diplomatic, economic, and military measures the two would take to remedy any violation of the treaty.[276] Specifically Washington committed itself to:

> ...consider, on an urgent basis, such measures as the strengthening of the United States presence in the area, the providing of emergency supplies to Israel, and the exercise of maritime rights in order to put an end to the violation.[277]

The United States also pledged its continuing military and economic assistance to Israel and promised to use its veto in the UN against measures deemed contrary to spirit and letter of the peace treaty.[278] Finally, America promised not to transfer weapons that might be used in an attack against Israel to any country in the area.[279]

NOTES

1. Washington Post, September 24, 1978.

2. New York Times, December 3, 1978.

3. Washington Post, October 3, 1978.

4. New York Times, December 3, 1978.

5. Washington Post, October 7, 1978; Christian Science Monitor, July 11, 1978.

6. Washington Post, October 6, 1978.

7. Ibid.

8. _Washington Post_, October 3, 1978.

9. Ehud Yaari, "Sadat's Pyramid of Power" in _The Jerusalem Quarterly_, Number 14, Winter 1980, p. 119–120.

10. _Ibid._

11. _Ibid._, p. 121.

12. _Ibid._, p. 117.

13. Eitan Haber, Zeev Schiff and Ehud Yaari, _The Year of the Dove_ (New York: Bantam Books, 1979), p. 284.

14. Equalizing status through promotion was a typical move engaged in by a patrimonial leader such as Anwar Sadat. See, Robert Springborg, "Patterns of Association in the Egyptian Political Elite" in George Lenczowski, ed. _Political Elites in the Middle East_ (Washington D.C.: American Enterprise Institute for Public Policy Research, 1975), p. 102–103.

15. Uzi Benziman, _Prime Minister Under Siege_ (Jerusalem: Adam Publishers, 1981) Translated from the Hebrew by Mordecai Schreiber, p. 203.

16. _Ibid._, p. 203–204.

17. _Ibid._, p. 205; also Moshe Dayan, _Breakthrough: A Personal Account of the Egypt–Israel Peace Negotiations_ (London: Weidenfeld and Nicholson, 1981), p. 191–192.

18. Dayan, _Breakthrough_, p. 193.

19. _Ibid._, p. 194–198.

20. _Ibid._

21. _Ibid._, p. 191.

22. See, Efraim Torgovnik, "Accepting Camp David: The Role of Party Factions in Israeli Policy Making" in _Middle East Review_, Volume 11, Number 2, Winter 1978–79, p. 22.

23.   Ibid., p. 22–23.

24   Ibid., p. 23.

25.   Ibid.; Dayan, Breakthrough, p. 191–198.

26.   Washington Post, September 28, 1978.

27.   Washington Post, September 25, 1978.

28.   Ibid.

29.   Ibid.

30.   Tamar Yegnes, "Saudi Arabia and the Peace Process" in The Jerusalem Quarterly, Number 18, Winter 1981, p. 117.

31.   See, Adam Garfinkle, "Negotiating by Proxy: Jordanian Foreign Policy and U.S. Options in the Middle East" in Orbis, Volume 24, Number 4, Winter 1981, p. 869–871.

32.   Ibid., p. 871–873.

33.   Ibid., p. 873.

34.   Ibid.

35.   Washington Post, October 2, 1978; October 16, 1978; October 20, 1978.

36.   Foreign Broadcast Information Service (Hereinafter FBIS), Middle East and North Africa, October 17, 1978, F3–F4.

37.   Rowland Evans and Robert Novak, "The Answers to Hussein's Questions" in Washington Post, October 30, 1978.

38.   Ibid.

39.   Ibid.

40.   Ibid.

292

41. Garfinkle, "Negotiating by Proxy..." _Orbis_, Winter 1981, p. 874.

42. Evans and Novak, "The Answers to Hussein's Questions" in _Washington Post_, October 30, 1978.

43. Garfinkle, "Negotiating by Proxy..." _Orbis_, Winter 1981, p. 874.

44. Dayan, _Breakthrough_, p. 201.

45. _Ibid._, p. 202.

46. Garfinkle, "Negotiating by Proxy..." _Orbis_, Winter 1981, p. 874.

47. Dayan, _Breakthrough_, p. 199.

48. _Ibid._, p. 205–206.

49. _Ibid._, p. 206.

50. _Ibid._, p. 206–207.

51. _Ibid._, p. 207.

52. _Ibid._

53. _Ibid._, p. 208.

54. _Ibid._, p. 211–212.

55. _Ibid._, p. 212–215.

56. _Ibid._, p. 213–214.

57. _Ibid._, p. 211–215.

58. _Ibid._, p. 215.

59. _Ibid._, p. 216.

60. _Ibid._, p. 216–217.

61. Ibid., p. 217.

62. Ibid., p. 218–221.

63. Ibid., p. 218.

64. Ibid.

65. Ibid., p. 238.

66. Ibid., p. 217–218.

67. Ibid., p. 214.

68. Ibid., p. 217–218.

69. Ibid., p. 232.

70. Ibid., p. 234.

71. Ibid., p. 205.

72. Ibid., p. 225.

73. Ibid., p. 226–227.

74. Ibid., p. 226.

75. Ibid., p. 226–227.

76. Ibid., p. 230.

77. Ibid., p. 227, 230.

78. Ibid., p. 209–210.

79. Ibid., p. 210.

80. Benziman, Prime Minister Under Siege, Translated from the Hebrew by Mordecai Schreiber, p. 209–211.

81. Dayan, Breakthrough, p. 210.

82. Ibid., p. 209.

83. Ibid., p. 210–211.

84. Ibid., p. 225.

85. Benziman, Prime Minister Under Siege, Translated from the Hebrew by Mordecai Schreiber, p. 217. Mr. Dan Patir –– Begin's Press Secretary at the time of the Blair Talks –– offered the opinion that Hammer's threat to resign was merely a ploy to secure government support for strengthening West Bank settlements. Interview with Dan Patir, Potomac, Maryland, January 31, 1982.

86. Benziman, Prime Minister Under Siege, Translated from the Hebrew by Mordecai Schreiber, p. 218.

87. Ibid., p. 217.

88. Dayan, Breakthrough, p. 225.

89. Benziman, Prime Minister Under Siege, Translated from the Hebrew by Mordecai Schreiber, p. 219.

90. Ibid., p. 216–217.

91. Ibid., p. 217.

92. FBIS, Middle East and North Africa, October 23, 1978, D–2.

93. Dayan, Breakthrough, p. 220. Also, see, FBIS, Middle East and North Africa, October 24, 1978, D–1.

94. FBIS, Middle East and North Africa, October 24, 1978, D–1.

95. Ibid., October 25, 1978, D–1.

96. Ibid., D–3.

97. Jake Wien, Saudi–Egyptian Relations: The Political and Military Dimensions of Saudi Financial Flows to Egypt (Santa Monica: The Rand Corporation) P–6327, p. 54; Dayan, Breakthrough, p. 230.

98. Washington Star, October 29, 1978; Washington Post, October 29, 1987.

99. Dayan, Breakthrough, p. 231.

100. Ibid., p. 231–232.

101. Ibid., p. 231–232.

102. Patricia Ann O'Connor, The Middle East: U.S. Policy, Israel, Oil and the Arabs, Fourth Edition (Washington: Congressional Quarterly, Inc., 1980), p. 18.

103. Ibid.; Washington Post, November 6, 1978.

104. Ibid.; Washington Post, November 7, 1978.

105. FBIS, Middle East and North Africa, November 8, 1978, D-1.

106. Joseph Kraft, "A Marshall Plan for Egypt" in Washington Post, November 7, 1978.

107. FBIS, Middle East and North Africa, November 8, 1978, D-1.

108. Dayan, Breakthrough, p. 235–236.

109. Ibid., p. 236–237.

110. Ibid., p. 238.

111. Ibid., p. 239.

112. Ibid., p. 242.

113. Ibid.

114. Ibid.

115. Ibid., p. 245.

116. Ibid., p. 245–246.

296

117. See, United States Department of State, The Camp David Summit — September 1978 (Washington: Department of State) Publication 8954, p. 10.

118. Ibid.

119. Dayan, Breakthrough, p. 212–213.

120. Ibid., . 213, 224.

121. Ibid.

122. Ibid., p. 233.

123. Benziman, Prime Minister Under Siege, Translated from the Hebrew by Mordecai Schreiber, p. 220–221.

124. Dayan, Breakthrough, p. 236.

125. Ibid., p. 239.

126. See, Ibid., p. 235, for Egyptian comments on its surprise at the depth of Arab dissatisfaction growing out of the Baghdad Conference. Also, New York Times, November 21, 1978.

127. Washington Post, November 16, 1978.

128. Washington Post, November 18, 1978.

129. FBIS, Middle East and North Africa, November 22, 1978, D-1.

130. New York Times, November 18, 1978; November 20, 1978; November 21, 1978.

131. New York Times, November 23, 1978.

132. New York Times, November 27, 1978.

133. New York Times, November 24, 1978.

134. FBIS, Middle East and North Africa, November 27, 1978, D–12, 13.

135. Washington Post, November 30, 1978.

136. Ibid.

137. Ibid.

138. Benziman, Prime Minister Under Siege, Translated from the Hebrew by Mordecai Schreiber, p. 225.

139. Ibid., p. 221.

140. Ibid., p. 225.

141. Dayan, Breakthrough, p. 248.

142. Benziman, Prime Minister Under Siege, Translated from the Hebrew by Mordecai Schreiber, p. 226.

143. Ibid.

144. Ibid.

145. Ibid.

146. New York Times, November 23, 1978.

147. Benziman, Prime Minister Under Siege, Translated from the Hebrew by Mordecai Schreiber, p. 226.

148. Washington Post, November 26, 1978.

149. Washington Post, November 25, 1978.

150. Dayan, Breakthrough, p. 248–249.

151. New York Times, December 6, 1978.

152. Dayan, Breakthrough, p. 250.

153. Ibid.

154. Ibid., p. 249–250.

155. Benziman, Prime Minister Under Siege, Translated from the Hebrew by Mordecai Schreiber, p. 226.

156. Ibid.

157. Ibid.

158. Ibid., p. 231–232.

159. Ibid., p. 232.

160. Ibid.

161. Ibid.

162. New York Times, December 17, 1978; December 20, 1978.

163. New York Times, December 7, 1978.

164. Dayan, Breakthrough, p. 252.

165. Ibid.

166. Ibid., p. 253.

167. Ibid.

168. Ibid., p. 254.

169. Ibid.

170. Ibid.

171. Ibid., p. 255.

172. Ibid., p. 255.

173. Andrew Lycett, "The Peacemaker Reorganizes Back Home" in African Business, December 1978, p. 31–32.

174. For discussion of U.S. preoccupation with Iran at the end of 1978 and the first weeks of 1979, see, Michael Ledeen and William Lewis, Debacle: The American Failure in Iran (New York: Alfred A. Knopf, 1981), p. 154–194; also, William Sullivan, Mission in Iran (New York: W. W. Norton and Company, 1981), p. 191–234.

175. Benziman, Prime Minister Under Siege, Translated from the Hebrew by Mordecai Schreiber, p. 234–235.

176. Ibid., p. 235.

177. New York Times, December 28, 1978.

178. New York Times, January 7, 1978.

179. Benziman, Prime Minister Under Siege, Translated from the Hebrew by Mordecai Schreiber, p. 236.

180. Ibid.

181. New York Times, January 14, 1979.

182. Ibid.

183. Dayan, Breakthrough, p. 256–257.

184. Ibid., p. 256.

185. Ibid., p. 257–258.

186. Ibid., p. 258.

187. Ibid.

188. FBIS, Middle East and North Africa, January 5, 1979, D-1.

189. New York Times, December 3, 1978.

190. New York Times, January 12, 1979.

191. New York Times, January 21, 1979.

192. New York Times, January 22, 1979.

193. New York Times, February 8, 1979.

194. New York Times, January 12, 1979.

195. Ibid.

196. New York Times, January 16, 1979.

197. New York Times, February 9, 1979.

198. New York Times, January 1, 1979; February 4, 1979.

199. Washington Post, February 10, 1979.

200. New York Times, February 12, 1979.

201. Dayan, Breakthrough, p. 259.

202. See, Benziman, Prime Minister Under Siege, Translated from the Hebrew by Mordecai Schreiber, p. 237. Dayan later regretted the remark and attempted to atone by sponsoring a government resolution favoring a program of water coordination in "Judea and Samaria" thereby demonstrating renewed commitment to Israeli retention of biblical lands. Ibid., p. 238.

203. Dayan, Breakthrough, p. 260.

204. Ibid.

205. Ibid., p. 260–261.

206. Ibid., p. 261.

207. Ibid., p. 262.

208. Ibid.

209. Ibid., p. 263.

210. Ibid., p. 264.

211. Ibid., p. 265.

212. Ibid.

213. Ibid., p. 266.

214. Benziman, Prime Minister Under Siege, Translated from he Hebrew by Mordecai Schreiber, p. 239.

215. Ibid.

216. Ibid.

217. Ibid., p. 239–240.

218. Ibid.

219. Ibid., p. 241.

220. Ibid.

221. Ibid.

222. Ibid., p. 241–242.

223. Ibid., p. 243.

224. Ibid.

225. Ibid.

226. Ibid., p. 243–244.

227. Ibid., p. 247.

228. Ibid., p. 248.

229. Ibid., p. 249.

230. Ibid., p. 250.

231. New York Times, March 9, 1979; March 11, 1979.

232. Dayan, Breakthrough, p. 270.

233. _Ibid._, p. 273.

234. See, United States Department of State, _The Egyptian-Israeli Peace Treaty — March 26, 1979_ (Washington: Department of State) Publication 8976, p. 19.

235. Dayan, _Breakthrough_, p. 271–272.

236. _Ibid._, p. 273.

237. _Ibid._, p. 269.

238. _Ibid._, p. 274; also, Jimmy Carter, _Keeping Faith: Memoirs of a President_ (New York: Bantam Books, 1982), p. 422–423.

239. Benziman, _Prime Minister Under Siege_, Translated from he Hebrew by Mordecai Schreiber, p. 256.

240. _Ibid._

241. _Ibid._

242. _Ibid._, p. 258–259.

243. Dayan, _Breakthrough_, p. 277–278.

244. _Ibid._, p. 269; Carter, _Keeping Faith_, p. 242.

245. Dayan, _Breakthrough_, p. 274.

246. Benziman, _Prime Minister Under Siege_, Translated from the Hebrew by Mordecai Schreiber, p. 256.

247. Dayan, _Breakthrough_, p. 276.

248. Department of State, _The Egyptian-Israeli Peace Treaty_, p. 19–20.

249. Dayan, _Breakthrough_, p. 277.

250. _Ibid._, p. 279–280.

251. New York Times, January 16, 1979.

252. New York Times, February 9, 1979.

253. New York Times, February 14, 1979.

254. New York Times, February 4, 1979.

255. New York Times, February 14, 1979.

256. New York Times, February 4, 1979.

257. New York Times, February 10, 1979.

258. Benziman, Prime Minister Under Siege, Translated from the Hebrew by Mordecai Schreiber, p. 251.

259. Dayan, Breakthrough, p. 270.

260. Benzlman, Prime Minister Under Siege, Translated from the Hebrew by Mordecai Schreiber, p. 253.

261. Ibid.

262. Ibid., p. 254-257, 262.

263. Ibid., p. 251.

264. Ibid., p. 255.

265. Ibid.

266. Ibid., p. 263.

267. New York Times, March 14, 1979.

268. Washington Post, February 17, 1979.

269. FBIS, Middle East and North Africa, March 12, 1979, D-13.

270. New York Times, March 27, 1979.

271.   Department of State, The Egyptian–Israeli Peace Treaty, p. 1–23.

272.   Ibid., p. 1.

273.   Ibid., p. 1–3.

274.   Ibid., p. 5–18.

275.   Ibid., p. 19–23.

276.   Dayan, Breakthrough, p. 279, 281, 356–357.

277.   Ibid., p. 356–357.

278.   Ibid., p. 357.

279.   Ibid.

8
The Peacemakers

Anwar Sadat and Menachem Begin overcame formidable challenges to their authority and political flexibility in negotiating the Egyptian–Israeli Peace Treaty. Their styles differed sharply, as did the nations and institutions each governed.

The Egyptian leader had to cope with domestic political rules he himself had established in the early years of his presidency. He had opened Egyptian society, elevated new faces to positions of leadership, and encouraged political discourse. He launched a new economic policy. Perhaps most important, he based his rule on a careful balance among individuals, groups, and classes, making Egyptian government less authoritarian and more benevolent. Paradoxically, the system Sadat had created proved difficult to manipulate as he embarked on his search for peace.

Sadat used cronies and confidants to explore privately opportunities for peace with Israel. He dispatched Marel and later Tuhamy to Romania and Morocco in the summer of 1977 with messages offering compromise. He concealed the missions from Cairo's bureaucracy, which continued to issue statements supporting traditional Arab positions. Then Foreign Minister Ismail Fahmy had even established himself as mediator between U.S. State Department officials and Palestinian representatives. The Soviet–American communique of October 1, 1977, forced Sadat's hand.

Sadat could not allow an open, broad–based debate among his advisers to occur for fear of generating widespread opposition to his peace plans. Rather, he attacked the Soviet–American statement from the perspective of an ardent supporter of Palestinian nationalism, and instructed Fahmy and others to voice the same official line. Sadat enlisted Arafat to remind Syria of the damage a solution imposed by the superpowers could cause, particularly if it ignored Palestinian statehood.

The Egyptian president toured the Middle East warning Arab leaders against the ills of a Geneva Conference based on the Soviet–American communique. He stopped off in Romania long enough to receive personal assurances of Begin's flexibility and commitment to peace. Then, back in Cairo, he startled the world by revealing that he would go to Jerusalem to seek peace.

The president chose his delegation for the Jerusalem trip with care, as he recognized the need to mobilize a strong leadership coalition to achieve peace with Israel. Most important, he would seek to counterbalance or split Mubarak's network of allies and clients, which espoused traditional Arab positions within and without the military–security establishment. Thus, Sadat selected personal confidants — Marei and Osman — technocratic leader Khalil, and officials from the military and foreign office — Ali, Ghali, and Usama al-Baz — to accompany him.

The foreign office joined Mubarak in opposing Sadat's visit to Jerusalem. Al-Baz, who remained necessary to the diplomatic maneuvering with Israel, became director of Vice President Mubarak's office. Sadat countered by forming a peace coalition around the Egyptian technocracy led by Khalil and the army under Gamassy. Both Khalil and Gamassy feared that Israel might use nuclear weapons in a future war with the Arabs. Moreover, they believed that only peace would provide them with the means to improve economic conditions for the rural and urban poor and reduce the constant threat of revolution. Gamassy also became a bridge to Ezer Weizman, the flamboyant Israeli defense minister. Sadat wished to ensure that Israel understood his real intentions and chose to use Weizman as his messenger.

Sadat regarded regaining the Sinai as his first and most critical goal. He had begun the peace process to achieve that result. The Palestinians mattered little to him. The PLO counted even less. Sadat regarded Arafat and his followers as a band of volatile extremists who had to be controlled. The Egyptian president's distrust of the movement turned to hatred following the murder of his friend Yusef el-Sabeh in Nicosia by Palestinian commandos. In a private conversation after the event he asserted that he had "excluded the PLO from my lexicon. By their own behavior they have excluded themselves from the negotiations." Even before the assassination, however, he did not support the PLO demand for Palestinian statehood.

Nevertheless, pressure from his own advisers and from important Egyptian constituencies prevented Sadat from concentrating solely on obtaining Israeli withdrawal from the Sinai. During his meeting with Begin on Christmas Day 1977, Sadat insisted on linking the Sinai settlement to resolution of Palestinian and West Bank issues.

The Egyptian president could not ignore mounting opposition to peace with Israel among pan-Arabist members of the Egyptian elite or widespread disenchantment toward the regime's policies from a small but growing group of fundamentalists. Although a strict Moslem, Sadat was viscerally antifundamentalist. He detested boisterous, self-righteous fanatics who wished to turn the clock back. Moreover, the fundamentalists — who enjoyed their greatest support among the urban poor and opposed Sadat's peace moves as heretical and self-serving — threatened the coalition of technocrats and urban leaders he had put together to support the peace process.

Under these circumstances, Sadat briefly resurrected the nationalist Wafd movement in order to dull the appeal of fundamentalists and leftists. He also moved swiftly to curtail the activities of the left, in particular the Nasserists. He thus avoided challenging directly the more numerous and influential, though less disciplined, fundamentalists, while sending them the clear message that he would no longer tolerate unremitting dissent. He ordered similar crackdowns whenever antigovernment activities increased in intensity. Each time, leftists, Nasserists, and other dissidents were rounded up and jailed, and their organizations were outlawed. But Sadat wisely refused to attack the fundamentalists directly, as he could not ensure that such action would not spark urban disorders.

Sadat also needed to keep the military satisfied. After the euphoria that followed the trip to Jerusalem subsided, it quickly became clear that peace with Israel and recovery of the Sinai would be enormously difficult to achieve. Mubarak and his allies gained strength as Arab hostility against the peace process mounted and Egyptian isolation increased. The Egyptian vice president temporarily took over monitoring of the peace process during the ill-fated political committee talks in Jerusalem. Mubarak also profited handsomely from his association with al-Baz, who remained one of two experts indispensable to the peace process. As a succession of foreign ministers were replaced for obvious disloyalty or incompetence, Egyptian diplomacy became increasingly dependent on al-Baz.

In the spring of 1978, Sadat convinced the skeptical U.S. government and Congress that they must supply Egypt with advanced weapons, particularly aircraft, to strengthen his hold on power. Mubarak, the former head of Egypt's Air Force, would thus be unable to argue that peace was diminishing Egyptian military strength and readiness.

Israel's military operation in Lebanon had unsettled Mubarak and his supporters. The absence of a firm Egyptian response to the invasion plunged Cairo's relations with other Arabs to a new low. Mubarak tried hard to reduce ties between Cairo and Jerusalem. But Sadat remained determined to improve the relationship. Sadat's March 30 meeting with Weizman in Cairo was a further attempt to move relations with Jerusalem forward.

He greeted the Israeli defense minister with the warning "I must tell my people that I have induced the Israelis to withdraw from the West Bank." The Egyptian president believed, however, that Israel would only need to declare its intention to withdraw rather than agree to a specific timetable. Sadat's eagerness to conclude a quick settlement on the Sinai was evident in the proposals he offered Weizman. Thus, Gamassy advanced two documents during the meetings -- one was a declaration of intent to withdraw from the West Bank and Gaza Strip; the other was a bilateral treaty. That Sadat reneged on the offer within twenty four hours provided significant evidence of his dependence on a military structure dominated by Mubarak.

The Egyptian president had attempted to barter away the Palestinians for Israeli assurances of an early Sinai settlement. He had promised that Egypt would prevent the formation of a Palestinian state. Sadat blamed his reversal on the displeasure of a group of Gazan leaders. But there exists little evidence that Sadat cared enough about Palestinian sensibilities to allow them to exercise such deep influence on his peace plans. Rather, military unease with peace prospects, the timidity of other Egyptian officials, deterioration in the economy, and pressure from the Arab world limited Sadat's room to maneuver.

Sadat's July meeting with Weizman in Salzburg occurred under even less favorable circumstances for the Egyptian leader. He had risked Western disapproval by cracking down on dissidents. Many of Sadat's advisers, in particular foreign office officials, did not support his peace strategy and placed political obstacles in his way. Sadat feared the excessive demands of his diplomatic team would drive Israel from the negotiating table. Sadat therefore courted Weizman both to soften the Israeli defense minister and to establish a direct line of communication with the Israelis that could be used to discuss controversial issues and proposals that his foreign office advisors might distort or oppose. The Egyptian leader sought to convince Weizman that Israel should take steps that might build Arab confidence in the peace process. Hence his suggestion that Israel return El-Arish and Mt. Sinai immediately to Egyptian control.

The Egyptian president understood, however, that he could not afford to wait for unilateral Israeli gestures toward peace. He needed to act in order to limit frustration and opposition to the peace process that continued to grow as time dragged on with little substantial progress. He took steps to reshuffle his regime and increase his personal control over the peace process. He created the New Democratic Party, brought leading figures from the important Coptic Christian community close to the seat of power, and foisted the role of political organizer on Khalil. Sadat could not break Mubarak's network of allies so he sought instead to counterbalance it with a coalition of his own.

When Israel refused to make a symbolic move in the Sinai, Carter had to rescue the floundering process by inviting Begin and Sadat to Camp David. Sadat left Mubarak behind, thus diminishing his influence on the bargaining. But more important, the Egyptian president went to Camp David secure that a revitalized party and restructured coalition would support his positions.

When he returned from Camp David Sadat moved quickly and deftly to defuse opposition at home. He appointed Khalil prime minister and swore in a new cabinet. He strengthened his authority over the military establishment by elevating new faces to senior levels in the army. He delivered a debilitating blow to Mubarak's coalition by reassigning General Ali from director of military intelligence to defense minister. Ali handled the Blair House talks temporarily, but Khalil soon assumed the added portfolio of foreign minister and directed the negotiations with Israel until signature of the peace treaty. Mubarak was effectively isolated from the peace talks, although al-Baz kept the vice president reasonably well-informed.

Placing daily responsibility for negotiating the treaty in Khalil's hands assured Sadat of a favorable outcome. The unanimous decision to quarantine Egypt by both moderates and radicals in the Arab camp delayed the result, however. Khalil initially advocated traditional Arab positions in alliance with Mubarak. But when Sadat adopted his Gaza-first strategy, Khalil moved away from Mubarak. The proposal became an effective bargaining tool, providing leverage with Israel, America, and moderate Arabs. In the end the strategy produced Israeli agreement to a loosely-defined timetable for autonomy negotiations -- the key to final Egyptian approval of the treaty Sadat had worked so hard to achieve. The length of time and difficult negotiations required to conclude the treaty predictably tarnished the agreement's image.

The absence of democratically elected institutions in Egypt led many to assume that Sadat possessed greater freedom in shaping the treaty than he actually did. In truth, he had to bargain, cajole, compromise, and coerce to assemble and preserve a coalition behind the peace process. The Egyptian president succeeding in negotiating and implementing a treaty that often went against the grain of Egyptian traditions because he was a master of the politics of maneuver, compromise, and coalition building usually associated with Western democratic government.

Menachem Begin employed many of the same techniques as Sadat to counter internal dissent against the peace treaty with equal dexterity. Begin had been elected on a platform calling for Israeli retention of the biblical lands -- Judea and Samaria -- affirming the permanent right of Jews to settle in the territories, and vowing to preserve secure and defensible borders in the Sinai and Golan Heights. The principles of revisionist Zionism had guided Begin for a half-century and explained his popularity among sephardic Jews. Begin was also the only remaining strong nationalist leader whose reputation was not tarnished by the corruption and division that had plagued the last years of Labor government.

Begin's cabinet selections and the composition of the Knesset reflected Israel's new majority and the growth in influence of right-wing, religious constituencies. Because Begin enjoyed only a narrow majority in the Knesset those right-wing groups and their representatives in the cabinet possessed a virtual veto over government decisions. Thus, Ariel Sharon, Zevulun Hammer, and other ministers provided strong, constant support for the positions of Gush Emunim zealots in their struggle to force the government to approve the expansion of settlements in the occupied territories. The religious right in Israeli society was represented in the cabinet by members of the vocal National Religious Party and associated smaller groups such as Auguda Israel. Hence, Begin presided over a government and parliament characterized by fervent nationalism and determined to retain the West Bank, Gaza Strip, Sinai, and Golan Heights and to protect cherished settlements in those areas.

Nevertheless, Begin ordered his Arab affairs adviser Moshe Sharon in July 1977 to search for a new formula that might interest Arab leaders while preserving Israeli security. The prime minister stimulated Egyptian interest by passing on raw intelligence data on Libyan plots against Sadat. He also accepted Romanian President Nicolae Ceausescu's offer to arrange a secret dialogue with Cairo. Begin even allowed his foreign minister to conduct discussions in Morocco with an Egyptian representative.

It was not until the unofficial meeting in September 1977 between Dayan and Tuhamy, however, that the extent of Egyptian interest in an eventual peace accord became clear. Israel's foreign minister told the Egyptian deputy prime minister that Israel would return the Sinai territory in exchange for full peace. Although a host of difficult issues would have to be negotiated, the parameters of a bilateral treaty were set.

The Soviet-American statement of October 1, 1977 surprised and dismayed Jerusalem as much as Cairo. Israel had no knowledge of Sadat's quiet but determined campaign to undermine the communique. Nevertheless, Jerusalem shared his objectives and pursued its own strategy to head off a Geneva Conference that might lead to the creation of a Palestinian state.

While the peace process was incubating, Begin moved to expand his coalition and thus his political authority. The Democratic Movement for Change (DMC) — a Labor Party splinter group — had captured 15 seats in the May 1977 election. It had declined to join the Likud coalition although Begin offered DMC leader Yigal Yadin ministerial positions. Yadin favored negotiations with the PLO and Jordan over the future of the West Bank. But Dayan's secret meeting with King Hussein near London in August provided convincing evidence that Jordan would barter neither with Israel nor the PLO over the West Bank. Eventually, Yadin accepted Begin's offer and solidified the government's control of the Knesset until the DMC's breakup a year later.

Begin secured a commitment from Yadin to support a Middle East settlement that precluded the formation of a Palestinian state, a return to 1967 borders, and contacts with the PLO. The union of Likud and DMC reflected both the dictates of practical politics and the impact in Israel of the Soviet-American communique. Thus, on the eve of Sadat's visit to Jerusalem Begin enjoyed wide-spread domestic strength for a tough stand on West Bank and Palestinian issues.

The Israeli prime minister designed and presented an autonomy plan that would sustain this internal base of support and remain faithful to his political creed. The self-rule program would preserve Israeli security in the West Bank and Gaza Strip and allow him to negotiate a Sinai settlement. The secret conversations between Dayan and Hussein had confirmed Jordanian opposition to a PLO role in the West Bank. Subsequent discussions between Weizman and Sadat satisfied Israeli officials that the Egyptian president also harbored little enthusiasm for the PLO. Thus, Begin believed the plan could satisfy Egypt and, if it joined the process, Jordan. The prime minister's proposal called for an Israeli military presence to remain in the area, thus reassuring the religious and hard-line ministers who favored maintaining total control over the West Bank and Gaza Strip.

But the disappointing results of the Ismailia conference revived the fears of hardline cabinet officials and right-wing zealots that the peace process would leave the Israeli settlements defenseless and lead inexorably to the creation of a Palestinian state. Begin rejected both views. But to counter right-wing pressure, he allowed Agriculture Minister Ariel Sharon to first erect dummy settlements in the Sinai and then strengthen existing ones in the Rafah salient. The twin moves earned him the opprobrium of Washington and Cairo but important political support at home. In January 1978 the Gush Emunim embarrassed the Israeli government -- as it would several more times during succeeding months -- by adding additional, unauthorized encampments in the West Bank. But Begin's support in the cabinet and among the public had already declined because of his self-rule plan, and he decided to ignore the affront.

Begin also refused to accept American mediation in the application of Resolution 242 to the West Bank or agree to limited Israeli withdrawal from the territory, a decision influenced by a terrorist attack against unarmed women and children in Tel Aviv. During the same period political talks

with Egypt ended in stalemate, hardening public attitudes.
Ideologues within Herut who had advocated severing contact with
Cairo gained ascendancy in Begin's party by summer.

As the negotiations dragged on and the belief grew within
ruling circles in Israel that Washington was working in
collusion with Cairo, Begin's popularity declined sharply.
Weizman's propinquity to Sadat and Dayan's lack of commitment
to traditional Herut Party positions damaged the government's
reputation with hardliners. The opposition Labor Party had
joined a split DMC and the peace movement to criticize government resistance to compromise on the West Bank. Inflation
spiraled above 40 percent, hurting Begin's constituents most.
Begin courted the smaller religious parties as he strove to
assemble a working majority in the Knesset. It was in those
circumstances that Begin went to Camp David.

In September 1978 Begin merely wished to secure the goal
that had eluded him since Ismailia -- trade the Sinai for total
peace with Egypt. He recognized that return of the Sinai would
not suffice, that he would have to make some sort of gesture
toward a settlement on the West Bank and Gaza Strip. Thus, he
offered his self-rule plan. In order to ensure that neither
the Sinai agreement nor the autonomy plan would threaten
Israeli security, Jerusalem insisted that it must retain its
settlements and airfields in the Sinai and a permanent military
presence in the West Bank. Israel also made clear that it
would agree to withdraw from the West Bank and Gaza Strip only
under conditions that would exclude establishment of a
Palestinian state.

The composition of Israel's Camp David delegation,
however, did not reflect either the influence of the religious
right in the Jerusalem cabinet or the national will expressed
in rallies and public forums. Dayan, Weizman, Barak, and
Tamir had labored long and hard to construct a peace with
Egypt. Weizman understood the Egyptian president's views and
requirements perhaps better than any other Israeli. Thus,
although the defense minister's own positions and activities
had damaged his reputation among hardliners and reduced his
influence on Begin, he remained an important figure in the Camp
David negotiations. Barak employed his formidable legal
talents to help draft and interpret the accords, thus erasing
many of Begin's concerns that the agreements might lock him
into positions detrimental to Israel's security. These and
other conributions by the members of the Israeli delegation
helped produce the accords. But ultimately, it was Begin's

ability to compromise on lifelong positions that ensured success at Camp David. Faced with a choice between peace and rigid adherence to his ideology, Begin quietly but forcefully chose peace.

Twenty five hours of debate in the cabinet and Knesset produced large margins of victory in both bodies for the Camp David Accords but not without leaving scars. Some of the prime minister's closest advisers emerged from the experience permanently disaffected. More important, in order to achieve quick and decisive approval of the accords in the Knesset Begin circumvented the normal process of submitting important matters to full review by the party caucus and appropriate parliamentary committees. He would pay for these unorthodox moves later when his cabinet insisted on severely limiting the freedom of Israeli negotiators in future dealings with Egypt.

Dayan, Israel's chief negotiator, was therefore forced to resort to political maneuver and deception in the cabinet to ensure success in talks with Egypt at Blair House, in Brussels, and at the second Camp David Conference. His task was made more complicated by the gradual deterioration of his relationship with Begin. During early stages of negotiation with Egypt and the United States, Dayan performed valuable services for the Israeli prime minister. The foreign minister commanded respect abroad among both Israel's friends and its adversaries. He was technically skilled, creative, and possessed a better memory of the historical record than Begin. After all, Dayan had been a member of nearly every cabinet since independence.

Even before Camp David, however, their relationship had soured. Dayan fought to preserve his freedom to make judgements and decisions during talks with Washington and Cairo. He showed his creativity most during difficult and tense negotiations and objected to attempts at imposing restrictions on his ability to employ his talents fully. He regarded himself as the most intelligent cabinet member, and submitting to the control of inferiors was humiliating.

Begin, nevertheless, wisely went along with his foreign minister's maneuvers. The agreement to give up the settlements in the Sinai automatically raised fears in Jerusalem that a similar arrangement might follow in the West Bank. The prime minister rejected the U.S. and Egyptian interpretations of Israel's agreement to limit its settlement activities after Camp David. Dayan endorsed future expansion of the settlements along the Jordan Valley both out of conviction and as a device

to secure ministerial support for further compromises with
Egypt on linkage. In this manner, he won Zevulun Hammer's
endorsement for a draft treaty at a crucial stage in the
bargaining with Cairo. Begin accepted the Dayan strategy in
late October and again at the end of November 1978.

But the prime minister maintained his dominant role in the
peace process. He would permit no deviation from his vision of
a settlement. All agreements and language were subject to
his personal review and approval.

Although the Peace Now movement virtually vanished at the
start of 1979, inflation was undermining government support
among Sephardic Jews. Growing fears that the negotiations with
Egypt would produce a Palestinian state also contributed to
enormous pressures on the government. Once again, storm clouds
hovered over Begin when he met with Carter in Washington to
negotiate the final details of the peace treaty. The fall of
the shah of Iran and resulting Israeli loss of its main oil
supply added an extra measure of urgency and tension to the
negotiations. But, faced with difficult issues -- the timing
and extent of linkage between the autonomy talks and mutual
recognition -- and beset by political problems at home, Begin
again chose statesmanship over the politically safe adherence
to rigid ideologic precepts. He then crowned the achievement
by persuading his ministers in Jerusalem to support his choice.

The political constraints and pressures the Israeli
cabinet and parliament imposed on Begin would have intimidated
a lesser leader. Begin fought with both bodies and was
sometimes forced to submit to their authority. But he never
merely accepted official direction in setting the parameters of
peace with Egypt. Begin was the government. Before him, only
late Prime Minister David Ben Gurion had achieved such a
position of power and prestige.

Anwar Sadat and Menachem Begin succeeded in March 1979 to
lay the cornerstone for peace in the Middle East. Sadat lost
his life in that effort. Begin has implemented the Sinai
settlement and has maintained his commitment to negotiate
autonomy for the West Bank and Gaza Strip. Yet the world looks
on and wonders whether the opportunities created by their
efforts have not been squandered. The Egyptian-Israeli Peace
Treaty bears testimony to what can be achieved with political
will, courage, and determination. Sadat and Begin had all
three and used it to bring peace to the area. Their
considerable skill and acumen should not be wasted. "Blessed
are the Peacemakers."

Selected Bibliography

Primary Sources

Brzezinski, Zbigniew. <u>Power and Principle: Memoirs of the National Security Adviser, 1977–1981</u>. New York: Farrar, Straus and Giroux, 1983.

Carter, Jimmy. <u>Keeping Faith: Memoirs of a President</u>. New York: Bantam Books, 1982.

Dayan, Moshe. <u>Breakthrough: A Personal Account of the Egypt–Israel Peace Negotiations</u>. London: Weidenfeld and Nicholson, 1981.

Israeli, Raphael. <u>The Public Diary of President Sadat: The Road to War</u> October 1970–October 1973. Leiden: E. J. Brill, 1978.

_____. <u>The Public Diary of President Sadat: The Road to Pragmatism</u> June 1975–October 1976. Leiden: E. J. Brill, 1978.

Kissinger, Henry. <u>The Years of Upheaval</u>. Boston: Little Brown and Company, 1982.

Rabin, Yitzhak, <u>The Rabin Memoirs</u>. Boston: Little Brown and Company, 1979.

Sadat, Anwar. <u>In Search of Identity</u>. New York: Harper and Row, 1977.

Shazly, Saad el. <u>The Crossing of the Suez</u>. San Francisco: American Mideast Research, 1980.

Sullivan, William H. <u>Mission to Iran</u>. New York: W. W. Norton and Company, 1981.

Weizman, Ezer. The Battle for Peace. New York: Bantam Books, 1981.

Personal Interviews

Atherton, Alfred. U.S. Ambassador to Cairo, Cairo, Egypt. Interview, August 18, 1981.

Dessouki, Ali. Professor, University of Cairo, Cairo, Egypt. Interview, August 18, 1981.

Kadishai, Yehiel. Chief of Staff to Prime Minister Begin, Jerusalem, Israel. Interview, August 27, 1981.

Patir, Dan. Press Secretary, Israel, Potomac, Maryland. Interview, January 31, 1982.

Saunders, Harold. U.S. Assistant Secretary of State, Middle East, Washington, D.C. Interview, September 3, 1981.

Quandt, William. NSC Advisor, Middle East. Interview, September 23, 1981.

Vance, Cyrus. Secretary of State. Telephone Interview, March 3, 1983.

U.S. Government Documents

U.S. Department of State. The Camp David Summit — September 1978. Washington: Department of State, 1978.

U.S. Department of State. The Egyptian-Israeli Peace Treaty — March 26, 1979. Washington: Department of State, 1979.

U.S. House of Representatives. 95th Congress. First Session. The Soviet Union: Internal Dynamics of Foreign Policy. Washington: U.S. Government Printing Office, 1978.

Secondary Sources

Books

Ajami, Fouad. The Arab Predicament: Arab Political Thought and Practice Since 1967. London: Cambridge University Press, 1981.

Aronson, Shlomo. Conflict and Bargaining in the Middle East: An Israeli Perspective. Baltimore: The Johns Hopkins University Press, 1978.

Benziman, Uzi. Prime Minister Under Siege. Jerusalem: Adam Publishers, 1981.

Berger, Monroe. Islam in Egypt Today: Social and Political Aspects of Popular Religion. London: Cambridge University Press, 1970.

Binder, Leonard. In a Moment of Enthusiasm: Political Power and the Second Stratum in Egypt. Chicago: University of Chicago Press, 1978.

Burrell, R. Michael and Kelidar, Abbas R. Egypt: The Dilemmas of a Nation — 1970-1977. Beverly Hills: Sage Publications, 1977.

Dekmejiian, R. Hrair. Patterns of Political Leadership, Egypt, Israel, Lebanon. Albany: State University of New York Press, 1975.

Greenberg, Harold I. and Nadler, Samuel. Poverty in Israel: Economic Realities and the Promise of Social Justice. New York: Praeger, 1977.

Haber, Eitan. Menachem Begin: The Legend and the Man. New York: Delacorte Press, 1978.

Hirst, David and Beeson, Irene. Sadat. London: Faber and Faber, 1981.

Leeden, Michael and Lewis, William. Debacle: The American Failure in Iran. New York: Alfred A. Knopf, 1981.

McLaurin, R. D., Mughisuddin, Mohammed and Wagner, Abraham. Foreign Policy Making in the Middle East. New York: Praeger, 1977.

Moore, Clement Henry. Images of Development: Egyptian Engineers in Search of Industry. Cambridge, Massachusetts: MIT Press, 1980.

Nasser, Munir K. Press, Politics and Power: Egypt's Heikal and Al-Ahram. Ames, Iowa: Iowa University Press, 1979.

Nyrop, Richard F. ed. Israel: A Country Study. Washington: The American University, 1978.

O'Conner, Patricia. The Middle East: U.S. Policy, Israel, Oil and the Arabs. 4th Edition. Washington: Congressional Quarterly, 1980.

Quandt, William. Decade of Decisions: American Policy Toward the Arab-Israeli Conflict, 1967-1976. Berkely: University of Caliornia Press, 1977.

Sachar, Howard. Egypt and Israel. New York: Richard Marek, 1981.

Safran, Nadav. Israel: The Embattled Ally. Cambridge, Massachusetts: Harvard University Press, 1978.

Schectman, Joseph. Rebel and Statesman: The Vladimir Jabotinsky Story, The Early Years. New York: Thomas Yoseloff, Inc., 1956.

Schiff, Gary. Tradition and Politics: The Religious Parties of Israel. Detroit: Wayne State University Press, 1977.

Sicherman, Harvey. Broker or Advocate? The U.S. Role in the Arab-Israeli Dispute, 1973-78. Monograph 25. Philadelphia: Foreign Policy Research Institute.

Springborg, Robert. Family, Power and Politics in Egypt: Sayed Bey Marei His Clan, Clients and Cohorts. Philadelphia: University of Pennsylvania Press, 1982.

320

Talbott, Strobe. Endgame: The Inside Story of SALT II. New York: Harper and Row, 1979.

Vatikiotis, P. J. The History of Egypt. 2nd Edition. Baltimore: The Johns Hopkins University Press, 1980.

Waterbury, John. Egypt: Burdens of the Past/Options for the Future. Bloomington: University of Indiana Press, 1978.

Weber, Max. The Theory of Social and Economic Organization. New York: Free Press, 1947.

Wien, Jake. Saudi–Egyptian Relations: The Political and Military Dimensions of Saudi Financial Flows to Egypt. P–6327. Santa Monica: The Rand Corporation.

Yanai, Nathan. Party Leadership in Israel: Maintenance and Change. Ramat Gan: Turtledove Publishing, 1981.

Secondary Sources

Articles

Abu–Lughod, Janet. "Rural Migration and Politics in Egypt" Rural Politics and Social Change in the Middle East ed. by Iliya Harik. Bloomington: Indiana University Press, 1972.

Akzin, Benjamin. "The Likud" Israel at the Polls, ed. by Howard Penniman. Washington: American Enterprise Institute for Public Policy Research, 1979.

Altman, Israel. "Islamic Movements in Egypt" The Jerusalem Quarterly. Number 10, Winter 1979.

Aly, Abd Al-Monein Said and Wenner, Manfred W. "Modern Islamic Reform Movements: The Muslim Brotherhood in Contemporary Egypt" The Middle East Journal. Volume 36, Number 3, Summer 1982.

Arian, Asher. "The Electorate: Israel 1977" Israel at the Polls. ed. by Howard Penniman. Washington: American Enterprise for Public Policy Research, 1979.

Aronson, Shlomo. "Israeli View of the Brookings Report" Middle East Review. Volume 10, Number 1, Fall 1977.

Aronoff, Myron. "The Decline of the Israeli Labor Party" Israel at the Polls. ed. by Howard Penniman. Washington: American Enterprise for Public Policy Research, 1979.

Ayubi, Nazih, N. M. "The Political Revival of Islam: The Case of Egypt" International Journal of Middle East Studies. Volume 12 (1980).

Avnery, Uri. "Menachem Begin: The Reality" Worldview. May 1978.

Ben–Zvi, Abraham. "Full–Circle on the Road to Peace? American Preconceptions of Peace in the Middle East: 1973–78" Middle East Review. Volume 11, Number 2, Winter 1978–79.

Brenner, Marie. "The Very Strange Life of the Yitzhak Rabin's" New York. February 13, 1978.

Brezinski, Zbigniew, Duchene Francois, and Saeki Kiichi. "Peace in the International Framework" Foreign Policy. Number 19, Summer 1975.

Burzonsky, Mark. "Interview with Ismail Fahmy" The Middle East. July 1979.

Cohen, Raymond. "Israel and the Soviet–American Statement of October 1, 1977: The Limits of Patron–Client Influence" Orbis. Volume 22, Number 3, Fall 1978.

Crittenden, Ann. "Israel's Economic Plight" Foreign Affairs. Volume 57, Number 5, Summer 1979.

Dawisha, Adeed. "Syria and the Sadat Initiative" The World Today. Volume 34, Number 5, May 1978.

Dessouki, Ali E. Hillal. "Policymaking in Egypt: A Case Study of the Open Door Economic Policy" Social Problems. Volume 28, Number 4, April 1981.

Dowty, Alan. "Current Perceptions of the Conflict: Cairo, Damascus, Amman" Middle East Review. Volume 11, Number 2, Winter 1978–79.

Elazar, Daniel J. "Israel's Compound Polity" Israel at the Polls. ed. by Howard Penniman. Washington: American Enterprise for Public Policy Reserach, 1979.

Eyal, Eli. "The Democratic Movement for Change: Origins and Perspectives" Middle East Review. Volume 10, Number 1, Fall 1977.

Garfinkle, Adam. "Negotiating by Proxy: Jordanian Foreign Policy and U.S. Options in the Middle East" Orbis. Volume 24, Number 4, Winter 1981.

Harik, Ilyia F. "Mobilization Policy and Political Change in Rural Egypt" Rural Politics and Social Change in the Middle East. ed. by Ilyia Harik. Bloomington: Indiana University Press, 1972.

Hinnebusch, Raymond A. "Egypt Under Sadat: Elites, Power Structure, and Political Change in a Post–Populist State" Social Problems. Volumer 28, Number 4, April 1981.

Horowitz, Dan. "More Than a Change in Government" The Jerusalem Quarterly. Number 5, Fall 1977.

Ibrahim, Saad Eddin. "Anatomy of Egypt's Militant Islamic Groups: Methodological Note and Preliminary Findings" International Journal of Middle East Studies. Volume 12 (1980).

Isaac, Rael and Jean. "The Impcat of Jabotinsky on Likud's Policies" Middle East Review. Volume 10, Number 1, Fall 1977.

Kondracke, Morton. "A Medieval Maze" New Republic. March 5, 1977.

Korayem, Karima. "The Rural–Urban Income Gap in Egypt and Biased Agricultural Pricing Policy" Social Problems. Volume 28, Number 4, April 1981.

Lurie, Runan R. "Israel's General Sharon: As Tough as Ever" Playboy. March 1978.

Lycett, Andrew. "The Peacemaker Reorganizes Back Home" African Business. December 1978.

Moshen, Assem Abdul. "Democracy Revisited" The Middle East. October 1978.

Peretz, Don. "The Earthquake — Israel's Ninth Knesset Elections" Middle East Journal. Summer 1977.

Perlmutter, Amos. "Begin's Strategy and Dayan's Tactics: The Conduct of Israeli Foreign Policy" Foreign Affairs. January 1978.

_____. "Ariel Sharon: Iron Man and Fragile Peace" The New York Times Magazine. October 18, 1981.

_____. "Clevage in Israel" Foreign Policy. Number 27, Summer 1977.

Peri, Yoram. "Ideological Portrait of the Israeli Military Elite" The Jerusalem Quarterly. Number 3, Spring 1977.

Pierre, Andrew J. "Beyond the 'Plane Package': Arms and Politics in the Middle East" International Security. Volume 3, Number 1, Summer 1978.

Reich, Bernard. "Israel's Foreign Policy and the 1977 Parliamentary Elections" Israel at the Polls. ed. by Howard Penniman. Washington: American Enterprise for Public Policy Reserach, 1979.

Spiegel, Steven A. "The Carter Approach to the Arab-Israeli Dispute" The Middle East and the United States: Perceptions and Policies. ed. by Haim Shaked and Itamar Rabinovich. New Brunswick: Transaction Books, 1980.

Springborg, Robert. "Patterns of Association in the Egyptian Political Elite" Political Elites in the Middle East. ed. by George Lenczowski. Washington: American Enterprise Institute for Public Policy Research, 1975.

324

_____. "Patrimonialism and Policy–Making in Egypt" Middle
Eastern Studies. Volume 15, Number 1, January 1979.

_____. "Sayed Bey Marei and Political Clientalism in Egypt"
Comparative Political Studies. Volume 12, Number 3,
October 1979.

Sullivan, Earl. "The U.S. and Egypt: The Potential Crisis"
Worldview. December 1979.

Rubinstein, Elikaim. "The Lesser Parties in the Israeli
Elections of 1977" Israel at the Polls. ed. by Howard
Penniman. Washington: American Enterprise for Public
Policy Research, 1979.

Tolchin, Susan and Martin. "The Feminist Revolution of Jihan
Sadat" The New York Times Magazine. March 16, 1980.

Torgovnik, Efraim. "Accepting Camp David: The Role of Party
Factions in Israeli Policy–Making" Middle East Review.
Volume 11, Number 2, Winter 1978–79.

_____. "A Movement for Change in a Stable System" Israel
at the Polls. ed. by Howard Penniman. Washington:
American Enterprise for Public Policy Research, 1979.

Warburg, Gabriel. "Islam and Politics in Egypt: 1952–1980"
Middle Eastern Studies. Volume 18, Number 2, April 1982.

Yaari, Ehud. "Sadat's Pyramid of Power" The Jerusalem
Quarterly. Number 14, Winter 1980.

Yaniv, Avner and Yishai, Yael. "Israeli Settlements in the
West Bank: The Politics of Intransigence" Journal of
Politics. Volume 43, Number 4, November 1981.

Yegnes, Tamar. "Saudi Arabia and the Peace Process" The
Jerusalem Quarterly. Number 18, Winter 1981.

Newspapers

Washington Post, 1977–1979.

Washington Star, 1977–1979.

New York Times, 1977–1979.

Jerusalem Post, 1978–1979.

Christian Science Monitor, 1978–1979.

Index